MEDICAL MASTERCLASS

EDITOR-IN-CHIEF

JOHN D FIRTH DM FRCP

Consultant Physician and Nephrologist
Addenbrooke's Hospital
Cambridge

SCIENTIFIC BACKGROUND TO MEDICINE 1

EDITOR

JOHN D FIRTH DM FRCP
Consultant Physician and Nephrologist
Addenbrooke's Hospital
Cambridge

Second Edition

1

D1439538

Royal College
of Physicians
Setting higher medical standards

Disclaimer

LIST OF CONTRIBUTORS

Dr EH Baker PhD FRCP
Reader and Consultant in Clinical
Pharmacology
Division of Basic Medical Sciences
St George's, University of London
London

Dr KM Bowles MBBS PhD MRCP(UK)
MRCPath
Consultant Haematologist
Norfolk and Norwich University
Hospital NHS Trust
Norwich

Dr GG Dark FRCP
Clinical Senior Lecturer
Northern Centre for Cancer Treatment
Newcastle General Hospital
Newcasthe-upon-Tyne

Dr JD Firth DM FRCP
Consultant Physician and Nephrologist
Addenbrooke's Hospital
Cambridge

Dr SJ Fowler MD MRCP(UK)
Lecturer and Honorary Consultant in
Respiratory Medicine
University of Manchester and Lancashire
Teaching Hospitals NHS Trust
Royal Preston Hospital
Preston

Dr FM Gribble DPhil MRCPath
Wellcome Senior Research Fellow and
Honorary Consultant in Clinical Biochemistry
Cambridge Institute for Medical Research
and Department of Clinical Biochemistry,
Addenbrooke's Hospital
Cambridge

Dr M Gurnell PhD FRCP
University Lecturer and Honorary Consultant
Physician
Department of Medicine, University of
Cambridge and Addenbrooke's Hospital
Cambridge

Dr AD Hingorani FRCP
Senior Lecturer
Centre for Clinical Pharmacology and
Therapeutics
University College London
London

Dr GM Hirschfield MA MB BChir PhD
MRCP(UK)
Clinical Lecturer (Hepatology)
Addenbrooke's Hospital
Cambridge

Dr S Jacob MBBS MS (Anatomy)
Formerly Senior Lecturer
Department of Biomedical Science
University of Sheffield
Sheffield

Dr F Reimann Dr rer. nat.
Meres Research Associate
Cambridge Institute for Medical Research
and Addenbrooke's Hospital
Cambridge

Dr PR Roberts MD FRCP
Consultant Cardiologist
Southampton General Hospital
Southampton

Dr MG Robson PhD MRCP(UK)
Senior Lecturer and Honorary Consultant
Nephrologist
King's College London
London

Professor TJ Vyse MA PhD MRCP(UK)
Honorary Consultant in Rheumatology/
Medicine and Wellcome Trust Senior Fellow
Imperial College London, Faculty of
Medicine and Hammersmith Hospital
London

Dr NS Ward MRCP(UK)
Consultant Neurologist
National Hospital for Neurology and
Neurosurgery and Institute of Neurology
University College London
London

Royal College
of Physicians
Setting higher medical standards

Published by:
Royal College of Physicians of London
11 St. Andrews Place
Regent's Park
London NW1 4LE
United Kingdom

Set and printed by Graphicraft Limited, Hong Kong

First edition published 2001
Reprinted 2004
Second edition published 2008

ISBN: 978-1-86016-264-0 (this book)
ISBN: 978-1-86016-260-2 (set)

Distribution Information:
Jerwood Medical Education Resource Centre
Royal College of Physicians of London
11 St. Andrews Place
Regent's Park
London NW1 4LE
United Kingdom
Tel: +44 (0)207 935 1174 ext 422/490
Fax: +44 (0)207 486 6653
Email: merc@rcplondon.ac.uk
Web: http://www.rcplondon.ac.uk/

CONTENTS

CONTENTS

FOREWORD

Since its initial publication in 2001, *Medical Masterclass* has been regarded as a key learning and teaching resource for physicians around the world. The resource was produced in part to meet the vision of the Royal College of Physicians: *'Doctors of the highest quality, serving patients well'*. This vision continues and, along with advances in clinical practice and changes in the format of the MRCP(UK) exam, has justified the publication of this second edition.

The MRCP(UK) is an international examination that seeks to advance the learning of and enhance the training process for physicians worldwide. On passing the exam physicians are recognised as having attained the required knowledge, skills and manner appropriate for training at a specialist level. However, passing the exam is a challenge. The pass rate at each sitting of the written papers is about 40%. Even the most prominent consultants have had to sit each part of the exam more than once in order to pass. With this challenge in mind, the College has produced *Medical Masterclass*, a comprehensive learning resource to help candidates with the preparation that is key to making the grade.

Medical Masterclass has been produced by the Education Department of the College. A work of this size represents a formidable amount of effort by the Editor-in-Chief – Dr John Firth – and his team of editors and authors. I would like to thank our colleagues for this wonderful educational product and wholeheartedly recommend it as an invaluable learning resource for all physicians preparing for their MRCP(UK) examination.

Professor Ian Gilmore MD PRCP
President of the Royal College of Physicians

PREFACE

The second edition of *Medical Masterclass* is produced and published by the Education Department of the Royal College of Physicians of London. It comprises 12 textbooks, a companion interactive website and two CD-ROMs. Its aim is to help doctors in their first few years of training to improve their medical knowledge and skills; and in particular to (a) learn how to deal with patients who are acutely ill, and (b) pass postgraduate examinations, such as the MRCP(UK) or European Diploma in Internal Medicine.

The 12 textbooks are divided as follows: two cover the scientific background to medicine, one is devoted to general clinical skills [including specific guidance on exam technique for PACES, the practical assessment of clinical examination skills that is the final part of the MRCP(UK) exam], one deals with acute medicine and the other eight cover the range of medical specialties.

The core material of each of the medical specialties is dealt with in seven sections:

- Case histories – you are presented with letters of referral commonly received in each specialty and led through the ways in which the patients' histories should be explored, and what should then follow in the way of investigation and/or treatment.

- Physical examination scenarios – these emphasise the logical analysis of physical signs and sensible clinical reasoning: 'having found this, what would you do?'

- Communication and ethical scenarios – what are the difficult issues that commonly arise in each specialty? What do you actually say to the 'frequently asked (but still very difficult) questions?'

- Acute presentations – what are the priorities if you are the doctor seeing the patient in the Emergency Department or the Medical Admissions Unit?

- Diseases and treatments – structured concise notes.

- Investigations and practical procedures – more short and to-the-point notes.

- Self assessment questions – in the form used in the MRCP(UK) Part 1 and Part 2 exams.

The companion website – which is continually updated – enables you to take mock MRCP(UK) Part 1 or Part 2 exams, or to be selective in the questions you tackle (if you want to do ten questions on cardiology, or any other specialty, you can do). For every question you complete you can see how your score compares with that of others who have logged onto the site and attempted it. The two CD-ROMs each contain 30 interactive cases requiring diagnosis and treatment.

I hope that you enjoy using *Medical Masterclass* to learn more about medicine, which – whatever is happening politically to primary care, hospitals and medical career structures – remains a wonderful occupation. It is sometimes intellectually and/or emotionally very challenging, and also sometimes extremely rewarding, particularly when reduced to the essential of a doctor trying to provide best care for a patient.

John Firth DM FRCP
Editor-in-Chief

ACKNOWLEDGEMENTS

Medical Masterclass has been produced by a team. The names of those who have written or edited material are clearly indicated elsewhere, but without the support of many other people it would not exist. Naming names is risky, but those worthy of particular note include: Sir Richard Thompson (College Treasurer) and Mrs Winnie Wade (Director of Education), who steered the project through committees that are traditionally described as labyrinthine, and which certainly seem so to me; and also Arthur Wadsworth (Project Co-ordinator) and Don Liu in the College Education Department office. Don is a veteran of the first edition of *Medical Masterclass*, and it would be fair to say that without his great efforts a second edition might not have seen the light of day.

John Firth DM FRCP
Editor-in-Chief

We have created a range of icon boxes that sit among the text of the various *Medical Masterclass* modules. They are there to help you identify key information and to make learning easier and more enjoyable. Here is a brief explanation:

> Iron-deficiency anaemia with a change in bowel habit in a middle-aged or older patient means colonic malignancy until proved otherwise.

This icon is used to highlight points of particular importance.

> Dietary deficiency is very rarely, if ever, the sole cause of iron-deficiency anaemia.

This icon is used to indicate common or important drug interactions, pitfalls of practical procedures, or when to take symptoms or signs particularly seriously.

GENETICS AND MOLECULAR MEDICINE

Author:

TJ Vyse

Editor:

JD Firth

Editor-in-Chief:

JD Firth

Introduction

Using the term 'molecular medicine' to describe the application of molecular biology to disease, this section provides an introductory account of molecular biology and the impact of this scientific discipline on clinical medicine. The second component discussed is genetics. Historically, genetics arose as a separate field of investigation, pre-dating any knowledge of the molecular basis of the inheritance processes observed.

Recently, the boundaries between molecular biology and genetics have become increasingly blurred. A well-known example demonstrating this convergence is the Human Genome Project: the DNA sequence of the human genome now provides a fundamental resource for researchers attempting to delineate both rare and common genetic variants that contribute to disease phenotypes.

In this section, a brief survey of molecular biology is set out, including:

- nucleic acid structure;
- genomic organisation;
- how various techniques have been employed to elucidate the molecular mechanisms underlying some common genetic diseases.

In the sections describing advances in genetics, the means by which genetic data are obtained provide the main area of focus, together with the close relationship of genetics and molecular biology. Although some of the examples used, particularly of single-gene traits, may seem obscure, the influence of molecular medicine on clinical practice cannot fail to grow. At the most basic level, discovery of molecular pathology generates substantial insight into disease mechanisms and pathophysiology. However, there are more direct clinical uses for the techniques of molecular medicine, including potential applications in diagnostics, especially with reference to prognosis; furthermore, individualising drug therapy in the future is also likely to be influenced by genetic make-up.

Structure of nucleic acids

> The central dogma of molecular biology states that a gene encoded in DNA is transcribed into mRNA. The mRNA is then translated into polypeptide.

Unit structure

Both deoxyribonucleic acid (DNA) and ribonucleic acid (RNA) comprise a polymer of nucleotide monophosphates. Table 1 illustrates the interrelationship of the bases, pentose sugars and phosphates that constitute nucleic acids. The structure is shown in Fig. 1. Nucleic acid bases are divided into two categories depending on their structure.

- Purines: adenine (A) and guanine (G).
- Pyrimidines: cytosine (C), thymine (T) and uracil (U).

Individual bases are bound to one side of the sugar moiety through N-9 in pyrimidines or through N-1 in purines. On the other side of the pentose ring, attached to the 5′-carbon atom, up to three phosphate groups are present, designated α through γ with respect to the proximity to the sugar.

It is the sugar group that distinguishes DNA from RNA. In RNA the sugar is ribose, and the 2′- and 3′-carbon atoms are hydroxylated; in DNA the sugar deoxyribose carries a hydroxyl

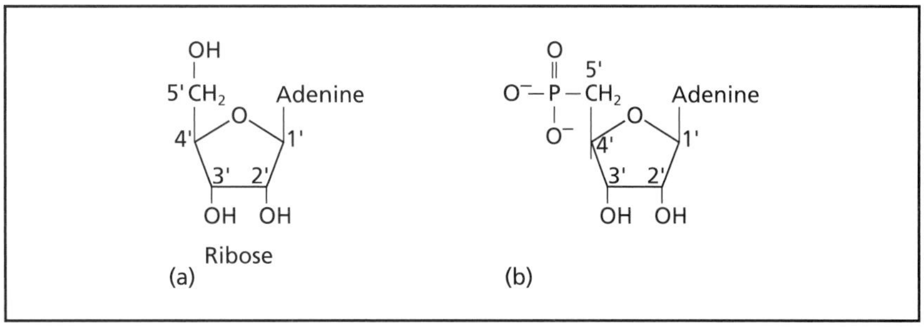

▲ **Fig. 1** (a) Nucleoside and (b) nucleotide structure. (a) In RNA, ribose is hydroxylated at the 2′- and 3′-carbons. Deoxyribose is hydroxylated only at the 3′-position. (b) The structure of AMP shows one (α) phosphate group attached to the 5′-carbon.

TABLE 1 THE COMPONENTS OF NUCLEIC ACIDS[1]

Base	Nucleoside [base + (deoxy)ribose]	Nucleotide (nucleoside + phosphate)
Purines (R)		
Adenine (A)	Adenosine	Adenosine 5′-monophosphate (AMP)
Guanine (G)	Guanosine	Guanosine 5′-monophosphate (GMP)
Pyrimidines (Y)		
Cytosine (C)	Cytidine	Cytidine monophosphate (CMP)
Thymine (T)	Thymidine[2]	Thymidine monophosphate (dTMP)[2]
Uracil (U)	Uridine	Uridine monophosphate (UMP)

1. DNA contains the same components as RNA with the exception that the ribose sugar in RNA is replaced by deoxyribose in DNA. The abbreviation for the DNA deoxynucleotides is hence prefixed by 'd'.
2. DNA contains the base thymine, which is transcribed into uracil in RNA. Uracil differs from thymine in the lack of a methyl on the 5′-carbon atom of the pyrimidine ring.

only on the 3′-carbon. The 3′-hydroxyl is essential for polymerisation. Nucleic acid chains are formed by binding the 3′-hydroxyl group on the (deoxy)ribose sugar to the α phosphate group, which is attached to the 5′-carbon.

Structure of the double helix of DNA

What is the double helix famously described by Watson and Crick using the X-ray diffraction data of Wilkins and Franklin? First, it is important to understand that the purine–pyrimidine bases pair in an invariant fashion (Fig. 2). Under physiological conditions, nucleic acid comprises A–T and G–C pairs. The bases are held together by hydrogen bonds. It is these pair bonds that form the basis of the constancy of the genetic code, and hence they lie at the heart of the molecular basis of the hereditary process. The base-pair alignment forms the bridge between two parallel strands of DNA. The direction of the individual DNA strands is opposite (Fig. 3). To complete the description of the two-dimensional structure of the DNA molecule, the two strands are intertwined in a double helix.

Messenger RNA

RNA is generally single-stranded. There are three main types and each type exhibits a different secondary structure.

- Messenger RNA (mRNA), as shown in Fig. 4.

- Ribosomal RNA (rRNA), which is a constituent of ribosomes.

- Transfer RNA (tRNA).

Genes encoding polypeptides are transcribed by RNA polymerase II. In general, rRNAs and tRNAs are transcribed by other RNA polymerases. After primary transcription, the intronic sequence is removed by splicing. Other changes include the addition of a poly(A) tail at the 3′-end that is usually 50–500 base pairs (bp) in length. At the 5′-end, a methyl-G residue is added in reverse. These two modifications promote mRNA stability.

The nucleosome and higher-order structure

The complete human genome consists of about 3×10^9 bp of DNA and the nucleus of every somatic cell contains about this amount of DNA. This incredible feat of packaging is achieved by virtue of multiple coiling at successive structure levels.

The double helix of DNA is initially supercoiled in association with several proteins, including positively charged histones. At physiological pH, DNA is, as would be expected from an acid, negatively charged.

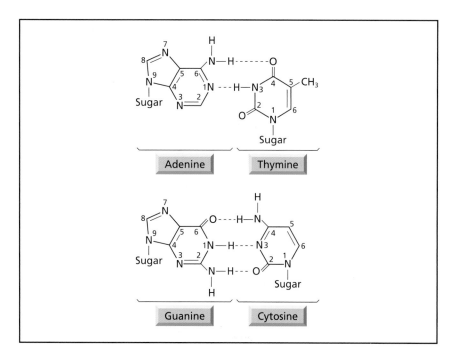

▲ **Fig. 2** Structure of nucleotide bases showing how the hydrogen bonds between them form. The dashed lines show hydrogen bonds between the A–T and G–C pairs. Note that the pairing is always purine with pyrimidine, and that the G–C pair is bound together more strongly than the A–T pair.

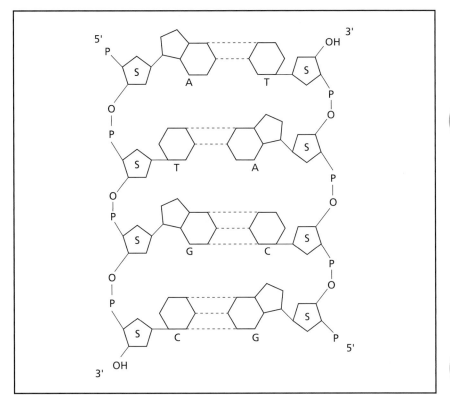

▲**Fig. 3** DNA antiparallel strands. The two strands of DNA are bound together to form double-stranded DNA by hydrogen bonding. The direction of each strand, described as 5′ to 3′ with respect to the deoxyribose carbon atoms, is opposite for each strand.

expression: densely packed chromatin, termed 'heterochromatin', tends to be less transcriptionally active than open chromatin.

Serum autoantibodies to double-stranded DNA are a characteristic feature of systemic lupus erythematosus. DNA is targeted by the immune system after sensitisation to the histone–DNA complex as chromatin. In some forms of drug-induced lupus, only individual histone components act as autoantigens.

Genomic DNA: coding vs non-coding sequences

Genomic DNA

- 3% encodes protein.
- 97% has regulatory or unknown function.

The DNA–histone complex is organised so that DNA is coiled around an octamer of four different histones: H2a, H2b, H3 and H4. This unit, the nucleosome, produces a string-of-beads type of structure.

The string is further coiled into a 30-nm chromatin fibre. At a further level of organisation, non-histone scaffold proteins are involved in the condensation of supercoiled DNA. This influences the level of gene

A typical gene has:

- a promoter that binds RNA polymerase;

- a transcriptional start site, where production of RNA begins;

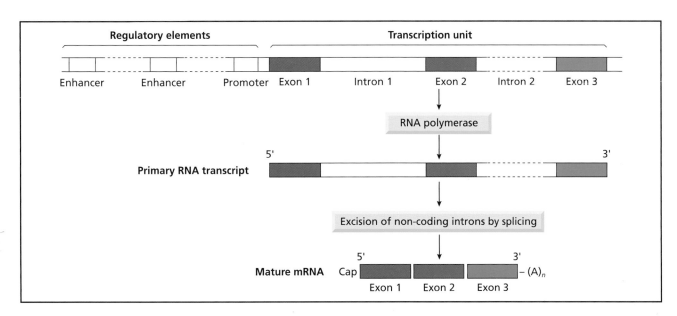

▲**Fig. 4** Organisation of genes.

TABLE 2 VARIATIONS IN GENE SIZE (KB = KILOBASE = 1000 BASES)

Gene	Size (kb)	Exon number
β-Globin	1.4	3
Complement C3	41	29
Dystrophin	2400	79

- exons (which contain the coding sequence);

- introns (non-coding sequence between exons, the function of which is largely unknown);

- a transcriptional stop site.

There is enormous variation in gene size, the greatest variables being the size and frequency of introns (Table 2).

It can be estimated that about 3% of the human genome encodes sequences that are eventually translated into functional proteins. The DNA that carries the protein-coding sequence in a gene is not usually contiguous. Coding DNA is frequently divided into segments (exons) that are separated by non-coding intervening regions (introns). These are shown in Figs 4 and 5. At the start of the gene, upstream of the first exon, lie sequences that influence either the expression of the gene or the efficiency with which it is transcribed into mRNA.

Between 20 and 30 bp upstream from the transcriptional start site there are promoter elements that bind RNA polymerases. Genes encoding polypeptides are transcribed by RNA polymerase II. The binding sequences for this polymerase are characteristic; such a run of conserved sequence is termed a 'consensus sequence'. Promoters, for example, commonly include:

- a TATA box (consensus, TATAA);

- a GC box (consensus, GGGCGG).

Other consensus elements, at a variable distance from the start site, bind to protein factors that influence tissue specificity of gene expression. Additional regulation may be provided by protein signals elicited by various stimuli, eg hormones and cytokines.

Other types of non-coding sequences are listed in Table 3. Introns have already been alluded to above, but there are many other types of non-coding genomic DNA. Some of these non-coding elements share homology with retroviral sequences, and hence may represent previous proviral sites that have become modified and have lost full replicative competence. Many mechanisms exist to check single base-pair mismatches, but there are limited processes for the excision of large tracts of DNA and this may

account for the persistence of the viral-related sequence in the genome.

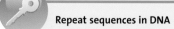

Repeat sequences in DNA

Although the function, if any, of many repeat sequences is not known, some repeats, such as microsatellites and minisatellites, have been exploited by molecular biologists. Minisatellites are used in 'DNA fingerprinting' and microsatellites have been employed as genetic markers owing to the variability of their length.

Codons

A polypeptide amino acid sequence is determined by the base sequence of its mRNA. The RNA bases are 'read' in a 3-bp or triplet code, each 3-bp unit being referred to as a codon (Table 4). Translation is the process of decoding the protein sequence from mRNA (Fig. 6). The details of the biochemistry of translation are not discussed here, except to say that small transfer (tRNA) molecules decode the triplet (see *Biochemistry and Metabolism*, Section 5.2). They recognise each codon by virtue of a complementary RNA sequence, the anticodon, which forms a unique part of each tRNA molecule.

There are over 30 types of cytoplasmic tRNA, which carry 20 amino acids as well as stop signals that terminate a polypeptide. It is apparent from Table 4 that there is degeneracy in the amino acid code. A total of 4^3 nucleotide

Exon

| A_{64} | G_{73} | g_{100} t_{100} a_{68} a_{68} g_{84} t_{63} ·········· y n y y r a y ··········· y y y y y n c_{65} a_{100} g_{100} | N N |

Exon

Purine = G or A = R   Pyramidine = C or T = Y   N = G or A or T or C

▲**Fig. 5** Splice-site consensus sequence. The exonic sequence is shown in upper case and the intronic sequence in lower case. The degree of consistency is indicated by a percentage value, indicating the frequency of the nucleotide at that site. The consensus sequences provide a recognition signal for the ribonucleoprotein spliceosome complex.

TABLE 3 NON-CODING GENOMIC DNA

Description	Position/size	Possible function
Intron	Within genes, separating exons A few genes lack introns, eg histones	May contain regulatory elements Contain splice site sequences Division of coding sequence into exons may facilitate movement of genetic material (exon shuffling)
Alphoid DNA	170 bp tandem repeats Located around centromeres	Unknown
Telomeric repeats	TTAGGG tandem repeats Located close to telomeres	These runs of hexanucleotide sequence promote chromosomal stability
Minisatellites	9–24 bp repeats often several kb in length Frequently subtelomeric	May function as recombination hotspots
Microsatellites	1–3 bp tandem repeats Usually several hundred bp long Randomly distributed	Unknown (used as genetic markers)
SINES (short interspersed nuclear elements)	In the human genome, the most abundant SINES are *Alu* repeats (contain the restriction site of the *Alu* I enzyme) Up to 10^6 copies/genome Repeats are about 280 bp long	*Alu* elements tend to be more prevalent in relatively gene-rich regions of the genome It is speculated that SINES align during meiosis; multiple SINES within a gene-rich locus may promote unequal crossing-over and hence generate genetic diversity
LINES (long interspersed nuclear elements)	LINE-1 or *Kpn* (another restriction enzyme) repeats are up to 6 kb in length They are homologous with retroviruses	LINES encode a reverse transcriptase and hence may be self-perpetuating They tend to occur in areas of low gene density
HERV (human endogenous retroviruses)	These sequences do carry a more complete representation of the retroviral genome than LINES, including flanking long terminal repeats (LTRs)	Unknown function Endogenous retroviruses may exist within genes without consequence, eg complement *C2* in the MHC; they may disrupt transcription at other sites, eg *F8* gene (haemophilia) or the *lpr* mutation in mouse which abrogates the apoptotic function of Fas

MHC, major histocompatibility complex.

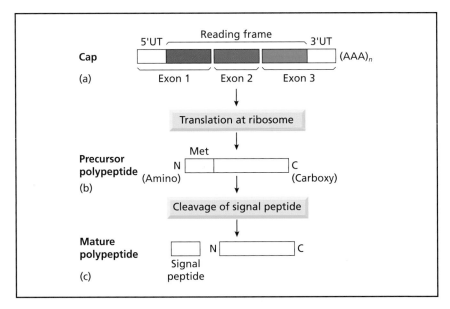

triplets encode only 20 different amino acids and three termination codons. The third base of the triplet exerts the least influence over amino acid specificity, which is sometimes referred to as the wobble hypothesis.

Precursor polypeptides leaving the ribosome undergo post-translational modification to form mature protein. These modifications include the following.

- Protease cleavage into distinct chains, often held together by disulphide bonds.

- *N*-glycosylation in the endoplasmic reticulum: this occurs in the sequence N-X-S/T, where X is any amino acid except proline, S is serine and T is threonine.

▲ **Fig. 6** Protein translation. (**a**) The reading frame (shaded sequence) encodes the peptide sequence. At the 3′ and 5′ ends of the mRNA, there are untranslated sequences (UT). 5′-UT and 3′-UT maintain mRNA stability. (**b**) Translation at a ribosome produces a precursor polypeptide. Polypeptides destined to become secreted proteins or transported across intracellular membranes contain a short peptide signal at the amino (N)-terminal end. (**c**) Cleavage of the signal peptide produces a mature polypeptide.

TABLE 4 THE UNIVERSAL GENETIC CODE

First[1] letter	Second letter				Third letter
	U	C	A	G	
U	UUU Phe (F)	UCU Ser (S)	UAU Tyr (Y)	UGU Cys (C)	U
	UUC Phe (F)	UCC Ser (S)	UAC Tyr (Y)	UGC Cys (C)	C
	UUA Leu (L)	UCA Ser (S)	UAA Stop	UGA Stop	A
	UUG Leu (L)	UCG Ser (S)	UAG Stop	UGG Trp (W)	G
C	CUU Leu (L)	CCU Pro (P)	CAU His (H)	CGU Arg (R)	U
	CUC Leu (L)	CCC Pro (P)	CAC His (H)	CGC Arg (R)	C
	CUA Leu (L)	CCA Pro (P)	CAA Gln (Q)	CGA Arg (R)	A
	CUG Leu (L)	CCG Pro (P)	CAG Gln (Q)	CGG Arg (R)	G
A	AUU Ile (I)	ACU Thr (T)	AAU Asn (N)	AGU Ser (S)	U
	AUC Ile (I)	ACC Thr (T)	AAC Asn (N)	AGC Ser (S)	C
	AUA Ile (I)	ACA Thr (T)	AAA Lys (K)	AGA Arg (R)	A
	AUG Met (M)*	ACG Thr (T)	AAG Lys (K)	AGG Arg (R)	G
G	GUU Val (V)	GCU Ala (A)	GAU Asp (D)	GGU Gly (G)	U
	GUC Val (V)	GCC Ala (A)	GAC Asp (D)	GGC Gly (G)	C
	GUA Val (V)	GCA Ala (A)	GAA Glu (E)	GGA Gly (G)	A
	GUG Val (V)*	GCG Ala (A)	GAG Glu (E)	GGG Gly (G)	G

1. Each triplet designates the nucleotide sequence in the mRNA (not the DNA).
Two codons, AUG and GUG (indicated by asterisks), are recognised by the initiator $tRNA_i^{Met}$, although only in the context of adjacent signal sequence. At internal sites, AUG is recognised by $tRNA^{Met}$ and GUG by $tRNA^{Val}$. Three codons, UAA, UAG and UGA, specify polypeptide chain termination and bind specific protein release factors.

One-letter amino acid code

A Alanine (Ala)	C Cysteine (Cys)	D Aspartic acid (Asp)	E Glutamic acid (Glu)	F Phenylalanine (Phe)
G Glycine (Gly)	H Histidine (His)	I Isoleucine (Ile)	K Lysine (Lys)	L Leucine (Leu)
M Methionine (Met)	N Asparagine (Asn)	P Proline (Pro)	Q Glutamine (Gln)	R Arginine (Arg)
S Serine (Ser)	T Threonine (Thr)	V Valine (Val)	W Tryptophan (Trp)	Y Tyrosine (Tyr)

- *O*-glycosylation in the Golgi apparatus at the S or T amino acids.

Splicing

The removal of an intronic sequence to create mature mRNAs is illustrated in Fig. 4. Splicing may also be used to increase the number of polypeptide products from a single gene, eg omitting a transmembrane coding region or altering a cytoplasmic tail may allow the production of a soluble secreted protein and a membrane-bound protein. Examples are listed in Table 5.

Chromosome structure

Most human cells contain 23 pairs of chromosomes: 22 different autosomes (Fig. 7) and one pair of sex chromosomes (X or Y). Cells that contain chromosome pairs are referred to as diploid. Specialised gametes or sex cells (sperm or egg cells) contain a single copy of the autosomes and either the X or Y sex chromosome. They are described as haploid.

TABLE 5 ALTERNATIVE SPLICING

Gene	Tissue/state	Function of different transcripts
Calcitonin	Thyroid	Calcium homeostasis
Calcitonin gene-related peptide (CGRP)	Hypothalamus	Neurotransmitter
Tumour necrosis factor receptors (TNFR1/2)	Membrane bound Soluble	Transduces signals from ligand Circulating inhibitor of TNF
IgM	Membrane bound Soluble	B-cell antigen–receptor complex Low-affinity, polyvalent antibody, IgM
Type IIb receptors for Fc region of IgG (FCGR2B)	B lymphocytes Macrophages, mostly secreted	b1 membrane bound, full cDNA b2 membrane bound: deletion of 23 amino acids from proximal cytoplasmic domain b3 fluid phase: transmembrane region

Telomeres and ageing

During replication, the telomeres are extended using a specialised enzyme, telomerase. The length of this extension progressively lessens over consecutive cell divisions, hence telomeres normally shorten with age. This is believed to be one facet of the cellular ageing process.

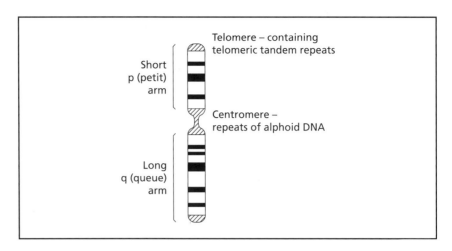

▲ **Fig. 7** Chromosome structure. The p and q arms are subdivided into regions p1, p2, . . . and q1, q2, . . . , respectively. The divisions are based on banding patterns. Dark bands produced by Giemsa staining are individually numbered and used as the gross map of a chromosome. Chromosomes are grouped on the basis of gross morphology. The position of the centromere varies, and may be central (metacentric) or very asymmetrical (acrocentric).

Cell division

Somatic cells divide by a process of mitosis (Fig. 8). In this process, nuclear genetic material is duplicated, each daughter

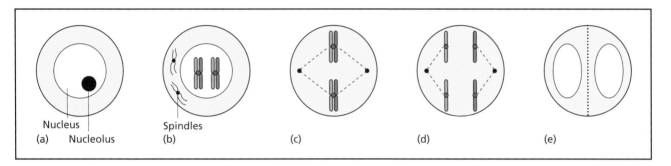

▲ **Fig. 8** Mitosis. (**a**) Interphase: before mitosis, the cell undergoes a synthesis (S) phase. After this, there is doubling of the amount of genetic material to four times the haploid content. (**b**) The chromosomes condense during prophase. (**c**) During metaphase, the chromosome pairs line up along the central line. (**d**) The centromere splits during anaphase and the chromatids are pulled apart. (**e**) In the final stage, telophase, the chromosomes condense and a nuclear membrane starts to form. Thereafter, the cell physically divides.

cell therefore receiving a full complement of chromosome pairs. Gametes arise by a process termed 'meiosis'. This is a two-stage reductive procedure, which in the male generates four gametes from a single progenitor cell. During meiosis, there is an exchange of genetic material between chromosome pairs (Fig. 9). This exchange is the basis of the diversity produced by sexual reproduction.

Chromosomal abnormalities

Most genetic disorders are secondary to events at the molecular level. However, large-scale losses or gains of

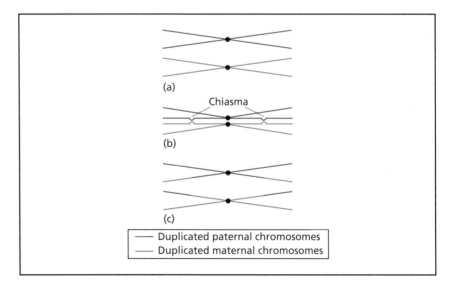

▲ **Fig. 9** Meiosis is a two-phase process. (**a**) As in mitosis, there is duplication of genetic material before cell division. (**b**) Recombination nodules form at points where cross-overs occur. Each connection is called a chiasma. (**c**) Exchange of genetic material occurs between paternal and maternal chromosome pairs. During anaphase I, the recombined chromosomes separate into daughter cells. A second round of cell division occurs so that each gamete is haploid.

TABLE 6 EXAMPLES OF ANEUPLOIDY

Syndrome	Karyotype	Frequency	Outline of phenotype
Turner's syndrome	45,X (monosomy X)	1 in 2,500	Female, no functional ovaries, short stature, retarded sexual development (see *Endocrinology*, Section 1.1.7)
Klinefelter's syndrome	47,XXY (disomy X)	1 in 500	Male, subfertile, breasts, long limbs, mental impairment
Trisomy 13	47,XX,+13	1 in 20,000	Mental deficiency and deafness, cleft palate, polydactyly
Down's syndrome	47,XY,+21	1 in 700	Short stature, broad head, epicanthic folds, macroglossia, mental impairment, cardiac malformations
Translocation	46,XX,t(14q;21q),+21		Down's syndrome

When describing the karyotype, the total chromosome number is followed by the sex chromosome composition and a description of aneuploidy.

genetic material or gross alterations of chromosomal architecture do cause more severe genetic diseases. These disorders tend to be rare, probably because gross genetic abnormalities are usually incompatible with life.

The gross structure and number of chromosomes are described by the karyotype. One of the more common pathological disturbances in karyotype is an abnormality of chromosome number, which is termed 'aneuploidy' (Table 6). The following are examples of aneuploidy:

- one extra copy of an entire chromosome (trisomy);

- loss of one of the chromosomes of a pair (monosomy).

Both trisomy and monosomy can arise as a consequence of failure of the chromosome pairs to separate during cell division. Thus, in meiosis, one gamete might receive no copies of a given chromosome, whereas its partner would then receive both copies. This process of non-disjunction would, on fertilisation, generate monosomy or trisomy, provided that the fertilising gamete was monoploid.

The recent explosion of activity and knowledge in molecular biology has been facilitated and driven by the development of a wide range of investigative techniques. The most widely used of these include:

- blotting;

- polymerase chain reaction (PCR);

- copy DNA (cDNA) and reverse transcriptase;

- DNA sequencing;

- cloning.

Blotting

Blotting refers to the transfer of either nucleic acid or protein on to a membrane so that it is immobilised. This transfer is usually preceded by electrophoresis to separate the molecules under investigation on the basis of their size.

- Proteins are often separated on vertical polyacrylamide gels.

- Large nucleic acid fragments are separated on agarose gels.

- When very fine resolution is required, as in DNA sequencing, fragments are electrophoresed on thin vertical polyacrylamide gels.

Proteins or nucleic acids can be run in a native state, during which secondary and tertiary structure will influence mobility in a gel. Alternatively, a denaturing gel (containing urea, formamide or some other agent that inhibits complex structure formation) is used. Denaturing gels allow more rigorous delineation of fragments with respect to size (useful for DNA sequencing). Denaturing protein gels permit visualisation of subunit structure.

The original blotting technique, described by Ed Southern (hence 'Southern blot'), involves the transfer of DNA fragments from an agarose gel on to a membrane (either nylon or nitrocellulose). Once bound to the membrane, DNA can be interrogated by hybridisation with DNA or RNA probes. Thus, to detect the presence of any particular gene, a short nucleic acid sequence (the probe) from that gene can be incubated with the membrane, onto which genomic DNA fragments are bound. If non-specifically bound probe is removed by vigorous washing, specific complementary DNA sequences will be detected. The probe is usually labelled with an enzyme tag or with the β-emitting isotope ^{32}P and can be used in the detection of restriction fragment length polymorphisms (RFLPs) (see below).

Other blotting techniques, following a geographical analogy with Southern blotting, include Northern blotting, where RNA is bound to a membrane and detected with a nucleic acid probe, and Western blotting, where proteins are transferred to a membrane that is usually interrogated with an enzyme-labelled antibody.

Polymerase chain reaction

It would not be hyperbole to state that PCR has revolutionised molecular biology since its introduction in the mid-1980s. The technique allows the exponential amplification of a target DNA sequence. Provided that sufficient information is already known to design short oligonucleotide primers that flank the target region, any region of the genome (termed the 'template') can theoretically be amplified by PCR.

Ingredients for PCR include the following:

- template to be amplified, eg 100 ng genomic DNA;

- oligonucleotide primer pair (in excess);

- free deoxynucleotides (dNTPs);

- buffer;

- magnesium 1.5–4.5 mmol/L;

- thermostable DNA polymerase, eg from *Thermus aquaticus* (*Taq* polymerase).

The basis of the PCR reaction is that DNA polymerase can, under the correct conditions, copy the template by extending from the designed oligonucleotide primers (Fig. 10). The PCR cycle involves the following steps.

1. A 94°C melting phase: all nucleic acid strands separate, after which the reaction is allowed gradually to cool.

2. A 50–65°C annealing phase: oligonucleotide primers (in excess) adhere to complementary sequences, and initial synthesis of complementary DNA strands occurs. The temperature is then

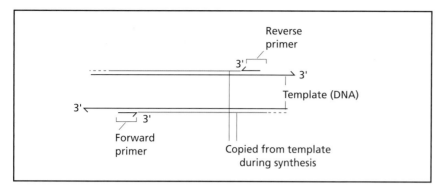

▲ **Fig. 10** Polymerase chain reaction.

increased to 72°C, which is optimal for the action of *Taq* polymerase.

3. 72°C synthesis: full synthesis of the template region occurs. The amount of template DNA has now been doubled.

The template is amplified geometrically using repeated cycles (usually 30–40) of heating and cooling.

Clinical applications of PCR

• Mutation detection: PCR can be used to amplify regions within a gene that are known to contain single base-pair point mutations, short insertions or deletions. The size of fragments that can be subject to PCR is a limiting factor in this application. Targets greater than 5 kb in length can be difficult; regions larger than 10 kb are not usually amenable to PCR. The presence of a mutation can be detected by several means, including DNA sequencing.
• Microbiological diagnosis: the fact that PCR will amplify a very limited amount of starting material means that nucleic acid from pathogens can be detected. The DNA sequence from pathogens allows accurate identification and will probably be utilised in the future to predict antibiotic resistance.
• Genetic markers such as microsatellites and single nucleotide polymorphisms are detected using PCR (see Genetic markers, Section 4).

• Forensic analysis of blood and other body fluids: these can be amplified by PCR and used to type individuals using methods such as DNA fingerprinting.
• PCR may be used as an adjunct to other methods for major histocompatibility complex (MHC) typing.

As the use of PCR in clinical medicine increases, it is important to realise that it does have limitations. The enormous amplification that occurs during PCR cycles presents the potential for error by contamination. Contamination from the environment is more likely to occur in a laboratory in which many similar PCRs are performed. Cross-contamination of reaction components with any product from previous reactions must be prevented. Finally, the DNA polymerase used will have a small but definite error rate for nucleotide incorporation; if such an error occurs during an early cycle, a significantly mixed product may be obtained.

cDNA and reverse transcriptase
The analysis of mRNA is a major source of information for molecular biologists. However, mRNA comprises only about 2% of the total RNA of most cells, and RNA itself is an unstable molecule

that is prone to degradation. DNA is more stable and more amenable to manipulation. For this reason, mRNA is frequently studied indirectly by making DNA copies, termed 'cDNA'. To produce cDNA, the retroviral enzyme reverse transcriptase is employed. The enzyme is 'reverse' in the sense that it synthesises DNA from an RNA template.

Information about the transcriptional activity of cells can be obtained by cloning cDNA (see below) from total mRNA. mRNA can also be examined using PCR to amplify cDNA, a process called reverse transcriptase PCR or RT-PCR.

DNA sequencing
By far the most commonly employed method of DNA sequencing is that developed by Sanger's group, the dideoxy termination method (Fig. 11). Modifications of the original method allow both single-stranded and double-stranded templates to be sequenced. All protocols require the use of an oligonucleotide primer (often the same primer as used to perform PCR, as described above) because DNA polymerases depend on a site containing a 3'-hydroxyl group onto which new nucleotides can be added.

Template copies are randomly terminated by the incorporation of complementary dideoxynucleotides, which are included at low concentration in the reaction mixture in addition to the usual deoxynucleotides that allow sequence extension.

To read the sequence, template copies must be carefully size separated. This is achieved on denaturing polyacrylamide gels on which the fragments may be

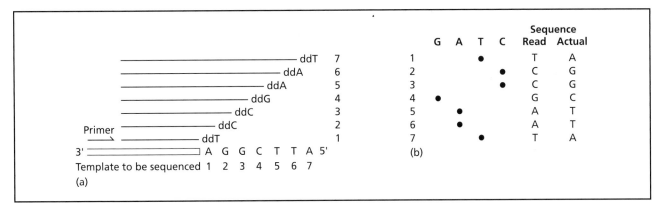

▲ **Fig. 11** DNA sequencing. (**a**) DNA sequencing is often performed using a single-stranded DNA template. A DNA polymerase copies the single-stranded DNA template, extending from the oligonucleotide primer. This reaction is randomly halted by the incorporation of limited amounts of dideoxynucleotides (ddNTPs). These ddNTPs lack a hydroxyl group on the 3′-carbon of the sugar group, and thus terminate the DNA polymer. If these copies are then size separated by electrophoresis, they will form a ladder, reflecting the complementary sequence to the original template (**b**).

detected by labelling with ^{32}P. In this circumstance, four separate reactions are performed simultaneously, each terminating with one of the four ddNTPs. If each nucleotide is labelled with a distinct fluorescent tag, the four ddNTP reactions may be pooled and the products detected by characteristic emission.

Cloning

Cloning is a process whereby regions of DNA are selectively amplified using some form of cell-based multiplication, in contrast to PCR.

Cloning exploits restriction enzymes, endonucleases that are normally produced by bacteria. Their nomenclature denotes the species from which they originate. An individual restriction enzyme recognises a unique DNA sequence, usually between 4 and 12 bp in length, and cleaves it at this point, which is known as a restriction site. The consistency of these sites allows DNA derived from different sources to be joined (Fig. 12).

Regions of DNA of interest are often cloned into vectors derived from bacterial plasmids or bacteriophage viruses, the type of vector used being contingent on the size of DNA fragment to be cloned. The vector

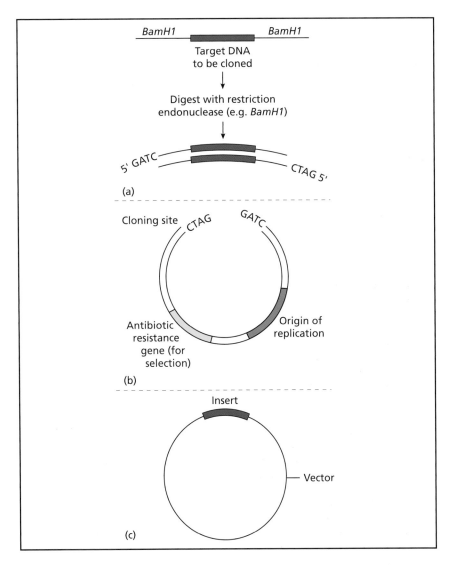

▲ **Fig. 12** Cloning. (**a**) The target DNA to be cloned is digested with restriction endonuclease, eg *Bam*HI, to produce characteristic overhangs at each end of the double strands. The endonuclease used must not cut within the target sequence itself. (**b**) The cloning vector is also cut with *Bam*HI to reveal complementary ends to the target insert. Vectors are often modified plasmids that contain multiple restriction enzyme sites which are limited to the insert region. (**c**) After incubation of the insert with the plasmid and a DNA ligase, a complete double-stranded circular plasmid is formed. This DNA can be introduced into a host bacterium (DNA transformation). If the bacteria are grown in culture, multiple copies of the original insert are obtained.

containing cloned DNA is then introduced into host bacteria by DNA transformation, whereby nucleic acid enters through pores chemically or electrically punched into the bacterial cell membrane. The cloned DNA is then amplified every time that the vector replicates.

Embryonic stem cell technology and gene targeting

Gene targeting is a technology that can be used to explore the function of a gene in the mouse. The gene in question is modified by a process that relies on homologous recombination (Fig. 13). A vector is made that contains a DNA sequence very similar to the gene but missing an essential part. In the event of recombination, the DNA sequence carried on the vector replaces the endogenous DNA sequence such that the gene will now no longer generate a functional product. The recombination event is conducted in embryonic stem (ES) cells from the 129 inbred mouse strain, and these modified 129 ES cells can be grown after injecting them into the blastocyst derived from a different inbred mouse, the C57BL/6 (Black 6) mouse. By a process of selection that exploits the different coat colours of the 129 and Black 6 mice, progeny can be selected that carry the modified, knockout gene (as described in Fig. 14).

Fluorescence-based *in situ* hybridisation and comparative genome hybridisation

These techniques can be used to visualise large regions of the genome that are not readily studied by PCR-based techniques. Fluorescence-based *in situ* hybridisation (FISH) is applied to chromosomes in metaphase (Fig. 15), when the chromosome pairs are aligned. Regions of the genome are visualised by

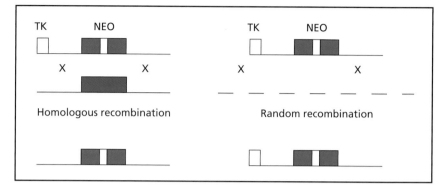

▲ **Fig. 13** Homologous recombination. The gene to be knocked out is represented by a blue box. The targeting vector contains the same sequence as the gene, although essential sequence has been deleted (shown as a red box), and also two markers that allow for selection. The NEO marker encodes a gene providing neomycin resistance that allows successfully recombined ES cells to be positively selected *in vitro*. However, random incorporation in the genome by the vector is possible, which would clearly leave the native gene intact and fully functional. To obviate this possibility an additional negative selection step using the gene encoding a viral thymidine kinase (TK) is employed. Ganciclovir produces a toxic phosphorylation product in the presence of TK, so that after selection of clones with neomycin, ganciclovir can be used to eliminate those arising as a result of random recombination.

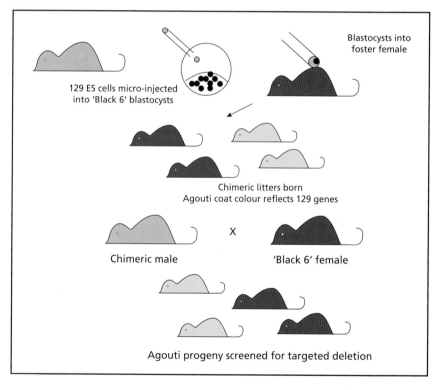

▲ **Fig. 14** How to make a gene 'knockout'. Embryonic stem (ES) cells (from the 129 strain) that have screened positive for the relevant recombination (see Fig. 13) are injected into the blastocyst of the C57BL/6 (Black 6) mouse. Eight to twelve injected blastocysts are transferred into the uterus of a foster mouse (rendered pseudo-pregnant by hormone treatment), where they implant. A litter is born, usually some black pups (reflecting the coat colour of the Black 6 recipient) where the cells have failed to integrate, but hopefully also some chimeras that are a brown (agouti) colour, reflecting a mixture of black and white coat colour (from the 129 donor). The best male chimeras are initially mated with black females (C57BL/6 strain). If the ES cells have been incorporated into the germline of the chimera, ie have made sperm in the testes, the resulting litters should have agouti pups, 50% of which should carry the modified target gene. The agouti pups are screened and any heterozygous carriers for the targeted gene are mated together: 25% of the resulting offspring would be expected to be homozygous for the modified target gene, or knockout. Note that these animals will be of mixed (129 × C57BL/6) genetic background. Once germline transmission is established, the chimeras can be bred onto the pure 129 background by repeated mating with 129 and then mating heterozygous carriers. The knockout mice can also be backcrossed onto other genetic backgrounds if required.

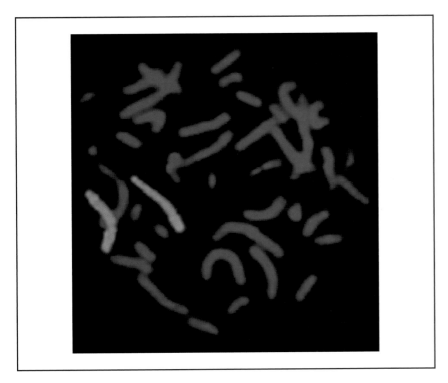

▲ **Fig. 15** FISH: a single chromosome pair displayed in pink. It would be easy to see if a significant part of one of these chromosomes was deleted or translocated.

large probes that are directly or indirectly labelled with a fluorochrome. FISH is commonly used in preimplantation genetic diagnosis, when it can be used to detect chromosome copy number variants and large genomic deletions or duplications, or to determine the sex of embryos. The main limitation of FISH is related to probe design: probes need to be specific for target regions whilst being robust to target sequence polymorphism.

Examination of deletions and duplications around the 10 Mb size range can be conducted using comparative genome hybridisation (CGH), which compares two DNA samples, referred to as 'test' and 'reference'. In the simplest form of this technique, metaphase CGH, each DNA sample is labelled with a different fluorochrome and then competitively hybridised to normal metaphase chromosomes on a glass slide. The ratio of signals from the two fluorochromes reflects the relative copy number in the test compared with the reference DNA sample. A more advanced technique, array-CGH, works on the same principle but in array-CGH the targets are mapped genomic clones instead of whole chromosomes. The advantage of using clones is that it increases the resolution of CGH dramatically, such that it has the capability to detect copy number variation at the resolution of kilobases. Array-CGH can therefore be employed in fields outside preimplantation genetic diagnosis, including cancer genetics, dysmorphology and complex trait genetics.

Whole genome expression analyses
The functional consequences of any changes in the genome will in part be manifest by changes in the

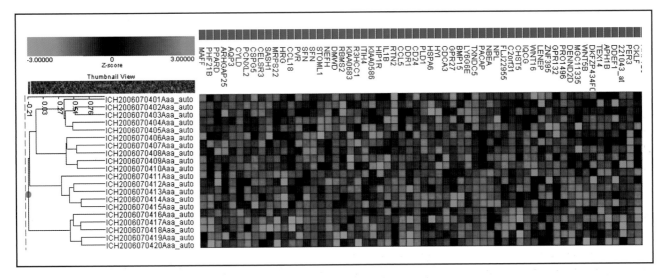

▲ **Fig. 16** Selection from a transcript profile. The results of the transcript array are colour-coded so that green and red represent increased and decreased expression. The genes whose transcripts are being assessed are listed at the top. A cluster analysis of the results is provided on the left-hand side which attempts to seek relationships between the transcript profiles in different samples. (Courtesy of Dr L. Game, Hammersmith Microarray Centre.)

magnitude of gene expression. With recent advances in technology it is now feasible to study expression on a genome-wide basis at both the transcript and protein level. Owing to its simpler structure, RNA is more readily studied in large scale, using transcript microarrays. Such arrays originally were based on representations of full-length cDNA on slides, with differentially labelled RNA extracted from 'test' and 'reference' cells (as with CGH arrays) competitively hybridised to such cDNA slides to quantify differences in expression. With improved bioinformatics, knowledge of the different RNA sequences expressed in cells has meant that transcripts can be analysed using shorter oligonucleotide sequences (usually from the 3'-end of the transcript) located on microchips. Using multiple RNA sequences with well-characterised levels of expression and deliberate introduction of known RNA sequences, absolute levels of RNA expression can be obtained from any given sample. This technology, sometimes referred to as transcriptomics, allows cells under different conditions to be compared. An example of a transcriptomic profile is shown in Fig. 16. Clinical applications are still being developed, but such approaches have generated valuable information for categorising malignancies such as breast cancer and lymphoproliferative disorders in order to allow better prediction of prognosis and likelihood of response to particular treatments. Genome-wide approaches to study protein expression have also been developed: using two-dimensional gels, thousands of cytosolic proteins can be separated and semi-quantified.

MOLECULAR BASIS OF SIMPLE GENETIC TRAITS

Mendelian inheritance patterns

Some hereditary conditions in humans and other species follow a predictable pattern of inheritance, sometimes referred to as Mendelian inheritance. In humans, three common classifications can be observed:

- autosomal recessive;
- autosomal dominant;
- X-linked.

At the most basic level, recessive diseases require the inheritance of defective genes from both parents, whereas in autosomal dominant disease one defective allele encoding a gene generates a disease phenotype.

As males have only one X chromosome, a defective allele on this chromosome will produce a phenotype. Although most of the genetic material carried by one of the X pairs in a female is inactive, the process of inactivation in each cell appears to be random; hence the less severe or absent phenotype in X-linked conditions in females.

Clinical characteristics of Mendelian inheritance patterns

- Recessive: appears sporadic; unaffected parents; much more likely with consanguineous marriage/ partners; both sexes affected.
- Dominant: one parent affected; both sexes affected; often milder phenotype or a high rate of spontaneous mutation if severe.
- X-linked: males affected; unaffected parents; may have affected male relatives.

More complex genetic effects

In contrast to predictable patterns of inheritance, many examples of human disease exhibit some genetic component in aetiology, but not one that can be described in simple terms. In these situations, multiple genes contribute to susceptibility in conjunction with environmental influences. The majority of human chronic illness can be considered to lie within this spectrum of what are now termed 'complex genetic traits'. Examples include hypertension, atherosclerosis, diabetes mellitus, osteoarthritis, asthma, many autoimmune diseases, schizophrenia, Alzheimer's-type dementia and bipolar affective disorder.

It has also recently become apparent that the simple model of single gene disorders described above is an oversimplification. Single gene traits are also subject to additional genetic influences. Sickle cell disease provides a good example. The mutation in the β-globin gene is known and the molecular pathology has been described, but there is a wide range of severity in the phenotype with which this mutation is associated. Some of this variation is probably the result of environmental factors. However, genetic mapping studies have implicated additional genetic loci, outside the globin locus, which modify the sickle cell phenotype. The nature of these genetic influences is not well characterised at present.

Mutational basis of disease

Mutations that disrupt gene function may be grouped into several categories on the basis of their molecular characteristics (Table 7). Single-nucleotide or point mutations may have several consequences. The most likely outcome is that of no functional change. As only a fraction of the genome is transcribed, or has a direct effect on transcription, many single-base changes are silent. Such changes can be exploited for genetic mapping (see below).

- Point mutations in coding DNA may result in no amino acid change (synonymous mutation). This is most likely to occur in the third base of the codon triplet.

- Missense mutations result in an amino acid change. However, the functional consequence is contingent on the extent of the chemical change in the amino acid wrought by the mutation.

Examples of conservative changes include the following.

- GAA → GAC produces Glu (E) → Asp (D): acidic side chain preserved.

- CTA → ATA produces Leu (L) → Ile (I): hydrophobic side chain preserved.

An example of a non-conservative change includes the following.

- GCA → CCA produces Ala (A) → Pro (P): small side chain replaced by bulky chain, will potentially disrupt secondary structure.

TABLE 7 MOLECULAR LESIONS THAT ABROGATE GENE FUNCTION

Classification	Molecular pathology	Examples
Deletion	Removal of entire gene	α-Thalassaemia Complement C4A deficiency
	Excision of part of a gene: may cause additional frameshift	X-linked muscular dystrophies
	Removal of a single codon	ΔF508 mutation in cystic fibrosis
Insertion	Insertion of LINE-1 element	*F8* gene in haemophilia A
	Triplet repeats	Myotonic dystrophy, etc. (see Table 8)
Nonsense mutation	Base change creating new stop codon	(A→T) transversion in β-globin codon 6 causing E→V
Missense mutation	Base change causing amino acid substitution	
Promoter mutation	Reduction in mRNA levels	−29 (A→G) β⁺-thalassaemia
Splice-site mutation	Complex effects (see Fig. 17)	

Nomenclature

A nucleotide change is described as follows: 403 (G→A). In this case, a guanine to adenine mutation has occurred at nucleotide 403 in the cDNA. As the base change is from purine to purine, the mutation may be referred to as a 'transition'. If this transition results in an amino acid substitution, eg arginine (R) replaced by histidine (H) at amino acid 131 in the mature polypeptide, then it is written as R131H.

In contrast, a thymine to guanine base change is termed a 'transversion'. The pyrimidine, T, is replaced by a purine, G. If this transversion occurred at the second nucleotide at the 5′-end (see Fig. 5) of an intron (and the adjacent base at the end of the preceding exon is nucleotide 421), this would be written 421 + 2 (T→G).

Functional consequences of point mutations

The most obvious consequence of a point mutation in DNA is the large number of potential effects that a non-conserved amino acid substitution may have on protein function.

- Most simply, the amino acid substitution might occur at a site critical to protein function, eg the active site of an enzyme or the binding site for another protein or nucleic acid.

- More subtle effects can also occur, eg protein folding may be affected so that stable secondary and hence tertiary structures cannot be adopted. One example is a proline substitution that can disrupt a helix. Other structural alterations include changes to glycosylation sites such as N-X-S/T (single letter code).

- Changes in the signal peptide or at post-translational cleavage sites may impede polypeptide processing. In many cases the mutant protein will therefore never reach its physiological destination.

Mutations in DNA can also affect the stability of the transcribed mRNA. This is difficult to predict, because many of the factors influencing mRNA half-life are uncharacterised, although mutant mRNA may never be translated in a detectable amount.

Splice-site mutations

Details of physiological splicing are shown in Figs 4 and 5. Mutations at splice sites are relatively common forms of molecular pathology. The consequences of splice-site lesions are complex. Three possible outcomes of a mutation at an acceptor splice site are shown in Fig. 17.

- The removal of a splice site may simply result in exon skipping: two non-adjacent exons are conjoined in the transcript.

- The spliceosome may identify a sequence within the exon or intron with sufficient similarity to the consensus acceptor splice site to function as such in the absence of the usual acceptor site. The cryptic site is often inefficient and hence several transcripts may originate from one abnormal allele.

The degree of disruption to protein function caused by splice-site lesions is dependent on whether the intron phase is altered. Introns interrupt codons, hence the position of the splice site within the coding triplet provides a method for classifying introns into three phases (Fig. 18).

Consider the transcripts elicited by the acceptor-site mutation in Fig. 17. If exon 2 is omitted from the transcript, the changes wrought in the mRNA are contingent on the phases of the first and second introns. If both are in phase 0, the allele may generate a readable transcript, albeit missing the sequence encoded by one exon. Alternatively, if the phases of the two

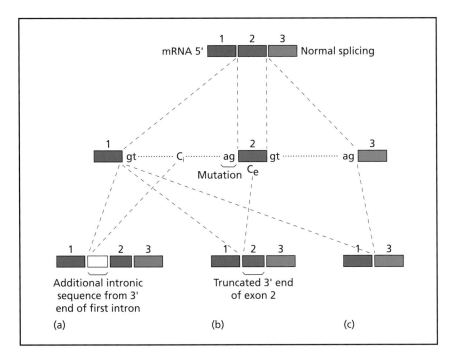

▲**Fig. 17** Splice-site mutations: (**a**) intronic cryptic splice site; (**b**) exonic cryptic splice site; (**c**) exon skipping. Ci, intronic cryptic site; C_e, exonic cryptic site.

Phase	Exon		Intron		Exon		
0	AGT	TGG	gt ·········· ag		TAT	GAC	
	S	W			Y	N	
1	AGT	TG	gt ·········· ag	G	TAT	GAC	
	S	(W		W)	Y	N	
2	AGT	T	gt ·········· ag	GG	TAT	GAC	
	S	(W		W)	Y	N	

(a)

Phase 0 to phase 1 splice

AGT	TGG	GTA	TGA	TGA
S	W	V	Stop	

Phase 0 to phase 2 splice

AGT	TGG	GGT	ATG
S	W	G	M

(b)

▲**Fig. 18** Intron phase: (**a**) across splice site showing translated sequence; (**b**) consequences of incorrect splicing.

introns are not identical, a highly aberrant mRNA will be produced.

Figure 18 provides examples of the formation of a premature stop codon and a completely novel polypeptide sequence distal to the mutation. A change of intron phase is said to produce a frameshift.

- Over 50% of cases of cystic fibrosis in white people are related to the loss of codon 508, the ΔF508 mutation. There is no frameshift and the protein product from the cystic fibrosis transmembrane regulator (*CFTR*) gene retains some function.

- Deletions in the dystrophin gene, *DMD*, cause X-linked muscular dystrophies. Deletions constitute the predominant lesion in both the milder Becker dystrophy phenotype and the more severe Duchenne dystrophy type. The difference between them is frequently whether the particular deletion produces a frameshift.

Anticipation and triplet repeats

Within the last decade, the molecular basis of several disorders, predominantly neurological, has been attributed to the insertion of an increased number of triplet repeats. Some of these diseases are listed in Table 8. Many share a dominant mode of inheritance. The repeat size appears to be meiotically unstable, ie expansion of the number of triplets can occur during meiosis. This provides the molecular explanation for two clinical observations.

- Anticipation is the tendency for diseases such as Huntington's disease and dystrophia myotonica to exhibit progressively worsening features and show earlier onset with successive generations within a family. This may be explained by progressive expansion of the repeat during successive meioses.

- It has also been observed that in some diseases, eg dystrophia myotonica, paternal meioses are inherently more unstable than female meioses, thus explaining the more marked anticipation seen with paternal inheritance.

The mechanism by which triplet expansions induce disease phenotype is for the most part uncertain, but must be variable because they have been described within untranslated as well as within coding DNA.

TABLE 8 EXAMPLES OF GENETIC DISEASES RELATED TO EXPANSION OF TRIPLET REPEATS

Disease	Gene locus	Normal repeat size	Pathological repeat size	Possible mechanism
Huntington's disease (HD)	4p16.3	$(CAG)_{9-35}$	$(CAG)_{37-100}$	Repeats are translated into polyglutamine tracts in HD protein
Bulbospinal muscular atrophy	Xp21	$(CAG)_{19-25}$	$(CAG)_{40-52}$	Repeats are translated into polyglutamine tracts in androgen receptor (*AR*)
Spinocerebellar ataxia type I	6p23	$(CAG)_{19-36}$	$(CAG)_{43-85}$	Coding: mechanism uncertain *SCA1*
Dentatorubral pallidoluysian atrophy	12p	$(CAG)_{7-23}$	$(CAG)_{49-150}$	Coding: mechanism uncertain
Myotonic dystrophy	19q13	$(CTG)_{5-35}$	$(CTG)_{50+}$	Repeat occurs in 3'-untranslated region of a kinase gene (*DMK*)
Friedreich's ataxia	9q13	$(GAA)_{7-22}$	$(GAA)_{200-900}$	Repeat occurs in intron 1 of *FRDA*, and appears to cause instability of DNA structure
Fragile-X site A	Xq27.3	$(CGG)_{6.54}$	$(CGG)_{200+}$	Repeat occurs in 5'-untranslated region of the fragile-X A gene (*FRAXA*)

- In the Huntington's disease gene, the CAG triplet is translated into polyglutamine tracts and the mutant Huntington's disease protein appears to be resistant to normal mechanisms of proteolysis and is prone to intracellular aggregation; how this influences cell function is not yet known.

- In dystrophia myotonica, the mRNA expression and stability of *DMK* is reduced, although this would not account for the dominant inheritance and there may be contributions from neighbouring genes.

Molecular basis of Mendelian dominance

Several different mechanisms have been described that may underlie a dominant mode of inheritance. Examples of these are given in Table 9. The mechanisms have been categorised into three types, although in some circumstances several modes of action may coexist:

- gain of function;

- haploinsufficiency;

- tumour suppressor.

Gain of function

A gain-of-function effect is self-explanatory: either the mutant protein gains a new function or it is not subject to the same constraints and regulatory influences as the wild-type molecule.

Complex structural proteins may exhibit a related form of aberrant function: a dominant negative effect. This occurs when one mutant component can disrupt a whole complex edifice. These lesions are particularly common in the collagen genes. The mature collagen molecule is dependent on aggregation of multiple gene products, the final structures being built on triple amino acid repeats, with abnormalities within any of these appearing to destabilise the entire molecule.

Haploinsufficiency

Haploinsufficiency is a term used to describe a locus at which a single gene product is insufficient to produce a normal phenotype. Such loci would self-evidently be more likely to generate dominant disorders. However, the mechanism of dominance is usually more complex than simple insufficiency.

Tumour suppressor

Dominance may arise when an inherited defect is combined with a somatic defect, the latter usually arising within particular tissues. Examples include many inherited tumour syndromes and growth disturbances such as tuberous sclerosis and autosomal dominant polycystic kidney disease. Retinoblastoma provided the first well-characterised disease exhibiting this phenomenon.

Single gene/multiple phenotypes

It cannot always be assumed that an inherited disease phenotype will invariably be the consequence of the mutation in a single gene. Mutations in the collagen genes provide good examples in simple genetic disease, although this scenario is most often encountered in complex traits (see below).

Somewhat more surprising is the concept that different defects within the same gene can lead to different diseases as a consequence of contrasting molecular lesions. This has been alluded to with respect to phenotype severity (X-linked muscular dystrophies). Examples in which the phenotype is

TABLE 9 MOLECULAR BASIS OF DOMINANT INHERITANCE

Mechanism		Gene	Disease	Comment
Gain of function	Structural change	*COL1A1* (collagen 1, αI)	Osteogenesis imperfecta, various types	Disruption of collagen fibrils exerts a dominant negative effect
			Ehlers–Danlos syndrome VII	
		COL1A2 (collagen 1, αII)	Osteogenesis imperfecta, various types	Ehlers–Danlos syndrome mutations confined to exon 6
			Ehlers–Danlos syndrome VII	Mutation causes constitutive activity of G_s protein
	Receptor activation	*GNAS1* (stimulatory protein α-subunit)	McCune–Albright syndrome	
			Loss of function mutations in *GNAS1* cause pseudohypoparathyroidism type IA	McCune–Albright syndrome patients are invariably mosaics for the lesion, otherwise the defect would be lethal
	Extension of sequence	*HD*	Huntington's disease	Polyglutamine runs from triple repeats
	Gene duplication	*PMP22* (peripheral myelin protein 22)	Charcot–Marie–Tooth syndrome type 1A (CMT1A). Other mutations cause HNPP and Déjerine–Sottas syndrome	*PMP22* belongs to a group of growth arrest proteins: activity arises from increased copy number in CMT1A
Haploinsufficiency	Enzyme deficiency	*C1NH* (C1 esterase inhibitor)	Hereditary angio-oedema (HANE)	Mutations in one allele also reduce transcription and translation from the wild-type allele
	Structural proteins	*FBN1* and *FBN2* (fibrillins)	Marfan's syndrome (*FBN1*) Congenital contractural arachnodactyly (*FBN2*)	In both cases, the abnormal alleles have a dominant negative influence
Tumour suppressor		*TSC2* (tubarin)	Tuberous sclerosis	The gene product has GTPase-activating activity
		RB1 (retinoblastoma 1)	Retinoblastoma	Example of a tumour-suppressor gene Inherited loss of *RB1* produces a phenotype in the context of a somatic mutation eradicating the wild-type gene

more diverse include the peripheral myelin protein 22 (*PMP22*) gene. Excess activity as a result of gene duplication causes a Charcot–Marie–Tooth syndrome, whereas point mutations and deletions in the same gene are associated with Déjerine–Sottas syndrome and hereditary neuropathy with pressure palsy (HNPP).

Phenotypes influenced by differential gene expression

Genetic polymorphism may alter the level of gene expression and such variation may be associated with different phenotypes, as in the following for example.

- The enzyme hypoxanthine adenine phosphoribosyltransferase is encoded by *HPRT* on the X chromosome. Virtual absence of enzyme activity causes Lesch–Nyhan syndrome with self-mutilation, extrapyramidal movement disorder and learning disability. Partial deficiency is associated with hyperuricaemia and gout because the enzyme functions in the salvage pathway in purine metabolism. A defect in purine recycling results in an increase in uric acid production.

- Apolipoprotein(a) is a major constituent of the lipoprotein Lp(a). The apolipoprotein(a) or *I* gene exhibits variation in the number of its 'krinkle 4' domains and the most important influence on Lp(a) plasma levels is the krinkle 4 I polymorphism.

Elevated plasma levels of Lp(a) are:

- associated with an increased risk of atherosclerosis as manifested by myocardial infarction and stroke;
- refractory to manipulation by drug treatment and/or dietary alteration.

Polymorphisms of the apolipoprotein(a) gene, which affects plasma levels of Lp(a), therefore contribute to a non-malleable genetic risk of ischaemic heart disease.

TABLE 10 MITOCHONDRIAL GENETIC DISEASES

Disease	Clinical features	Molecular pathology
MELAS	Mitochondrial myopathy Encephalopathy Lactic acidosis Stroke-like episode	Loss of Leu-tRNA
MERRF	Myoclonic epilepsy Ragged red fibre myopathy	Loss of Lys-tRNA
Kearns–Sayre syndrome	Ophthalmoplegia Retinal degeneration Cardiomyopathy	Deletions in mtDNA
Leber optic atrophy	Adult-onset optic atrophy Cardiac conduction defects (variable)	Multiple different point mutations

Mitochondrial diseases

Mitochondria possess their own genome, a circular mitochondrial DNA (mtDNA) of 16 kb. The genome encodes 37 genes, including tRNAs and subunits of enzymes involved in oxidative phosphorylation. In comparison with the nuclear genome, the mitochondrial genome is entirely maternally derived. Several genetic neurological diseases are caused by mutations in mtDNA (Table 10).

Imprinting

Imprinting is the term used to refer to the differential expression of alleles contingent on their parental origin. Several regions of the human genome demonstrate imprinting. The mechanism is poorly understood, although it does involve DNA methylation, and the effect is complex. Within a given region, some genes may be maternally imprinted, others paternally so; examples are given in Table 11. Disease may occur as a result of a defect in only one allele if the other allele is imprinted and hence not expressed. Alternatively, in circumstances of uniparental disomy (inheritance of both alleles from one parent), two imprinted alleles may not be expressed.

> **DNA methylation**
> • Indicates the addition of a methyl group to a base, usually the formation of 5-methylcytosine.
> • Associated with a general suppression of transcription.

5-Methylcytosine bases are also found in the promoters of selectively expressed genes (in tissues that do not express the gene) and occur during physiological inactivation of the X chromosome in females.

Linkage

> **Linkage** is observed because particular genes or DNA sequences are in physical proximity on the same chromosome and hence tend to be inherited together.

Linkage is a term that seems to strike fear in many, but the basic concept is simple. Linkage is observed because particular genes or DNA sequences are in physical proximity on the same chromosome and hence tend to be inherited together. The difficulties arise in trying to prove or deduce the probability of linkage.

Quantifying recombination

To understand the quantification of linkage, it is vital to be familiar with recombination and the concept of genetic distance. Recombination may be defined as the production of genetic combinations not found in either of the parents. In humans, this is predominantly created by crossing-over between homologous chromosomes during meiosis.

> **Recombination distance**
>
> The maximum possible recombination distance is 50%, because a marker and gene may be inherited together at random on 50% of occasions. Note also that two loci may still lie on the same chromosome with a recombination fraction of about 0.5, provided that they are sufficient distance apart.

The inheritance of an autosomal recessive disorder is shown in Fig. 19 in two families. The disease gene, D, is situated close to another locus, A, which is utilised as a genetic marker, ie locus A has four different alleles that are readily distinguished.

In the parents, it is apparent that the mutant D allele, D*, is linked with allele A_1. This inheritance of D* is predicted by the inheritance of A_1 in family 1. In family 2, there has been a recombination event between A_1 and D* in the affected sibling (proband). If, when observing the inheritance of D* and A_1, there was such a recombination event between them in only 1 of 100 times that the alleles were inherited, the

TABLE 11 REGIONS OF GENOMIC IMPRINTING

Disease	Clinical features	Gene	Expression
Beckwith–Wiedemann syndrome	Obesity Macroglossia Abnormal glucose tolerance	11p15.5: region includes insulin-like growth factor 2 (*IGF2*) and *H19*	*IGF2* paternal *H19* maternal
Prader–Willi syndrome	Hypotonia Mental handicap Obesity Hypogonadism	Deletion 15q12	Maternal
Angelman's syndrome	Clonic jerks Mental handicap Hypopigmentation	Deletion 15q12	Paternal

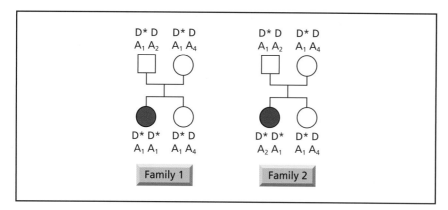

▲**Fig. 19** The inheritance of an autosomal recessive disorder. Consider a locus *A* that is linked to disease locus *D*. Locus *A* has four alleles, A_1–A_4. Locus D has two alleles, D and D*. D* is a mutant allele that causes disease in the homozygous state. See text for further explanation.

recombination distance between them would be 1% and the genetic distance would be said to be 1 centimorgan (cM), after the pioneering *Drosophila* geneticist Thomas Hunt Morgan.

Relationship between mapping distance and physical distance

A genetic mapping distance between two loci must have some relationship to the physical separation of the two sites. For regions of the genome that have been physically mapped in detail, it is apparent that a genetic distance of 1 cM is equivalent to about

10^6 bp (or 1 Mb of genomic DNA). This equivalence is subject to wide regional variation. However, in the absence of a detailed genome-wide physical map, a genetic map based on recombination frequencies was the only means of genomic navigation.

With the completion of the Human Genome Project, a base-by-base physical map of the human genome is available. Some of the methods used in the construction of this molecular map are illustrated in Fig. 20. The anchoring of a framework of markers was an essential first step and was

achieved using mapping data as well as artificially recombined chromosomes, termed 'radiation hybrids'.

The LOD score

How do you know whether two sites on the DNA are linked? Now that the genome has been sequenced, this should become clear from reference to the human genome database, but previously this was not possible, and statistical methods were derived for determining whether two things (perhaps a putative gene for a disease trait and a known genetic locus, or two known genetic loci) were likely to be linked with each other. A LOD (logarithm of the odds) score was the most widely employed means of quantifying linkage, and many papers make reference to this. The principle is straightforward, but calculating a LOD score for anything but the simplest family pedigrees is a complex process. The LOD score for linkage of a given marker with a disease is determined as follows.

1. The inheritance pattern of each marker allele is followed through the pedigree and the probability that it is linked with the disease gene is calculated, based on the observed recombination (if any) between it and the putative disease gene.

2. This probability is aggregated for all alleles to determine an overall likelihood. This calculation can be performed assuming different recombination distances (θ) between the marker and disease gene. The aggregate of these probabilities is the likelihood of linkage, $L(\theta)$.

3. A null hypothesis would be that there is no linkage, ie $\theta = 0.5$, which can be written $L(\theta = 0.5)$.

4. The LOD score (*Z*) calculation is usually performed for varying

Physical maps figure

Cytogenetic map	
Framework map	Genetic markers spaced regularly throughout interval. Markers include microsatellites, ESTs
Initial overlapping map of clones (YAC contigs)	Individual YAC clones overlapping with one another anchored onto framework map
Smaller clones	Contigs of smaller clones such as BACs and eventually cosmids
DNA sequence from subclones	G T T A C T G G A

▲**Fig. 20** Physical maps. BAC, bacterial artificial chromosome; EST, expressed sequence tags; YAC, yeast artificial chromosomes.

TABLE 12 EXAMPLES OF DIFFERENT GENETIC MARKERS

Marker	Method	Comments
Restriction fragment length polymorphisms (RFLPs)	Mutations are detected that occur at the consensus sequence recognised by restriction enzymes. The alleles are distinguished by restriction digestion followed by gel electrophoresis and Southern blotting	RFLPs are limited in availability. Time-consuming and expensive to analyse
Minisatellites or variable number tandem repeat (VNTR) probes	Specific probes are used after Southern blotting of digested DNA. The probes show the length of the VNTR	Restricted number of VNTRs Time-consuming and expensive to analyse
Microsatellites or simple sequence length polymorphic (SSLP) markers	Short tandem repeats, typically of dinucleotides, are amplified by PCR using primers that flank the repeat sequence	Distributed throughout genome and amenable to rapid and relatively inexpensive genotyping[1]
Single nucleotide polymorphism (SNP)	Single-point mutations occur every 500–1,000 bp. Usually detected by PCR	Densely distributed throughout the genome. Amenable to rapid automated typing. Various means of identification, biallelic[2]

1. The Whitehead Institute and Massachusetts Institute of Technology, Boston have screened both human and murine genomes with dinucleotide probes. Thousands of microsatellite markers have been identified spanning the entire genome in both species.
2. Collections of SNP markers are being collected and published in the public domain. However, at present these markers do not provide the genome-wide coverage of microsatellites. Their very density indicates that, in the human genome, there will be over 10^6 useful SNPs.

values of θ and the maximum values stated, Z_{max}:

$$Z = \log_{10} [L(\theta)/L(\theta = 0.5)]$$

For a single gene trait, a LOD score of 3.0 indicates odds in favour of linkage of 1,000 to 1. Note that LOD = 3.0 does not imply $P = 1 \times 10^{-3}$; a P value can be determined for a LOD score using Bayesian analysis.

Genetic markers

Examples of different clinical markers are given in Table 12.

A genetic marker is a polymorphic sequence of DNA from a single locus that is used in genetic mapping. The following are attributes of an ideal marker:

- originates from one locus and is readily distinguishable from other sites;
- stable over generations;
- highly polymorphic;
- easily identified and characterised;
- may be screened on a large scale;
- exhibits prevalent (and not rare) allelic differences.

In the field of forensic science, hypervariable minisatellites have been used as a means of 'DNA fingerprinting'. These minisatellites contain a variable number of tandem repeats – GGGCAGGANG. The fingerprint is read by Southern blotting of DNA and interrogating the blot with a probe comprising a run of tandem repeats. The size and density of the bands thus revealed represent the fingerprint.

Simple vs complex genetic traits

Complex genetic traits are those in which many different genes contribute to susceptibility; examples include ischaemic heart disease, hypertension, asthma, diabetes types 1 and 2 and systemic lupus erythematosus (SLE), to name but a few. Their genetic complexity, combined with confounding factors from the environment, has delayed their characterisation. However, the clinical importance of complex traits (Table 13) provides the impetus for their investigation.

Gene identification

Steps in gene identification

1. With the use of linkage studies, map regions that are linked with disease.
2. Identify the most likely known genes that are located within an area (candidate genes):
   (a) Biological function.
   (b) Genetic analyses from animal models.
   (c) Data from other genetic investigations, eg association studies.
   (d) Functional biological data implicating gene.
   (e) Data implicating genes of related function or within the same biological pathway.
3. When there are no good candidate genes available, try:
   (a) Expression profiling (study differentially expressed genes in disease state vs healthy).
   (b) Identification of novel genes within defined genomic regions.
   (c) Cloning.
4. Sequencing of the putative disease gene and characterisation of mutations.
5. Corroboration of mutational analyses in additional cohorts.
6. Functional biology.

TABLE 13 COMPARISON OF SIMPLE AND COMPLEX GENETIC TRAITS

Simple traits	Complex traits
Genetic influence predominantly from one locus. The penetrance of the mutation at this locus is high	Multiple genes contribute to susceptibility; each gene has a relatively low penetrance
There may be consistent or many different molecular lesions at the disease locus. Mutations often have a dramatic effect on the function of the gene product	No disease system has been completely characterised: current models suggest that the genetic influences come from polymorphisms within the population, variations having subtle effects on the function of gene products, although through interactions between gene products the overall influence is magnified
Molecular basis of many simple traits is well defined	Susceptibility genes remain for the most part unidentified
Mode of inheritance is usually weighted towards a recessive or dominant pattern for autosomal diseases	Non-Mendelian inheritance overall
Amenable to genetic screening	Screening not useful at present owing to paucity of identified genes and the complexity of risk associated with them
Genetic heterogeneity, ie mutations in different genes producing same phenotype, is unusual	Genetic heterogeneity is usual. Not all affected individuals will possess the same constellation of susceptibility genes
Limited interaction with other genes to generate phenotype	Genetic interaction is usual
Accounts for relatively rare diseases	Complex traits include some of the most prevalent human ailments

Methods used to map disease genes

Pedigree-based linkage studies

Large pedigrees in which there are many affected individuals can be used in linkage analyses. The complexity of the process necessitates the use of computer programs to determine LOD scores. This approach is most suited to simple disease traits because the mathematical analyses require the estimation of disease gene frequencies and penetrance.

Non-parametric linkage studies

A non-parametric analysis is one in which no a-priori models are used and hence no assumptions are made about penetrance and disease-susceptible gene frequencies. These types of studies are particularly useful in complex traits.

One of the most commonly used methods is that of affected sib pairs (Fig. 21). The principle in this approach is to examine families in which there are at least two affected siblings. Individuals are genotyped,

either in regions of interest or across the entire genome with microsatellite markers. Using Mendelian principles, it can be determined which alleles siblings would be expected to share given random segregation of alleles. Linkage with disease may be inferred if affected siblings share alleles at a locus in a disproportionate fashion, ie over and above that predicted by chance.

As illustrated in Fig. 21, because of recombination between disease-susceptibility genes and marker alleles, different alleles may be

shared in different families. Using this method large regions of the genome (20 cM) are linked with disease: given that an average gene is 40 kb, a region of 20 cM would be expected to encode 5,000 genes.

Number of genetic markers

When conducting any linkage analysis, individuals may be genotyped over selected regions if there is evidence that supports linkage at these sites. Alternatively, the entire genome may be screened using suitable markers, eg microsatellites.

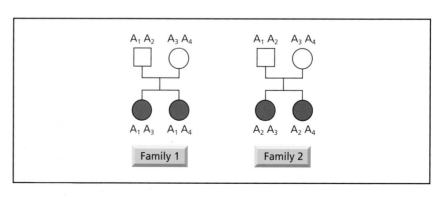

▲ **Fig. 21** Allele sharing. A genetic locus *A* has four distinguishable alleles, A_1–A_4. Both siblings are affected in each family. They share alleles, albeit different ones. See text for further explanation.

Association studies

An association study examines the frequency of a particular allele in a population with disease compared with that in a control population.

In an association study, the frequency of a given allele in a disease population is compared with its frequency in a control population. This method has the advantage of simplicity of design, but inherent in the simplicity are some major drawbacks.

The reliability of the data is dependent on the appropriateness of the control group with respect to the disease population, and securing DNA from a well-matched control sample is fraught with difficulties. Any bias in sample ascertainment may affect allele frequencies in the control population and hence lead to spurious positive associations with respect to disease.

Another caveat that needs to be considered is that of linkage disequilibrium. An association study examines the relationship of disease with a particular allele; it does not, for example, examine a single gene. Figure 22 shows a region of DNA with two loci A and B. There are two known alleles at each locus in a given population, each with the frequency shown. If loci A and B are inherited entirely separately (without linkage between them), the frequencies of individuals with the combination A_1B_1 and A_2B_2 are shown. If these frequencies are not observed, the loci A and B are said to be in linkage disequilibrium, meaning that alleles do not segregate independently. Following the example in Fig. 22, an association between A_1 and disease might simply reflect the actual role of an allele at another (possibly unknown) locus such as B, if A and B are in linkage disequilibrium with each other. Linkage disequilibrium has been described for many alleles in the major histocompatibility complex, in part reflecting a high gene density in a region that has been well studied.

The HapMap

The pattern of linkage disequilibrium across the human genome is an essential component for interpreting association data. Following the Human Genome Project, whose primary goal was to delineate the basic sequence of the genome, the HapMap consortium was established as a second phase of analysis that involved genotyping polymorphisms across the entire genome to build up a pattern of linage disequilibrium. These data are publicly available through the HapMap consortium website (http://www.hapmap.org/) for white, Japanese, Chinese and Yoruban African populations.

Animal models

The most commonly used genetic model for human disease is the mouse. The use of mice stems from the similarity of murine and human physiology (the murine immune system being particularly well studied), and also from practical considerations, eg the size of the animal and its breeding potential. Examples of the use of murine genetic models include the following.

- The susceptibility gene was first cloned in the murine system.

- Single gene mutations in the mouse model of Mendelian human disease: this can be useful in the study of rare human genetic disease, eg the *beige* mutation in the mouse has a similar phenotype to Chédiak–Higashi syndrome.

▲ Fig. 22 Linkage disequilibrium. Two loci are shown, *A* and *B*. There are two possible alleles at each locus, designated 1 and 2, with frequencies in the population as shown. In any one individual studied in isolation it would not be possible to determine which of these alleles was situated on the paternal or maternal chromosome. Two possible scenarios are given that represent two extreme possibilities in how the alleles are distributed on the two chromosomes. If the two alleles are in equilibrium, then there is complete correlation between them, with the genotype at locus *A* unfailingly predicting that at locus *B* on the haplotype. In contrast, if there is no linkage between them, the alleles show no correlation with one another and all possible combinations are present, the frequencies of which are represented by the product of the individual allele frequencies. The further apart the two loci on a chromosome, the more likely that the correlation between allelic variants breaks down.

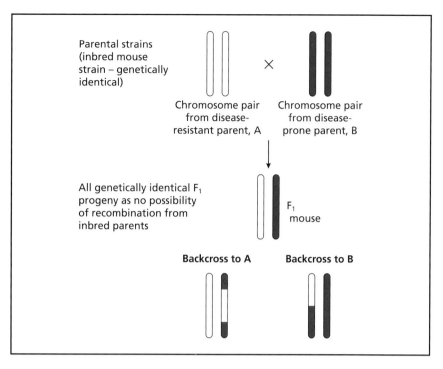

▲ **Fig. 23** Mapping genes in animal models. Diversity can be created by crossing the F₁ mice with either of the parental strains, ie a backcross. The segregation of disease-prone genes from B will lead to a spectrum of severity of the disease phenotype in the backcross mice. The inheritance of a particular region from B in severely affected backcross progeny will mark the site of disease genes.

• With the advent of analyses in complex human traits, murine models can also be useful, eg the non-obese diabetic (NOD) mouse as a model for human type 1 diabetes, and the New Zealand black/white hybrid mouse as a model for human SLE.

How murine models can be used to map disease genes is depicted in Fig. 23.

Murine systems offer additional advantages. With the use of embryonic stem cell technology, copies of human genes (as transgenes) can be introduced into the mouse and functional studies performed. Similarly, using homologous recombination, segments of coding sequence can be excised from murine genes and the phenotype of targeted gene disruption (or knockout) observed. Using these methods, putative human disease susceptibility genes can be tested in an *in vivo* situation.

Genetic testing

Genetic testing is currently applicable for some simple genetic traits when:

• the aetiological mutation(s) is known (a direct test);

• the locus involved is well characterised (an indirect test).

Many different methods may be employed; examples include PCR and DNA sequencing of the PCR products, and oligonucleotide hybridisation. The following are some of the technical limitations to genetic screening.

• Allelic heterogeneity: the same phenotype resulting from many different mutations, eg β-thalassaemias.

• Complexity of the genetic lesion with respect to risk calculation, eg triplet repeats.

• Other (unknown) genetic polymorphisms influencing the phenotype.

• Some mutations not identified, eg X-linked muscular dystrophies.

• Mosaicism: the genetic composition of the individual cells in an organism vary as a consequence of some somatic event.

Ethical issues

The explosion of knowledge in molecular medicine and genetics raises a number of very important ethical issues, ranging from the possibilities produced by cloning to considerations of the use to which genetic information about individuals might be put by insurance companies, employers and the like. These are beyond the scope of this book, but comment about the use of genetic testing in clinical practice is warranted. In some situations genetic tests are different from other tests that doctors perform. For instance, they may have the following consequences.

• Profound implications for an individual who is perfectly well at the moment of testing: 'You will get Huntington's disease' and not 'You might get . . .'

• Equally profound implications for other family members, who might be totally unaware of any issues being raised, and who may prefer to remain unaware of such issues: 'Your mother must be a carrier' or 'Your brother has a 50% chance of having this'.

It is therefore vitally important that genetic tests must be:

• voluntary;

• confidential (information gained must not be revealed to third parties, leading to complex considerations when the third party is a family member who may or may not be at risk of a particular condition);

- explained (possible outcomes and uncertainties must be thoroughly discussed before any testing is performed).

FURTHER READING

Bronchud MH, *et al.*, eds. *Principles of Molecular Oncology*, 2nd edn. Totowa, NJ: Humana Press, 2004.

Cox T and Sinclair J, eds. *Molecular Biology in Medicine*. Oxford: Blackwell Science, 1997.

Elliott WH and Elliott DC, eds. *Biochemistry and Molecular Biology*, 3rd edn. Oxford: Oxford University Press, 2005.

Hancock JT, ed. *Molecular Genetics*. Biomedical Sciences Explained Series Oxford: Butterworth-Heinemann, 1999. (There are other quite useful books in this series.)

Kingston HM. *ABC of Clinical Genetics*, 3rd edn. London: BMJ Books, 2002.

Lemoine NR, ed. *Understanding Gene Therapy*. Oxford: BIOS, 1999.

Levitan M, ed. *Textbook of Human Genetics*, 3rd edn. New York: Oxford University Press, 1988.

Lewin B. *Genes VII*, 7th edn. Oxford: Oxford University Press, 2000.

Miesfeld RL. *Applied Molecular Genetics*. New York: Wiley, 1999.

Ott J. *Analysis of Human Genetic Linkage*, 3rd edn. Baltimore: Johns Hopkins University Press, 1999.

Primrose SB and Twyman RM. *Principles of Genome Analysis and Genomics*, 3rd edn. Malden, MA: Blackwell Science, 2003.

Runge MS and Patterson C, eds. *Principles of Molecular Medicine*, 2nd edn. Totowa, NJ: Humana Press, 2006.

Snustad DP and Simmons MJ. *Principles of Genetics*, 4th edn. Hoboken, NJ: Wiley, 2006.

Strachan T and Read AP. *Human Molecular Genetics 3*, 3rd edn. London: Garland Science, 2004.

Sudbery P. *Human Molecular Genetics*, 2nd edn. Harlow: Prentice Hall, 2002.

Turnpenny PD and Ellard S. *Emery's Elements of Medical Genetics*, 12th edn. Edinburgh: Elsevier Churchill Livingstone, 2005.

Websites
Online Mendelian Inheritance in Man (OMIM): database of textual information and references covering human genes and genetic disorders. Available at http://www.ncbi.nlm.nih.gov/Omim/

US National Center for Biotechnology Information (NCBI): Human Genome Resources website. Available at http://www.ncbi.nlm.nih.gov/genome/guide/human/

5.1 Self-assessment questions

Question 1

In the field of molecular biology, the term 'recombination' means:

Answers

A The coming together of chromosomes at meiosis

B The separation of chromosomes at mitosis

C The combination of alleles from both parents at fertilisation

D The production of genetic combinations not found in either of the parents

E The tendency of some genetic disorders to run true in families

Question 2

In the field of molecular biology, a codon is:

Answers

A a 2-base pair unit of DNA that codes for an amino acid

B a 3-base pair unit of DNA that codes for an amino acid

C a 4-base pair unit of DNA that codes for an amino acid

D a 2-base pair unit of RNA that codes for an amino acid

E a 3-base pair unit of RNA that codes for an amino acid

Question 3

A Mendelian X-linked dominant condition would be transmitted to:

Answers

A All of the sons of an affected woman

B All of the children of an affected man

C None of the sons of an affected woman

D All of the sons of an affected man

E Half of the daughters of an affected woman

Question 4

The nucleic acid bases in RNA are:

Answers

A Adenine, cytosine, guanine and uracil

B Adenine, cytosine, guanine and thymine

C Adenine, cytosine, uracil and thymine

D Cytosine, guanine, uracil and thymine

E Adenine, guanine, uracil and thymine

Question 5

The process of producing mRNA from DNA is called:

Answers

A Translation

B Transcription

C Translocation

D Splicing

E Promotion

Question 6

If an allele at locus *A* and an allele at locus *B* are in linkagedisequilibrium, this means that they are:

Answers

A Found together on the same chromosome on all occasions

B Never found together on the same chromosome

C Found together on the same chromosome as often as you would expect by chance

D Found together on the same chromosome more often than you would expect by chance

E Found together on the same chromosome less often than you would expect by chance

Question 7

In the field of molecular biology, what is meant by the term 'anticipation'?

Answers

A That having a particular genetic mutation anticipates the development of a disease

B That having a particular genetic mutation anticipates the development of a disease if there is a particular environmental exposure

C That a disease shows earlier onset and worsening features in successive generations of a family

D That two parents who are carriers of a recessive gene can anticipate a 25% likelihood of having an affected child

E That the expression of a gene can be anticipated by knowing its parental origin

Question 8

A man with a genetic condition caused by mutation in mitochondrial DNA will pass it on to:

Answers

A All of his children

B None of his children

C All of his sons, but none of his daughters

D All of his daughters, but none of his sons

E Any child with a 50% probability

Question 9

The following are purines:

Answers

A Cytosine and thymine

B Cytosine and guanine

C Cytosine and adenine

D Adenine and thymine

E Adenine and guanine

Question 10

The coding regions of DNA are called:

Answers

A Codons

B Introns

C Exons

D Promoters

E Transcriptons

5.2 Self-assessment answers

Answer to Question 1

D

Recombination is the production of genetic combinations not found in either of the parents, which in humans is predominantly created by crossing-over between homologous chromosomes during meiosis.

Answer to Question 2

E

Translation is the name of the process of decoding protein sequence from mRNA, the polypeptide amino acid sequence being determined by the base

sequence of its mRNA. The RNA bases are 'read' in a 3-bp or triplet code, each 3-bp unit being referred to as a codon. The 'decoding' is performed by tRNA, which recognises each codon by virtue of a complementary RNA sequence (the anticodon), which forms a unique part of each tRNA molecule.

Answer to Question 3

E

A Mendelian X-linked condition can affect and be transmitted by both males and females. Affected males will pass the condition on to all their daughters but to none of their sons (since no X chromosome is transmitted to them from their father). Affected females will transmit the condition to 50% of their children, whether male or female.

Answer to Question 4

A

The nucleic bases in DNA are adenine, cytosine, guanine and thymine. In RNA the thymine is replaced by uracil, which differs from thymine in the lack of a methyl on the 5'-carbon atom of the pyrimidine ring.

Answer to Question 5

B

The process of producing RNA from DNA is called transcription, after which intronic sequence is removed by splicing. Other changes include the addition of a poly(A) tail at the 3'-end and a methyl-G residue (in reverse) at the 5'-end, both promoting mRNA stability. Translation is the process by which codons of mRNA are read to produce a polypeptide sequence.

Answer to Question 6

D

Linkage is observed because particular genes or DNA sequences are in physical proximity on the same chromosome and hence tend to be inherited together. If two loci, *A* and *B*, are on different chromosomes or a long way apart on the same chromosome, then alleles at these loci are likely to be inherited independently, ie their inheritance will not be linked and the chances of them being inherited together will be as expected by chance (linkage equilibrium). In contrast, if they are inherited together more often than expected by chance, then the two loci are said to be in linkage disequilibrium.

Answer to Question 7

C

Anticipation describes the tendency for some diseases to show earlier onset and worsening features in successive generations of a family. This occurs in the 'triplet repeat diseases', eg Huntington's disease and myotonic dystrophy, which are associated with the insertion of an increased number of triplet repeats in successive generations. The term used to refer to the differential expression of alleles contingent on their parental origin is imprinting.

Answer to Question 8

B

The mitochondrial genome is entirely maternally derived, so a man cannot pass mitochondrial DNA to any of this children. In contrast, a woman with a mitochondrial mutation will pass it on to all of her offspring.

Answer to Question 9

E

Adenine (A) and guanine (G) are purines; cytosine (C), thymine (T) and uracil are pyrimidines. Base pairing in DNA always involves one purine and one pyrimidine, ie GC or AT.

Answer to Question 10

C

Coding DNA is frequently divided into segments (exons) that are separated by non-coding intervening regions (introns), whose function is largely unknown. Codons are the nucleotide triplet code in mRNA that determine the amino acid sequence as polypeptides are made. The promoter is the sequence of DNA that binds RNA polymerase at the start of a gene.

BIOCHEMISTRY AND METABOLISM

Authors:

FM Gribble and F Reimann

Editor:

JD Firth

Editor-in-Chief:

JD Firth

BIOCHEMISTRY AND METABOLISM: **SECTION 1**
REQUIREMENT FOR ENERGY

Introduction

Biochemistry is the study of how living organisms function at the molecular level. It includes:

- the generation and storage of energy;

- the metabolism of basic molecules such as sugars, amino acids and fatty acids;

- the biosynthesis and functions of complex macromolecules such as proteins, DNA, glycogen and lipids.

Energy is required to power many cellular processes, for example:

- biosynthesis of macromolecules;

- performance of mechanical work;

- active transport of ions and molecules.

Cells generate energy by the metabolism of carbohydrates, fats and protein, and store it in the form of high-energy phosphate bonds in adenosine triphosphate (ATP) or guanosine triphosphate (GTP).

The central pathways involved in the release of energy from glucose are:

- glycolysis;

- citric acid cycle (Krebs cycle, tricarboxylic acid or TCA cycle).

The metabolism of other fuels such as amino acids and fatty acids produces molecules that feed into these pathways at various points.

The metabolic pathways can generate high-energy phosphate bonds in two principal ways:

- some reactions are coupled directly to the formation of ATP and GTP;

- other reactions release electrons that are carried by molecules such as NAD^+ (nicotinamide adenine dinucleotide) and then transferred to the mitochondrial electron transport chain which generates ATP by oxidative phosphorylation.

Glycolysis

> **Glycolysis** is a cytoplasmic series of reactions by which glucose, a six-carbon sugar, is metabolised to two molecules of the three-carbon unit, pyruvate.

The glycolytic pathway is shown in Fig. 1.

1. Glucose enters cells on a glucose transporter and is then phosphorylated by hexokinases to form glucose-6-phosphate. This reaction, although consuming ATP, traps glucose within the cell because glucose-6-phosphate cannot pass back through the membrane.

2. Glucose-6-phosphate is isomerised to fructose-6-phosphate and is then further phosphorylated to form fructose-1,6-bisphosphate. The latter reaction is catalysed by phosphofructokinase and consumes a second molecule of ATP. This is the first committed

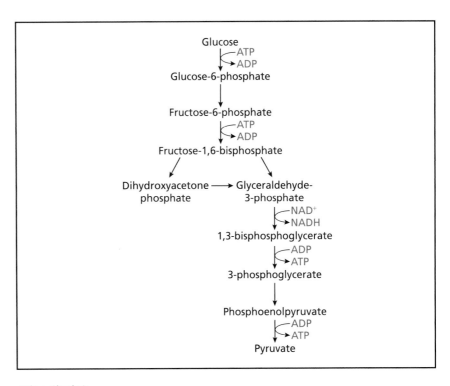

▲ **Fig. 1** Glycolysis.

step in glycolysis and is one of the main steps at which flux through the pathway is regulated. ATP and citrate, whose levels are increased by glycolysis, act as feedback inhibitors of phosphofructokinase and thereby prevent the unnecessary entry of further glucose into the glycolytic pathway.

3. Fructose-1,6-bisphosphate is cleaved into two three-carbon units: glyceraldehyde-3-phosphate and dihydroxyacetone phosphate, which are themselves interconvertible.

4. Glyceraldehyde-3-phosphate is further phosphorylated to form 1,3-bisphosphoglycerate, in a reaction which is coupled to the generation of NADH from NAD^+.

5. In a further series of reactions the two phosphate groups of 1,3-bisphosphoglycerate are transferred to adenosine diphosphate (ADP), forming ATP. The final step of glycolysis, catalysed by pyruvate kinase, results in the formation of pyruvate.

For each molecule of glucose undergoing glycolysis, there is therefore a net synthesis of two pyruvate, two ATP and two NADH molecules.

- A low-affinity hexokinase, known as glucokinase, regulates glycolytic flux in pancreatic β cells and contributes to coupling insulin release to glucose concentration. Mutations in glucokinase that reduce its affinity for glucose result in an inherited form of diabetes (maturity-onset diabetes of the young, type 2). Mutations that increase the affinity of glucokinase cause neonatal persistent hyperinsulinism.

- Pyruvate kinase deficiency is an inherited disorder of glycolysis affecting the red blood cells. Haemolytic anaemia results because mature red blood cells depend on glycolysis for ATP production, needed to maintain ionic gradients and hence red blood cell size and shape. Immature erythrocytes still have mitochondria and therefore an alternative energy supply.

The two common dietary sugars, sucrose and lactose, are disaccharides, containing one residue of glucose and one residue of either fructose (in sucrose) or galactose (in lactose). Fructose and galactose also feed into the glycolytic pathway.

- Fructose is phosphorylated to fructose-1-phosphate or fructose-6-phosphate, and subsequently cleaved to three-carbon units that are metabolised by glycolysis.

- Galactose is first phosphorylated and then coupled to uridine diphosphate (UDP). UDP-galactose is an activated form of the sugar that is converted into UDP-glucose and subsequently glucose-1-phosphate.

- Deficiency of the enzyme galactose-1-phosphate uridyltransferase, which catalyses the coupling of UDP and galactose-1-phosphate, causes galactosaemia. Infants with the condition present with failure to thrive, vomiting, hepatomegaly and jaundice, due to the accumulation of toxic levels of galactose-1-phosphate.
- Hereditary fructose intolerance is caused by an inherited deficiency in fructaldolase B, the enzyme that cleaves fructose-1-phosphate in the liver. A fructose load therefore results in the accumulation of fructose-1-phosphate, which inhibits

enzymes in gluconeogenesis and glycogenolysis and thereby causes hypoglycaemia. It should be distinguished from the more benign condition of essential fructosuria, which is due to a deficiency of fructokinase. This results in slower fructose metabolism and consequently higher plasma levels following ingestion of fructose-rich meals.

The fate of pyruvate

Aerobic metabolism of pyruvate by the citric acid cycle results in the generation of large quantities of ATP. Anaerobic conversion of pyruvate to lactate releases less ATP, but allows glycolysis to continue even in the absence of oxygen.

The fate of pyruvate depends on the metabolic environment (Fig. 2).

Aerobic Under aerobic conditions, pyruvate passes into mitochondria and is metabolised by the citric acid cycle. Some steps of the citric acid cycle are oxidative, ie electrons are released. The electrons are used to reduce specialised carrier molecules, NAD^+ and FAD (flavine adenine dinucleotide), thereby forming NADH and $FADH_2$. Subsequent electron transfer to the electron transport chain, and thence to O_2, generates large amounts of ATP (see Citric acid cycle and Oxidative phosphorylation, below). The regenerated NAD^+ and FAD are used for further activity of the citric acid cycle.

Anaerobic Under anaerobic conditions O_2 is not available, and the electron transport chain becomes saturated with electrons. The reduced forms of NADH and $FADH_2$ therefore accumulate in the mitochondria, and concomitant

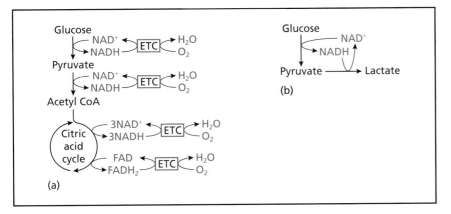

▲ **Fig. 2** (**a**) Aerobic and (**b**) anaerobic pathways. ETC, electron transport chain.

depletion of NAD^+ and FAD prevents further turns of the citric acid cycle. NADH also accumulates in the cytosol, where the depletion of NAD^+ inhibits further glycolysis.

This would result in a total block of ATP production in the absence of O_2 if it were not for an alternative pathway for the regeneration of cytoplasmic NAD^+. For this purpose, tissues such as muscle contain lactate dehydrogenase which converts pyruvate to lactate. This reaction reoxidises NADH back to NAD^+, thereby removing the block on glycolysis. It allows a flux of glucose to lactate with the simultaneous generation of ATP.

There is, as expected, a pay-off for this reaction. The amount of energy released by the anaerobic metabolism of glucose to lactate (2 ATP for each molecule of glucose) is very small compared with that obtained when glucose is oxidised completely in the citric acid cycle (36–38 ATP per glucose).

Lactate produced in the muscle is carried to the liver where, provided the oxygen supply is adequate, it is reconverted to glucose by gluconeogenesis. The glucose can then return to the muscle for a further passage through glycolysis. This circulation is known as the Cori cycle, and enables energy production

to continue in exercising muscle when insufficient oxygen is available for aerobic metabolism.

> **Lactic acidosis can result from either increased lactate production or decreased lactate clearance.**
>
> - Increased lactate synthesis arises in conditions of generalised tissue hypoxia such as shock and congestive cardiac failure.
> - Decreased lactate clearance may result from hepatocyte damage or impaired liver perfusion.
> - Inherited deficiency of pyruvate dehydrogenase also results in lactic acidosis as more pyruvate is converted to lactate.

Citric acid cycle

> **The citric acid cycle is a mitochondrial set of reactions with two major roles.**
>
> - Large amounts of energy are released from the metabolism of pyruvate or other intermediates.
> - Intermediates in the cycle act as precursors or end-points for other pathways, such as the metabolism of certain amino acids.

The main fate of pyruvate under aerobic conditions is to enter the

mitochondrial matrix (the innermost space of the mitochondria) where it acts as a fuel for the citric acid cycle. The substrate for the cycle is the two-carbon unit, acetyl coenzyme A (CoA), which is formed from pyruvate by pyruvate dehydrogenase.

The principle of the cycle is that, with each turn, two carbons enter as acetyl CoA and two carbons are lost as CO_2 (Fig. 3).

Acetyl CoA combines with oxaloacetic acid (OAA), a four-carbon unit, to form the six-carbon compound citrate. Rearrangement and removal of the first molecule of CO_2 leaves α-ketoglutarate (a five-carbon unit), release of the second CO_2 generates succinate (a four-carbon unit), and a series of reactions then regenerates OAA.

Energy is released by the cycle in two ways (Fig. 3):

- conversion of succinyl CoA to succinate is coupled directly to the phosphorylation of GDP to GTP;

- electrons released at several points in the cycle are carried by NADH and $FADH_2$ to the electron transport chain, where ATP is generated by oxidative phosphorylation.

Alternative fates of citric acid cycle intermediates

The citric acid cycle also provides intermediates for the biosynthesis of other molecules, eg many amino acids are formed from α-ketoglutarate and OAA, and succinyl CoA is the basic starting point in haem synthesis (Fig. 4).

Removal of intermediates in this way reduces the supply of OAA for future turns of the cycle, so metabolism can only proceed efficiently if carbon atoms are also fed back into the cycle. One way in which citric acid cycle intermediates are replenished is by direct

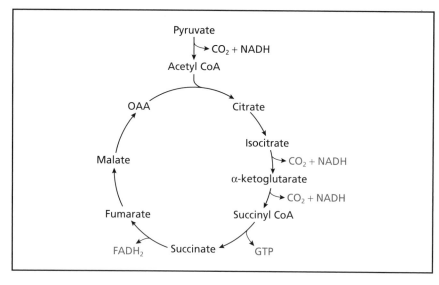

▲**Fig. 3** Citric acid cycle.

carboxylation of pyruvate to OAA, catalysed by the enzyme pyruvate carboxylase (Fig. 4).

Oxidative phosphorylation

- The cytochrome chain collects electrons from NADH and $FADH_2$ and passes them to O_2.
- Electron transfer is coupled to the pumping of protons across the mitochondrial membrane and the generation of a proton gradient.
- Energy stored in the proton gradient is used by ATP synthase to generate ATP.

$NADH$ and $FADH_2$ carry electrons from the sites of oxidative reactions to the electron transport chain in the inner mitochondrial membrane. This chain is composed of four large enzyme complexes that ultimately pass the electrons to O_2 (Fig. 5):

- NADH-ubiquinone oxidoreductase (complex I);

- Succinate-ubiquinone oxidoreductase (complex II);

- Ubiquinol-cytochrome c oxidoreductase (complex III);

- cytochrome oxidase (complex IV).

As electrons move down the chain, protons are translocated out of the mitochondrial matrix, forming a proton gradient across the inner mitochondrial membrane.

1. NADH-ubiquinone oxidoreductase accepts electrons from NADH and passes them to ubiquinone (Q), forming ubiquinol (QH_2). Energy released during this process is used to pump protons. While electrons from $FADH_2$ are also used to reduce Q via complex II, the energy difference between these compounds is not large enough to allow concomitant proton translocation.

2. Ubiquinol-cytochrome c oxidoreductase again couples proton translocation to the flux of electrons from ubiquinol to cytochrome c. Several cytochromes contribute to the cytochrome reductase complex, and as with other cytochromes the electrons are carried by prosthetic haem groups.

3. Cytochrome oxidase collects electrons from cytochrome c and transfers them to molecular O_2, coupled to further proton pumping. Four electrons ultimately combine with each molecule of O_2 to produce two molecules of H_2O.

$$4e^- + 4H^+ + O_2 \rightarrow 2H_2O$$

Cyanide poisoning results from the inhibition of cytochrome oxidase. It is one of the most potent and rapidly acting poisons known, due to the widespread inhibition of mitochondrial energy production.

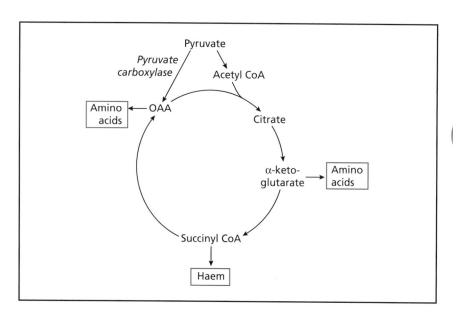

◄**Fig. 4** Supply of intermediates from the citric acid cycle.

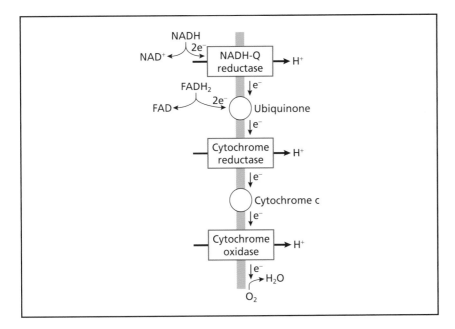

▲**Fig. 5** The electron transport chain.

Fate of cytosolic NADH

NADH generated in the cytosol by glycolysis also passes its electrons to the mitochondrial electron transport chain, but does so indirectly because it cannot diffuse through the inner mitochondrial membrane. Instead the electrons enter the mitochondria via shuttles, which use molecules such as glycerol phosphate or malate to feed electrons towards intramitochondrial NAD^+ or FAD.

ATP synthesis

Complexes I, III and IV use the energy from electron transport to translocate protons out of the mitochondrial matrix against an electrochemical gradient. The H^+ gradient, called the proton-motive force, thus formed is then used by ATP synthase to generate ATP (Fig. 6).

ATP synthase, often called complex V, consists of a catalytic particle located on the matrix side of the inner mitochondrial membrane, and a membrane-spanning region which acts as a proton channel. The passage of protons through the channel domain is coupled to the rotation of a shaft inside the catalytic head group, driving the synthesis of ATP from ADP and phosphate. ATP formed in the matrix is then transported to the cytosol by the ATP–ADP translocator.

Stoichiometry of ATP synthesis

Approximately three molecules of ATP are formed for each NADH, and approximately two molecules of ATP are formed for each $FADH_2$ (since the proton-pumping NADH-Q oxidoreductase is bypassed with $FADH_2$). Some of the proton-motive force is also used for transport in and out of the matrix, eg during the exchange of ATP^{4-} for ADP^{3-} and of phosphate for hydroxide. Mitochondria also contain uncoupling proteins, which can dissipate the mitochondrial H^+ gradient without forming ATP. One role for such proteins is to generate heat in brown fat.

Pentose phosphate pathway

The pentose phosphate pathway (hexose monophosphate pathway) is an alternative route for the metabolism of glucose, which generates NADPH and ribose.

Glucose is utilised for the synthesis of ribose and NADPH by the pentose phosphate pathway.

- Since ribose is a precursor of DNA and RNA, the pathway is active in actively dividing cells. Ribose is also the sugar component of CoA and NAD^+.

- NADPH is required for many biosynthetic reactions such as fatty acid synthesis. It is not interchangeable with NADH in these pathways.

The pentose phosphate pathway comprises two parts (Fig. 7).

Part 1

In the first part, ribose and NADPH are generated from glucose-6-phosphate. This phase is active

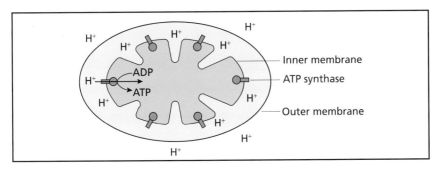

▲**Fig. 6** ATP synthesis is driven by the proton gradient across the inner mitochondrial membrane.

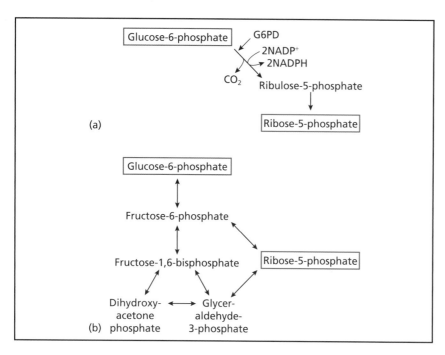

▲ **Fig. 7** The pentose phosphate pathway: (**a**) Part 1; (**b**) Part 2.

only in liver, adipose tissue, lactating mammary gland, adrenal cortex and red blood cells. These tissues require the reducing power of NADPH for synthetic reactions such as the biosynthesis of cholesterol and fatty acids, and in erythrocytes for the formation of glutathione.

This first step in the pathway is catalysed by the enzyme glucose-6-phosphate dehydrogenase (G6PD). A further series of reactions generates ribulose-5-phosphate, which is isomerised to ribose-5-phosphate.

The overall reaction is oxidative, since it results in the formation of two NADPH and one ribose-5-phosphate for each molecule of glucose-6-phosphate. In the production of a five-carbon sugar (ribose) from a six-carbon sugar

(glucose) a molecule of CO_2 is released. This makes the oxidative phase of the pentose phosphate pathway irreversible.

Flux through the pentose phosphate pathway is determined by the activity of G6PD. This enzyme is regulated by the concentration of $NADP^+$ and therefore matches the generation of NADPH to demand.

Part 2
In the second part of the pathway, ribose is reconverted into glycolytic intermediates. This phase is both reversible and ubiquitous.

This second stage occurs when the demands for NADPH and ribose are not exactly matched. If more NADPH than ribose is needed, the excess ribose is recycled by a series of non-

oxidative reactions. Three pentoses are converted into two hexoses and one triose, and the products can thereby feed back into glycolysis:

3 ribulose-5-phosphate ↔ 2 fructose-6-phosphate + glyceraldehyde-3-phosphate

When the demand for ribose exceeds the demand for NADPH, ribose-5-phosphate is produced from glycolytic intermediates by the reverse set of reactions.

Red blood cells do not possess mitochondria and therefore rely on the pentose phosphate pathway for the synthesis of NADPH and thereby reduced glutathione. These compounds are essential for maintenance of erythrocyte structure and to keep haemoglobin in a reduced state.

Inherited G6PD deficiency impairs the formation of NADPH by the pentose phosphate pathway and thereby renders the red cells more susceptible to haemolysis, particularly following exposure to certain drugs (dapsone, nitrofurantoin, primaquine, sulphonamides such as co-trimoxazole, or quinolones such as ciprofloxacin).

See *Haematology*, Section 2.1.3.

Transketolase is an enzyme of the second stage of the pentose phosphate pathway. It requires thiamine pyrophosphate as a cofactor. Genetic defects in transketolase, or thiamine deficiency in alcoholics, result in Wernicke–Korsakoff syndrome, with its symptoms of memory loss and partial paralysis.

Gluconeogenesis

> **Gluconeogenesis is the synthesis of glucose from non-carbohydrate precursors, principally lactate and alanine.**

The gluconeogenic pathway is used to generate glucose when carbohydrate intake and glycogen stores are low. Glucose generated in the liver is carried in the bloodstream to tissues that are unable to metabolise alternative fuels such as fatty acids.

Gluconeogenic substrates

The principal substrates for gluconeogenesis are:

- amino acids (such as alanine), from the diet or proteolysis (eg in starvation);

- lactate, from exercising muscle;

- glycerol, from the breakdown of triacylglycerols.

These compounds enter the gluconeogenic pathway as shown in Fig. 8.

Gluconeogenic pathway

Gluconeogenesis is controlled independently of glycolysis. In converting pyruvate to glucose, gluconeogenesis is effectively, though not exactly, a reversal of glycolysis (Fig. 8). Some steps are simply glycolytic reactions running in reverse. At other points gluconeogenesis uses its own set of enzymes, enabling:

- flux through the pathway to be controlled independently of glycolysis;

- routes to be taken around irreversible reactions.

The reactions which differ between gluconeogenesis and glycolysis are as follows.

- The conversion of pyruvate to phosphoenolpyruvate (PEP) in gluconeogenesis occurs via the intermediate oxaloacetic acid (OAA). This is catalysed by the enzymes pyruvate carboxylase and PEP carboxykinase, and is driven by the hydrolysis of two high-energy phosphate bonds (one ATP and one GTP). In glycolysis, the reverse reaction is performed by a single enzyme, pyruvate kinase, yielding a single ATP.

- The dephosphorylations of fructose-1,6-bisphosphate to fructose-6-phosphate and of glucose-6-phosphate to glucose do not result in the regeneration of high-energy phosphate bonds in gluconeogenesis. In contrast, the reverse reactions that occur in

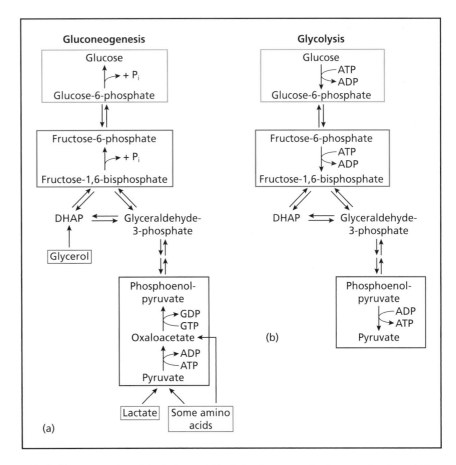

▲ **Fig. 8** Gluconeogenesis and glycolysis are not identical pathways operating in reverse. Reactions which differ between glycolysis and gluconeogenesis are boxed. DHAP, dihydroxyacetone phosphate.

glycolysis both split high-energy phosphate bonds of ATP.

> Alcohol metabolism by the liver inhibits gluconeogenesis. In conditions where glycogen strores are low, eg following strenuous exercise or undernourishment, alcohol consumption can result in hypoglycaemia because of the combined decrease in gluconeogenesis and glycogenolysis. The effects are particularly severe in insulin-treated diabetics who already have a tendency to hypoglycaemia.

Glycogen

> Glycogen is the storage form of carbohydrate, found predominantly in liver and muscle.
> - Liver glycogen acts as a rapidly releasable glucose reservoir that is used to regulate blood glucose concentration.
> - Muscle glycogen provides a local supply of glucose during exercise.

Tissues store carbohydrate as cytoplasmic granules of glycogen, which is a large branched polymer of glucose residues (Fig. 9a). These act as a readily releasable pool of glucose in liver and muscle.

Chains of glucose residues are linked in glycogen by α-1,4-glycosidic bonds (ie between the first carbon of one glucose and the fourth carbon of the next). Branches occur approximately every 10 residues, and are formed by α-1,6-glycosidic linkages (Fig. 9b). Glycogen synthesis and degradation occur at the tips of the branches, so the branching structure increases the number of sites at which glucose residues can be added or removed.

Glycogen synthesis

Glycogen synthase adds glucose residues to the free ends of an existing glycogen molecule.

- α-1,4 linkages are formed by the addition of glucose from an activated donor molecule, UDP-glucose:

$$\text{glycogen}_n + \text{UDP-glucose} \rightarrow \text{glycogen}_{n+1} + \text{UDP}$$

- α-1,6 links are formed by a separate branching enzyme, which transfers a block of (usually seven) residues from the end of a growing chain to a new position in the middle of the molecule.

Glycogenolysis

Removal of glucose from the free ends of glycogen is not a simple reversal of glycogen synthesis.

- The α-1,4 glycosidic linkages are cleaved by the enzyme phosphorylase, which catalyses the reaction:

$$\text{glycogen}_n + P_i \rightarrow \text{glycogen}_{n-1} + \text{glucose-1-phosphate}$$

- The α-1,6 links are broken by a separate debranching enzyme.

Glucose-1-phosphate is converted into glucose-6-phosphate, the fate of which depends on the tissue.

- In liver the further action of glucose-6-phosphatase releases free glucose that can pass into the bloodstream.

- In muscle there is no glucose-6-phosphatase, and since glucose-6-phosphate cannot diffuse through the plasma membrane it remains trapped for use as a substrate for glycolysis.

> **Glycogen storage diseases**
>
> Glycogen storage diseases are caused by inherited deficiencies of enzymes involved in glycogen synthesis or breakdown. The clinical features are determined by the particular enzyme affected. Two major types are von Gierke's disease and McArdle's disease.

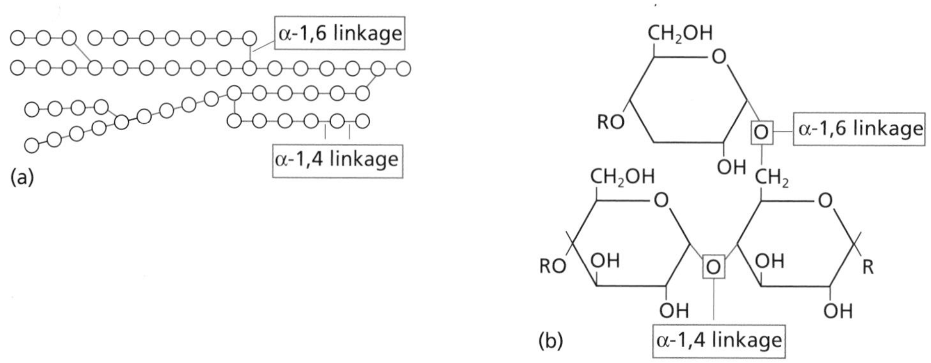

▲ **Fig. 9** Structure of glycogen. (**a**) Glycogen is a branched chain of glucose residues. (**b**) Glucose residues are linked by two types of bond. R, side chain.

Type I (von Gierke's disease)

Results from a deficiency of glucose-6-phosphatase. This enzyme is principally involved in releasing free glucose from glucose-6-phosphate in the liver. Massive hepatomegaly and fasting hypoglycaemia develop, because liver glycogen cannot be mobilised under conditions of starvation.

Type V (McArdle's disease)

Caused by a deficiency of muscle phosphorylase. Patients have normal blood glucose control but cannot mobilise muscle glycogen. They therefore have impaired exercise tolerance and accumulate glycogen in muscle tissue.

Glycosaminoglycans (mucopolysaccharides)

Glycosaminoglycans are secreted macromolecules that form the ground substance of connective tissue. They are composed of chains of disaccharides.

Glycosaminoglycans are high-molecular-weight polysaccharides that form a major component of the ground substance of connective tissue. They are made up of repeating disaccharide units, comprising an amino sugar (such as glucosamine or galactosamine) linked usually to a hexuronic acid (glucuronic acid or iduronic acid). One or both residues may be carboxylated or sulphated. The major glycosaminoglycans are hyaluronic acid, chondroitin sulphate, dermatan sulphate, keratan sulphate, heparin and heparan sulphate. They are usually linked in a comb-like structure to a protein core (forming a proteoglycan).

Glycosaminoglycans are normally degraded in lysosomes. Inherited deficiencies of lysosomal enzymes can result in the lysosomal storage diseases known as the mucopolysaccharidoses.

Hurler's syndrome and Hunter's syndrome are caused by defects in enzymes that degrade heparan and dermatan sulphate: these accumulate in lysosomes resulting in bone dysplasia and mental retardation.

Regulation of glucose metabolism

The fluxes of glucose to (and from) glycogen and pyruvate are determined by overall nutritional status and the requirement of different tissues for glucose. Key enzymes in the pathways of glycogen synthesis/glycogenolysis and of gluconeogenesis/glycolysis are therefore under the regulation of hormones such as insulin, glucagon and adrenaline (epinephrine). Important actions of these hormones are summarised in Fig. 10.

Response to hypoglycaemia

When glucose levels are low, glucagon is released to promote glucose production, mainly by the liver. Glucagon binds to its cell-surface receptor and increases

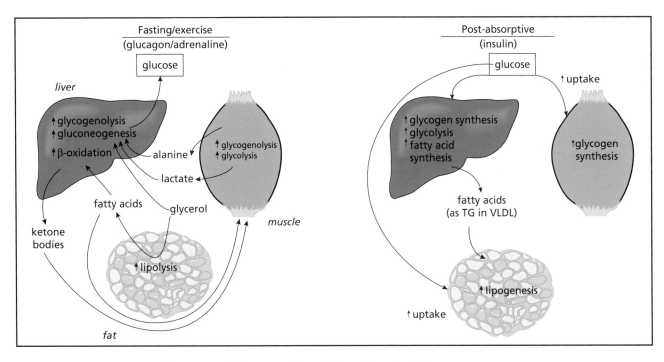

▲**Fig. 10** Hormonal control of glucose homeostasis in the fasting/exercising and the post-absorptive states.

intracellular cAMP levels, causing activation of protein kinase A (PKA). The subsequent phosphorylation of both glycogen phosphorylase and glycogen synthase leads to activation of the former and inhibition of the latter, thereby stimulating an overall increase in glycogen breakdown and glucose release into the plasma. Glucagon also promotes gluconeogenesis over glycolysis. This is partly due to the PKA-dependent phosphorylation and consequent inhibition of the glycolytic enzyme pyruvate kinase. In addition, PKA promotes the conversion of fructose-1,6-bisphosphate to fructose-6-phosphate in the gluconeogenic pathway, and inhibits the reverse reaction due to the reduced production of the allosteric modulator fructose-2,6-bisphosphate.

Response to exercise or stress

Exercise and stress trigger hepatic glucose release and mobilisation of muscle glycogen as a consequence of rising adrenaline levels. Adrenaline, like glucagon, triggers cAMP elevation in liver, but also elevates cAMP in skeletal and cardiac muscle through the activation of β-adrenergic receptors. In muscle, as in liver, elevated cAMP causes glycogenolysis, but as muscle lacks glucose-6-phosphatase, the glucose-6-phosphate produced is retained in the cells for further metabolism. Unlike liver, muscle is not a site of gluconeogenesis.

Response to raised glucose levels

When the blood glucose level rises, insulin is released to coordinate and promote energy storage. Insulin opposes many of the actions of glucagon, resulting in net glycogen synthesis and enhanced glycolysis. On binding to its cell-surface receptor in the liver, insulin triggers a protein kinase cascade resulting in the inactivation of glycogen synthase kinase 3, thereby releasing glycogen synthase from inhibition by this enzyme. Insulin also results in the phosphorylation of an ancillary subunit of protein phosphatase 1, recruiting this enzyme to glycogen, where it activates glycogen synthase and inhibits glycogen phosphorylase. Glycolytic flow is enhanced by the dephosphorylation, and consequent activation, of pyruvate dehydrogenase.

Insulin also promotes the uptake of glucose into skeletal muscle and adipose tissue by causing the translocation of the glucose transporter GLUT4 from intracellular storage vesicles into the plasma membrane. The absorbed glucose is then stored as glycogen in muscle and fat in adipocytes. Note that once glucose has been converted to fatty acids via acetyl CoA, humans are unable to reconvert these carbons back to glucose. However, the greater molecular energy content and lesser impact on osmolarity of fat versus carbohydrate storage seems to outweigh this disadvantage.

BIOCHEMISTRY AND METABOLISM: **SECTION 3**
FATTY ACIDS AND LIPIDS

3.1 Fatty acids

Fatty acids contain a carboxylic acid head and a hydrocarbon tail. Their principal roles are as:

- fuel molecules;
- components of phospholipid and glycolipid;
- intracellular signalling molecules.

Fatty acids consist of a long hydrocarbon chain with a carboxylic acid head group. The hydrocarbon chain is hydrophobic, preferring a non-aqueous environment such as that found in a lipid membrane. The carboxylic acid group is the reactive moiety that forms linkages with other molecules, eg to form triacylglycerols.

Saturated vs unsaturated

If the hydrocarbon chain is formed entirely by single bonds, a fatty acid is said to be 'saturated', whereas the presence of one or more double bonds makes it 'unsaturated' or 'polyunsaturated'.

Unsaturated fatty acids have lower melting points, a property essential for the maintenance of membrane fluidity at normal body temperature. The enhanced fluidity arises because *cis* double bonds (Fig. 11), in particular, introduce kinks into the hydrocarbon chain and increase disorder in a lipid bilayer.

Polyunsaturated fatty acids have even lower melting points,

accounting for their occurrence in animals such as fish whose membranes must remain fluid at very low temperatures.

Nomenclature

Fatty acids (Fig. 11) derive their names from the length of the parent hydrocarbon chain, which usually possesses an even number of carbon atoms (typically 14–24). The chain length may be indicated by a subscript, eg C_{18}, C_{20}.

The number of double bonds is indicated by an additional subscript, eg the fatty acid $C_{18:2}$ has two double bonds. The position of double bonds can be indicated in several ways.

- The carbons may be numbered sequentially from the carboxyl group (carbon 1), and the position of the double bond is denoted by a Δ, eg *cis*-Δ^3 indicates that there is a *cis* double bond between carbons 3 and 4 (Fig. 11a).

- The methyl carbon furthest from the carboxyl group may be termed the ω-carbon, or $n-1$ carbon, and the position of the double bond is denoted by the distance from this carbon, eg an $\omega3$ or $n-3$ fatty acid has a double bond three positions away from the $\omega(n-1)$ carbon (Fig. 11b).

Synthesis

Fatty acids are built up from acetyl CoA units in the cytosol using energy derived from NADPH and ATP.

Biosynthesis of fatty acids occurs in the cytosol, catalysed by an enzyme complex known as fatty acid synthase. The acyl backbone is constructed on a carrier protein and is released when it is 16–18 carbons long. It is built up from two-carbon units derived from acetyl CoA.

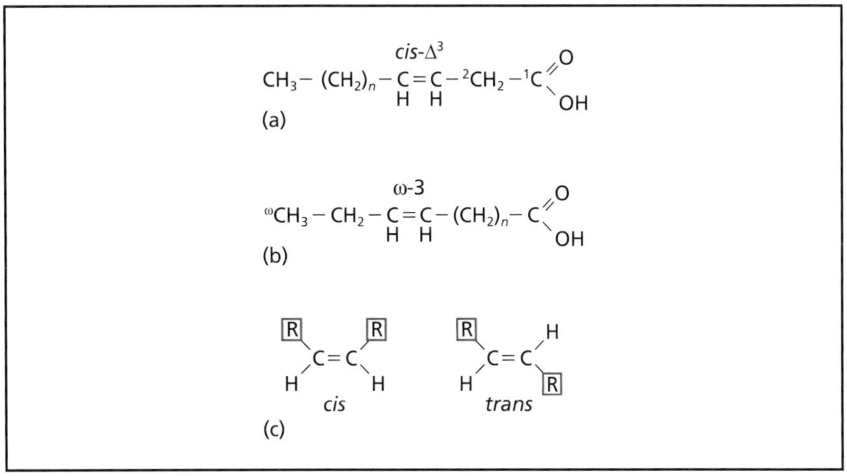

▲ **Fig. 11** Fatty acid nomenclature. Methods for describing double bond position (a and b) and double bond configuration (c) are shown. The nomenclature of fatty acids is complicated; see text for further explanation.

Exit of acetyl CoA from the mitochondrion

Acetyl CoA is produced in the mitochondrial matrix. When present in abundance, it is transported into the cytosol in the form of citrate (Fig. 12).

1. Oxaloacetate combines with acetyl CoA in the mitochondrion to form citrate.

2. Citrate exits the mitochondrion.

3. A cytoplasmic enzyme, citrate lyase, utilises ATP to cleave citrate into acetyl CoA and oxaloacetate.

4. Oxaloacetate is converted into pyruvate, concomitantly forming NADPH from NADH.

5. Pyruvate re-enters the mitochondrion and is converted back into oxaloacetate.

Acetyl CoA carboxylation

Acetyl CoA in the cytosol destined for fatty acid synthesis is carboxylated to malonyl CoA. The reaction is catalysed by acetyl CoA carboxylase, using energy from ATP and a carboxyl group from bicarbonate. The activity of acetyl CoA carboxylase controls flux through the fatty acid synthetic pathway. Acetyl CoA carboxylase activity is enhanced by high levels of substrate (citrate) and inhibited by the product of fatty acid synthesis (palmitoyl CoA). The malonyl group is subsequently transferred from CoA to an acyl carrier protein (ACP), forming malonyl-ACP.

Growth of the acyl chain

Formation of a new chain (Fig. 13) begins when a malonyl-ACP combines with an acetyl-ACP. This generates a four-carbon unit attached to the ACP. Loss of the carboxyl group as CO_2 drives the reaction forwards.

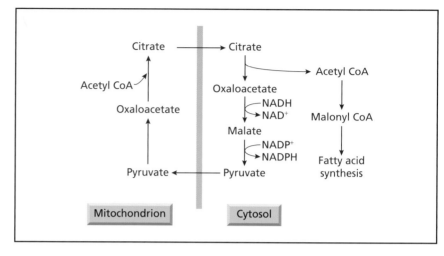

▲ **Fig. 12** Transport of acetyl CoA out of the mitochondrion.

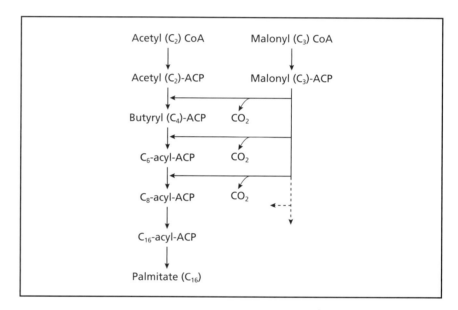

▲ **Fig. 13** Fatty acid synthesis. ACP, acyl carrier protein.

Subsequent elongations use malonyl-ACP as substrate, driven each time by loss of a molecule of CO_2. Addition of each two-carbon unit utilises two molecules of NADPH (derived, in part, from the pentose phosphate pathway).

The cycle continues until the acyl chain is 16 (or 18) carbons long, at which point the fatty acid palmitate (or stearate) is released from the carrier protein.

Elongation and desaturation

If fatty acids are required which are either longer or unsaturated, these are produced by additional enzyme systems. The most important of these are located on the cytosolic surface of the endoplasmic reticulum.

- Elongation: this uses NADPH and acetyl groups donated from malonyl CoA. An additional elongation pathway occurs in the mitochondria, and may be important for elongating shorter (<14 carbon) fatty acids.

- Desaturation: only three desaturases (enzymes that introduce double bonds) are present in humans, namely Δ^5-, Δ^6- and Δ^9-fatty acyl desaturases. They are associated with the membrane of the smooth endoplasmic reticulum, particularly in liver.

Certain 'essential' fatty acids cannot be synthesised in humans because of the limited range of desaturating enzymes. The most important essential fatty acids are linoleic acid (an ω6 fatty acid) and α-linolenic acid (an ω3 fatty acid). These are precursors of arachidonate, prostaglandins and leukotrienes and must be obtained from the diet.

Degradation

> The energy stored in fatty acids is released by β-oxidation occurring in the mitochondria. The hydrocarbon chain is sequentially shortened by the removal of two-carbon acetyl CoA units which feed into the citric acid cycle.

Fatty acids are largely metabolised in the mitochondrial matrix by β-oxidation.

1. They enter the mitochondria having first been activated by acyl CoA synthetase, an enzyme on the outer mitochondrial membrane that links the acyl group to CoA.

2. The activated fatty acids then cross the inner mitochondrial membrane with the assistance of carnitine.

3. Once in the matrix, a series of reactions occurs which sequentially removes two-carbon units in the form of acetyl CoA from the acyl chain.

4. Energy is produced by β-oxidation itself, since removal of each acetyl CoA unit produces a molecule of both NADH and $FADH_2$. These pass their electrons to the mitochondrial electron transport chain.

5. Further energy is derived by oxidation of acetyl CoA in the citric acid cycle.

Thus, one molecule of palmitate yields 35 molecules of ATP from β-oxidation, and 96 molecules of ATP from metabolism of acetyl CoA units by the citric acid cycle.

The rate of β-oxidation is modulated by the flux of fatty acids into the mitochondria. As the carnitine palmitoyl transferase shuttle is inhibited by malonyl CoA, β-oxidation is blocked under conditions favouring fatty acid synthesis.

Oxidation of unsaturated fatty acids

Oxidation of unsaturated fatty acids requires additional enzymes. Some of these are present in mitochondria, but others are located in specialised organelles called peroxisomes.

Peroxisomes are responsible for a proportion of β-oxidation. Their capacity increases under conditions of peroxisomal proliferation, eg due to fibrate therapy or a high-fat diet. They are capable of oxidising a range of polyunsaturated fatty acid analogues such as prostaglandins. In addition they can shorten very long chain fatty acids (>22 carbons), and the shorter fatty acid products may be passed to mitochondria for further β-oxidation. Peroxisomes are also responsible for α-oxidation and are therefore necessary for the metabolism of branched-chain fatty acids such as phytanic acid, which is produced by chlorophyll breakdown and is present at high levels in dairy products and meat from ruminants.

> Defects in a peroxisomal membrane protein (an ATP-binding transporter of uncertain function) result in X-linked adrenoleukodystrophy. This disease is characterised by the accumulation of very long chain fatty acids due to their defective β-oxidation in peroxisomes. The clinical outcome is progressive cerebral demyelination.

Ketone bodies

> Ketone bodies act as a transportable form of acetyl CoA. They are produced by the metabolism of fatty acids in the liver and are used by tissues such as the brain during starvation.

Fatty acids are an important fuel during starvation. However, certain tissues, eg the brain, cannot metabolise fatty acids but are able to metabolise glucose and ketones. Ketone bodies, derived from fatty acid oxidation, act as a transportable form of acetyl CoA under these conditions.

In starvation, the rates of fatty acid β-oxidation and gluconeogenesis in the liver are enhanced. β-Oxidation results in the production of acetyl CoA and NADH, but the acetyl CoA is not immediately metabolised by the citric acid cycle because:

- NADH produced by β-oxidation has an inhibitory action on the citric acid cycle;

- oxaloacetate, which normally combines with acetyl CoA to form citrate, is diverted into gluconeogenesis.

The acetyl CoA is instead converted into the ketone bodies acetoacetate, D-3-hydroxybutyrate and acetone (Fig. 14). This occurs as follows.

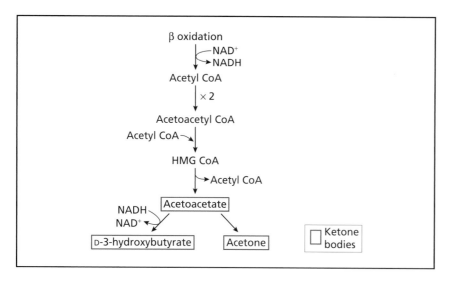

▲ **Fig. 14** Ketone body production.

1. Two molecules of acetyl CoA in the mitochondria combine to form acetoacetyl CoA.

2. A third molecule of acetyl CoA is added to form 3-hydroxy-3-methylglutaryl (HMG) CoA.

3. HMG CoA is cleaved into acetoacetate and acetyl CoA.

High levels of NADH favour the reduction of acetoacetate to D-3-hydroxybutyrate. Some acetoacetate is non-enzymically decarboxylated to acetone, the ketone responsible for the characteristic odour associated with excess ketone body production.

Ketone body utilisation Tissues that consume ketone bodies do so by reconverting them into acetoacetyl CoA and thence into acetyl CoA. Liver mitochondria lack the enzyme responsible for reconverting ketone bodies into acetoacetyl CoA. Ketones synthesised in the liver are therefore not degraded at their site of production but are diverted to other tissues.

3.2 Lipids

Lipids are biomolecules that are highly insoluble in water, but which dissolve in organic solvents such as chloroform. They occur in a variety of forms and serve a number of roles.

> Ketone bodies are produced during starvation and in untreated diabetes mellitus. Although their production is a positive response in that they act as a fuel supply to the brain, excessive ketone body synthesis presents problems.
>
> Acetoacetic acid and D-3-hydroxybutyric acid are both acids and their associated H$^+$ ions can overwhelm the buffering capacity of the blood, resulting in acidosis. This acidosis, rather than the presence of the ketones themselves, is the dangerous feature of ketoacidosis.

> Lipids occur in a number of forms (eg triglycerides, phospholipids, glycolipids and cholesterol) and play vital roles in the cell. They contribute to energy storage, membrane structure and intracellular signalling.

- Triacylglycerols: a concentrated transportable and storable fuel supply.

- Phospholipids, glycolipids and cholesterol: components of membranes.

- Diacylglycerols and inositol phospholipids: signal molecules.

Triacylglycerols

Triacylglycerols (triglycerides, neutral fats) are largely synthesised and stored in adipose tissue. They comprise a glycerol backbone with three fatty acyl groups.

Biosynthesis

1. Glycerol contains three hydroxyl groups, each of which can potentially form a linkage with a fatty acyl side chain. The starting point in triacylglycerol synthesis (Fig. 15) is glycerol-3-phosphate, which has a phosphate group attached to the third carbon (C-3).

2. Fatty acyl groups, donated from acyl CoAs, are linked to the first and second carbons to form phosphatidic acid, a simple phosphoglyceride. The C-1 position of glycerol usually contains a saturated fatty acid, whereas unsaturated fatty acids are often found attached to C-2.

3. The phosphate group can be either modified to form more complex phospholipids (see below) or removed by hydrolysis and replaced with a third fatty acid, forming a triacylglycerol (Fig. 15).

Degradation

Triacylglycerol is hydrolysed by hormone-sensitive lipase to release fatty acids and glycerol. Glycerol is converted into dihydroxyacetone

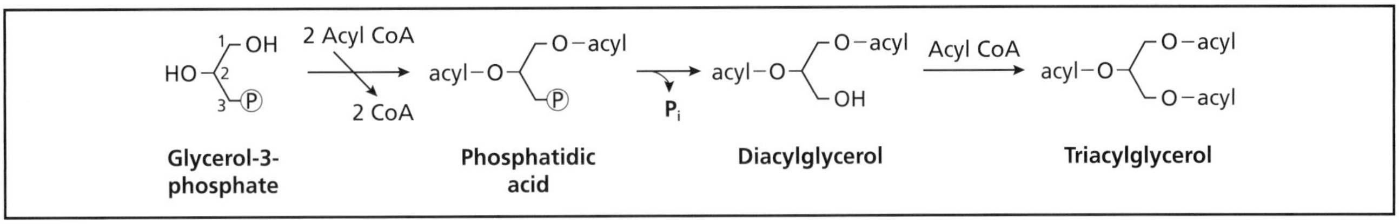

$$\text{Glycerol-3-phosphate} \xrightarrow[\text{2 CoA}]{\text{2 Acyl CoA}} \text{Phosphatidic acid} \xrightarrow{P_i} \text{Diacylglycerol} \xrightarrow{\text{Acyl CoA}} \text{Triacylglycerol}$$

▲ **Fig. 15** Biosynthesis of triacylglycerols.

phosphate and thereby metabolised to glucose or pyruvate. The fatty acid moieties are oxidised as described above.

Hormonal regulation of fat metabolism

Like glycogen and glucose production, the formation of ketone bodies, fatty acids and triacylglycerides is under the opposing control of glucagon and insulin (see Fig. 10). In adipose tissue, raised cAMP levels triggered by glucagon activate hormone-sensitive lipase and thereby promote triglyceride hydrolysis. Insulin opposes this action by activating a phosphodiesterase that degrades cAMP. Insulin also promotes the uptake and storage of fatty acids by activating lipoprotein lipase and stimulating triacylglycerol synthesis.

In the liver insulin promotes fatty acid synthesis from glucose as it activates pyruvate dehydrogenase and acetyl CoA carboxylase. In contrast, glucagon inhibits acetyl CoA carboxylase, thereby decreasing malonyl CoA levels and blocking fatty acid synthesis. This stimulates fatty acid flux into the mitochondria and β-oxidation, due to the de-inhibition of the carnitine palmitoyl transferase shuttle as malonyl CoA levels fall. As any excess acetyl CoA produced by β-oxidation cannot be converted to glucose, it is channelled into the production of ketone bodies.

Phospholipids

> 🔑 Phospholipids are a major component of lipid membranes and surfactant. As well as serving a structural role, they are also involved in intracellular signalling.

Phospholipids are lipids that have a hydrophilic moiety comprising either a phosphate group or a modified phosphate group, and are derived from glycerol (phosphoglycerides) or sphingosine (sphingolipids).

Phosphoglycerides

The simplest phosphoglyceride is phosphatidic acid, which has already been described (see above). In most phosphoglycerides the phosphate group is modified by esterification with an alcohol such as serine, ethanolamine, choline, glycerol or inositol. The resulting molecules are known, respectively, as phosphatidylserine, phosphatidylethanolamine,

phosphatidylcholine, diphosphatidylglycerol (cardiolipin) and phosphatidylinositol.

Hydrolysis of phosphoglycerides is catalysed by the family of enzymes known as phospholipases (A_1, A_2, C and D). These preferentially target different bonds in the molecule (Fig. 16).

- Phospholipase A_2 cleaves unsaturated fatty acids such as arachidonic acid from their linkage to the second carbon of the glycerol moiety.

- Phospholipase C plays an important role in intracellular signalling, since its action on phosphatidylinositol bisphosphate releases the second messengers diacylglycerol and inositol trisphosphate.

Sphingolipids

Sphingolipids are based on sphingosine rather than glycerol (Fig. 17). Sphingosine is synthesised from palmitoyl CoA and serine. Linkage of an acyl chain to the amino side group of sphingosine

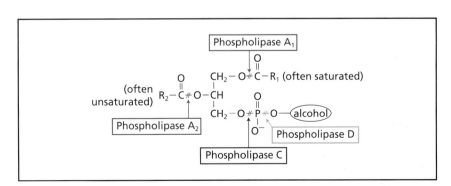

▲ **Fig. 16** Phospholipases hydrolyse phospholipids.

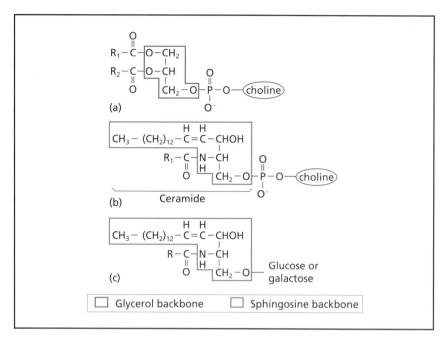

▲ **Fig. 17** Comparison of glycerolipids and sphingolipids: (a) phosphatidylcholine, (b) sphingomyelin and (c) cerebroside.

Gangliosides contain an acidic sugar, *N*-acetylneuraminic acid, which is added to an existing ceramide–glucose–galactose molecule. The resulting GM$_3$ ganglioside can be converted into GM$_2$ and then GM$_1$ gangliosides by further sugar additions.

Gangliosides are found at high concentrations in the central nervous system, particularly in the grey matter. The sugar hydrolases that degrade the oligosaccharide chain are located in lysosomes.

> Inherited defects in the sugar hydrolases and other enzymes involved in glycolipid turnover result in some of the lysosomal storage diseases, such as those of Gaucher, Niemann–Pick, Fabry, Tay–Sachs and metachromatic leukodystrophy (Fig. 18). The clinical picture depends on the severity of the enzyme defect, and on the nature and location of the accumulated lipid.

produces ceramide. The terminal hydroxyl of ceramide can then be further substituted.

Sphingomyelin is a membrane phospholipid that is formed when a phosphorylcholine is donated to ceramide from CDP-choline. The conformation of sphingomyelin resembles that of other phospholipids, since it also possesses two long hydrocarbon chains and a hydrophilic head group (Fig. 17b).

Glycolipids

> Glycolipids are the sugar-containing lipids, such as gangliosides, which are components of lipid membranes.

Glycolipids are formed from ceramide by the addition of one or more sugar residues. The sugars are donated by activated precursors, UDP-glucose or UDP-galactose.

• Addition of the first glucose or galactose forms a cerebroside (Fig. 17c).

• Addition of further sugar residues to form an oligosaccharide side chain results in the formation of the gangliosides, globosides and lipid sulphates (Fig. 18).

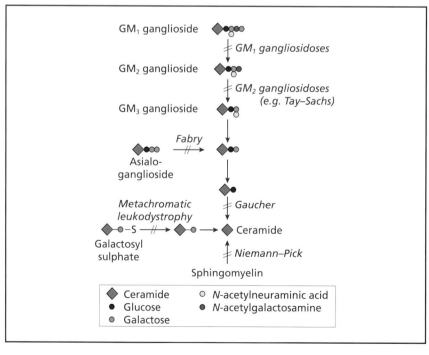

▲ **Fig. 18** Glycolipids and associated lysosomal storage diseases.

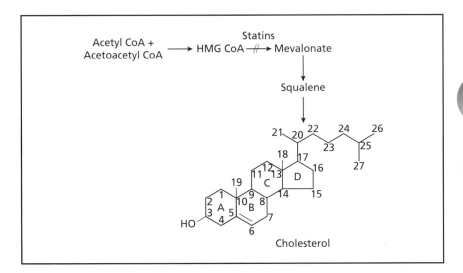

Cholesterol is a structural component of lipid membranes and the precursor for steroid hormone synthesis. It is obtained from the diet or synthesised *de novo*.

Cholesterol is a steroid molecule located largely in lipid membranes. It plays a major role in maintaining normal membrane function since it modifies membrane fluidity. It is synthesised in the liver and further modified in tissues such as the adrenal cortex and gonads to form the steroid hormones.

Biosynthesis

The multiple ring structure of cholesterol is built up from acetate units (Fig. 19).

1. Acetoacetyl CoA and acetyl CoA first combine to form 3-hydroxy-3-methylglutaryl (HMG) CoA.

2. HMG CoA reductase then converts HMG CoA into mevalonate. This reaction is the first committed step in cholesterol synthesis. Activity of HMG CoA reductase is under negative feedback control by the amount of dietary cholesterol.

3. Six molecules of mevalonate are combined to form squalene, a hydrocarbon possessing 30 carbon atoms.

4. Squalene cyclises to form the multi-ring structure of cholesterol.

High levels of circulating cholesterol contribute to the formation of atherosclerotic plaques. The statin family of cholesterol-lowering drugs operates by inhibiting the enzyme HMG CoA reductase, thereby reducing the rate of

cholesterol synthesis. In response, many cells, particularly hepatocytes, increase their number of low-density lipoprotein (LDL) receptors to enhance cholesterol uptake, and thereby contribute further to reduction in the circulating LDL concentration.

Elimination

Cholesterol is eliminated by excretion in the bile, either as cholesterol itself or by secretion as bile salts.

Bile salts are produced in the liver by metabolism of cholesterol to cholyl CoA. Cholyl CoA is conjugated with glycine or taurine to form glycocholate or taurocholate, respectively. It is the combination of both hydrophobic and hydrophilic moieties that allows bile salts to play a key role in the solubilisation of dietary fat. They are reabsorbed in the intestine as part of the enterohepatic circulation.

Anion-exchange resins such as cholestyramine lower plasma cholesterol by binding bile salts in the intestine. This prevents their reabsorption and promotes the hepatic synthesis of bile salts from cholesterol. The increased utilisation of cholesterol in the hepatocytes results in an increase in LDL receptor number, and enhanced cholesterol uptake from the plasma.

▲ **Fig. 19** Cholesterol synthesis.

Steroid hormones

Steroid hormones are derivatives of cholesterol. They include the progestagens, androgens, oestrogens, corticosteroids and mineralocorticoids. Their targets, and hence their physiological properties, are determined by the nature of the side chains.

Cholesterol is converted into progestagens, androgens, oestrogens, corticosteroids and mineralocorticoids in the adrenal cortex, testis and ovary. The interconversions occur by modifications to the basic structure of cholesterol (Fig. 20).

- The side chain (carbons 22–27) of cholesterol is excised to form the progestagens.

- Additional hydroxyl and ketone groups are added to form the corticosteroids and aldosterone.

- Androgens are formed by further modification of the progestagens, including the loss of C-20 and C-21.

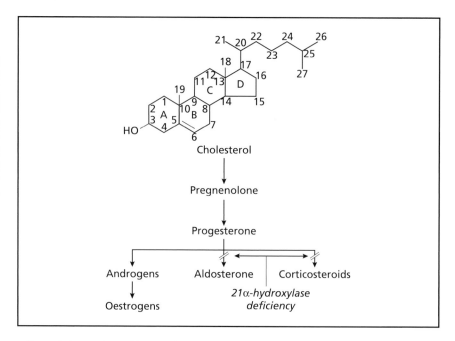

▲ **Fig. 20** Pathways of steroid hormone biosynthesis.

- Aromatisation of the 'A' ring converts the androgens into oestrogens.

Inherited defects can occur at a number of steps in the steroid biosynthetic pathway, but the most common is 21α-hydroxylase deficiency

(Fig. 20). Since corticosteroids and mineralocorticoids are hydroxylated at C-21, the syndrome results in deficiencies of both these types of hormone. Adrenocorticotrophic hormone (ACTH) levels are raised because normal feedback control is impaired, and enhanced synthesis of progestagens and overflow down the androgen pathway causes virilisation.

AMINO ACIDS AND PROTEINS

5.1 Amino acids

🔑 Amino acids are the building blocks of proteins. They contain an amino group, an acid group and a side chain. The nature of the side chain determines the specific properties of the amino acid.

Structure

Amino acids contain amino and carboxylic acid groups, and a variable side chain (R). Twenty different side chains, which vary in shape, size, charge, hydrogen-bonding capacity and reactivity, make up the basic set of amino acids.

Biosynthesis

Humans can synthesise 11 of the basic set of 20 amino acids. The rest must be obtained from the diet, and are known as the 'essential' amino acids (Table 1).

The carbon skeletons of most amino acids originate from metabolic intermediates such as oxaloacetate and pyruvate (Fig. 21). The amino groups are donated by other amino acids in transamination reactions.

If extra amino groups are required, they are derived from ammonia after first being incorporated into glutamate by the enzyme glutamate dehydrogenase:

α-ketoglutarate + NH_4^+ + NADPH + H^+ → glutamate + $NADP^+$

TABLE 1 ESSENTIAL AND NON-ESSENTIAL AMINO ACIDS

Non-essential amino acids	Essential amino acids
Alanine	Histidine
Arginine	Isoleucine
Asparagine	Leucine
Aspartate	Lysine
Cysteine	Methionine
Glutamate	Phenylalanine
Glutamine	Threonine
Glycine	Tryptophan
Proline	Valine
Serine	
Tyrosine	

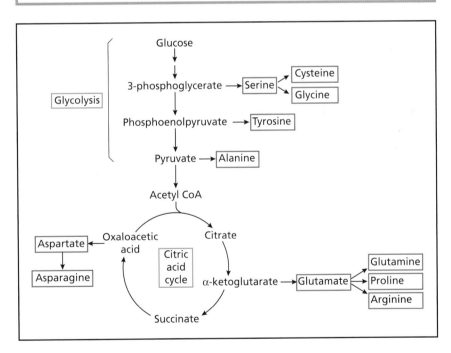

▲ **Fig. 21** The origins of the amino acid backbones.

Glutamate can also carry a second amino group, forming glutamine:

glutamate + NH_4^+ + ATP → glutamine + ADP + P_i

The amino groups can then be swapped between different carbon skeletons by enzymes known as transaminases (Fig. 22). These use

pyridoxal phosphate (vitamin B_6) as a cofactor and catalyse the general reaction:

amino acid$_1$ + α-keto acid$_2$ ↔ amino acid$_2$ + α-keto acid$_1$

Some amino acids are simply formed by the one-step transfer of the amino group to a different

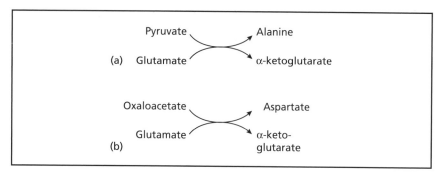

▲**Fig. 22** Examples of transamination reactions.

backbone, eg transamination of pyruvate forms alanine. Tyrosine is formed in another one-step reaction from the essential amino acid phenylalanine:

phenylalanine + O_2 + NADPH + H^+ → tyrosine + $NADP^+$ + H_2O

Other non-essential amino acids are derived by multistep reactions, but still the backbones originate from intermediates of glycolysis and the citric acid cycle (Fig. 21). The conversion from serine to glycine involves the formation of N^5,N^{10}-methylenetetrahydrofolate (derived from the B vitamin, folic acid). N^5,N^{10}-Methylenetetrahydrofolate is the starting point of the so-called 'one-carbon' metabolism, as the methylene group is used in the synthesis of purines and thymidine monophosphate (see below) or can be transferred to the general methyl-group donor S-adenosylmethionine (SAM). When the methyl group of

SAM is transferred, for example in the synthesis of adrenaline and choline, homocysteine is formed.

Degradation

The first step in the degradation of many amino acids involves transfer of the α-amino group back to α-ketoglutarate, thereby forming glutamate (Fig. 23). These reactions are catalysed by the transaminases that are also involved in amino acid synthesis. Glutamate subsequently releases its ammonium ion, which is converted into urea and excreted (see below).

The carbon skeletons that remain after deamination are converted into various citric acid cycle intermediates (Fig. 24).

• Most carbon skeletons enter metabolic pathways at positions from which they can be converted into glucose by gluconeogenesis. These amino acids are said to be 'glucogenic'.

• Others result in the formation of acetyl CoA or acetoacetyl CoA, and are said to be 'ketogenic'. Acetyl CoA cannot act as a substrate for gluconeogenesis in humans, because of a lack of the appropriate enzymes. However, it can be converted into ketone bodies or metabolised by the citric acid cycle.

Inborn errors of metabolism resulting from defects in amino acid metabolism

Maple syrup urine disease

Caused by a block in a common step in the metabolism of leucine, isoleucine and valine. Failure to break down the carbon skeletons of these amino acids results in an increase in the blood and urinary concentrations of both the amino acids themselves and their α-keto acids. Affected infants present with poor feeding, vomiting and lethargy within the first week of life.

Phenylketonuria and alkaptonuria

Phenylalanine metabolism normally involves its conversion to tyrosine and thence, via a series of intermediates, to fumarate and acetoacetate. Defects can occur at several steps (Fig. 25), with varying clinical consequences.

• Phenylketonuria: caused by failure of conversion of phenylalanine to tyrosine, resulting in severe mental retardation.
• Alkaptonuria: caused by a defect later in the pathway, which results in a relatively benign condition. Homogentisate accumulates due to a block in its oxidation, and high levels in the urine are converted into a melanin-like substance that causes darkening of the urine on standing.

Homocystinuria

Caused by a defect in the metabolism of homocysteine, an intermediate in the pathway linking methionine to cysteine. The commonest enzyme defect impairs cysteine production from homocysteine, and is associated clinically with lens dislocation, mental retardation and a physical appearance similar to that of Marfan's syndrome.

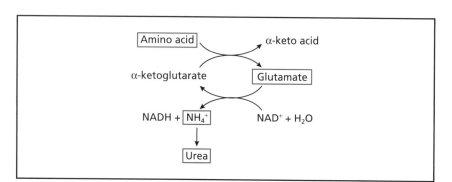

▲**Fig. 23** Fate of the amino acid amino group.

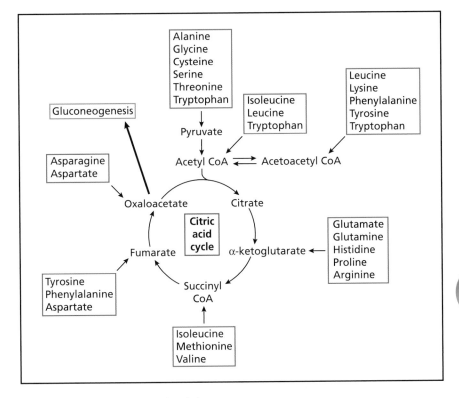

▲ **Fig. 24** Fates of the amino acid carbon skeleton.

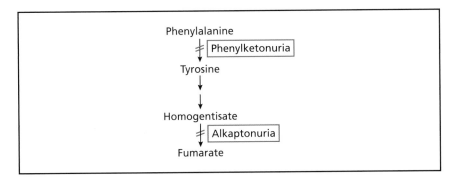

▲ **Fig. 25** Inborn errors of phenylalanine metabolism.

The urea cycle

> The urea cycle is responsible for the formation of urea from ammonia, hence allowing the safe disposal of nitrogenous waste.

Ammonia, which is released during amino acid breakdown, is highly toxic. It is therefore converted into urea and excreted by the kidneys. The pathway by which urea is formed from ammonia is known as the urea cycle. Ammonium ions that are not captured by the urea cycle may be scavenged instead by glutamate (forming glutamine).

In the urea cycle, an ammonium ion is combined with a molecule of CO_2 and the amino group from aspartate to form urea (Fig. 26). The cycle occurs partly in the cytosol and partly in the mitochondria.

1. ATP is consumed in the initial formation of carbamoyl phosphate from $NH4^+$ and CO_2.

2. The carbamoyl group enters the urea cycle by transfer to the carrier molecule ornithine, thereby forming citrulline.

3. A second amino group is donated by aspartate, resulting in the formation of arginine.

4. Hydrolysis of arginine releases urea and re-creates ornithine, ready to start the cycle again.

Hormones derived from amino acids

> The amino acids glycine and glutamate are important neurotransmitters in the central nervous system. A number of other neurotransmitters and hormones are derived from amino acids by simple reactions such as decarboxylation.

Dopamine, adrenaline and noradrenaline

Dopamine, adrenaline (epinephrine) and noradrenaline (norepinephrine) are derived from tyrosine via the intermediate dopa (Fig. 27). Dopa decarboxylation produces dopamine, which is subsequently hydroxylated to noradrenaline and further methylated to form adrenaline.

Hormone inactivation is mediated by two enzymes:

- catechol-*O*-methyltransferase (COMT), as its name implies, transfers a methyl group onto the hormone and is reponsible for forming the metabolites metadrenaline and normetadrenaline;

- monoamine oxidase (MAO) removes the amine group.

The combined effects of COMT and MAO produce hydroxymethoxymandelic acid (HMMA), formerly known as vanillylmandelic acid.

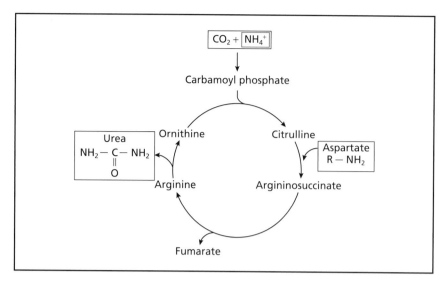

▲**Fig. 26** The urea cycle.

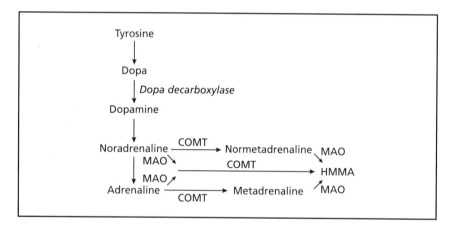

▲**Fig. 27** Catecholamine metabolism. COMT, catechol-*O*-methyltransferase; HMMA, hydroxymethoxymandelic acid; MAO, monoamine oxidase.

Serotonin is secreted by carcinoid tumours, and in some cases up to 50% of dietary tryptophan (rather than the usual 1%) may be diverted into serotonin synthesis. This may precipitate symptoms of tryptophan deficiency, ie pellagra (dermatitis, dementia and diarrhoea).

GABA and glycine

GABA (γ-aminobutyric acid) and glycine act as neurotransmitters, opening specific chloride channels and thereby affecting membrane excitability. GABA is derived from glutamate by decarboxylation and is inactivated by metabolism to succinate.

Histamine

Histamine is a paracrine hormone derived from histidine by decarboxylation.

5.2 Proteins

Proteins play a wide variety of critical roles on account of their diverse structures. They are formed from strings of amino acids, the sequence of which determines the functional property of a protein. Different proteins are targeted to the cytosol, membranes, organelles or secretory vesicles.

• Metadrenaline, normetadrenaline and HMMA are used as markers for phaeochromocytomas and other disorders of excessive catecholamine secretion.
• Dopa decarboxylase inhibitors are used in combination with levodopa (L-dopa) in the treatment of Parkinson's disease. The dopa decarboxylase inhibitors reduce side effects by preventing the peripheral formation of dopamine from levodopa.

Thyroxine

Thyroxine is also derived from tyrosine and is produced specifically in the thyroid gland. Each molecule is derived from two tyrosine molecules and three or four iodines (hence T_3 and T_4). Most of the hormone is metabolised by deiodination in the peripheral tissues, or by hepatic conjugation and excretion in the bile.

Serotonin

Serotonin (5-hydroxytryptamine, 5-HT) is synthesised from tryptophan by hydroxylation and decarboxylation. The majority of 5-HT is degraded into 5-hydroxyindoleacetic acid (5-HIAA).

The functions of proteins are as myriad as their structure. The following are just a few of their roles:

• enzymes;

• receptors, channels and transporters;

- structural proteins, eg actin;

- proteins of the immune system, eg immunoglobulins, complement;

- proteins involved in locomotion, eg myosin;

- proteins involved in the transport of other molecules, eg haemoglobin;

- proteins coordinating growth, differentiation and protein expression, eg transcription factors;

- hormones, eg thyroid-stimulating hormone, insulin.

Proteins are formed from chains of amino acids, the order of which is encoded by the DNA. The three-dimensional structure and the functional properties of a protein are determined by the amino acid sequence. This is because of the ability of different amino acid side chains to interact with:

- other residues within the same protein;

- other residues on different proteins;

- non-protein elements such as lipid, water and DNA.

Strongly hydrophobic regions, for example, prefer to be buried in a hydrophobic environment such as the protein core or a lipid membrane. A cysteine residue may form a disulphide bridge with

▲ **Fig. 28** The peptide bond.

another cysteine at a distant region of the peptide. Other side chains are capable of hydrogen bonding, and some are charged at physiological pH. Bonds formed by the peptide backbone also contribute to the structure and function of proteins.

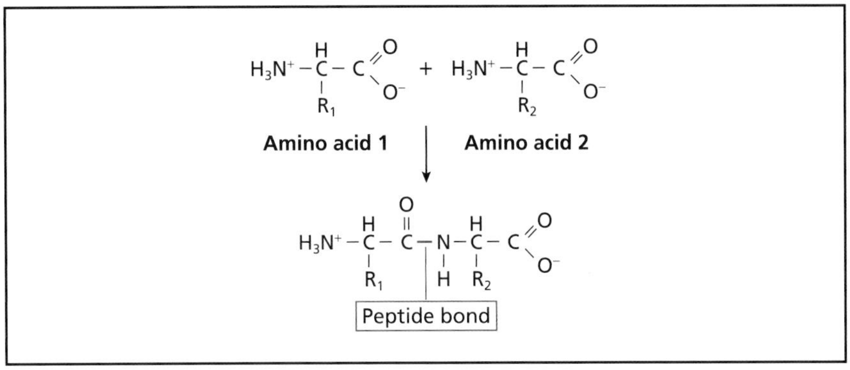

Synthesis

Amino acids are linked together in proteins by peptide bonds. These linkages occur between the carboxylic acid group of one amino acid and the amino group of the next, and result in the peptide backbone (Fig. 28).

The amino acid sequence of a protein is translated from the sequence of a messenger (m)RNA. This is encoded in blocks of three bases, known as codons. Amino acids are carried to the sites of protein synthesis by specific transfer (t)RNAs. A tRNA donates its amino acid to a growing peptide chain

when its anticodon matches the next codon of the mRNA (Fig. 29).

Proteins are synthesised on ribosomes. Translation is initiated at a start codon and continues until a stop codon is reached. The completed protein is then released from the ribosome. The peptide may contain a signal sequence that targets the protein to its appropriate destination, such as the plasma membrane, secretory vesicles or mitochondria. Some proteins are modified by post-translational processing, eg in the Golgi or secretory vesicles.

- Some secreted proteins must be cleaved, eg to form an active hormone from a prohormone, or to remove a signal sequence.

- Many membrane proteins and secreted proteins (eg immunoglobulins and clotting factors) are glycosylated by the

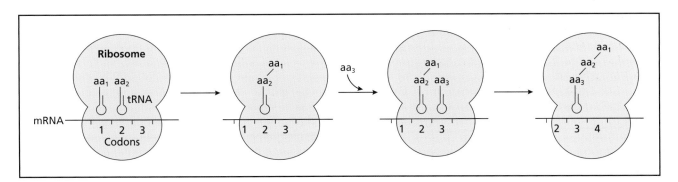

▲ **Fig. 29** Protein synthesis. aa, amino acid; mRNA, messenger RNA; tRNA, transfer RNA.

addition of carbohydrate side chains. These are added in the endoplasmic reticulum and are further modified in the Golgi complex. Up to 85% of a glycoprotein may be formed from carbohydrate.

Degradation

Proteins are broken down into their constituent amino acids by enzymes known as proteases.

Major sites for the degradation of proteins and glycoproteins are the lysosome and the proteasome. Lysosomes are vesicular structures containing enzymes for the digestion of both proteins and the carbohydrate domain of glycoproteins. Proteins destined for destruction by the proteasome, a cytoplasmic protein complex, may become tagged with a molecule called ubiquitin.

A defect in lysosomal cystine transport causes cystinosis, a lysosomal storage disease in which cystine accumulates in the lysosomes. It may either follow a benign course or result in renal tubular damage and the development of Fanconi's syndrome. Cystinosis should not be confused with cystinuria, which is caused by a defect in renal tubular transport.

> Haem is a multi-ring (porphyrin) structure that chelates an iron ion. It is a key component of cytochromes and haemoglobin.

Haem consists of an iron ion chelated within a porphyrin ring. A large proportion of haem is used in the formation of haemoglobin. Much of the rest is synthesised in the liver and is incorporated into enzymes of the cytochrome P450 series.

Biosynthesis

Porphyrins are formed from glycine and succinyl CoA (Fig. 30).

1. The first committed step in the pathway involves the condensation of glycine and succinyl CoA to form δ-aminolevulinic acid (ALA).

2. Two molecules of ALA then combine into a monopyrrole structure (porphobilinogen, PBG).

3. Four PBG join to a form the linear tetrapyrrole, hydroxymethylbilane (HMB).

4. HMB readily cyclises into a tetrapyrrole ring, forming the first of the porphyrinogens. Under physiological conditions the cyclisation involves an enzyme that introduces asymmetry into the ring and forms uroporphyrinogen III. If HMB accumulates, it cyclises symmetrically to form uroporphyrinogen I, which cannot subsequently be converted into haem.

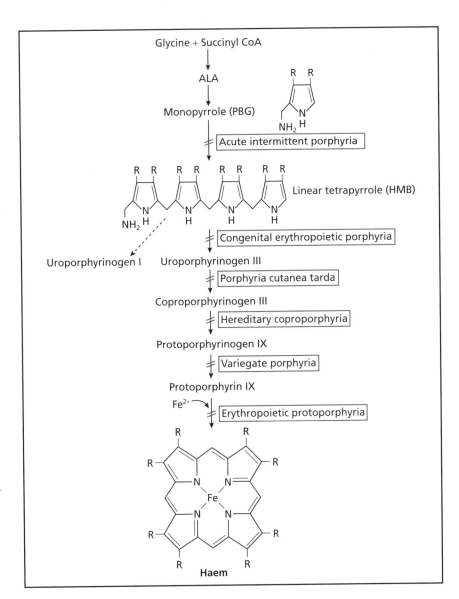

▲ **Fig. 30** Biosynthesis of haem. ALA, δ-aminolevulinic acid; HMB, hydroxymethylbilane; PBG, porphobilinogen; R, side group.

5. The final stages in porphyrin synthesis involve modifications of the side chains and conjugation of the porphyrin ring to form protoporphyrin IX.

6. Insertion of ferrous iron completes the haem structure.

Regulation of haem synthesis

In liver the rate of haem synthesis is strongly controlled by demand. The first committed step in porphyrin synthesis (the formation of ALA) is under negative feedback control by haem, which operates by depressing synthesis of the enzyme

ALA synthase. Drugs that induce enzymes of the cytochrome P450 series enhance ALA synthase activity (and thereby flux through the entire pathway) because the haem pool is depleted as molecules are incorporated into newly formed cytochrome P450 enzymes.

In red blood cells the rate of haem synthesis is less flexible, and the overall rate of production reflects the number of differentiated erythroid cells. The rate of globin synthesis is coupled to the availability of haem.

> Inherited disorders of porphyrin metabolism result in the porphyrias (Fig. 30). The clinical picture depends on which intermediates accumulate, and therefore on the position of the defective enzyme in the pathway.
>
> - The porphyrins themselves are strong photosensitisers, and their overproduction results in cutaneous lesions in sun-exposed areas.
> - Overproduction of the early precursors ALA and PBG is associated with acute neurovisceral attacks. Stimulation of ALA synthase activity by drugs that induce cytochrome P450 enzymes accounts for the ability of these drugs to precipitate acute attacks.

Degradation

Breakdown of haemoglobin occurs in the spleen and reticulendothelial system as red blood cells are removed from the circulation. The iron is recycled, and the porphyrin ring is converted into biliverdin, and thence to bilirubin.

In the first step, haem oxygenase breaks the porphyrin ring to reform a linear tetrapyrrole (biliverdin):

$$\text{haem} + O_2 + \text{NADPH} \rightarrow$$
$$\text{biliverdin} + \text{NADP}^+ + Fe^{3+} + H_2O + CO$$

A second molecule of NADPH is then used to form bilirubin:

$$\text{biliverdin} + \text{NADPH} + H^+ \rightarrow$$
$$\text{bilirubin} + \text{NADP}^+$$

Unconjugated bilirubin is relatively insoluble and is transported in the bloodstream as a complex with albumin. It is not excreted in the urine.

Hepatocytes take up unconjugated bilirubin and conjugate it to form the soluble diglucuronide, using residues donated by UDP-glucuronate. Conjugated bilirubin is excreted by a specific transporter into the bile.

Further metabolism by gut bacteria forms the soluble colourless compound urobilinogen. Some urobilinogen enters the bloodstream and can be excreted in the urine. Urobilinogen remaining in the gut is converted into the brown pigment, urobilin, and is excreted.

> Jaundice is caused by excessive bilirubin in the bloodstream, either conjugated or unconjugated.
>
> - Unconjugated hyperbilirubinaemia most often results from haemolysis (or Gilbert's syndrome, see below), since excessive bilirubin release exceeds the conjugating capacity of the liver. Unconjugated bilirubin is not excreted by the kidney.
> - Conjugated bilirubin does not enter the bloodstream unless there is liver damage, either obstructive or non-obstructive. If it does enter the bloodstream, conjugated bilirubin is excreted by the kidney, resulting in darkening of the urine. In complete biliary obstruction no bilirubin reaches the gut, so urobilinogen and urobilin are not formed.

> Inherited hyperbilirubinaemias arise from defects in enzymes involved in bilirubin degradation.
>
> - Mutations in the gene encoding bilirubin UDP-glucuronosyltransferase, the enzyme that conjugates bilirubin with UDP-glucuronate, result in either Gilbert's syndrome or Crigler–Najjar syndrome, depending on the severity and location of the mutation.
> - Mutations in the transporter responsible for biliary excretion of conjugated bilirubin cause Dubin–Johnson syndrome.

NUCLEOTIDES

Base — ribose — phosphate tail

Purine ring   **Pyrimidine ring**

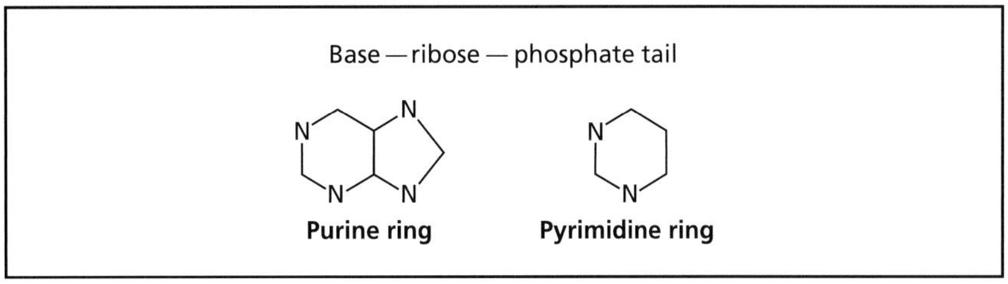

▲ **Fig. 31** Nucleotides.

Nucleotides consist of a purine or pyrimidine base, a ribose moiety and a phosphate chain (Fig. 31). They have many roles in the cell, including acting as:

- building blocks for DNA and RNA synthesis;

- energy stores, eg ATP and GTP;

- components of coenzymes, eg NAD^+, FAD and CoA;

- intracellular signalling molecules, eg cyclic adenosine monophosphate (cAMP) and cyclic guanosine monophosphate (cGMP);

- activated carrier molecules, eg UDP-glucose.

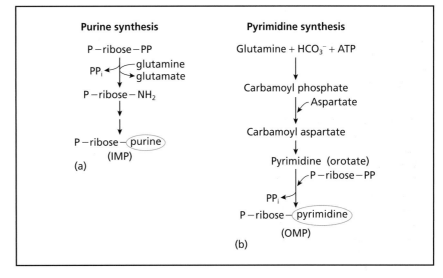

▲ **Fig. 32** Biosynthesis of (**a**) purines and (**b**) pyrimidines. IMP, inosine monophosphate; OMP, orotidine monophosphate, PP_i, pyrophosphate.

Purine synthesis
The principal purines are adenine and guanine. Purines are synthesised *de novo* in a multistep pathway that is energetically expensive (Fig. 32).

- The nitrogen atoms arise from glycine, aspartate and the side-chain amide groups of two glutamine residues.

- The carbon atoms come variously from glycine, CO_2 and tetrahydrofolate.

The process is as follows:

1. The base is synthesised by additions to a ribose phosphate unit, starting with the precursor, 5-phosphoribosyl-1-pyrophosphate (PRPP) (Fig. 32). This molecule consists of a ribose sugar with a single phosphate in the position of the eventual phosphate tail, and a pyrophosphate group where the base will grow. The pyrophosphate is replaced in the first committed step of

purine synthesis by an amide group from glutamine:

P-ribose-PP + glutamine → P-ribose-NH_2 + glutamate + PP_i

2. The purine ring is then constructed by a series of additions and modifications to the amide side group, resulting in the eventual formation of inosine monophosphate (IMP).

3. Other purine nucleotides are formed by modifications to IMP.

Pyrimidine synthesis

The principal pyrimidines are cytosine, thymine and uracil. Unlike the purine ring, the pyrimidine ring is assembled before it is coupled to the ribose phosphate unit (Fig. 32). The pyrimidine ring contains atoms from carbamoyl phosphate and aspartate.

1. The supply of carbamoyl phosphate is separate from that which enters the urea cycle. Whereas the urea cycle uses mitochondrially derived carbamoyl phosphate, pyrimidine synthesis makes use of a cytosolic enzyme that produces carbamoyl phosphate from bicarbonate and the side-chain amine of glutamine:

$$\text{glutamine} + 2\text{ATP} + \text{HCO}_3^- \rightarrow$$
$$\text{carbamoyl phosphate} + 2\text{ADP} + \text{P}_i + \text{glutamate}$$

2. The committed step in pyrimidine synthesis is the combination of carbamoyl phosphate with aspartate to form *N*-carbamoyl aspartate.

3. A further series of reactions forms the first pyrimidine, orotate.

4. Addition of a ribose phosphate moiety from PRPP forms OMP (orotidine monophosphate).

5. OMP acts as the precursor for synthesis of the other pyrimidine nucleotides:

$$\text{OMP} \rightarrow \text{UMP} \rightarrow \text{UTP} \rightarrow \text{CTP}$$

The phosphate tails can be moved between nucleotides to form the diphosphates and triphosphates:

$$\text{UMP} + \text{ATP} \leftrightarrow \text{UDP} + \text{ADP}$$

and in general:

$$X\,\text{DP} + Y\,\text{TP} \leftrightarrow X\,\text{TP} + Y\,\text{DP}$$

The deoxyribonucleotides, which are the components of DNA, are formed by reduction of the ribonucleotide

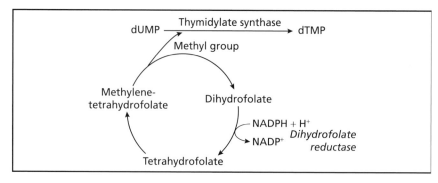

▲ **Fig. 33** Biosynthesis of thymine bases. dTMP, deoxythymidine monophosphate; dUMP, deoxyuridine monophosphate.

diphosphates (eg ADP → dADP, CDP → dCDP):

$$\text{PP-ribose-base} + \text{NADPH} + \text{H}^+ \rightarrow$$
$$\text{PP-deoxyribose-base} + \text{NADP}^+$$

DNA contains the base thymine, which is not found in RNA, and is formed by methylation of dUMP by thymidylate synthase (Fig. 33). The methyl group is donated by the carrier molecule methylenetetrahydrofolate. The dihydrofolate formed in this reaction is subsequently reduced to tetrahydrofolate by dihydrofolate reductase.

> 🔑 Several anticancer drugs target the production of dTMP since this nucleotide is specifically required for incorporation into DNA in rapidly dividing cells. Thus, fluorouracil inhibits thymidylate synthase and methotrexate blocks dihydrofolate reductase.

Salvage pathways

The *de novo* synthesis of purines, in particular, is a long and energetically expensive pathway. Free purine bases released in the course of normal cell turnover are therefore salvaged and reused.

Two salvage enzymes (for different purines) recombine the bases with ribose phosphate, thereby reforming the nucleotide monophosphate.

- Adenine phosphoribosyltransferase (APRT) is involved in the salvage of adenine, and catalyses the reaction:

$$\text{adenine} + \text{PRPP} \rightarrow \text{AMP} + \text{PP}_i$$

- Hypoxanthine-guanine phosphoribosyltransferase (HGPRT) catalyses the equivalent reactions for guanine and hypoxanthine:

$$\text{hypoxanthine} + \text{PRPP} \rightarrow \text{IMP} + \text{PP}_i$$

$$\text{guanine} + \text{PRPP} \rightarrow \text{GMP} + \text{PP}_i$$

The nucleotides thus formed exert feedback inhibition on the *de novo* synthetic pathway, thereby preventing the unnecessary synthesis of new purine bases.

> 🔑 Inherited deficiencies of the phosphoribosyltransferases can occur, such as the severe defects in HGPRT that cause Lesch–Nyhan syndrome. Affected individuals have very high levels of uric acid (see below), and the clinical features of spasticity, self-mutilation and mental retardation.

Purine degradation

Purine nucleotides are degraded to urate (Fig. 34). First the phosphate tail is removed and then the ribose moiety is excised to leave the free base:

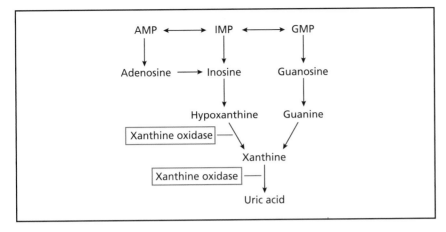

▲ **Fig. 34** Degradation of purines.

- GMP is converted to guanosine and thence to guanine;

- IMP is degraded via inosine to hypoxanthine;

- adenosine is degraded to hypoxanthine via conversion to inosine.

The free bases are then either salvaged for reincorporation into nucleotides, or are further catabolised via xanthine to uric acid.

The enzyme xanthine oxidase catalyses the oxidation of hypoxanthine to xanthine, and of xanthine to uric acid.

Increased serum levels of uric acid result in gout.

- Gout may arise from conditions in which uric acid excretion is impaired, or when rapid tissue breakdown (eg in malignancy) releases excessive quantities of purines into the bloodstream.
- In rare cases the cause is an inherited enzyme defect, eg in HGPRT.
- Allopurinol, an analogue of hypoxanthine, reduces uric acid production by inhibiting the enzyme xanthine oxidase.

Vitamins

Apart from the so-called macronutrients, which include sugars, amino acids and fats, several micronutrients are required. These include vitamins and trace elements. Vitamins can be divided into water soluble (B family and C) and fat soluble (A, D, E and K).

Vitamin A

Provitamin A (β-carotene) can be cleaved to generate two vitamin A molecules (retinol). Like other members of the carotenoid family (eg lycopene found in tomato products), provitamin A can act as an antioxidant. Retinol and its derivative retinoic acid are ligands for transcription factors important in cell differentiation and development; high doses should therefore be avoided especially during pregnancy. Another derivative, retinal, is the light-absorbing component of rhodopsin. Vitamin A deficiency is characterised by night blindness and follicular hyperkeratosis.

Vitamin B

This is a family of water-soluble substances, many of which are important cofactors in enzymes.

Deficiencies of several of these have overlapping or similar symptoms, as they are most often due to malnutrition (eg in chronic alcoholism).

- Thiamine (vitamin B_1) as its pyrophosphate is a cofactor of pyruvate dehydrogenase and α-ketoglutarate dehydrogenase, and as its triphosphate is an integral part of peripheral nerve membranes. Deficiency results in beriberi, or in a milder form as Wernicke–Korsakoff syndrome, most often seen in chronic alcoholism.

- Riboflavin (vitamin B_2) and niacin are incorporated into $NAD(P)^+$ and FAD/FMN respectively. These molecules carry electrons and hydrogen ions produced by oxidative reactions such as those of the citric acid cycle. Reduced carriers, such as NADPH, supply electrons in many biosynthetic reactions. As niacin can be synthesised from tryptophan, pellagra is usually only seen when tryptophan availability is low, eg on a diet mostly based on maize, during malabsorption (Hartnup's desease) or during general malnutrition.

- Biotin, the coenzyme of many carboxylases (eg pyruvate carboxylase) and pantothenic acid, a component of coenzyme A, are rarely associated with avitaminoses, as they are widely abundant in many foods or can be synthesised by intestinal bacteria.

- Folate is the cofactor in 'one-carbon' metabolism and its deficiency affects rapidly dividing tissues, causing megaloblastic anaemia. During pregnancy, higher levels are required and deficiency can lead to neural tube defects.

- Pyridoxine (vitamin B_6) plays an important role in metabolism as it is converted into pyridoxal phosphate, the cofactor for amino acid transaminases and decarboxylases.

- Vitamin B_{12} (cobalamin) is scarce and requires a special binding protein, intrinsic factor, to be secreted into the gut lumen to aid its absorption. It is a cofactor for the transfer of methyl groups from tetrahydrofolate to homocysteine and the rearrangement of methylmalonyl CoA, necessary in the oxidation of odd chain length fatty acids. Deficiency results in pernicious anaemia, as under these conditions folate is trapped in its N^5-methylene-tetrahydrofolate form, and accumulation of homocysteine and methylmalonate result in progressive demyelination of nervous tissue.

Vitamin C

Ascorbic acid can act as an antioxidant and protects against damage by oxygen-derived radicals. It is also a cofactor for dopamine, carnitine, lysine and proline hydroxylases. As hydroxyproline and hydroxylysine are important for the stability of collagen, ascorbate deficiency leads to scurvy.

Vitamin D

Vitamin D is either obtained from the diet or formed by the photolytic opening of the cholesterol B ring in the presence of ultraviolet light. The active 1,25-dihydroxycholecalciferol, formed by regulated hydroxylations, binds to its nuclear receptor and is involved in calcium homeostasis. Deficiency of vitamin D due to insufficiencies in dietary intake and exposure to sunlight results in rickets in children and osteomalacia in adults. Since the main site of 1α-hydroxylation is the kidney, deficiency of active 1,25-dihydroxycholecalciferol is a feature of renal failure.

Vitamin E

Vitamin E consists of tocopherols and tocotrienols, which act as antioxidants in lipophilic compartments (eg membranes and low-density lipoprotein). They protect polyunsaturated fatty acids from attack by radicals (eg oxygen derived). α-Tocopherol might also bind to transcription factors, thereby having effects beyond its antioxidant potential. Avitaminoses are rare.

Vitamin K

Two natural sources of vitamin K are phytylmenaquinone from plants and multiprenylmenaquinone from (intestinal) bacteria. It is a cofactor for the conversion of glutamate side chains in some proteins (eg thrombin and osteocalcin) into γ-carboxyglutamate, which is important in the binding of these proteins to Ca^{2+}. Vitamin K becomes oxidised during this reaction and needs to be reduced to be reactivated. Dicoumarins (eg wafarin) interfere with this reactivation. Vitamin K is routinely given to newborns to assist blood clotting because they have no intestinal source and low liver storage capacity.

Trace elements

Apart from the major minerals (sodium, potassium, calcium, magnesium, chloride, phosphate and carbonate), many trace elements are necessary, although their specific functions in humans are often obscure.

Iron

Iron is the ion in haem and its major function is to assist transport of oxygen by haemoglobin and myoglobin. In mitochondria, iron is involved in the electron transport chain as part of the cytochromes or in FeS clusters. Other important iron-containing enzymes are cytochrome P450, catalase and peroxidases. Microcytic hypochromic anaemia due to iron deficiency is probably the most common nutrient deficiency in the world.

Zinc

Zinc is a constituent of more than 300 metalloproteins. Zn^{2+} is an integral part of the active centre of enzymes such as RNA and DNA polymerases, alkaline phosphatase, carbonic anhydrase and superoxide dismutase. Alternatively, Zn^{2+} can have structural roles, eg as part of the so-called Zn^{2+} fingers that assist protein–DNA and protein–protein interactions, or as part of the insulin crystals found in the secretory vesicles of pancreatic β cells. Zinc deficiency results in dermatitis and poor wound healing.

Copper

Copper is an important cofactor in several enzymes, including cytochrome c oxidase (electron transport chain), dopamine-β-hydroxylase (catecholamine synthesis), lysyl oxidase (collagen cross-linking), Δ^9-desaturase (fatty acid desaturation) and ceruloplasmin (iron oxidation and absorption). Deficiency symptoms therefore include anaemia, leucopenia, hypercholesterolaemia, bone demineralisation, fragile arteries and demyelination. Menke's kinky hair syndrome is a rare X-linked copper malabsorption syndrome.

Selenium

Selenium occurs as the rare amino acid selenocysteine in a number of enzymes. Examples include glutathione peroxidase (reversal of oxidative damage to membrane lipids) and iodothyronine deiodinase (T_4 to T_3). Deficiency results in growth retardation.

Manganese and cobalt

Manganese is part of the active site of arginase (urea cycle), pyruvate carboxylase (gluconeogenesis) and mitochondrial superoxide dismutase. It can compete with Mg^{2+} and either activates (eg glutamine synthetase) or alters specificity (eg DNA polymerases and nucleases) when doing so. Cobalt is mostly restricted to its function in vitamin B_{12}, but both Co^{2+} and Mn^{2+} can replace Cu^{2+} in active centres of enzymes without abolishing activity. Manganese deficiency results in growth retardation, skeletal abnormalities and glucose intolerance, whilst cobalt deficiency results in anaemia.

Other (possible) trace elements

Fluoride is important in bone and tooth mineralisation. Iodine is an essential component of the thyroid hormones and deficiency leads to goitre. Chromium is found in chromodulin, a possible enhancer of insulin signalling. Chromium deficiency leads to glucose intolerance. Molybdenum is part of the active centre of aldehyde and xanthine oxidases. Vanadate can compete with phosphate, but its importance is unclear. Other trace elements of unclear functions include lithium, nickel, arsenic, boron, cadmium and silicon.

FURTHER READING

Berg JM, Tymoczko JL and Stryer L. *Biochemistry*, 6th edn. New York: WH Freeman, 2007.

Devlin TM, ed. *Textbook of Biochemistry: With Clinical Correlations*, 6th edn. Hoboken, NJ: Wiley-Liss, 2006.

Metzler DE. *Biochemistry: The Chemical Reactions of Living Cells*, 2nd edn (2 vols). San Diego: Academic Press, 2001–2003.

Nelson DL and Cox MM. *Lehninger: Principles of Biochemistry*, 4th edn. New York: Freeman, 2005.

Salway JG. *Metabolism at a Glance*, 3rd edn. Oxford: Blackwell Science, 2004.

Scriver CR, Childs B, Kinzler KW and Vogelstein B, eds. *The Metabolic and Molecular Bases of Inherited Disease*, 8th edn. New York: McGraw-Hill, 2001.

Voet D and Voet J. *Biochemistry*, 3rd edn. New York: Wiley, 2004.

8.1 Self-assessment questions

Question 1

Which of the following statements about glycolysis is true?

Answers

A Glycolysis is a net consumer of ATP

B Glycolysis results in the reduction of $NADP^+$ to NADPH

C $FADH_2$ produced by glycolysis feeds into the electron transport chain at the level of complex II

D Conversion of pyruvate to lactate is linked to the oxidation of NADH to NAD^+

E Glycolysis in muscle is inhibited by adrenaline

Question 2

Which one of the following is *not* a consequence of raised insulin levels?

Answers

A Hepatic fatty acid synthesis

B Increased β-oxidation in muscle

C Glycogen synthesis in muscle

D Triacylglycerol synthesis in adipose tissue

E Increased glycogen synthesis in the liver

Question 3

Which one of the following is *not* a true statement about the electron transport chain?

Answers

A Electron transport by the electron transport chain (ETC) is coupled to proton translocation into the mitochondrial matrix

B Dissipation of mitochondrial proton gradients by uncoupling proteins in brown fat generates heat

C Electrons from $FADH_2$ can enter the ETC at complex II

D More ATP is generated by oxidation of NADH than of $FADH_2$

E Exchange of ATP for ADP by the adenine nucleotide translocator dissipates some of the proton-motive force

Question 4

Which of the following is an essential fatty acid?

Answers

A Palmitate

B Oleate

C Linoleate

D Stearate

E Arachidonate

Question 5

Which one of the following *cannot* be formed using acetyl CoA as a starting point?

Answers

A Malonyl CoA

B Cholesterol

C Acetoacetate

D Pyruvate

E HMG CoA

Question 6

Which of the following conversions is a result of a transaminase reaction?

Answers

A Pyruvate to lactate

B Alanine to pyruvate

C Oxaloacetate to serine

D Citrate to glutamate

E α-Ketoglutarate to aspartate

Question 7

Which one of the following hormones is *not* an amino acid derivative?

Answers

A 5-HT

B Adrenaline

C GABA

D Thyroxine

E Aldosterone

Question 8

Which of the following vitamins is important in the hydroxylation of proline and lysine to form hydroxyproline and hydroxylysine?

Answers

A Vitamin A

B Vitamin B_6

C Vitamin C

D Vitamin D

E Vitamin E

Question 9

In which of the following reactions is methylenetetrahydrofolate an essential cofactor?

Answers

A ADP to dADP

B dUDP to dTDP

C CMP to dCMP

D dUMP to dTMP

E GMP to dGMP

Question 10

Which one of the following is *not* an essential amino acid?

Answers

A Histidine
B Isoleucine
C Tryptophan
D Lysine
E Proline

8.2 Self-assessment answers

Answer to Question 1

D

Conversion of pyruvate to lactate occurs under anaerobic conditions, as full oxidation by the mitochondria is not possible in the absence of oxygen. By converting pyruvate to lactate, NAD^+ is regenerated from NADH, allowing glycolysis to continue. Glycolysis itself produces ATP, although less so than mitochonrial oxidation, and supplies energy under anaerobic conditions. The lactate that is produced is recycled to the liver where it is reconverted to glucose. $FADH_2$ and NADPH are not produced by glycolysis. Adrenaline stimulates muscle glycogenolysis, providing a local supply of glucose that is used by glycolysis.

Answer to Question 2

B

β-Oxidation is the process by which fatty acids are metabolised in mitochondria to synthesise ATP, and is not stimulated by insulin when other substrates like glucose are readily available. Raised insulin levels in the post-absorptive state promote the storage of excess energy as fat and glycogen.

Answer to Question 3

A

Electron transport by the electron transport chain is coupled to the translocation of protons out of the mitochondrial matrix, not into it. Flow of electrons back into the matrix is coupled to the formation of ATP by the mitochondrial ATPase.

Answer to Question 4

C

Linoleate is an ω6 fatty acid and cannot be synthesised by the limited range of desaturases present in humans. α-Linolenic acid, an ω3 fatty acid, is also essential. These are required for the synthesis of arachidonic acid and prostaglandin/leukotriene relatives.

Answer to Question 5

D

Conversion of acetyl CoA to pyruvate cannot be performed by humans, hence acetyl CoA produced by β-oxidation of fatty acids cannot be channelled back into glucose. Excessive acetyl CoA formation, which occurs when glucose supplies are low and fatty acids are used as an energy source, results in the production of ketone bodies. These can be used as an energy source for brain and muscle, but are acids that can cause dangerous levels of acidosis, most typically in the context of diabetic ketoacidosis.

Answer to Question 6

B

Transamination reactions catalyse the transfer of an amino group from one keto acid to another. Transamination of pyruvate forms alanine. Other important transamination reactions involve the conversion of oxaloacetate to aspartate and of α-ketoglutarate to glutamate.

Answer to Question 7

E

Aldosterone is a steroid hormone. 5-HT is derived from tryptophan, adrenaline from tyrosine, GABA from glutamate and thyroxine from tyrosine.

Answer to Question 8

C

Hydroxyproline and hydroxylysine, produced by hydroxylation of proline and lysine using vitamin C as a cofactor, are essential components of collagen. Deficiency of vitamin C impairs collagen synthesis, with the consequent signs of scurvy.

Answer to Question 9

D

Thymine residues are found in DNA but not RNA. They are formed by the methylation of dUMP to form dTMP, in a reaction catalysed by thymidylate synthase. The methyl group is donated by methylenetetrahydrofolate. Inhibition of dTMP synthesis by inhibitors of thymidylate synthase (eg fluorouracil) or dihydrofolate reductase (eg methotrexate) affects rapidly dividing cells.

Answer to Question 10

E

Proline is formed from glutamate. All the others are essential amino acids and must be obtained from the diet in humans.

CELL BIOLOGY

Authors:

EH Baker, KM Bowles, GG Dark, JD Firth and AD Hingorani

Editor:

JD Firth

Editor-in-Chief:

JD Firth

The movement of ions across cell membranes is critical for normal homeostasis. For example, transmembrane ion transport contributes to:

- generation of electrical signals, eg in muscle and nerve cells;

- control of intracellular calcium and hence cell functions including intracellular signalling and muscle contraction;

- absorption and excretion of ions across epithelia, essential for whole-body homeostasis;

- control of ion concentration within cells and other body fluid compartments, essential for local homeostasis.

An understanding of ion transport is increasingly important in medicine as abnormalities of ion transport underlie the development of many diseases and many drugs in everyday use exert their therapeutic effects through actions on ion transport processes. In this section basic principles important to the understanding of ion transport are discussed and common examples of ion transport processes given. The reader should be aware that this only scratches the surface of what is a huge and rapidly expanding field in medicine.

Basic principles of ion transport

> Lipid membranes are virtually impermeable to water and ions. Transport of ions across cell membranes depends on the following mechanisms.
> - Ion channels: act as pores through which a specific ion(s) can pass; driven by electrochemical gradients.
> - Ion carriers: bind to a specific ion(s) on one side of the membrane, change shape, and release it on the other; driven by electrochemical gradients or chemical energy.

Cells and intracellular organelles are surrounded by lipid membranes, which are virtually impermeable to water and polarised ions. These membranes separate the contents of cells and organelles from each other and from extracellular fluid. Ions are able to move spontaneously across cell membranes by diffusion, but this movement is very slow and insufficient for electrical signalling and other cell functions: most movement of ions across cell membranes depends on a variety of ion transport proteins. Ion transport proteins sit in the cell membrane and assist the movement of ions across the lipid bilayer.

Ion channels

Ion channels (Fig. 1a) are assembled in the membrane from several subunits, which may be different proteins or multiple copies of the same protein. Subunits are usually identified using a letter from the Greek alphabet, eg three different proteins that are subunits of the epithelial sodium channel are designated α, β and γ. Each protein subunit is folded into a complex tertiary structure that causes it to cross the cell membrane at least twice. The regions of the subunits embedded in the membrane together form an ion-conducting pore. Movement of ions through ion channels is driven by electrical and chemical gradients for the ions across the cell membrane.

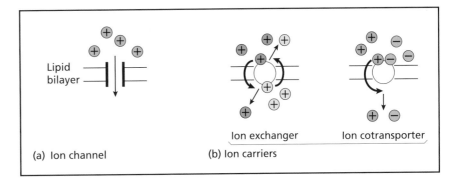

(a) Ion channel (b) Ion carriers Ion exchanger Ion cotransporter

Lipid bilayer

▲ **Fig. 1** Types of ion transport protein.

Ion carriers

Ion carrier proteins (Fig. 1b) move ions across the membrane by binding to the ion on one side of the membrane, then undergoing a conformational change that moves the ion to the other side of the membrane. This process may be driven by energy from:

- hydrolysis of ATP (active transport);

- an ion gradient generated by another transporter (secondary active transport).

Ion carriers may carry:

- only one ion, eg H^+-ATPase;

- two or more types of ion in the same direction, eg Na^+/HCO_3^- cotransporter, $Na^+/K^+/2Cl^-$ cotransporter;

- two types of ion in opposite directions across the membrane, eg Na^+/H^+ exchanger, Na^+/K^+-ATPase.

Thus transport by ion carriers is generally charge neutral, ie they either carry ions of opposite charge (eg Na^+/HCO_3^- cotransporter) in the same direction or ions of the same charge in opposite directions (eg Na^+/H^+ exchanger). Carriers that generate an electrical gradient by unbalanced movement of ions generally consume energy to do this (eg H^+-ATPase).

Types of ions moved by transport proteins

There are many different ion transport proteins. Ion transport proteins may move one or more simple cations (eg Na^+, K^+, Ca^{2+}, H^+) or anions (eg Cl^-, HCO_3^-). Transporters can also move larger, ionised molecules such as amino acids or drugs.

1.1 Ion channels

Ion channels have a wide range of different functions, determined by specific features of individual channels and by ion gradients across the channel (Fig. 2).

Factors determining transport through ion channels

Selectivity

The ions transported by a channel are determined by its structure. For example, the entrance to a cation channel may be negatively charged, repelling anions but permitting the entrance of cations. The entrance to selective Na^+ channels is big enough to permit the passage of Na^+ ions, but too small to admit larger cations, eg K^+.

Conductance

Passage of ions through ion channels may be rapid (high conductance) or slow (low conductance). Highly selective channels tend to have low conductance, whereas non-selective channels have high conductance.

Gating

Ion channels can be open or closed and movement between these states is called gating. Channels may be gated by voltage of the cell membrane, extracellular ligands or intracellular messengers (Fig. 2). Gating allows control of movement of ions into or out of the cell. Channels may move between open and closed states rapidly or slowly.

Coordination of ion channel activity and cell function

Individual cells may have many types of ion channels in their cell membranes. Coordination of function of channels of different selectivity and conductance by different gating methods is an important determinant of cell function.

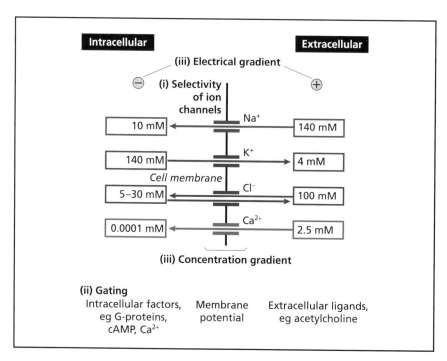

▲ **Fig. 2** Type and quantity of ion transport across a cell membrane are determined by (**i**) the channels (selectivity, conductance, numbers) present in the cell membrane; (**ii**) mechanisms for gating the channel (moving between open and closed states); and (**iii**) electrical and chemical gradients for different ion types that drive their movement across the membrane.

1.1.1 Ion channels in epithelial cells

- Epithelial cells form an interface between the body and the outside world.

- Epithelial cells are polarised, ie ion transporters in the apical (luminal) membrane differ from ion transporters in the basolateral (interstitial) membrane.

Ions can therefore be moved across the epithelium by coordinated action of basolateral and apical transporters. Ion channels in epithelial cells play a role in controlling the movement of ions into and out of the body and determining the content of transcellular fluid, for example of airway surface liquid.

There are many different types of ion channel in epithelial cells. Two examples are discussed here: the epithelial sodium channel and the cystic fibrosis transmembrane regulator.

Epithelial sodium channel

The epithelial sodium channel (ENaC) (Fig. 3) has the following features.

- Present in the apical membrane of cells in absorptive epithelia, eg the collecting duct of the renal tubule.

- Comprises α, β and γ subunits that each start in the cytoplasm, cross the cell membrane, form a large extracellular loop, then end in the cytoplasm. Assembly of these subunits forms a Na^+-conducting pore across the membrane.

- Permits reabsorption of Na^+ from the urine into the interstitium down a chemical gradient for Na^+ generated by the sodium pump in the basolateral membrane of the cell.

- Allows movement of Na^+ alone, but Na^+ reabsorption in the distal tubule promotes K^+ excretion into the urine.

- Controlled by hormones that regulate sodium balance and blood pressure: the sodium-retaining hormone aldosterone increases Na^+ reabsorption (and K^+ excretion) partly by stimulating an increase in the number and activity of epithelial sodium channels. Atrial natriuretic peptide, in contrast, promotes natriuresis in part by suppressing the activity of ENaC.

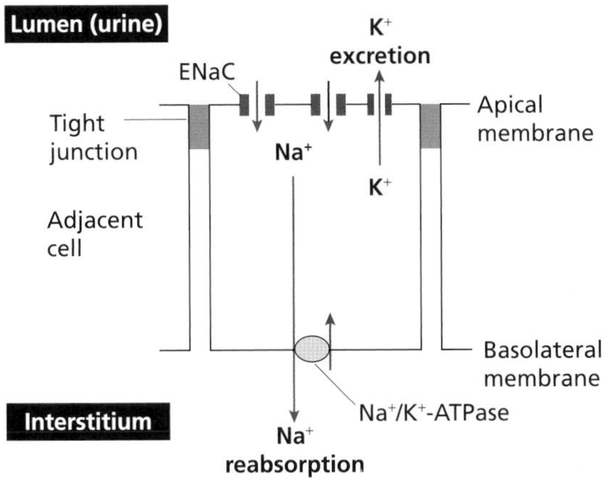

Abnormalities of ENaC have been shown to cause both high and low blood pressure, and the channel is a target for drug action.

Liddle's syndrome

This is an extremely rare autosomal dominant form of hypertension caused by mutations of the regulatory region of either the β or γ ENaC subunits. These regions are normally used to pull Na^+ channels out of the apical membrane into the cytoplasm as a means of reducing channel activity. Mutations of these regions cause channels to become stuck in the cell membrane, and hence ENaC activity and renal Na^+ reabsorption (and K^+ excretion) increases (Fig. 4a). Patients with Liddle's syndrome develop features of sodium overload, ie hypertension with suppression of the renin–aldosterone system, and hypokalaemia (see *Physiology*, Section 6.2).

Pseudohypoaldosteronism type 1

This is the opposite of Liddle's syndrome. Different mutations of ENaC cause disruption of the pore-forming region and loss of ENaC activity, with renal salt wasting and potassium retention (Fig. 4b). The clinical features of pseudohypoaldosteronism include low blood pressure, activation of the renin–aldosterone system and hyperkalaemia.

Drugs targeting ENaC activity

The diuretic drug amiloride works by blocking epithelial sodium channels (Fig. 4c). Its effect is to reduce renal Na^+ reabsorption and promote K^+ retention; hence it is called a 'potassium-sparing' diuretic.

▲ **Fig. 3** Normal function of the epithelial sodium channel in the renal collecting duct.

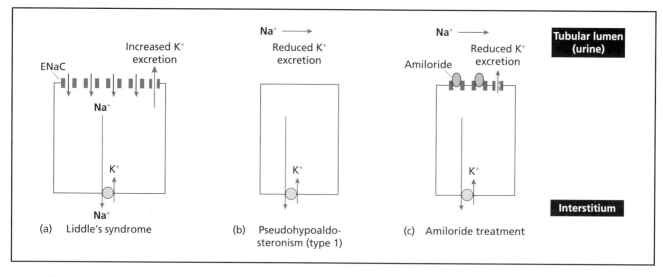

▲**Fig. 4** Effects of disease and drug therapy on epithelial sodium channel activity.

Cystic fibrosis transmembrane conductance regulator

The cystic fibrosis transmembrane conductance regulator (CFTR) is a large continuous protein that consists of two repeating structures, each of which cross the membrane six times. Between and on either side of these repeats are protein regions (domains) that sit in the cytoplasm and are important for channel regulation. It is not clear if functional CFTR consists of one or more of these CFTR molecules in the cell membrane.

CFTR is found in epithelial cells, most notably in the airway (Fig. 5) and ducts of the pancreas (Fig. 6) and sweat glands (Fig. 7), where it has dual functions.

• As a chloride channel, allowing transepithelial secretion or absorption of Cl⁻ ions across these epithelia.

• As a regulator of activity of other ion transporters. For example, in airway epithelium where CFTR and ENaC are both expressed, ENaC activity appears to be suppressed (down-regulated) by CFTR.

It is probable that, through both of these functions, CFTR has an integral role in regulating the volume and composition of airway surface liquid, pancreatic secretions and sweat.

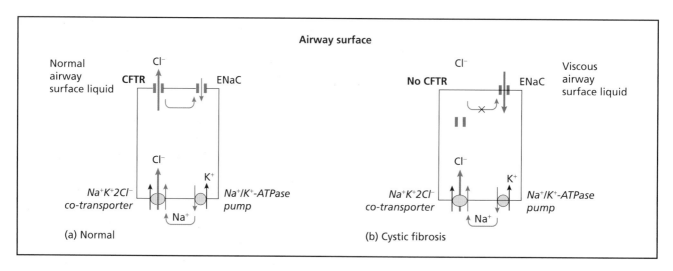

▲**Fig. 5** CFTR in the airway. (**a**) In normal airway epithelium CFTR secretes Cl⁻ into airway surface liquid and down-regulates Na⁺ absorption through ENaC. (**b**) In cystic fibrosis the most common mutation (ΔF508) prevents correct processing of CFTR protein, which does not reach the plasma membrane. Lack of CFTR causes reduced Cl⁻ secretion into and increased Na⁺ absorption from airway secretions, which become thick and viscous.

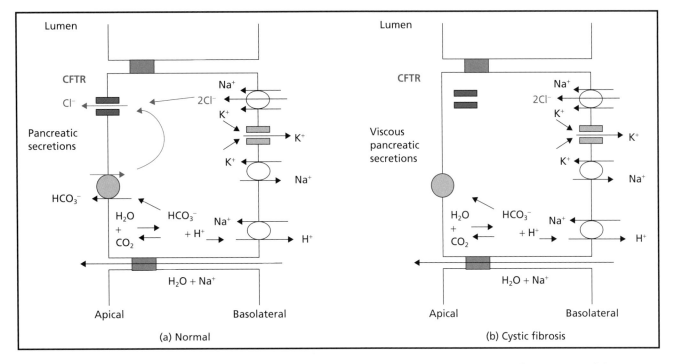

▲**Fig. 6** CFTR in the pancreatic duct. (**a**) In normal pancreatic duct epithelial cells, CFTR is expressed in the luminal membrane, allowing secretion of Cl^- into pancreatic secretions. This in turn drives bicarbonate secretion by HCO_3^-/Cl^- counter-transporters and these anions are followed by water and Na^+. (**b**) In cystic fibrosis, loss of CFTR reduces secretion of Cl^- and HCO_3^- into pancreatic secretions, which become more viscous.

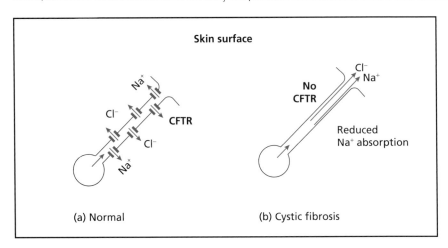

▲**Fig. 7** CFTR in the sweat duct. (**a**) In normal sweat duct epithelial cells CFTR is expressed in the luminal membrane but, unlike other epithelia, allows reabsorption of Cl^-. Reabsorption of Cl^- creates a lumen-positive electrical potential that drives Na^+ absorption and water is absorbed by osmosis. (**b**) In cystic fibrosis loss of CFTR reduces absorption of Cl^-, reduces electrical driving force for Na^+ absorption and results in wasting of Cl^-, Na^+ and water in sweat.

Cystic fibrosis

🔑 Cystic fibrosis is most commonly caused by mutations of the *CFTR* gene, which prevent synthesis or processing of the protein, resulting in lack of CFTR in the cell membrane. Other mutations alter

regulation or conduction of the channel. The net effect is that:

- transepithelial Cl^- transport is reduced;
- ENaC down-regulation is lost, so ENaC activity and transepithelial Na^+ transport are increased;
- changes in Cl^- and Na^+ transport cause osmotic changes that alter hydration of body secretions.

In the airway CFTR mutations cause decreased secretion of Cl^- and increased reabsorption of Na^+ from the airway surface liquid (Fig. 5b). These alterations result in this fluid becoming thick and viscous, blocking bronchi and bronchioles, causing bronchiectasis and allowing recurrent lung infections, particularly with *Pseudomonas*. The majority of people with cystic fibrosis die prematurely of respiratory failure.

In the pancreatic duct CFTR is involved in the secretion of Cl^-, HCO_3^- and water (Fig. 6). Failure of these processes in cystic fibrosis causes pancreatic secretions to become more viscous so that they plug pancreatic ducts, triggering autodigestion and pancreatic destruction. The clinical features of cystic fibrosis include pancreatic insufficiency with malabsorption and weight loss (or failure to thrive in children). Treatment is with replacement pancreatic enzymes taken with meals and a high-calorie diet. Diabetes mellitus, due in part to insulin deficiency from pancreatic destruction, is common in cystic fibrosis, affecting around 30% of cystic fibrosis patients who survive to age 30.

In the sweat duct CFTR channels are normally responsible for Cl$^-$ reabsorption from sweat (Fig. 7). People with cystic fibrosis are therefore unable to conserve Cl$^-$, which appears in high concentrations in their sweat. This finding forms the basis of the sweat test. In hot weather or climates, people with cystic fibrosis are vulnerable to dehydration because they cannot reduce the amount of Cl$^-$ (and Na$^+$ and H$_2$O) that is lost in their sweat.

For clinical details of cystic fibrosis, see *Respiratory Medicine*, Sections 1.1.3, 1.2.9 and 2.5.

1.1.2 Ion channels in non-epithelial cells

In epithelial cells, ion movement is often across cells and contributes to absorption or excretion of ions into or out of the body. In non-epithelial cells, eg muscle or nerve cells, ion channels regulate movement of ions into or out of the cell. This generates a transmembrane potential difference that is crucial for normal cell function. Controlled changes in cell membrane potential can be used to signal between cells or alter intracellular calcium.

Cell membrane potential

Why is there a potential difference across the cell membrane? It is worth taking a few moments to revisit the basic principles involved. Ohm's law states that voltage equals current multiplied by the resistance ($V = IR$), so the potential difference across the cell membrane must be proportional to the current that

flows across it, ie the number of ions moving across the membrane.

Movement of ions across the cell membrane depends on the:

- type of ion channels open in the cell membrane;
- electrical and chemical gradients driving ions across the cell membrane through the open channels.

Any ion will always tend to move down its chemical or electrical gradient, with movement ceasing when the electrical and chemical gradients are equal and opposite, the electrical potential at this point being known as the Nernst potential.

Resting cell potential

The resting cell potential of most cells is determined by the fact that the majority of channels open in the cell membrane are K$^+$ channels. As intracellular K$^+$ concentration is ~140 mmol/L and extracellular K$^+$ concentration is ~4 mmol/L, the chemical gradient drives movement of K$^+$ out of the cell

until the transmembrane potential is near the Nernst potential for K$^+$ (typically about –90 mV) (Fig. 8). The potential difference is denoted as being electrically negative as the movement of K$^+$ out of the cell renders the inside of the cell membrane negative with respect to the outside.

Changes in membrane potential

The cell membrane potential is usually negative inside the cell with respect to the outside.

- Hyperpolarisation occurs if the inside of the cell becomes more negative. This can be produced by movement of cations out of the cell (efflux) or anions into the cell (influx).

- Depolarisation occurs if the inside of the cell becomes more positive. This can be produced by efflux of anions or influx of cations.

There are many different types of ion channel in non-epithelial cells. One example is discussed here: voltage-gated sodium channels.

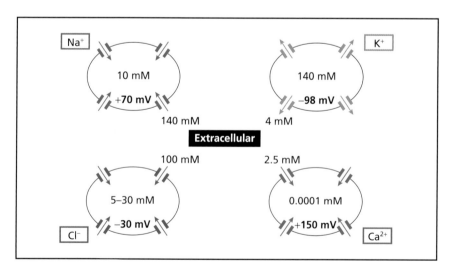

▲ **Fig. 8** Typical Nernst potentials for individual ions. Where ion channels selective for one type of ion are open in the cell membrane, the concentration gradient drives transport of that ion through the channel. Because ions are charged, their movement generates a potential difference across the membrane which exerts a force on the ions in the opposite direction to the concentration gradient. Once the electrical and chemical forces are equal, there is no further net ion movement and the resulting potential difference is known as the Nernst potential. Note that efflux of cations (K$^+$) and influx of anions (Cl$^-$) hyperpolarises the cell membrane, whereas influx of cations (Na$^+$, Ca^{2+}) depolarises the membrane.

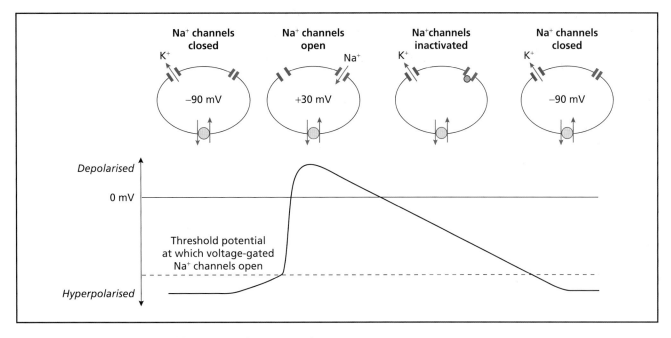

▲ **Fig. 9** Voltage-gated Na⁺ channels and the generation of action potentials.

Voltage-gated sodium channels

Voltage-gated Na⁺ channels consist of a principal α subunit that forms the channel and one or more β subunits that modify channel properties. Voltage-gated Na⁺ channels permit rapid changes in membrane potential (Fig. 9). In skeletal and cardiac muscle and in nerves this is critical for generation and potentiation of action potentials, which are generated as follows.

- At resting cell membrane potential, voltage-gated Na⁺ channels are closed.

- Depolarisation of the cell membrane triggers rapid channel opening, causing a flux of Na⁺ into the cell down the concentration gradient (extracellular Na⁺ ~140 mmol/L, intracellular Na⁺ ~10 mmol/L).

- The entry of Na⁺ ions depolarises the cell membrane.

- The Na⁺ channels inactivate as rapidly as they open, Na⁺ is extruded from the cell by the

Na⁺/K⁺-ATPase pump and resting membrane potential is restored by the action of K⁺ channels as described above.

To accomplish this, voltage-gated Na⁺ channels move between three states: open, inactivated and closed. After a channel has been open it becomes inactivated and cannot be reopened for a period of time. This period of channel inactivation is critical as it allows excitable cells a period of time to hyperpolarise before the next action potential commences. Once hyperpolarisation of the cell membrane is complete, the channels change to the closed state and are ready to open again.

Several mutations of voltage-gated Na⁺ channels have been identified as causing disease. The majority of these impair channel inactivation and disrupt the action potential, interfering with the function of excitable cells. Voltage-gated Na⁺ channels are also a target for drug action.

Skeletal muscle cells

In skeletal muscle, activation of normal voltage-gated Na⁺ channels and depolarisation of the cell membrane results in an increase in intracellular calcium that promotes muscle contraction. Inactivation and closure of voltage-gated Na⁺ channels allows hyperpolarisation of the cell membrane, a fall in intracellular calcium and muscle relaxation. Some mutations of the α subunit of the voltage-gated Na⁺ channel prevent inactivation of the channel, resulting in a persistent inward Na⁺ current that causes hyperexcitability of skeletal muscle, with myotonia or paralysis.

Myotonia

Mutations that cause a small persistent inward Na⁺ current make muscle cell membranes hyperexcitable by lowering the action potential threshold (Fig. 10b). This causes myotonia, a syndrome of impaired muscle relaxation: sufferers have difficulty opening their hand after clenching a fist or opening their eyes after shutting them tightly. (See *Neurology*, Sections 2.2.3 and 2.2.4.)

Periodic paralysis

More severe mutations result in a large inward Na$^+$ current, altering the membrane potential so that voltage-gated Na$^+$ channels do not open at all (Fig. 10c), an action potential cannot be generated and paralysis results. This is found in the syndrome of hyperkalaemic periodic paralysis, where intermittent attacks of muscle weakness occur spontaneously or can be precipitated by exercise, stress or K$^+$-rich foods.

Cardiac muscle cells

A normal action potential in cardiac cells starts when opening of voltage-gated Na$^+$ channels is triggered, leading to influx of Na$^+$ and rapid membrane depolarisation. Na$^+$ channels then quickly become inactivated and depolarisation is maintained by Ca^{2+} influx (plateau phase) before hyperpolarisation is restored by K$^+$ efflux.

Long QT syndrome

Mutations of voltage-gated Na$^+$ channels have been identified which slow Na$^+$ channel inactivation. These mutant channels allow persistent Na$^+$ influx, delay hyperpolarisation and prolong the action potential (Fig. 11a), seen as an increase in QT interval on an ECG.

Torsade de pointes

Patients with long QT syndrome are susceptible to sudden dysrhythmias, at worst leading to sudden death. The mechanism of dysrhythmia is uncertain: one hypothesis is that mutant Na$^+$ channels, which have failed to inactivate, reopen during the prolonged period of hyperpolarisation, initiating early 'after depolarisations' (Fig. 11b) and thereby triggering additional action potentials at multiple loci, which may initiate or maintain torsade de pointes (Fig. 11c). (See *Cardiology*, Sections 1.1.2 and 2.2.2.)

Nerve cells

A mutation of the β1 subunit of the voltage-gated Na$^+$ channel has been identified as a cause of familial epilepsy. The β1 subunit normally accelerates both the rate of inactivation and the speed of recovery from inactivation of voltage-gated Na$^+$ channels: loss of this function is predicted to cause a persistent inward Na$^+$ current that is probably responsible for neuronal hyperexcitability and seizures.

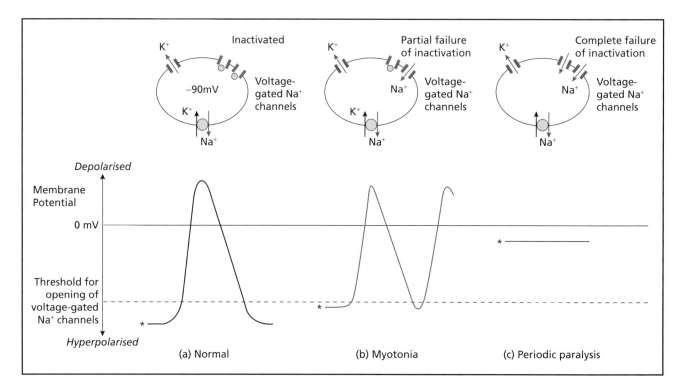

▲ **Fig. 10** Normal and abnormal function of voltage-gated Na$^+$ channel in skeletal muscle cells. The asterisk denotes resting potential of the cell membrane. (**a**) In normal skeletal muscle cells a resting potential of −90 mV is maintained by K$^+$ efflux and voltage-gated Na$^+$ channels are inactivated. (**b**) The small abnormal inward sodium current in patients with myotonia brings the resting potential closer to the threshold potential at which voltage-gated Na$^+$ channels open, which makes the cells hyperexcitable. (**c**) The large abnormal inward sodium current in patients with periodic paralysis depolarises the cell membrane to a level at which voltage-gated Na$^+$ channels do not open. Thus action potentials and muscle contraction cannot be initiated and paralysis results.

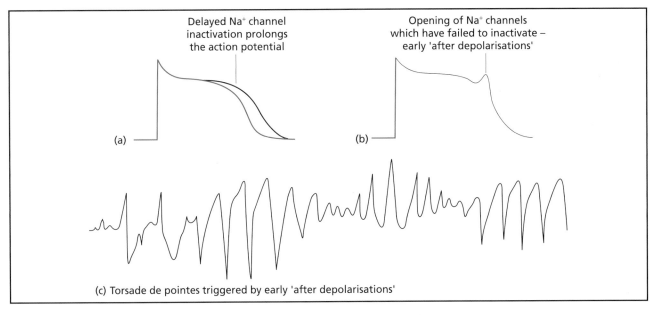

Delayed Na⁺ channel inactivation prolongs the action potential

(a)

Opening of Na⁺ channels which have failed to inactivate – early 'after depolarisations'

(b)

(c) Torsade de pointes triggered by early 'after depolarisations'

▲ **Fig. 11** Effects of abnormalities of the voltage-gated Na⁺ channel in cardiac cells on action potential and ECG.

Drugs targeting voltage-gated Na⁺ channels

Drugs that block voltage-gated Na⁺ channels are used as 'membrane stabilisers' in the treatment of dysrhythmias and epilepsy. They may act to restrict the rapid inflow of Na⁺, slowing the maximum rate of cell depolarisation and limiting cell responsiveness to excitation. Such drugs include class I antiarrhythmic agents (Vaughan Williams classification) such as quinidine, disopyramide, lidocaine (lignocaine) and flecainide; also the antiepileptic drugs phenytoin and carbamazepine. (See *Cardiology*, Section 2.2.2.)

1.2 Ion carriers

Carriers that utilise ATP (pumps)

Many carriers use energy supplied by ATP to drive ion transport. The most important of these is the Na⁺/K⁺-ATPase, which is a target for drug action.

Na⁺/K⁺-ATPase

Na⁺/K⁺-ATPase transporters are present in the membranes of all cells in the body. They have the following properties.

- They are composed of α and β subunits, which form a complex in the cell membrane.

- The α subunit contains regions that coordinate cation transport and regions that bind and hydrolyse ATP, releasing energy to drive ion transport.

- The transporter pumps three Na⁺ ions out of the cell in exchange for two K⁺ ions pumped into the cell, thus maintaining normal concentration gradients of Na⁺ and K⁺ across the cell membrane.

- In epithelial cells these gradients drive transepithelial Na⁺ and K⁺ transport (see Figs 3 and 5) and in non-epithelial cells they determine resting membrane potential and allow depolarisation and electrical signalling.

Drugs targeting Na⁺/K⁺-ATPase

Digoxin binds to and inhibits the ATPase enzyme of Na⁺/K⁺-ATPase pumps in cardiac cell membranes, preventing the hydrolysis of ATP. This removes the energy supply for pump activity and thus inhibits pumping of Na⁺ out of the cell and K⁺ into the cell. The rise in intracellular Na⁺ causes a rise in intracellular Ca²⁺ (Fig. 12), thereby enhancing actin–myosin interaction and increasing cardiac contractility. However, it remains controversial as to whether digoxin has clinically significant inotropic activity in the treatment of heart failure. Digoxin also enhances vagal activity, slowing conduction through the atrioventricular node, which at least partly accounts for its usefulness as an agent for rate control in atrial fibrillation.

Carriers that utilise secondary active transport mechanisms

Many carriers use energy supplied by the electrochemical gradient

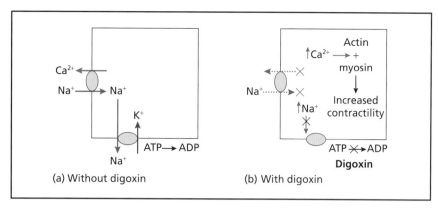

▲ **Fig. 12** Effect of digoxin on Na⁺/K⁺-ATPase and intracellular calcium.

of one ion to drive movement of another against its electrochemical gradient. Two examples are the Na⁺/K⁺/2Cl⁻ cotransporter and the Na⁺/Cl⁻ cotransporter: both are targets of drug action and mutations of both can lead to disease (see *Physiology*, Section 6.2).

Na⁺/K⁺/2Cl⁻ cotransporter

The Na⁺/K⁺/2Cl⁻ cotransporter mediates sodium transport across epithelia. In the kidney it is found in the thick ascending limb of the loop of Henle, where it contributes to reabsorption of 25% of the filtered load of sodium (Fig. 13a).

Drugs targeting Na⁺/K⁺/2Cl⁻ cotransporters The loop diuretic furosemide (frusemide) causes a natriuresis by blocking the actions of the Na⁺/K⁺/2Cl⁻ cotransporter and reducing sodium and chloride reabsorption across the thick ascending limb of the loop of Henle (Fig. 13b).

Disease caused by abnormal Na⁺/K⁺/2Cl⁻ cotransporters Mutations causing loss of function of the Na⁺/K⁺/2Cl⁻ cotransporter have been shown to cause one type of Bartter's syndrome, a rare condition presenting with profound hypokalaemia in infancy (Fig. 13b).

Na⁺/Cl⁻ cotransporter

The Na⁺/Cl⁻ cotransporter mediates sodium transport across epithelia. In the kidney this transporter is found in the distal tubule where it contributes to the reabsorption of 10% of the filtered load of sodium (Fig. 14a).

Drugs targeting Na⁺/Cl⁻ cotransporters Thiazide diuretics cause a natriuresis by blocking the actions of the Na⁺/Cl⁻ cotransporter and reducing sodium and chloride reabsorption across the distal tubule (Fig. 14b).

Disease caused by abnormal Na⁺/Cl⁻ cotransporters Mutations causing loss of function of the Na⁺/Cl⁻ cotransporter are the cause of Gitelman's syndrome, the commonest monogenic cause of hypokalaemia in adults (Fig. 14b).

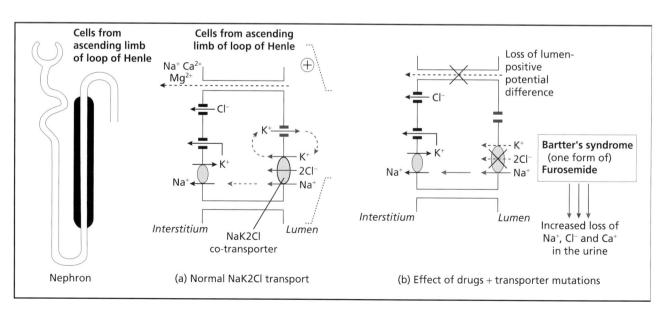

▲ **Fig. 13** Function of Na⁺/K⁺/2Cl⁻ cotransporters in the thick ascending loop of Henle (**a**) under normal conditions and (**b**) altered by drugs or transporter mutations.

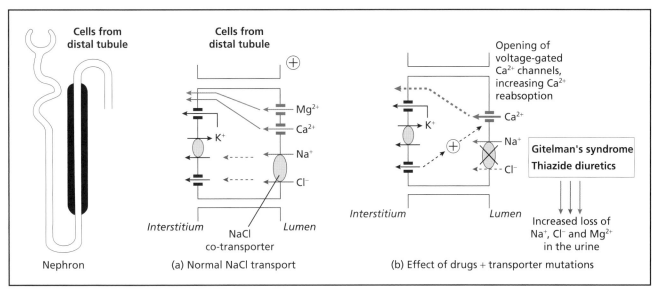

▲ **Fig. 14** Function of Na$^+$/Cl$^-$ cotransporters in the early distal renal tubule (**a**) under normal conditions and (**b**) altered by drugs or transporter mutations.

FURTHER READING

Ackerman MJ and Clapham DE. Ion channels: basic science and clinical disease. *N Engl J Med* 1997; 336: 1575–86.

Baker EH. Ion channels and the control of blood pressure. *Br J Clin Pharmacol* 2000; 49: 185–98.

Hebert SC. General principles of the structure of ion channels. *Am J Med* 1998; 104: 87–98. This article is the first in a series on ion transport disorders in *Am J Med* which cover dysrhythmias and antiarrhythmic drugs, Liddle's syndrome, cholera, malignant hyperthermia, cystic fibrosis, the periodic paralyses and Bartter's and Gitelman's syndrome.

Scheinman SJ, Guay-Woodford LM, Thakker RV and Warnock DG. Genetic disorders of renal electrolyte transport. *N Engl J Med* 1999; 340: 1177–87.

RECEPTORS AND INTRACELLULAR SIGNALLING

- Cells use chemical signals to communicate with one another and these control many biological processes.
- This communication depends on specific chemicals (ligands) binding to specific receptors, which then initiate specific intracellular events (signal transduction).
- There are three main types of chemical signalling mechanism: endocrine, paracrine and synaptic.

Basic principles of cell–cell signalling

The body relies on chemical signalling between cells to orchestrate and integrate complex biological processes as diverse as organogenesis and neuromuscular transmission. Despite this diversity, the fundamental components of intercellular communication are the same (Fig. 15).

- A generator cell produces a chemical signal (or ligand).

- This ligand binds with high affinity to a specific receptor protein, usually found in the plasma membrane of the target cell.

- The binding of ligand to its receptor initiates a series of intracellular events, commencing with the formation of an intracellular messenger and culminating in the biological response.

Since individual cells express only a limited repertoire of receptors, the response to chemical signals is highly specific.

The process by which ligand–receptor binding is converted to an intracellular response is termed signal transduction. The molecular structure of receptors reflects their dual function, with separate domains participating in ligand binding and signal transduction. Three broad patterns of intercellular communication are recognised (Fig. 16).

- Endocrine: specialised cells secrete a hormone that circulates in the bloodstream to act on distant target cells, integrating and harmonising responses in disparate cells and tissues. Endocrine signalling underlies major changes in the body such as growth, puberty and pregnancy.

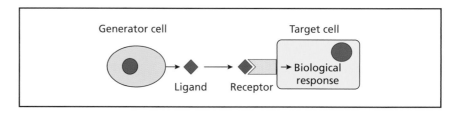

▲ **Fig. 15** Basic principle of cellular signalling.

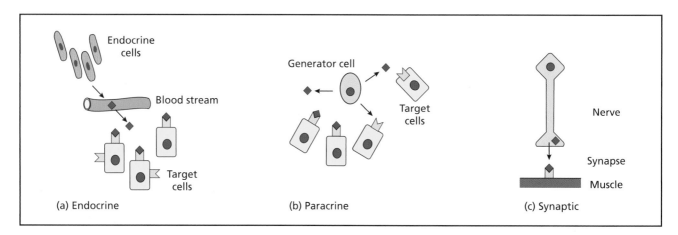

▲ **Fig. 16** Patterns of intercellular signalling.

- Paracrine: the secreted ligand diffuses locally to influence adjacent cells only. This occurs within organs and tissues, an example being tubuloglomerular feedback in the kidney.

- Synaptic: interneuronal or neuromuscular synaptic transmission is a specialised form of paracrine signalling characterised by the close physical proximity of generator and target cells at the synapse.

Membrane-bound receptors and signal transduction

- Signal transduction commonly results in the phosphorylation and activation of key intracellular proteins such as ion channels, enzymes or transporters that are the effectors of the biological response.

- Effector proteins are phosphorylated (often at serine or threonine residues) by a variety of kinase enzymes, which are themselves activated by the binding of intracellular messengers, as indicated in Table 1.

Most receptors are located on the surface of cells and are anchored in the plasma membrane. In contrast, receptors for steroid hormones and other lipophilic substances are located in the cytosol. Membrane-bound receptors can be classified into three basic types by their pattern of receptor activation and signal transduction:

- receptors with integral ion channel function (ionotropic receptors);

- G protein-coupled receptors;

- receptors with integral enzymatic function.

TABLE 1 KINASE ACTIVATORS

Kinase	Activated by
Protein kinase A	cAMP
Protein kinase G	cGMP
Protein kinase C	Diacylglycerol

Within each broad grouping there are families of receptors, each characterised by shared structural and functional features (Table 2), but with subtle variations in receptor structure that create different receptor isoforms with differing ligand-binding specificities or effector function. This receptor diversity allows a single ligand to produce different responses in different cells depending on the receptor subtype that is activated.

Ionotropic receptors

Ligand binding to ionotropic receptors (eg nicotinic acetylcholine,

TABLE 2 FEATURES OF MEMBRANE-BOUND RECEPTORS

	Ionotropic receptors	G protein-coupled receptors	Receptors with intrinsic enzymatic activity
Example	nAChR GABA$_A$ 5HT$_3$	mAChR α and β adrenoceptors Dopamine 5HT Opiate Peptides	Growth factors Insulin ANP
Basic structure	Multiple subunit with integral pore	Seven transmembrane domains Ligand- and G protein-binding domains	Extracellular (ligand binding), membrane-spanning and intracellular (enzymatic) domains
Signal transduction	Ligand gating of integral ion channel	Ligand binding induces receptor–G protein coupling and G-protein activation. G-protein activation leads in turn to activation of membrane-bound effector proteins, eg adenylate cyclase	Ligand binding to extracellular domain causes activation of cytosolic enzymatic function
Time scale of effector response	Milliseconds	Seconds to minutes	Minutes to hours
Effector molecules		cAMP IP$_3$/Ca^{2+}	GAP, PI3 kinase

nAChR, nicotinic acetylcholine receptor; mAChR, muscarinic acetylcholine receptor; cAMP, cyclic adenosine monophosphate; ANP, atrial natriuretic peptide; GABA, γ-aminobutyric acid; GAP, GTPase-activating protein; 5HT, 5-hydroxytryptamine; IP$_3$, inositol 1,4,5-trisphosphate; PI3 kinase, phosphatidylinositol 3-kinase.

GABA$_A$ and 5-HT$_3$ receptors) results in the rapid (millisecond) opening of an integral receptor ion channel (Fig. 17). The resulting changes in the membrane potential of the target cell are responsible for the ensuing biological response such as neurotransmission or muscle contraction.

G protein-coupled receptors

G protein-coupled receptors are characterised by an extracellular N-terminus, an intracellular C-terminus and seven membrane-spanning domains. The binding of ligand to a domain on the extracellular surface of the receptor leads to a conformational change that allows the binding of a guanine nucleotide-binding (G) protein to a cytoplasmic domain of the receptor and leads to signal transduction (Fig. 18).

G proteins act as relays, coupling receptors to a variety of proteins involved in the synthesis of intracellular messengers such as the following.

• cAMP: activates protein kinase A, an enzyme that activates intracellular proteins by phosphorylating them at serine or threonine residues.

• Inositol 1,4,5-trisphosphate (IP$_3$): binds to receptors on the endoplasmic reticulum and causes the release of stored

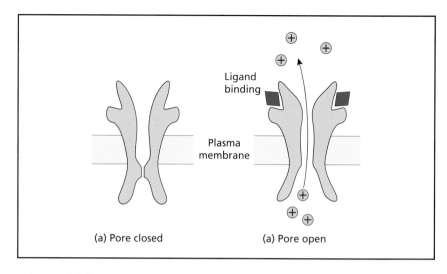

▲ **Fig. 17** Model of ionotropic receptor activation.

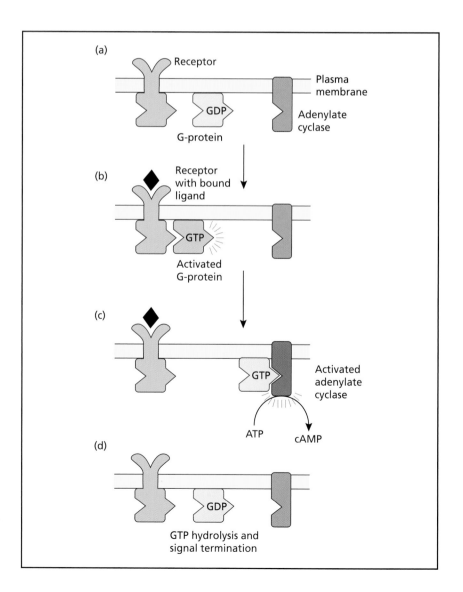

▶ **Fig. 18** Signal transduction via the stimulatory G protein (G$_s$), adenylate cyclase and cAMP. The stimulatory G protein, G$_s$, activates adenylate cyclase and leads to the synthesis of cAMP. (**a**) G$_s$ comprises three subunits α, β and γ. The α subunit retains a bound molecule of GDP. (**b**) Ligand binding to a G protein-coupled receptor induces the formation of a G protein–receptor complex. This interaction causes dissociation of GDP from the α subunit and allows the binding of GTP. (**c**) The G protein/GTP complex activates adenylate cyclase, resulting in the formation of the second messenger cAMP. cAMP activates protein kinase A, an enzyme that phosphorylates multiple intracellular proteins. (**d**) G$_s$α eventually hydrolyses GTP back to GDP, a process that terminates the activation of adenylate cyclase.

calcium ions, an important intracellular signal.

- Diacylglycerol (DAG): diffuses freely within the plane of the plasma membrane to activate protein kinase C (PKC).

Different families of G proteins are characterised by the relatedness of their α subunits, for example:

- G_i (which contains the α subunit, α_i) inhibits adenylate cyclase and activates K^+ channels;

- G_q activates phospholipase C to catalyse the formation of the intracellular messengers IP_3 and DAG.

An example of a process by which G proteins convert ligand–receptor binding into the synthesis of intracellular messengers is shown in Fig. 19. Adrenoceptors, muscarinic receptors, some 5HT receptors, receptors for opiates and receptors for many peptides are examples of G protein-coupled receptors.

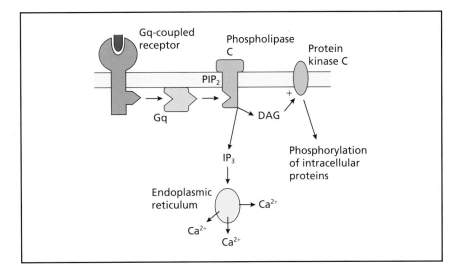

▲ Fig. 19 Signal transduction via G_q, phospholipase C, inositol trisphosphate (IP_3) and diacylglycerol (DAG). The G protein, G_q, activates phospholipase C leading to the synthesis of IP_3 and DAG. Receptors coupled to G_q initiate the synthesis of IP_3 and DAG from the membrane phospholipid phosphatidylinositol diphosphate (PIP_2). IP_3 causes Ca^{2+} release from intracellular stores and DAG activates the enzyme protein kinase C, which leads to the phosphorylation of intracellular proteins.

receptor guanylate cyclases (the receptors for natriuretic peptides) are examples in this group. These receptors (Fig. 20) all have a large extracellular N-terminal ligand-binding domain, a membrane-spanning α-helix, and an intracellular C-terminal domain with enzymatic activity.

Receptor tyrosine kinases Ligand binding to receptor tyrosine kinases results in conformational change that allows receptor dimerisation and activation of an integral tyrosine kinase activity, the primary target for tyrosine phosphorylation being the cytoplasmic domain of the receptor itself. Receptor autophosphorylation exposes binding sites for cytosolic proteins that contain a motif called an SH2 (src homology 2) domain. Examples of such proteins include phosphatidylinositol 3-kinase, GTPase-activating protein and phospholipase C-γ. These proteins couple the membrane signal to a variety of intracellular processes that include enzyme activation and alterations in gene transcription.

Receptors with integral enzymatic function

Tyrosine kinase-linked receptors for insulin, growth factors and the

---

What happens if a G-protein receptor malfunctions? An example from cholera

Cholera toxin produces its pathological effects by catalysing the ADP-ribosylation of the α_s subunit of G_s in enterocytes. This modification renders G_s incapable of hydrolysing guanosine triphosphate (GTP), which is a prerequisite for terminating G_s-mediated activation of adenylate cyclase (Fig. 18d). The massive increase in the level of intracellular cAMP then triggers a large efflux of Na^+ and water into the intestinal lumen, the result being profuse watery diarrhoea.

A clinical example of an overactive receptor tyrosine kinase

Multiple endocrine neoplasia type 2 (medullary thyroid carcinoma, phaeochromocytoma and hyperparathyroidism) is caused by mutations in the *RET* gene on chromosome 10, whose protein product is a membrane-bound tyrosine kinase. These mutations result in constitutive receptor activation and lead to an unchecked growth signal and tumour formation.

Using knowledge of receptors and signalling pathways for therapeutic benefit

Many proto-oncogenes (genes where mutations lead to the development of cancers) encode components of signal transduction pathways. Around 25% of invasive breast cancers overexpress the epidermal growth factor receptor tyrosine kinase, HER2, which is associated with an adverse prognosis. A recombinant monoclonal

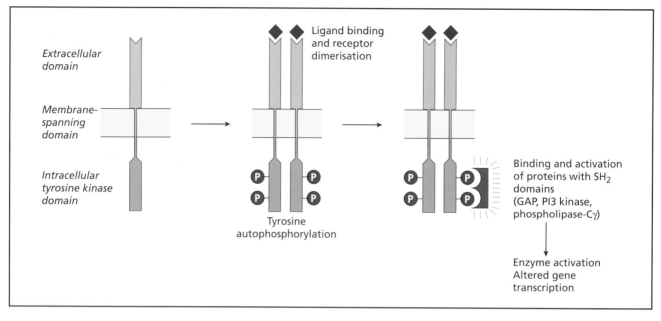

▲**Fig. 20** Model of tyrosine kinase receptor activation. GAP, GTPase-activating protein; PI3 kinase, phosphatidylinositol 3-kinase.

antibody that targets this receptor (trastuzamab) is used in the treatment of women with metastatic breast cancers that overexpress HER2. Erlotinib and gefitinib are monoclonal antibodies that target a different class of epidermal growth factor receptor and are used in the treatment of non-small-cell lung cancers.

Receptor guanylate cyclases
Receptors for atrial natriuretic peptides (ANPs) are examples of membrane-bound guanylate cyclases, which act as follows.

- Binding of ligand to the extracellular domain of the receptor activates an intracellular domain with guanylate cyclase activity.

- This catalyses the conversion of GTP to cyclic guanosine monophosphate (cGMP).

- cGMP activates protein kinase G (PKG).

- PKG in turn phosphorylates and activates the intracellular effector proteins that produce the biological response.

Nitric oxide

- Nitric oxide (NO) is a paracrine mediator produced by endothelial cells, some neurons and inflammatory cells.
- NO lacks a classical receptor and has a unique mechanism of action: it diffuses freely into cells where it activates a soluble cytosolic form of guanylate cyclase and causes an elevation in cGMP.
- Nitrovasodilator drugs in clinical use (eg glyceryl trinitrate and sodium nitroprusside) act as exogenous sources of NO, producing relaxation of blood vessels via increases in intracellular cGMP in vascular smooth muscle cells.

Cytosolic receptors

Steroids bind to cytosolic receptors that modify gene transcription.

The receptors for lipid-soluble ligands, which together form the steroid receptor superfamily, share the following common features:

- they are not membrane bound but are located in the cytosol;

- ligand binding results in receptor dimerisation and translocation of the ligand–receptor complex to the nucleus;

- the response to receptor activation is mediated by specific binding of the ligand–receptor complex to promoter or enhancer elements of genes and modulation of gene transcription.

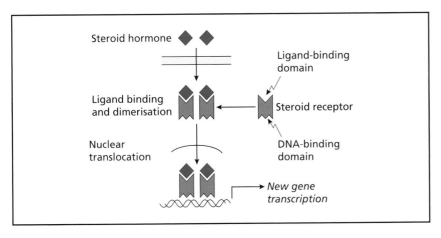

Fig. 21 Signal transduction via a steroid receptor.

Receptor monomers contain a ligand-binding domain and highly homologous domains mediating DNA binding and transcription activation.

A model for steroid receptor activation is shown in Fig. 21. Because the response to activation of receptors of this type is *de novo* gene transcription and protein synthesis, responses mediated by such receptors are slow in onset but long-lasting.

FURTHER READING

Hancock JT. *Cell Signalling*, 2nd edn. Oxford: Oxford University Press, 2005.

Basic principles of the cell cycle

The cell cycle (Fig. 22) consists of several ordered, strictly regulated phases.

Quiescent phase (G$_0$)

Normal cells grown in culture will stop proliferating once they become confluent or are deprived of serum or growth factors, and enter a quiescent state called G$_0$. Stimulation by the addition of growth factors or serum or by replating the cells as a less dense population will result in resumption of cell proliferation. The duration of individual phases may vary among cells of a particular population: most cells in normal tissue of adults are in a G$_0$ state.

First gap phase (G$_1$)

This occurs prior to the initiation of DNA synthesis and represents the period of commitment that separates M and S phases as cells prepare for DNA duplication. Cells in G$_0$ and G$_1$ are receptive to growth signals, but once they have passed a restriction point they are committed to DNA synthesis/chromosome replication (S phase).

DNA synthesis (S)

See *Genetics and Molecular Medicine*, Section 1.

Second gap phase (G$_2$)

This occurs after DNA synthesis and before mitosis (M) and completion of the cell cycle. An important function of this phase is to allow cells to repair errors that occur during DNA duplication and thus prevent the propagation of these errors to daughter cells.

Mitosis (M)

This completes the cell cycle (see *Genetics and Molecular Medicine*, Section 1).

Regulation of the cell cycle

The system is bewilderingly complex with a large number of parallel pathways, and interactions between pathways, probably because of the biological importance of controlling the cell cycle. Although it may seem complicated, the account given here is very simplified.

Checkpoints

Progress through the cell cycle is controlled by checkpoints, which prevent cells from entering the next stage until previous necessary stages have been completed.

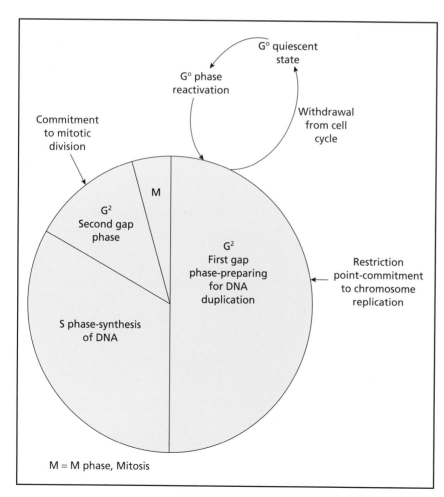

Fig. 22 The cell cycle.

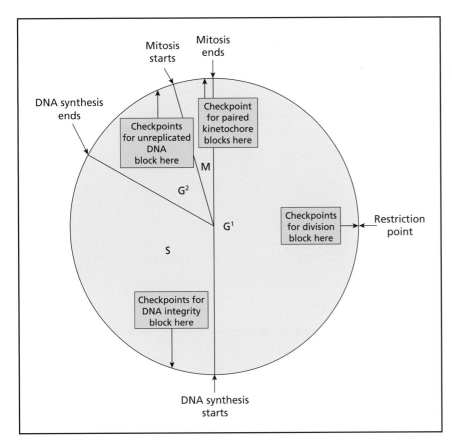

▲**Fig. 23** Checkpoints of the cell cycle.

The checkpoints of the cell cycle are shown in Fig. 23. Within G$_1$ these respond to DNA damage, within S phase to incomplete replication, within G$_2$ to DNA damage, and within mitosis to ensure that all necessary earlier events have been performed.

Before dividing a cell must replicate every DNA sequence once, and the mass of the cell must approximately double, so that there is sufficient of everything else to support two daughter cells.

Mechanisms of regulation

The critical events that regulate the cell cycle are phosphorylation and dephosphorylation of a wide variety of substrates, and these processes are also used to control the function of the regulatory molecules themselves.

M-phase kinase Mitosis is clearly one of the key steps in the cell cycle. This is regulated by M-phase kinase (of which there are at least two forms, both proteins that act by phosphorylating other proteins); hence events that activate M-phase kinase at G$_2$/M and inactivate it before the end of M phase are clearly critical (Fig. 24). M-phase kinase has two subunits.

- Catalytic: Cdc2, a kinase that phosphorylates serine and threonine residues in target proteins. Modification of Cdc2 is the critical event that triggers transition from G$_2$ to M.

- Regulatory: cyclin, which is necessary for the catalytic kinase to function on the right substrates. Destruction of cyclin by proteolysis leads to inactivation of M-phase kinase.

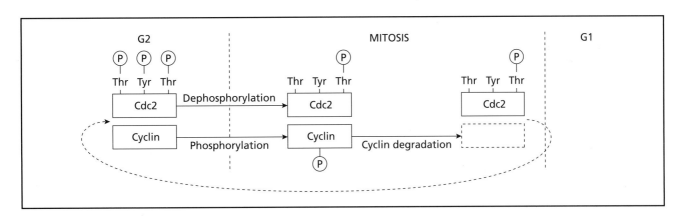

▲**Fig. 24** Regulation of activity of M-phase kinase. Thr, threonine; Tyr, tyrosine; P, phosphate.

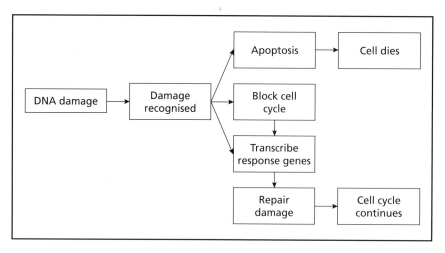

▲**Fig. 25** Consequences of DNA damage.

M-phase kinase phosphorylates a wide variety of substrates. Precisely how this triggers mitosis is not certain: it may act as a 'master regulator' of a cascade, or it may directly phosphorylate proteins that execute the necessary processes. The best-characterised substrate for M-phase kinase is H1 histone, one of the main proteins in chromatin.

Checkpoint pathways Damage to DNA triggers responses that block the cell cycle and lead to a number of outcomes (Fig. 25). There are also checkpoints to ensure that appropriate progress is made through specific stages of the cell cycle, eg replication must be completed before division can occur;

all kinetochores must be paired before metaphase can finish.

> A critical function of checkpoints in the cell cycle is to prevent progression if there is damage to DNA.

Each checkpoint pathway typically involves three groups of proteins.

• Sensor proteins: recognise an event that tiggers the checkpoint pathway.

• Transducer proteins: activated by the sensor proteins and have an amplification function.

• Effector proteins: activated by the transducer kinases to correct the event that triggered the checkpoint pathway, eg the protein kinase ATM, which has a central role in the DNA damage response, loss of whose function leads to the condition ataxia telangiectasia.

Cyclin-dependent kinases
Progression through the cell cycle is regulated by a large number of kinases (enzymes that can phosphorylate other proteins) that can each interact specifically with a large number of proteins called cyclins; hence they are known as cyclin-dependent kinases. There are inhibitors that can block the actions of these kinases, termed cyclin-dependent kinase inhibitors (CKIs) (Table 3). Mutations in cyclin-dependent kinases and other proteins involved in cell cycle regulation are found in many cancers.

Apoptosis

> During development unwanted cells are eliminated by a process called programmed cell death or apoptosis.

Regulatory mechanism	Effect	Implication for cell cycle
Retinoblastoma (RB) gene product phosphorylated by cdk–cyclin D complex	RB binding to transcription factor E2F prevents action of E2F and entry into S phase. Phosphorylation of RB leads to it being released from E2F	Release of cell cycle block in G_1
Action of CKI of INK4 family	Inhibits action of cdk4 and cdk6	Affects G_0 to G_1 transition
Action of CKI of Kip family	Inhibits action of all G_1 and S phase cdk enzymes	Affects progression through all stages of G_1 and S

TABLE 3 THREE IMPORTANT CELL CYCLE REGULATORY MECHANISMS INVOLVING CYCLIN-DEPENDENT KINASES (CDK) AND THEIR INHIBITORS

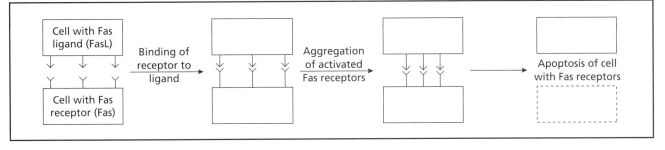

▲**Fig. 26** Interaction of Fas with FasL leads to apoptosis. Note that each Fas receptor shown in the diagram is a homomeric trimer.

TABLE 4 TRIGGERS OF APOPTOSIS	
Trigger	**Mechanism**
Ligand, eg FasL or TNF, activates receptor	Uses death domain (see below and Figs 26 and 27)
Cytotoxic lymphocyte attacks target	Involves release of granules containing serine proteases (granzymes) and other components such as perforin, which can make holes in the target cell membrane
Withdrawal of necessary growth factor	Unknown
Irradiation	Requires tumour suppressor p53, a key defence mechanism against cancer (see Cancer and the cell cycle)
Glucocorticoids	Unknown

Apoptosis is an active process that involves activation of a pathway that leads to suicide of the cell by a process whereby it becomes more compact, blebbing occurs at the membranes, chromatin becomes condensed and the DNA is fragmented into segments of about 180 bp. Apoptosis can be triggered by a variety of stimuli (Table 4).

Fas receptor
The Fas receptor (called Fas or FasR) is one of the main triggers for apoptosis. Key elements of the mechanism (Fig. 26) are as follows.

- Fas: a cell-surface receptor related to the tumour necrosis factor (TNF) receptor; normally present as a homomeric trimer (three identical molecules together); critical element responsible for

apoptosis is a region of 80 amino acids called the 'death domain'.

- Fas ligand (FasL): a transmembrane protein related to TNF.

- Fas binds to FasL: this causes Fas trimers to congregate into large aggregates, which activates apoptosis.

Interaction of TNF with its receptor (particularly TNF-R1) is also a trigger for apoptosis.

Downstream from the Fas receptor
The 'classical' pathway for apoptosis triggered by interaction of Fas with FasL or by TNF with TNF-R1 is shown in Fig. 27. Members of the caspase family (cysteine aspartate proteases) are important downstream components.

Fas and TNF-R1 can also activate apoptosis by a pathway involving the kinase JNK, whose main substrate is the protein c-Jun, activation of which leads to the activation of proteases (mechanisms uncertain). This pathway, in contrast to that shown in Fig. 27, is not blocked by Bcl2.

Cancer and the cell cycle

Cancers typically arise as a result of multistage processes that involve oncogenes or tumour-suppressor genes.

Cancer cells have escaped the usual mechanisms that control their growth. This typically occurs in stages, with several different types of event contributing at the molecular level. The two main changes include the following.

- Accumulation of somatic mutations: occurs particularly in genes responsible for proteins involved in the detection or repair of damaged DNA, which therefore increases the rate at which mutations occur (because they are not detected and repaired).

- Development of genetic instability: leads to changes in the number of genes in cancer cells through, for example, duplications or deletions of parts of chromosomes, translocations of DNA from one chromosome to another.

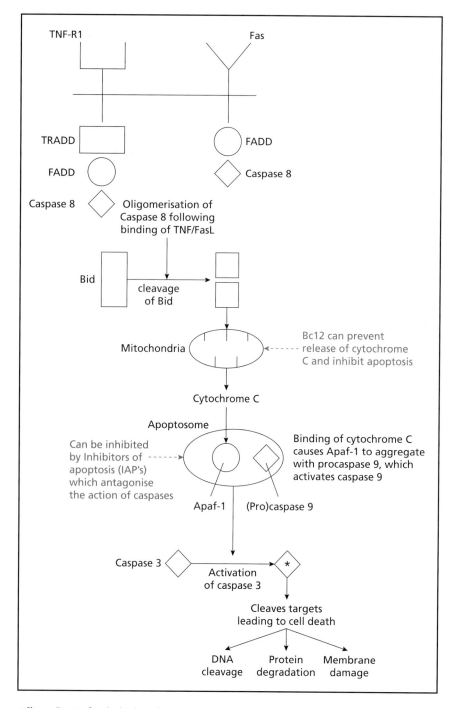

▲ **Fig. 27** Events after the binding of FasL to Fas or TNF to TNF-R1. Bcl2 was discovered as a proto-oncogene that is activated in lymphomas.

There are two types of gene where mutation causes cells to be transformed, ie released from normal growth constraints.

- Oncogenes: these were originally identified as viral genes that caused transformation of their target cell; proto-oncogenes are genes that exist within the normal DNA of every cell but which can be mutated or activated to form an oncogene that produces a product that can lead to a tumour.

- Tumour-suppressor genes: mutation leads to loss of function that normally restrains cell growth.

Oncogenes

Oncogenes can influence, directly or indirectly, any part of the signal transduction pathways involved in the cell cycle control mechanism. To give a classic example: one of the best-characterised pathways involved in control of cell growth is the mitogen-activated protein kinase (MAPK) pathway (Fig. 28); mutations occur that result in substitution of amino acids at position 12 or 61 in Ras in several different human tumours, which has the effect of activating the ERK MAPK pathway (and possibly other pathways), with downstream effects leading to tumours.

Tumour-suppressor genes

As with oncogenes, there are many possible examples. Brief details are given of two: the retinoblastoma (RB) gene and p53.

RB gene In the normal cell, non-phosphorylated RB prevents cell proliferation, and phosphorylation by cyclin-dependent kinases is necessary for the cell to proceed into S phase (see Table 3). If both copies of the *RB* gene are inactivated (in the inherited form of the disease one parental chromosome carries a mutated gene and a somatic event mutates the other copy), then retinoblastoma occurs.

p53 This is the most important tumour suppressor (named because its molecular mass is 53 kDa) and is lost or mutated in more than 50% of all human cancers. It is a nuclear phosphoprotein that is normally activated by damage to DNA, with the effect of blocking progression through the cell cycle (via p21, see Fig. 28) or causing apoptosis via several mechanisms. Its function

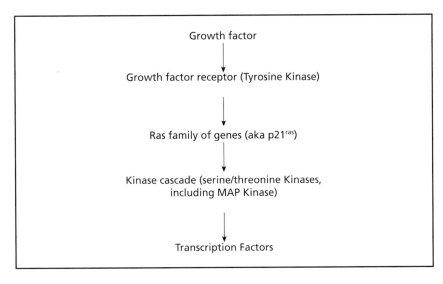

Growth factor

↓

Growth factor receptor (Tyrosine Kinase)

↓

Ras family of genes (aka p21^{ras})

↓

Kinase cascade (serine/threonine Kinases, including MAP Kinase)

↓

Transcription Factors

▲**Fig. 28** MAPK mitogenic pathway.

can be impaired by direct mutation of the p53 gene or by mutations of other genes that affect p53 expression or function.

FURTHER READING

Lewin B. *Genes VIII*. Upper Saddle River, NJ: Pearson Prentice Hall, 2004.

- - - - - - - - - - - - - - - - -

Morgan DO. *The Cell Cycle: Principles of Control*. Oxford: Oxford University Press, 2006.

- - - - - - - - - - - - - - - - -

Weinberg RA. *The Biology of Cancer*. New York: Garland Science, 2007.

Bone marrow structure

The bone marrow is the principal organ of adult haematopoiesis. Red cells, white cells and platelets, referred to as the formed elements of the blood, are produced in the bone marrow from a common pluripotent stem cell. The stem cell is capable of both self-renewal and differentiation down all cell lines (Fig. 29). A complex microenvironment of stromal cells and growth factors regulates haematopoiesis.

The bone marrow consists of:

• haematopoietic cells;

• fat cells;

• stromal cells.

Blood cells are produced in different places at different times.

• First 6 weeks of fetal life: yolk sac.

• Between 6 and 24 weeks of fetal life: liver and spleen.

• From week 24 of fetal life onwards: bone marrow.

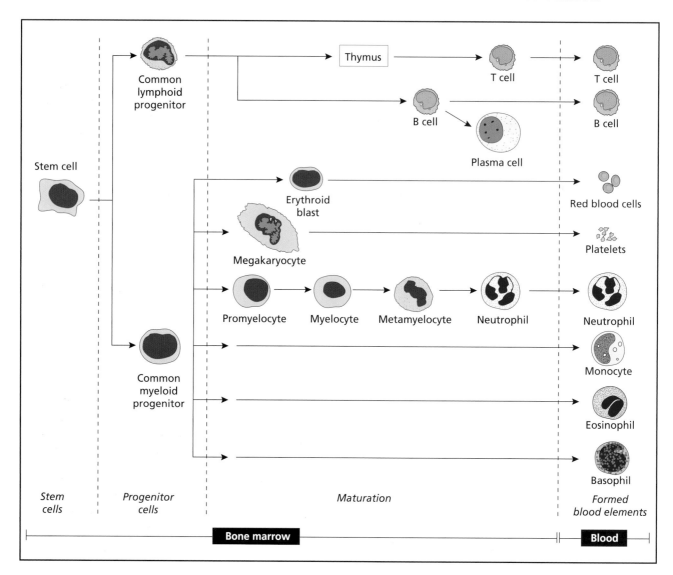

▲**Fig. 29** The process of differentiation and maturation from stem cell to formed blood elements.

In children, active haematopoiesis occurs in the axial skeleton and the long bones, with the marrow being relatively more cellular than in adults. In adults, fat replaces much of the cellular bone marrow, with haematopoiesis becoming limited to the axial skeleton, where about half the marrow space is taken up by blood cell production and half by fat. In some disease states cellularity of the marrow may increase and the long bones may once again become active in haematopoiesis. The spleen and liver may also be recruited into blood cell production as they were in fetal life, a phenomenon referred to as extramedullary haematopoiesis (and which may cause organomegaly). Examples of such conditions include the myeloproliferative disorders and the thalassaemias (intermedia and major).

The haematopoietic process

All cell lines, and subsequently all mature blood cells, are derived from a common pluripotent stem cell (Fig. 29). In the presence of growth factors, stem cells give rise to progenitor cells that are committed to a particular cell line. These progenitor cells in turn differentiate and undergo a series of further cell divisions. This process allows for amplification and maturation in haematopoiesis, with the mature cells eventually being released into the peripheral blood. The stem cell is also capable of self-renewal, ensuring lifelong haematopoiesis. Developing red cells lose their nucleus prior to release into the blood. Platelets are formed from megakaryocyte cytoplasm.

Role of growth factors

The process of differentiation and maturation is regulated by cell–cell and cell–matrix interactions, together with growth factors produced locally by:

- endothelial cells;
- fibroblasts;
- monocytes;
- lymphocytes.

There are many different growth factors that, via complex interactions with each other and the cells in the marrow, stimulate haematopoiesis at various stages of maturation and differentiation.

- Those that act on the early stages of haematopoiesis, eg stem cell factor (SCF), which promotes stem cell proliferation, will have an effect on the production of all cell lines.

- Those that act on more mature cells tend to be lineage specific, eg granulocyte colony-stimulating factor (G-CSF) specifically promotes the production of maturing granulocytes and is used in clinical practice.

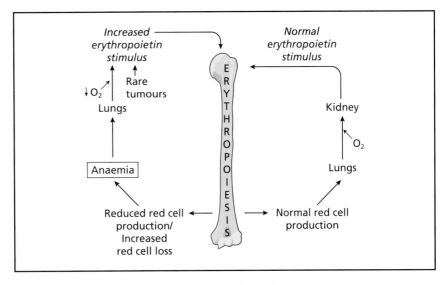

▲**Fig. 30** Control of erythropoiesis by erythropoietin. Erythropoietin production is stimulated physiologically by anaemia or hypoxia. Rare tumours can produce erythropoietin and cause polycythaemia.

Colony-stimulating factors (eg G-CSF, GM-CSF) can be used to shorten the duration of neutropenia in patients receiving chemotherapy (see *Haematology*, Sections 1.4.2 and 2.9).

Erythropoietin

Although most growth factors are produced locally in the bone marrow, erythropoietin, which controls erythropoiesis, is a hormone produced in the kidney (see *Cell Biology*, *Haematopoiesis*, and *Physiology*, Section 6.3).

Erythropoiesis is controlled by a negative feedback loop (Fig. 30). Erythropoietin is released by specialised interstitial cells in the cortex of the kidney in response to reduced oxygen delivery, which can occur as a result of the following.

- Anaemia: red cell production is increased until the haemoglobin concentration increases and oxygen delivery to the kidney is returned to normal.

- Reduced oxygen delivery to the peritubular cells: commonly the result of chronic hypoxia, when erythropoietin is released and red cell production is increased even in the absence of anaemia, leading to secondary polycythaemia.

Renal (and rarely other) tumours may secrete erythropoietin outside the control of the normal feedback loop and cause polycythaemia.

In chronic renal failure the kidney is unable to produce adequate amounts of erythropoietin to drive haemopoiesis and this is the main reason for the anaemia of chronic renal failure. Therapeutic erythropoietin is very effective treatment for the anaemia of chronic renal failure. (See *Nephrology*, Sections 2.1.2 and 2.1.3.)

FURTHER READING

Hoffbrand V, Catovsky D and Tuddenham EGD, eds. *Postgraduate Haematology*, 5th edn. Oxford: Blackwell Science, 2005.

5.1 Self-assessment questions

Question 1

After passing the restriction point in G_1 of the cell cycle, cells are/have:

Answers

A Committed to entering G_0 phase

B Committed to chromosome replication

C Replicated their DNA

D Committed to mitotic division

E No longer capable of dividing

Question 2

M-phase kinase is important in the control of mitosis, the end of which is associated with:

Answers

A Phosphorylation of Cdc2

B Proteolytic destruction of Cdc2

C Dephosphorylation of Cdc2 and cyclin

D Phosphorylation of cyclin

E Proteolytic destruction of cyclin

Question 3

One of the important triggers for apoptosis is the Fas receptor, a cell-surface receptor related to:

Answers

A T-cell receptor

B Tumour necrosis factor receptor

C Fc receptor

D IgG

E IgM

Question 4

Bcl2 can inhibit apoptosis by:

Answers

A Preventing the aggregation of Fas after binding with Fas ligand (FasL)

B Inhibiting the action of caspase 8

C Preventing caspase 8 from cleaving Bid

D Preventing the release of cytochrome c from mitochondria

E Inhibiting the action of caspases in the apoptosome

Question 5

P53 is:

Answers

A A cell-surface molecule activated by Fas ligand (FasL)

B A cell-surface molecule activated by tumour necrosis factor

C A component of the apoptosome

D An oncogene

E A tumour suppressor

Question 6

A skeletal muscle cell has a resting membrane potential of –90 mV. Which of the following transporters is most likely to have generated this potential?

Answers

A Cl^- channel

B Na^+/HCO_3^- exchanger

C Na^+/K^+-ATPase

D K^+ channel

E Voltage-gated Na^+ channel

Question 7

A 3-year-old boy presents with suspected cystic fibrosis. If the diagnosis is correct, lack of cystic fibrosis transmembrane conductance regulator (CFTR) will:

Answers

A Reduce Cl^- absorption and cause Cl^- loss in the airway

B Reduce down-regulation of epithelial sodium channels, increasing Na^+ absorption in the sweat duct

C Reduce drive for HCO_3^- secretion in the pancreatic duct

D Reduce movement of water across the airway epithelium

E Reduce potential difference across sweat duct epithelium

Question 8

Which one of the following drugs does *not* work by blocking ion channels?

Answers

A Amiloride

B Carbamazepine

C Digoxin

D Lidocaine

E Phenytoin

Question 9

Genetic mutations that impair inactivation of the voltage-gated Na^+ channel:

Answers

A Alter the threshold for channel activation

B Generate persistent outward Na^+ currents

C Hyperpolarise muscle cells

D Prolong the QT interval

E Shorten the action potential

Question 10

A 55-year-old man with heart failure requires diuretic treatment. Which of the following statements is most true?

Answers

A Amiloride is K⁺ sparing because it blocks K⁺ channels

B Excessive thiazide treatment will mimic Liddle's syndrome

C Furosemide therapy produces similar electrolyte disturbances to Gitelman's syndrome

D Mg^{2+} loss is predicted to be greater with thiazides than amiloride

E Na⁺ absorption by Na⁺/K⁺-ATPase counter-transporters is blocked by furosemide in the loop of Henle

Question 11

If a ligand exerts its action in a paracrine manner, this means that it:

Answers

A Can affect all cells

B Acts after circulating in the bloodstream to reach its target

C Acts only on the cell that has secreted it

D Can act via several cell-surface receptors

E Acts on cells adjacent to the cell that secretes it

Question 12

Protein kinase C is activated by:

Answers

A cAMP

B cGMP

C Diacylglycerol

D Acetylcholine receptor

E ATP

Question 13

Which one of the following receptors is *not* a G protein-coupled receptor?

Answers

A Muscarinic acetycholine receptor

B α-Adrenoreceptor

C β-Adrenoreceptor

D Opiate receptor

E Insulin receptor

Question 14

Steroids exert their biological effects by binding to:

Answers

A Ionotropic receptors

B G protein-coupled receptors

C Receptors with intrinsic enzymatic activity

D Cytosolic receptors

E Nuclear receptors

5.2 Self-assessment answers

Answer to Question 1

B

Replication of DNA occurs after the restriction point in G_1 and during the S phase. The commitment to mitotic division occurs towards the end of G_2.

Answer to Question 2

E

M-phase kinase is formed of Cdc2 and cyclin. Mitosis is triggered by dephosphorylation of Cdc2 and phosphorylation of cyclin. The end of mitosis is associated with cyclin degradation by proteolytic enzymes.

Answer to Question 3

B

The Fas receptor is a cell-surface receptor related to the tumour necrosis factor receptor. It is normally present as a homomeric trimer (three identical molecules together). After binding to Fas ligand (FasL), these trimers aggregate on the cell surface to trigger apoptosis, the critical element responsible for this being a region of 80 amino acids called the 'death domain'.

Answer to Question 4

D

Bcl2 was discovered as a proto-oncogene activated in some lymphomas. It is able to inhibit apoptosis by preventing release of cytochrome *c* from mitochondria, which in the apoptotic pathway triggered by interaction of Fas with FasL or tumour necrosis factor (TNF) with TNF-R1 is induced by Bid after this has been cleaved by the action of caspase 8, which is attached to the Fas and TNF-R1 complexes.

Answer to Question 5

E

P53 is the most important tumour suppressor and is lost or mutated in more than 50% of all human cancers. It is a nuclear phosphoprotein that is normally activated by damage to DNA, with the effect of blocking progression through the cell cycle (via p21) or causing apoptosis via several mechanisms.

Answer to Question 6

D

Movement of ions across the membrane is determined by the concentration gradient for each ion and the type of channels present in the cell membrane. A large concentration gradient (but not potential difference) for K⁺ is generated by the Na⁺/K⁺-ATPase (intracellular K⁺ concentration 140 mmol/L, extracellular K⁺ concentration ~4 mmol/L) and K⁺ exits the cell through K⁺ channels until the electrical potential generated is equal and opposite to the concentration gradient (the Nernst potential). Figure 8 illustrates the membrane potentials that are generated if only

Na$^+$ or Cl$^-$ channels are open in the cell membrane. Na$^+$/HCO$_3^-$ exchangers involve balanced exchange of ions and would not generate a membrane potential.

Answer to Question 7

C

Lack of Cl$^-$ secretion by CFTR across the apical membrane of pancreatic duct epithelial cells into the lumen increases intracellular Cl$^-$ and removes the drive for Cl$^-$/HCO$_3^-$ exchange (Fig. 6). In the airway, lack of CFTR decreases Cl$^-$ secretion and removes down-regulation of epithelial sodium channels. The resulting increase in Na$^+$ absorption drives increased water absorption, thickening respiratory secretions. In the sweat duct, channels are lined up the opposite way round and lack of CFTR causes reduction in Cl$^-$ and Na$^+$ absorption with loss of these ions and water in the sweat.

Answer to Question 8

C

Digoxin inhibits the Na$^+$/K$^+$-ATPase counter-transporter, which is an ion carrier. All the others block voltage-gated Na$^+$ channels except amiloride which blocks epithelial Na$^+$ channels.

Answer to Question 9

D

Genetic mutations of voltage-gated Na$^+$ channels have been identified in patients with long QT syndrome and cardiac arrhythmias as well as in patients with muscle disorders and familial epilepsy. Impaired activation of these channels generates a persistent inward Na$^+$ current that depolarises cells so that the resting membrane potential is closer to the threshold for channel activation and cells become hyperexcitable. Additionally, failure of these channels to inactivate prolongs the action potential.

Answer to Question 10

D

Thiazides act in the early distal tubule where Mg^{2+} absorption is affected, although the mechanisms underlying this remain unclear. Excessive thiazide treatment mimics Gitelman's syndrome, which has been attributed to genetic mutations of the Na$^+$/Cl$^-$ cotransporter. Amiloride acts in the late distal tubule where it blocks epithelial sodium channels (ENaC), causing a secondary reduction in K$^+$ loss. Amiloride can be used to treat Liddle's syndrome, a genetic disease caused by activating ENaC mutations. Furosemide blocks Na$^+$/K$^+$/2Cl$^-$ cotransport and

excessive use may mimic a form of Bartter's syndrome that has been attributed to genetic mutations of the same transporter.

Answer to Question 11

E

A ligand that acts after circulating in the bloodstream to reach its target is working in an endocrine manner.

Answer to Question 12

C

G proteins act as relays coupling receptors to proteins involved in the synthesis of intracellular messengers. One such messenger is diacylglycerol, which diffuses within the plasma membrane to activate protein kinase C.

Answer to Question 13

E

The insulin receptor is a receptor with intrinsic enzymatic activity.

Answer to Question 14

D

Steroids bind to monomeric cytosolic receptors, which then dimerise and move to the nucleus where they bind the promoter or enhancer elements of genes to activate their transcription.

IMMUNOLOGY AND IMMUNOSUPPRESSION

Author:

MG Robson

Editor:

JD Firth

Editor-in-Chief:

JD Firth

Immune system components

> Organisms have physical barriers and mechanical mechanisms to protect against external injury, but even primitive organisms have developed 'immune systems' to defend against pathogens. The immune system in humans has two main components.
>
> - Innate: available on first exposure to stimulus.
> - Adaptive: modified and more active on subsequent exposure to stimulus.

There are many different mechanisms that protect the human body against external injury. These include simple mechanical mechanisms and highly developed physical barriers such as the skin, which prevent pathogens and other potentially harmful agents from damaging the underlying tissue. These barriers often have specialised adaptations that facilitate their capacity to resist foreign invasion, eg sweat is rendered acidic by the presence of lactic acid, and the relatively low pH of the epidermis helps resist colonisation by potentially harmful bacteria. The epithelial linings of the gut and respiratory tract have a very effective local protective mechanism in the form of mucus, which serves to trap, solubilise and help in the disposal of unwanted foreign materials.

Species throughout the evolutionary spectrum have developed physical barriers of varying levels of sophistication that are adapted to their lifestyles. However, even relatively primitive organisms have developed complex systems of proteins and other molecules to defend themselves against any pathogen that succeeds in breaching the external surface barriers.

This 'immune system' comprises:

- macromolecules (most of which are proteins) that are found in the extracellular fluid compartment and in blood, and which serve to make these environments inhospitable to pathogens;

- highly specialised cells that can recognise and eliminate various types of pathogen or other harmful substances.

The immune system has both innate and adaptive components. Innate (sometimes referred to as 'natural') immunity describes defence mechanisms that:

- are available the first time a pathogen is encountered;

- do not necessitate previous exposure to that pathogen;

- are not modified by repeated exposure to the pathogen over time.

In contrast, adaptive (sometimes referred to as 'acquired') immune mechanisms are:

- modified after exposure to a pathogen;

- become more active when repeatedly exposed to the same pathogen.

Innate immunity

> In the acute-phase response, the liver responds to particular cytokines by producing proteins that are important in innate immunity.

In response to an insult of any kind, there are a number of processes that facilitate removal of a potential pathogen, the activation of the immune system and the subsequent repair of any injury. The most important of these is the acute-phase response.

Acute-phase response When an acute-phase response occurs, there is an increase in the production of key proteins involved in the innate immune system (Table 1). Many of these are synthesised in the liver, where increased production is driven by exposure of hepatocytes to key cytokines, namely interleukin (IL)-1, tumour necrosis factor (TNF) and IL-6.

Although the acute-phase response is primarily designed to facilitate defence and repair, the activation of this immune response, which occurs in many autoimmune diseases, can be harmful; this usually occurs when production of these key cytokines becomes chronic.

Toll-like receptors A family of more than 10 receptors has been described that is crucial for the cellular recognition of microbial products. Toll-like receptor (TLR)-4 was the first of these to be described as the

TABLE 1 SOME PROTEINS WITH IMPORTANT FUNCTIONS IN THE INNATE IMMUNE SYSTEM

Protein	Target pathogen	Effector mechanism
Complement protein C3	Binding of carbohydrates and other molecules on the bacterial surface	Opsonisation, complement activation and cell lysis (MAC)
Serum amyloid P component	Cell wall carbohydrates	Opsonisation
C-reactive protein	Microbial surface polysaccharides and other molecules	Complement activation and opsonisation
Mannose-binding lectin	Glycoproteins with a high mannose content	Complement activation via MASP and C3
Lysozyme	Cell wall peptidoglycans	Cell wall digestion
Soluble CD14	Lipopolysaccharide	Inhibits lipopolysaccharide

CD, cluster of differentiation; MAC, membrane attack complex; MASP, mannose-binding protein-associated serine protease.

receptor for endotoxin. Since then, ligands for the other receptors have been determined, including bacterial (various lipopeptides, flagellin, hypomethylated DNA), fungal (zymozan) and viral (single-stranded or double-stranded viral RNA) products. TLRs are widely expressed on leucocytes, but also on parenchymal cells. Their ligation has immediate effects, with release of pro-inflammatory cytokines. They also have effects on the adaptive immune response through the activation of antigen-presenting cells such as dendritic cells, and also through direct effects on B and T cells.

Local inflammatory response
The key components of the local inflammatory response that occurs following tissue injury are:

- dilatation and increased permeability of microscopic vessels;

- endothelial activation, which facilitates the adhesion of white blood cells;

- attraction and activation of phagocytic cells such as neutrophils and mononuclear cells.

Adaptive immunity

> The two parts of the adaptive immune system are humoral and cellular immunity.

There are two main components to the adaptive immune system, humoral immunity and cellular immunity, and these are inextricably interlinked.

- Humoral immunity: the most important factors are the complement system and antibody, produced by B cells.

- Cellular immunity: T lymphocytes are the most important factors.

Anatomy of the adaptive immune system Stem cells in the bone marrow are the origin of all red cells and leucocytes. The bone marrow is also the site at which B cells develop; T cells develop in the thymus. The thymus, situated in the anterior mediastinum, grows in childhood and then undergoes a process of gradual involution after puberty, but it continues to function during adult life. Immature T cells are found in the cortex, and mature

T cells in the medulla before passing into the blood.

The cells of the immune system are organised into lymph nodes, spleen and mucosal-associated lymphoid tissue (MALT). Most lymphocytes enter the spleen and lymph nodes through high endothelial venules. There is continual recirculation of B and T cells through the lymph nodes such that they are exposed to any foreign antigen.

Lymph nodes comprise a cellular cortex, where B cells are organised into follicles. During an active immune response, these follicles acquire pale germinal centres. As B cells mature they pass to the medulla and become antibody-secreting plasma cells. T cells are found in the deep cortex. Antigen-presenting cells such as dendritic cells and macrophages are found in both T and B cell areas of the lymph node. The white pulp of the spleen has a smilar organisation, with B-cell follicles and T-cell areas. The red pulp is a network of blood vessels responsible for removing old red blood cells. MALT is found in the gastrointestinal tract (eg Peyer's patches in the small intestine), respiratory tract (eg tonsils and adenoids) and urogenital tract.

B cells Bone marrow-derived (B) cells are primarily responsible for the development of the humoral antibody immune response. Sophisticated mechanisms have been developed that control the way in which B lymphocytes develop from precursors and acquire the capacity to make unique antibody molecules, including the following.

- Antigens induce an immune response from the appropriate B cells (in most cases T lymphocytes help in this process).

- B-cell responses are diversified to result in the production of different classes of immunoglobulin, eg IgM and IgG; these have different roles to play in the immune system.

- There are ways of maximising the affinity of antibodies produced in response to unwanted exogenous pathogens.

Impaired regulation of these mechanisms can result in the development of autoimmunity, with the production of self-reactive antibodies, ie antibodies that react with self.

T cells Thymus-derived (T) lymphocytes:

- have the ability to recognise and discriminate among a huge range of different foreign antigens;

- use receptors on their surface (T-cell receptors) to recognise antigen in the form of peptide fragments bound to HLA (human leucocyte antigen) molecules (classes I and II);

- have a diverse repertoire that is generated in a similar way to that for B cells.

The ways in which T cells, B cells and other antigen-presenting cells interact to facilitate the development of an effective immune response are considered in detail below.

Impaired regulation of the immune response: clinical examples

Disease can result from impaired regulation of immune responses in a variety of ways.

Clonal disorder

In multiple myeloma, there is overproduction of a specific monoclonal antibody, with impaired function of the rest of the humoral immune system.

Clonal disorders can result in a much more specific functional impairment of specific cells, eg in paroxysmal nocturnal haemoglobinuria there is impaired production of key molecules (eg decay-accelerating factor, or DAF, and CD59) that are involved in the control of complement activation. This increases the susceptibility of affected red blood cells to lysis mediated by complement, which results in the development of haemolytic anaemia.

Autoimmunity

Impaired regulation of humoral immune responses can result in autoimmunity, with the production of autoreactive antibodies ('autoantibodies'). These may be directed against:

- specific receptors;

- DNA or other intranuclear antigens;

- other plasma proteins and macromolecules.

In most autoimmune diseases, autoreactive T lymphocytes are also produced.

THE MAJOR HISTOCOMPATIBILITY COMPLEX, ANTIGEN PRESENTATION AND TRANSPLANTATION

Major histocompatibility complex

Class I and II molecules encoded in the HLA region present antigen to T cells.

The chromosomal region that was originally shown to encode molecules responsible for foreign tissue rejection in mice is known as the major histocompatability complex (MHC). In humans, this region is found on chromosome 6 and is also known as the human leucocyte antigen (HLA) region (Fig. 1).

The highly polymorphic class I and II molecules found within the HLA region have important functions in antigen presentation to T cells and the determination of the compatibility of certain tissues for transplantation (Table 2). Class III molecules are not structurally or functionally related to class I and II molecules and include complement proteins and genes for tumour necrosis factor.

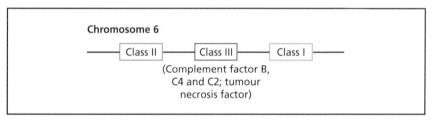

▲ **Fig. 1** Chromosomal HLA region.

	Class II	**Class I**
	TABLE 2 STRUCTURE AND FUNCTION OF MOLECULES OF THE HLA REGION	
Structure	Heterodimers consisting of α and β chains. There are three class II antigens (DP, DQ and DR)	Single chain found in close association with β_2-microglobulin. There are three class I antigens (A, B and C)
Expression	Professional antigen-presenting cells (monocytes/macrophages, dendritic cells, Langerhans' cells, B cells). Other cells may express class II when activated (eg T cells, epithelial cells)	All cell types except red blood cells
Function	Present exogenous foreign antigens to CD4 helper T cells, promoting antibody production and delayed-type hypersensitivity responses	Identify infected cells to CD8 T cells to promote cytotoxic killing
Processing pathway	*Exogenous* Exogenous protein is endocytosed and degraded. Late endosomes fuse with vesicles from the Golgi apparatus containing newly synthesised class II. At this stage, before class II contains peptide, it is associated with a non-polymorphic molecule known as the invariant chain. This stabilises it in the absence of peptide. Cleavage and degradation of the invariant chain allows peptide loading to occur. This process involves a molecule called DM. This has class II-like structure, but is not polymorphic. The vesicle containing peptide-loaded class II is then transported to the surface of the cell	*Endogenous* Newly synthesised proteins degraded in the cytosol are transported across the membrane into the endoplasmic reticulum. Protein degradation is carried out by particles known as proteasomes. These are complex dimers made up of 14 subunits. In response to interferon, two of these subunits may be replaced by two products of the class II region (LMP2 and LMP7) in order to tailor the function of these proteasomes for antigen processing. Peptides produced by these proteasomes are transported into the endoplasmic reticulum by TAP proteins, in a process dependent on ATP. Peptides are then loaded onto class I molecules which become non-covalently bound to β_2-microglobulin and the complex is transported to the cell surface

MHC and associated diseases

🔑 Susceptibility to certain diseases is associated with different HLA types, which is evidence that these diseases have an immune aetiology. Common disease associations with HLA are given in Table 3.

Antigen presentation

🔑 • B cells can recognise soluble antigens.
• T cells need antigen to be presented to them as small peptides by class I and II molecules on the surface of antigen-presenting cells (APCs).

B cells can recognise soluble antigens, but T cells require peptides to be presented on the surface of APCs that are bound to an MHC molecule.

- Both class I and II MHC molecules have a groove that binds peptides for antigen presentation.

- Class I molecules present peptides derived from endogenously synthesised proteins to CD8-positive cytotoxic T cells.

- Class II molecules present peptides derived from proteins taken up exogenously to CD4-positive T-helper cells (see Section 3).

See Table 2 and Fig. 2 for further details.

Transplantation

🔑 Transplants, unless from an identical twin, are recognised as foreign by direct and indirect pathways of immune recognition. Suppression of these pathways is necessary to prevent transplant rejection.

TABLE 3 HLA TYPES ASSOCIATED WITH DISEASE

Class	Type	Disease
Class I	HLA-B27	Ankylosing spondylitis Reactive arthritis Psoriatic arthropathy Reiter's syndrome
	HLA-CW6	Psoriasis
Class II	HLA-B8-DR3	Systemic lupus erythematosus Addison's disease Graves' disease Coeliac disease Type 1 diabetes
	HLA-DR4	Rheumatoid arthritis
	HLA-DR2	Multiple sclerosis

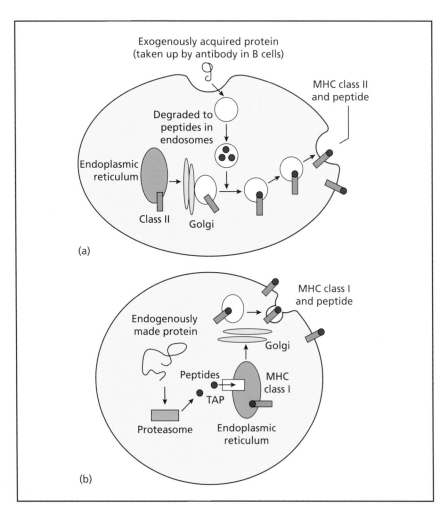

▲ **Fig. 2** Routes of antigen processing and presentation on MHC class II (**a**) and class I (**b**).

107

Two pathways of immune recognition are thought to occur after transplantation.

- Direct pathway: recognition of donor MHC molecules and peptides.

- Indirect recognition: recognition of MHC molecules on host APCs that have acquired exogenous foreign antigen from the transplant.

Effector mechanisms of rejection

Humoral mechanisms Antibody is thought to be most important in mediating the immediate rejection that occurs when preformed antibody to donor MHC antigens is present. This is characterised by complement activation (see Section 6), thrombosis and ischaemia of the organ. In clinical practice this is avoided by performing an in vitro cross-match between recipient serum and donor cells before proceeding to transplantation: if the cross-match is positive, then transplantation is precluded (except in special circumstances).

Cell-mediated mechanisms

Delayed-type hypersensitivity mechanisms involving CD4 cells and macrophages, and cytotoxic effects caused by CD8 T cells and natural killer (NK) cells, are both thought to play a role in mediating acute rejection episodes. Commonly used anti-rejection drugs, eg ciclosporin and tacrolimus, are designed to inhibit T-cell-mediated rejection mechanisms (see Section 8).

Chronic rejection Obliterative

vascular changes occur in the long term in most if not all transplants. The role of the immune system in this process still needs to be clarified.

Immunosuppression

Suppression of rejection is necessary for transplantation to be effective (see Section 8).

Xenotransplantation

A great deal of effort has been invested in developing the possibility of using pig kidneys for human recipients. Studies in non-human primates have shown that the first major barrier is hyperacute rejection as a result of complement-dependent damage to the kidney by preformed natural antibodies to the carbohydrate epitope galactose-[1,3]-galactose. This happens because porcine membrane-bound complement inhibitors are ineffective against human complement, a problem that can be circumvented by making a pig transgenic for the human complement inhibitors CD59 and decay-accelerating factor. However, there are substantial concerns, including transmission to humans of porcine infectious agents and to what extent the viability of porcine organs in humans will be limited by other rejection processes.

T-cell receptors

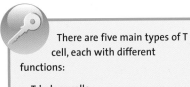

Each clone of T cells has a unique antigen-specific receptor.

T cells have antigen-specific receptors on their surface known as T-cell receptors. These have similarities to and differences from antibody, which acts as the B-cell antigen receptor (see below). Diversity results from rearrangement of germline genes, with each T cell producing only one specificity of T-cell receptor (a process known as allelic exclusion).

The structure of the T-cell receptor is shown in Fig. 3. Unlike antibody,

there is no secreted form. The two chains (α and β) comprising the molecule have one variable (V) and one constant (C) region each. The α and β chains do not have a cytoplasmic domain, and an associated complex with a cytoplasmic tail, CD3, is important in signalling.

T-cell functions

There are five main types of T cell, each with different functions:

- T-helper cells;
- cytotoxic T cells;
- natural killer T cells;
- regulatory T cells;
- $\gamma\delta$ T cells.

T-helper cells

T-helper cells are distinguished by the presence of CD4 on their surface and their ability to recognise peptides presented on MHC class II molecules. Their functions include:

- promoting delayed-type hypersensitivity reactions, characterised by monocyte recruitment;

- providing help for B-cell antibody production (described below).

Cytotoxic T cells

Cytotoxic T cells have CD8 on their surface and recognise peptide presented on MHC class I molecules. Cytotoxic T cell-mediated cell killing occurs by the release of granule products after binding of the T cell to its target. Products released include perforin, which forms pores, and proteases such as granzymes.

Natural killer T cells

Natural killer T cells are a subset of T cells that express the T-cell receptor and develop in the thymus. They are not to be confused with natural killer (NK) cells (described in the next paragraph), although they share the NK cell marker NKR-P1. They produce high levels of interleukin (IL)-4, have a limited T-cell repertoire and recognise antigen presented by an atypical MHC class I. They may be negative for both CD4 and CD8, or express intermediate levels of CD4. Both immunosuppressive and protective antimicrobial roles have been attributed to these natural killer T cells.

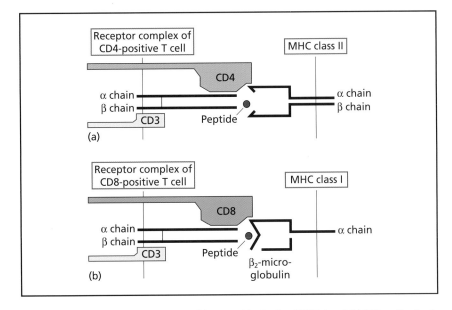

▲**Fig. 3** T-cell receptor and MHC interaction: (**a**) CD4-positive T cell and MHC class II; (**b**) CD8-positive T cell and MHC class I.

NK cells are not T cells but are described here to avoid confusion with natural killer T cells. NK cells kill target cells in a non-MHC-restricted manner. They do not develop in the thymus and do not use T-cell receptor genes (the nature of their receptors is poorly understood). They are inhibited by the recognition of self class I molecules, and play a role in recognising and killing tumour cells.

Regulatory T cells

There are several types of regulatory T cell that are CD4 positive. These have suppressive actions on the immune system and may play a role in the prevention of autoimmunity or the induction of tolerance. Two of the best described are naturally occurring T regulatory cells characterised by their high expression of CD25 and the transcription factor foxP3. Another type is known as Tr1 cell, which does not express CD25, is induced by IL-10, and then produces high levels of IL-10 itself.

γδ T cells

γδ T cells express a receptor comprising γ and δ chains rather than conventional α and β chains. The genes for these chains are somatically rearranged like the conventional T-cell receptor genes, but the receptor has more limited diversity. The ligands for the receptor are not yet known.

These cells are found at epithelial barriers such as the skin and the gastrointestinal tract.

Helper cell differentiation

After their development in the thymus, CD4-positive T cells undergo further differentiation into two types of cell with different but complementary functions, called Th1 and Th2 cells. Th1 and Th2 groups of T-helper cells were originally described in mice, but there appear to be analogous populations in humans.

Many of the effector functions of T cells are mediated by cytokines: Th1 and Th2 cells produce different cytokine profiles. Table 4 shows the main cytokines produced by different T cells.

T-cell development

> T cells undergo complex development in the thymus, where gene rearrangement allows each T cell to develop a unique T-cell receptor. T cells that are likely to be ineffective or dangerous are removed.

T cells develop in the thymus and when mature can be divided into two groups, helper cells and cytotoxic cells, based on the expression of CD4 and CD8, respectively. These mature cells develop from progenitor cells that go through three stages:

- negative for both CD4 and CD8 ('double negative');

- positive for both ('double positive');

- positive for one antigen only.

During this process of development, gene rearrangement to form the T-cell receptor occurs, together with two other important processes.

- Positive selection: probably occurs on thymic epithelial cells and produces 'MHC-restricted' T cells that have receptors capable of binding self-MHC.

- Negative selection: probably occurs on bone marrow-derived cells and eliminates strongly self-reactive T cells.

Activation of T cells

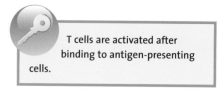

> T cells are activated after binding to antigen-presenting cells.

Two types of signals are delivered to T cells after binding to the antigen-presenting cell (APC).

- Signal 1 is delivered to the cell by the T-cell receptor complex (CD3 delivers the signal) and by CD4 or CD8 interacting with MHC class I or II, respectively.

- Signal 2 is delivered by other 'co-stimulatory' interactions, the best characterised of which is the signal mediated by CD28 (on T cells) interacting with B7-1 or B7-2 on APCs (B cells, dendritic cells, monocytes). CTLA4 is another ligand for B7 molecules that is found on activated T cells, delivering an inhibitory signal. In the absence of this second signal, anergy or cell death may occur.

T cell	CD4 (helper) Th1	CD4 (helper) Th2	CD8 (cytotoxic)
Function	Delayed-type hypersensitivity	Allergy, atopy, antibody production	Cytotoxic killing
Cytokines	IFN, TGF-β, IL-2	IL-4, IL-5, IL-6, IL-10	IFN, GM-CSF

TABLE 4 CYTOKINES PRODUCED BY DIFFERENT KINDS OF T CELLS

GM-CSF, granulocyte–macrophage colony-stimulating factor; IFN, interferon; TGF, transforming growth factor.

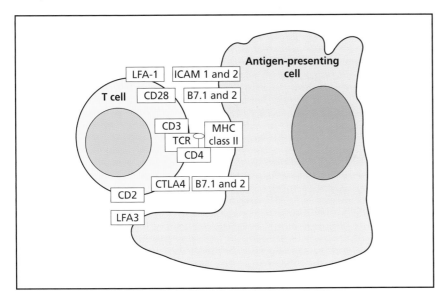

▲ **Fig. 4** Molecules involved in interactions of T cells and APCs. B, HLA class B; CD, cluster of differentiation; CTLA, cytotoxic T-lymphocyte antigen; ICAM, intercellular adhesion molecule; LFA, lymphocyte function-associated antigen; MHC, major histocompatibility complex; TCR, T-cell receptor.

Other interactions (Fig. 4) aid adhesion of the T cell to the APC and delivery of signals to the T cell. These include lymphocyte function-associated antigen (LFA)-1 on T cells binding to ICAMs (intercellular adhesion molecules) on APCs, and CD2 binding to LFA-3.

Memory cells

T cells are part of the adaptive immune system. Memory cells persist after initial (primary) exposure to an antigen, allowing an accelerated response if there is further (secondary) exposure.

During primary immune responses, naive T cells proliferate, acquire effector functions and die. However, some persist and form memory cells. These allow an accelerated response if the same antigenic stimulus is encountered. Naive, activated and memory T cells display characteristic surface markers that can be used to distinguish between them.

- Naive T cells have a high-molecular-weight form of CD45 (CD45RA).

- Memory T cells have a low-molecular-weight form of CD45 (CD45RO).

- Activated T cells also display CD45RO but have other markers in addition, including MHC class II.

T-cell immunodeficiencies: clinical example

There are many clinical T-cell immunodeficiency disorders, the most important being congenital thymic aplasia, of which the major immunological features are:

- congenital hypoplasia of the thymus and parathyroid glands;

- absent T-cell function in the peripheral blood;

- lymphopenia.

Levels of antibodies in these patients are variable, but there are characteristic facial abnormalities and congenital heart disease may also occur. Chronic candidal infection of the skin, nails and mucous membranes can occur, with and without an associated endocrinopathy. The patients characteristically have negative delayed hypersensitivity skin tests to *Candida* antigen, despite chronic infection, but T-cell immunity to most other antigens is intact.

Antibody structure and function

> - Each antibody is made of two light and two heavy chains.
> - The type of heavy chain determines the class of antibody (IgM, IgG, etc.).
> - The variable regions of one light and one heavy chain make one antigen-binding site.

Immunoglobulins are the B-cell antigen receptor. Unlike T-cell receptors, these may be secreted or bound to the membrane. As for the T-cell receptor, the membrane-bound form does not have a cytoplasmic tail. Signalling is mediated by Ig-α and Ig-β (CD79a and CD79b), which are associated with the ligand-binding immunoglobulin (Fig. 5). These activate signalling pathways such as those mediated by phospholipase.

The basic structure of antibody is two light chains (with two domains each) and two heavy chains (with four or five domains each), as shown in Fig. 5. The two antigen-binding sites are made from the variable (V) domains of one light chain and one heavy chain, with other domains being less variable (constant or C domains). The heavy chain C domains define the class or subclass of antibody (IgM, IgG1, IgG2, IgG3, IgG4, IgA, IgD or IgE) and this part of the molecule influences interactions with important antibody receptors (Fc receptors). There are only two kinds of light chain, kappa (κ) and lambda (λ).

Table 5 shows the functions of different classes of antibody. As with T cells, B cells show allelic exclusion, and each B cell only produces one antibody specificity (although the class may 'switch').

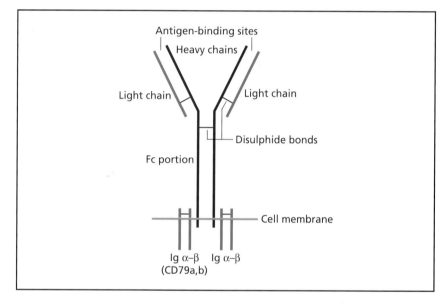

▲ **Fig. 5** Antibody structure.

TABLE 5 ANTIBODY CLASSES AND THEIR FUNCTIONS

Class	Affinity	Function	Complement fixation
IgM	Low	Main class in serum of primary response	Fixes complement well
IgG (four subclasses: IgG1–IgG4)	High	Main class in serum of secondary response. Interactions with Fc receptors on phagocytes important in antibody-mediated inflammation	Fixes complement (varies with subclass)
IgA	High	Secreted across mucosal surfaces	Activates alternative complement pathway
IgE	High	Activates mast cells and basophils via Fc receptors for IgE. Important in allergy and reactions to parasites	Does not fix complement
IgD	Low	Surface marker expressed during development	Does not fix complement

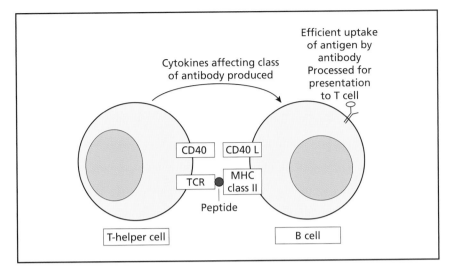

▲ **Fig. 6** T- and B-cell interaction. CD40, cluster of differentiation 40; CD40L, cluster of differentiation 40 ligand; TCR, T-cell receptor.

Early development

- B cells develop in the bone marrow.
- Self-reactive B cells are eliminated.

Development of B cells occurs in the bone marrow. During this process, B cells rearrange their immunoglobulin genes to generate antigen receptors with a large number of different specificities. Just as T cells that react with self-antigens are eliminated in the thymus, there are also mechanisms to exclude self-reactive B cells by inducing deletion or anergy. Mature B cells leave the bone marrow and circulate around the body, expressing surface IgM and IgD.

T-cell-dependent and T-cell-independent responses

The activation of B cells by most antigens requires signals that are delivered by T cells. However, some repeating protein or sugar structures can stimulate B cells without the help of T cells by cross-linking surface IgM. These are known as T-cell-independent responses and do not show any of the features of affinity maturation, class switching

or memory cell generation (see below), all of which depend on T cells.

Figure 6 shows the interactions that occur between B and T cells in a simplified diagrammatic way.

Primary response

In a primary response the B cell produces IgM. It then undergoes the following processes.

- Class switching: changing from IgM to IgG.
- Affinity maturation: antibody is developed that binds more tightly to antigen.
- Memory cell formation: enables high-affinity antibody to be produced immediately upon subsequent contact with an antigen.

When a naive B cell is stimulated by antigen binding, IgM is the main class of antibody produced. The processes that follow this are class switching, affinity maturation and memory cell formation.

Antibody production and class switching

While retaining the same antigen-binding portion of the

immunoglobulin molecule, gene rearrangement of the heavy chain locus changes the class of antibody. The interaction with T cells through the binding of CD40 (B cell) and CD40L (T cell) promotes class switching. This is shown by the fact that patients with X-linked deficiency of CD40L develop the hyper-IgM syndrome and fail to switch class.

T-helper (CD4) cells produce different types of cytokines, as discussed above, which:

- determine whether the effector response will be primarily antibody or cell mediated;
- influence the class of antibody and the IgG subclasses that will be produced, eg IL-4 promotes IgE production.

Affinity maturation

Naive B cells have low-affinity antigen receptors. This changes during the primary response, when a reaction takes place in the germinal centres of lymphoid tissue. Mutations occur in the variable region of the immunoglobulin gene and generate binding sites with different affinities for antigen. The high-affinity variants are selected and the low-affinity ones deleted.

T-cell help is required for affinity maturation, providing a safeguard against mutations that produce autoreactive B cells.

Generation of memory cells

Some of the B cells that are selected on the basis of high affinity become long-lived memory cells rather than antibody-secreting plasma cells. The interaction of CD40L with CD40 on T cells is necessary for memory cell formation.

Regulation of B-cell activation

A number of other signals also regulate B-cell activation.

Examples of inhibitory signals include CD22 (which binds sialic acids on glycoproteins) and FcγRIIb receptors (which bind IgG). An important interaction that lowers the activation threshold is that between the complement receptor CR2 (CD21) and fragments of complement protein, C3, bound to immune complexes.

B-cell immunodeficiency disorders: clinical examples

These disorders result in relative or absolute antibody deficiency. There is a broad spectrum of disease, ranging from complete absence of all classes of immunoglobulin to selective deficiency of a single class or subclass. The extent to which these deficiency states constitute a clinical problem reflects the degree of antibody deficiency. The main clinically important subgroups are:

- X-linked agammaglobulinaemia;

- transient hypogammaglobulinaemia of infancy;

- common variable immunodeficiency;

- immunodeficiency with hyper-IgM;

- selective IgA deficiency;

- selective IgM deficiency;

- deficiency states resulting in selected deficiency of specific immunoglobulin subclasses.

The two most clinically important B-cell immunodeficiency disorders are X-linked agammaglobulinaemia and selective IgA deficiency.

X-linked agammaglobulinaemia

Symptoms of recurrent pyogenic infections usually begin by about 6 months of age. The most common organisms responsible for infection are *Streptococcus pneumoniae* and other Gram-positive pathogens, but patients are susceptible to a wide range of different infections. Malabsorption can occur, but normally does not become symptomatic until early childhood; it may be associated with *Giardia* infection. An arthropathy resembling rheumatoid arthritis has been reported.

IgG levels are characteristically less than 200 mg/dL, with absent IgM, IgD, IgE and IgA. B cells are not detected in peripheral blood.

The mainstay of treatment is replacement therapy with intravenous immunoglobulin: serum levels of IgG approaching normal can usually be achieved within 2–4 days of intravenous administration, but repeated treatment is needed because the half-life of intravenous immunoglobulin is only 2–4 weeks.

Selective IgA deficiency

Selective IgA deficiency occurs in 1 in 600 to 1 in 800 people, and there is debate about whether they should be regarded as 'normal' or as having a true 'disease'. The IgA level is usually below 5 mg/dL, whereas other immunoglobulin levels are either normal or, in some cases, increased. Cell immunity is usually normal and the most common clinical associations are recurrent sinus infection and autoimmune diseases such as lupus, rheumatoid arthritis, autoimmune haemolytic anaemia and Sjögren's syndrome.

Patients with selective IgA deficiency should not be treated with intravenous gamma-globulin as this has only a small quantity of IgA.

- The immune system has evolved to protect the host against a wide range of antigens, whilst simultaneously avoiding harmful reactivity with self-antigens. Sometimes things go wrong and self-reactivity manifests itself as autoimmune disease.
- Tolerance is the term used to describe a specific lack of reactivity with a particular antigen.

Mechanisms that maintain tolerance

For B and T cells, both 'central' and 'peripheral' tolerance mechanisms are described.

- Central tolerance refers to the elimination of autoreactive clones during lymphocyte development in the bone marrow for B cells and the thymus for T cells. There are low-affinity self-reactive T and B cells in the periphery.

- Peripheral mechanisms provide the next level of defence for eliminating self-reactive cells that escape into the periphery. As B-cell and cytotoxic T-cell (CD8) responses generally require help from CD4 T cells, mechanisms that make CD4 cells unreactive also limit self-reactivity for these types of responses. Naive T cells that are stimulated through their T-cell receptor in the absence of a second co-stimulatory signal may become anergic or die.

Mechanisms of loss of tolerance

Polyclonal B-cell activation

Non-specific B-cell activation may contribute to the pathogenesis of systemic lupus erythematosus.

Cross-reactivity

Exposure to foreign antigens that are similar to self-antigens may stimulate a response that is harmful. This has been postulated as a possible mechanism for the development of autoimmune sequelae such as reactive arthritis following bacterial or viral infections.

Exposure to previously sequestered antigens

Although the host has not strictly been made tolerant to a sequestered antigen that has not been seen before, exposure to this antigen may generate autoimmunity.

Modification of self-antigen

New epitopes may be generated on self-antigens by a variety of mechanisms, eg in lupus antibodies arise that react to a neoepitope (previously unseen epitope) on activated complement C1q.

Autoimmune diseases: clinical examples

Autoimmunity can affect every organ in the body, but autoimmune diseases can be broadly divided into systemic diseases and organ-specific conditions.

Systemic diseases

Systemic lupus erythematosus is the classic systemic autoimmune disease and is characterised by:

- antinuclear antibodies and antibodies to a range of intracellular components;

- immune complex-mediated damage and low levels of serum complement;

- glomerulonephritis, associated with intrarenal immune complex and complement deposition (Fig. 7).

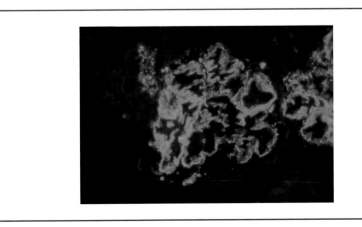

▲ **Fig. 7** Immunofluorescent staining with an anti-IgG antibody of a biopsy from the kidney of a patient with systemic lupus erythematosus, readily demonstrating deposition of immunoglobulin within the glomerulus.

Other systemic autoimmune diseases include rheumatoid arthritis, Sjögren's syndrome, progressive systemic sclerosis (associated with anticentromere antibodies or antibodies against topoisomerase 1, ie Scl-70), polymyositis/dermatomyositis (characterised by lymphocytic and plasma cell infiltration of affected muscle and antibodies to the nuclear antigens Jo-1, PMScl, MI2 or RNP) and seronegative arthritides (associated with HLA-B27).

Organ-specific diseases

A very wide range of organ-specific diseases have an autoimmune basis, for details of which see the relevent sections of the speciality modules of *Medical Masterclass*.

The proteins of the complement system:

- are involved in inflammatory and immune responses;
- can be activated by three pathways (classical, alternative and lectin).

Complement system

The complement system is a group of plasma proteins with a range of biological functions, including:

- recruitment of inflammatory cells;

- cellular activation;

- cell lysis;

- antimicrobial defence;

- clearance of immune complexes;

- amplification of the immune response.

Activation of the complement system

There are three ways in which the complement system may be activated.

- The classical pathway is activated by immune complexes, initiated by the binding of C1q to the Fc portion of immunoglobulin.

- The alternative pathway occurs either spontaneously in the fluid phase or on foreign 'activator' surfaces lacking control mechanisms. It is initiated by C3 activation.

- The lectin pathway is initiated by mannose-binding lectin (MBL)

and its associated serine protease (MASP). These have homology with C1q and C1r/s, respectively. MBL binds to carbohydrate residues on bacteria, and can activate C4 and the classical pathway.

The activation of C3 is the central event in activation of both the classical and the alternative pathways. This allows formation of C3b and C3a, as well as formation of the C5 convertases; this in turn allows terminal pathway formation. A simplified diagram of the complement system is shown in Fig. 8.

Functions and regulation of the complement system

The functions of the products of complement activation are shown in Table 6. The complement system

is tightly regulated by a number of membrane-bound and fluid phase inhibitors (Table 7).

Complement deficiencies: clinical examples

Serum complement levels are often measured in clinical practice and a number of conditions are associated with hypocomplementaemia. These may be divided into those that usually result in a low C3 only and those that result in both a low C3 and a low C4, as shown in Table 8.

Inherited deficiencies of complement proteins are associated with particular clinical features. Autoantibodies to complement proteins may arise and can be associated with disease, although their role in pathogenesis is not clear. Examples are given in Table 9.

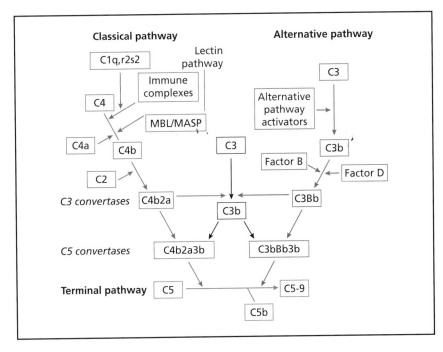

▲ **Fig. 8** The complement pathway. MBL, mannose-binding lectin; MASP, MBL-associated serine protease.

TABLE 6 COMPLEMENT PROTEINS AND THEIR FUNCTIONS*

Complement proteins	Function
C3a, C5a	Chemotaxis (C5a) Neutrophil and macrophage activation. Mast cell degranulation causing vasodilatation (C3a and C5a)
C3b, C3Bb, iC3b	Adhesion of macrophages and neutrophils (via complement receptors CR1, CR3 and CR4)
Terminal pathway	Lysis of cells. Sublytic amounts may cause activation of inflammatory cells (C5–9)
iC3b, C3dg, C3d	Amplification of the B-cell response to antigen via binding to complement receptor CR2
C3b, C4b	Clearing immune complexes (C3b and C4b bound covalently to immune complexes are ligands for complement receptor CR1 on erythrocytes)

* C3b is metabolised to iC3b and C3dg and C3d by factor I-mediated cleavage.

TABLE 7 COMPLEMENT INHIBITORS

Inhibitor	Location	Target
CR1	Red blood cells, B cells, FDCs, PMNs, macrophages	Inhibits both AP and CP convertases. Also a cofactor for factor I-mediated cleavage of C3b and C4b
MCP	B and T cells, neutrophils, macrophages	Cofactor for factor I-mediated cleavage of C3b and C4b
DAF	Cell surface: widespread	Dissociation of C3 and C5 convertases
CD59	Cell surface: widespread	Inhibits insertion of MAC into cell membrane
Factor H and C4-binding protein	Plasma	Inhibit AP and CP convertases respectively. Also cofactors for factor I-mediated cleavage of C3b and C4b, respectively
Factor I	Plasma	Cleavage of C3b and C4b
C1 inhibitor	Plasma	Causes release of C1r and C1s from C1 complex

AP, alternative pathway; CP, classical pathway; CR1, complement receptor 1; DAF, decay accelerating factor; FDC, follicular dendritic cell; MAC, membrane attack complex; MCP, membrane cofactor protein; PMN, polymorphonuclear cells.

TABLE 8 CAUSES OF HYPOCOMPLEMENTAEMIA

Abnormality	Disease
Low C3 and C4	Systemic lupus erythematosus, bacterial endocarditis and other chronic infections (osteomyelitis, arteriovenous shunt infections) Cryoglobulinaemia types I, II and III Mesangiocapillary glomerulonephritis (low C3 more common than low C4)
Low C3 only (low C4 occasionally seen but low C3 dominates in these conditions)	Poststreptococcal nephritis Cholesterol emboli Haemolytic–uraemic syndrome

TABLE 9 CLINICAL CONSEQUENCES OF COMPLEMENT PROTEIN DEFICIENCIES

	Abnormality	Clinical consequence
Inherited	C1q, C2 and C4	Leads to a disease with features of systemic lupus erythematosus. May be caused by abnormal clearance of immune complexes
	C3	Deficiency leads to pyogenic infections
	Terminal pathway	Deficiencies predispose to neisserial infections
	Hereditary C1 inhibitor	Uncontrolled C1 activation and formation of vasoactive kinins leads to angioneurotic oedema
	Factor H	Low C3 as a result of alternative pathway activation and mesangiocapillary glomerulonephritis
Acquired	C3 nephritic factor	This is an autoantibody to the alternative pathway C3 convertase C3bBbC3b, which stabilises it and causes uncontrolled alternative pathway activation and a low C3. Like factor H deficiency, the presence of this antibody is associated with mesangiocapillary glomerulonephritis
	Antibodies to C1q	Associated with lupus nephritis
	Clonal deficiency of DAF	Associated with paroxysmal nocturnal haemoglobinuria

Inflammation

- A non-specific response to tissue damage.
- Mediated by a variety of systems: kinin, complement, eicosanoid.
- Involves controlled migration of neutrophils and monocytes from the circulation into tissues.
- Uses neutrophils and macrophages (derived from monocytes) to remove microorganisms, damaged cells and debris.

Inflammation is a non-specific response to tissue damage that does not involve the immune system and which includes:

- increased vascular permeability;
- enhanced blood flow;
- migration of leucocytes into the tissues.

A range of soluble mediators and cellular mechanisms, classified by function in Table 10, is important in the inflammatory response, including the following.

- Kinin system: bradykinin is the most important product, causing an increase in vascular permeability and vasodilatation.

- Complement system: C3a and C5a increase vascular permeability and cause vasodilatation. C5a is a powerful chemoattractant.

- Eicosanoids: arachidonic acid is released from cell membranes by phospholipases and is metabolised to leukotrienes and prostaglandins by cyclooxygenase and lipoxygenase. These have vasoactive effects, and leukotriene (LT)B_4 is a potent chemoattractant.

Mast cells

These cells are found in the tissues and can be stimulated by complement C3a and C5a as well as by IgE (in immune reactions). Mast cells produce products of arachidonic acid metabolism (see below) and the powerful vasoactive mediators histamine and serotonin (5-hydroxytryptamine or 5HT).

Cell migration

Leucocytes enter a site of inflammation by:

- loose adhesion, mediated by selectins;
- firm adhesion, mediated by integrins;
- migration, mediated by chemotactic factors.

Three well-defined steps allow leucocytes to enter a site of inflammation, as shown in Fig. 9.

1. Loose adhesion to the vascular endothelium, mediated by molecules of the selectin family.

2. Firm adhesion, mediated by the binding of integrin family molecules on leucocytes to endothelial adhesion molecules (inflammatory stimuli such as IL-1 and TNF up-regulate endothelial selectin expression and integrin adhesiveness).

3. Migration to sites of inflammation, directed by chemotactic factors that include complement components

TABLE 10	**SOME KEY MEDIATORS OF INFLAMMATION**

Function	Mediator
Vasodilatation/increased vascular permeability	Bradykinin Histamine Complement C3a and C5a Prostaglandins, thromboxanes and leukotrienes
Chemotaxis of leucocytes	Complement C5a Chemokines C-X-C chemokines, mainly acting on neutrophils, eg IL-8, CINC, ENA 78 C-C chemokines, mainly acting on macrophages, eg MCP-1, MIP-1α, MIP-1β Leukotrienes, eg LTB$_4$
Macrophage activation	Interferon-γ, endotoxin
Increased endothelial adhesion	TNF-α, IL-1

CINC, cytokine-induced neutrophil chemoattractant; ENA 78, epithelial cell-derived neutrophil-activating protein 78; IL, interleukin; MCP, monocyte chemoattractant protein; MIP, macrophage inflammatory protein; TNF, tumour necrosis factor.

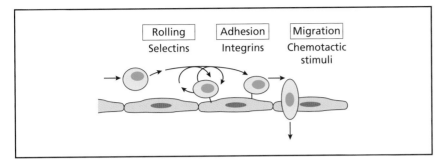

▲ **Fig. 9** Mechanisms of adhesion and migration.

(C5a) and leukotrienes (LTB$_4$), as well as a large family of small molecules known as chemokines.

Adhesion molecules

Figure 9 and Table 11 show the adhesion molecules involved in leucocyte–endothelial interactions. There are three main groups:

- selectins, which contain a lectin-like domain that recognises carbohydrates;

- integrins;

- members of a superfamily that have homology with immunoglobulin molecules.

Chemokines

These small molecules are important in chemotaxis and are produced by endothelium, leucocytes and other cell types. They are divided into two groups.

- The α-chemokines or C-X-C chemokines have two cysteine residues separated by another amino acid and are mainly

chemoattractants for neutrophils.

- The β-chemokines or C-C chemokines do not have an intervening residue and are mainly chemoattractive for monocytes and lymphocytes.

Examples of these groups of chemokines are given in Table 10. Chemokines bind to a series of receptors with overlapping specificities. Recently, there has been a great deal of interest in the association of a polymorphism of these receptors (CCR5) with HIV infection.

Phagocyte effector functions

Neutrophils and macrophages are the main effector cells of inflammation, with circulating neutrophils and monocytes leaving the blood to enter tissues. Neutrophils are short-lived mediators of acute inflammation; monocytes differentiate into

TABLE 11 ADHESION MOLECULES

Adhesion molecule	Expression	Ligand
Selectins		
L-selectin	Lymphocytes, monocytes, neutrophils	MadCAM, GlyCAM
E-selectin	Endothelium	Sialyl Lewis X
P-selectin	Endothelium and platelets	Sialyl Lewis X
Integrins		
β1		
VLA-1–4	Leucocytes	VCAM-1, MadCAM
β2		
LFA-1	Leucocytes	ICAM-1, ICAM-2
CR3, CR4	Phagocytes	ICAM-1, iC3b, iC4b
β3		
GPIIb/IIIa	Platelets	Fibrinogen, collagen, vWF
Vitronectin receptor	Leucocytes	Vitronectin
Immunoglobulin superfamily		
ICAM-1	Lymphocytes, endothelium	CR3, LFA-1
ICAM-2	Endothelium	LFA-1
VCAM-1	Endothelium	VLA-4
PECAM	Platelets and lymphocytes	PECAM (homotypic)
MadCAM	Endothelium	L-selectin, VLA-4

CR, complement receptor; GlyCAM, glycosylation-dependent cell adhesion molecule; GP, glycoprotein; ICAM, intercellular adhesion molecule; LFA, lymphocyte function-associated antigen; PECAM, platelet endothelial cell adhesion molecule; MadCAM, mucosal addressin cell adhesion molecule; VCAM, vascular cell adhesion molecule; VLA, very late antigen; vWF, von Willebrand factor.

macrophages, which are more complex cells that develop through a series of activation steps leading to enhanced functional abilities.

> **Phagocytes clear pathogens and immune complexes by the following mechanisms.**
>
> - Opsonisation: the target is coated with specific IgG or complement fragments.
> - Internalisation of target: cell-surface receptors for Fc fragment of IgG.
> - Killing/degradation by proteases and reactive oxygen species.

Opsonisation The internalisation of pathogens and immune complexes by neutrophils and macrophages is greatly increased by opsonisation, when a target is coated with the following.

- Specific IgG, which enables binding to the Fc receptors for IgG on neutrophils and macrophages.

- Complement fragments, which enable binding to complement receptors CR1 (binds C3b, iC3b and C4b) and CR3 (binds iC3b) on neutrophils and macrophages.

Intracellular killing Neutrophils and macrophages kill and degrade ingested microbes by a combination of reactive oxygen intermediates and proteases. The respiratory burst occurs during the formation of the phagosome, generating toxic reactive oxygen intermediates. Other toxic oxidant products are also generated.

Neutrophils

Neutrophils possess specialised membrane proteins that facilitate the binding of opsonised organisms. Examples of these membrane receptors are those for complement receptor 3 (CR3) and the immunoglobulin Fc.

Neutrophils contain a range of soluble proteins, mainly in three different types of granule.

- Azurophilic granules: contain myeloperoxidase, lysozyme and a group of proteins called defensins, as well as lysosomal acid hydrolases, proteinase 3, cathepsin G and elastase.

- Specific granules: contain lysozyme, gelatinase and collagenase, as well as lactoferrin, β_2-microglobulin and vitamin B_{12}-binding protein.

- Gelatinase granules: contain the enzyme gelatinase.

Macrophages

Mononuclear phagocytic cells in the blood are called monocytes; they comprise 2–5% of all nucleated blood cells and contain cytoplasmic lysosomes that have the same enzymatic constituents as neutrophils.

Within some organs, monocytes develop into macrophages, which do not circulate but are fixed within the tissues and have a lifespan of 2–4 months. They facilitate:

- phagocytosis of microorganisms;

- breakdown of unwanted tissue components and damaged cells;

- processing of immune complexes.

These functions are closely regulated; in some situations impaired control of tissue macrophages can cause the aggregation of large numbers around cellular or other targets, resulting in the formation of granulomas. This process is important in a number of diseases, eg tuberculosis and sarcoidosis.

Macrophages produce a range of secretory products, including:

- enzymes;

- mediators, such as interferon-α and -β;

- colony-stimulating factors;

- interleukins (IL-1, IL-6, IL-8, IL-10 and IL-12);

- chemokines;

- TNF-α;

- platelet-derived growth factor;

- platelet-activating factor;

- transforming growth factor (TGF)-β;

- nitric oxide;

- arachidonic acid derivatives;

- factors involved in angiogenesis.

Inflammation: clinical examples

Increased inflammation
The following are two examples of conditions in which increased inflammation leads to disease.

Familial Mediterranean fever This is an autosomal recessive condition affecting Mediterranean populations. Some patients have a mutation in a gene whose protein product has two names, pyrin and marenostrin. Its function is unclear, but it may normally suppress inflammation because it is expressed exclusively in neutrophils. Clinical features include recurrent fever, peritonitis, pleuritis, pericarditis, arthralgia, rashes and secondary amyloid. The clinical response to colchicine is usually dramatic.

Secondary amyloid Any chronic inflammatory condition (eg rheumatoid arthritis, bronchiectasis, osteomyelitis) may cause the formation of amyloid as a result of excess serum amyloid A (SAA, an acute-phase reactant). The liver, kidney, adrenals and spleen are particularly affected. Amyloid may be detected by the injection of radioactive serum amyloid P component (a constituent of AL and AA amyloid) and gamma scintigraphy.

Defective inflammation

Neutrophil disorders can result from either neutropenia or a defect in cell function. Neutropenia is most frequently the result of myelosuppressive drugs, although it can be autoimmune in origin or caused by hypersplenism. Defects of neutrophil function are rare, the following being two examples.

Leucocyte adhesion deficiency

Defective function of β_2-integrin results from a defect in the chain CD18, which combines with CD11a, -b and -c to form LFA-1, CR3 and CR4, respectively. There is failure in the migration of neutrophils from the intravascular compartment in response to infection or an inflammatory stimulus. Patients have recurrent infections and severe skin ulceration, which is slow to heal (Fig. 10). Bone marrow transplantation has been used successfully to treat severe cases.

Chronic granulomatous disease

Phagocyte function is impaired as a result of a defective respiratory burst. Inheritance is X-linked or autosomal. Chronic granulomas or abscesses occur in the skin, lung, liver and bone. There is increased risk of mycobacterial and *Salmonella* infections.

Anti-inflammatory therapy

> 🔑 Anti-inflammatory drugs are commonly used in clinical practice. These include NSAIDs and corticosteroids, and also recently developed novel agents.

Non-steroidal anti-inflammatory drugs

These drugs work by inhibiting cyclooxygenase (COX) activity and prostaglandin and thromboxane synthesis (Fig. 11). There are two forms:

- COX-1 (widely expressed, including in the gastrointestinal tract);
- COX-2 (induced at sites of inflammation).

This is the basis for the selectivity of the new COX-2-specific NSAID agents, which are said to spare the gastrointestinal tract. COX-2-specific agents include meloxicam, celecoxib and rofecoxib. Unfortunately, some these drugs have been found to have serious adverse cardiac effects.

Corticosteroids

Steroids act on the leucocyte cell nucleus, affecting the transcription of cytokines involved in both inflammation and the immune response.

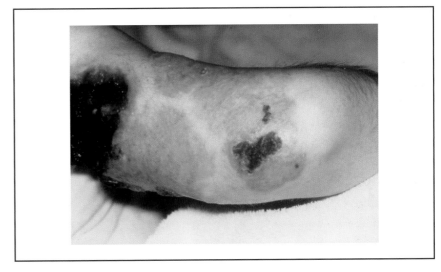

▲ **Fig. 10** Necrotic skin ulceration on the arm of a man with leucocyte adhesion deficiency disease.

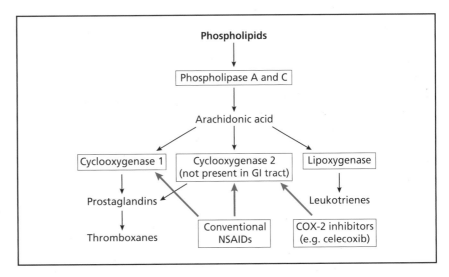

▲ **Fig. 11** Eicosanoid production and sites of action of NSAIDs. COX, cyclooxygenase; GI, gastrointestinal.

Novel agents

- The leukotriene LTB_4 is a potent chemoattractant; an inhibitor of LTB_4 has been used in asthma.

- Monoclonal antibodies and soluble receptors to TNF have been used to good effect in Crohn's disease and rheumatoid arthritis.

- Anticytokine therapy and antibodies to endotoxin have proved disappointing in the treatment of septic shock in humans.

> 🔑 Most immunosuppressive agents available are non-specific inhibitors of the immune response and/or inflammation.
>
> - Corticosteroids have complex effects, including reducing the activity of nuclear factor (NF)-κB and thereby stopping the production of many cytokines and cellular adhesion molecules.
> - Cytotoxic drugs kill cells that are capable of self-replication; lymphocytes are particularly susceptible.
> - Ciclosporin and similar agents selectively inhibit the activation and proliferation of T cells.

- antibodies or soluble ligands /receptors acting on lymphocytes or cytokines.

The ways in which various immunosuppressants affect lymphocytes are shown in Fig. 12.

Corticosteroids

> 🔑 Corticosteroids are amongst the most widely used drugs in medicine. They have many actions, including:
>
> - transiently altering the numbers of circulating leucocytes;

> - inhibiting T-cell responses, in part by reducing synthesis/secretion of interleukin (IL)-2;
> - impairing function of transcription factor NF-κB, which prevents synthesis of a variety of cytokines.

These drugs are widely used to suppress the inflammation of an autoimmune disease. One of their most important effects is to alter transiently the numbers of circulating leucocytes.

Effect on neutrophils
After injection of an intravenous steroid there is a prompt fall in

Most autoimmune diseases result from impaired regulation of the immune response, with the production of harmful autoantibodies or autoreactive cells that cause tissue damage and perpetuate the production of harmful antibodies. Impaired regulation of inflammatory mechanisms is also a key component of autoimmune disease. Most of the therapies currently available to clinicians for treating the panoply of 'autoimmune' diseases are non-specific inhibitors of the immune response and/or inflammation. The same agents are employed to prevent rejection of organ transplants. The agents most commonly used include:

- corticosteroids;

- cytotoxic drugs;

- ciclosporin and related drugs;

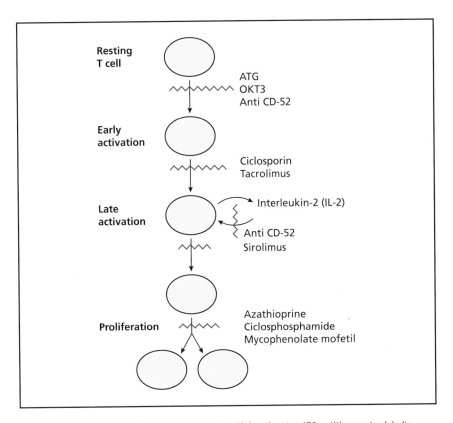

▲ **Fig. 12** Sites of interaction of immunosuppressants with lymphocytes. ATG, antithymocyte globulin; OKT3, monoclonal anti-CD3 antibody.

the numbers of neutrophils and a subsequent decrease in the total number of lymphocytes, monocytes and eosinophils. Maximum changes occur at around 4 hours after injection. More chronically, steroid administration provokes a neutrophilia as a result of the release of mature neutrophils from marrow reserves. The half-life of circulating neutrophils is increased from the normal of around 6 hours.

Effect on lymphocytes and monocytes

Corticosteroids have important effects on the function of both lymphocytes and monocytes. Functions such as chemotaxis and the action of lysosomal enzymes are not significantly impaired, but:

- there is a reduction in the capacity of these cells to release non-lysosomal proteolytic enzymes;

- lymphoproliferative responses of T cells are inhibited, partly by a reduction in synthesis and secretion of IL-2 (this cytokine is required for the clonal expansion of activated lymphocytes);

- the effects of corticosteroids on B lymphocytes are less marked; on modest doses of prednisolone, immune responses to most test antigens are not usually impaired, but with high-dose corticosteroids there are modest reductions in circulating immunoglobulin (IgG and IgA) levels.

Effects on NF-κB

One of the major activities of steroids is impairment of the functions of the transcription factor NF-κB, which regulates the genes for many cytokines and cellular adhesion molecules. In the cytoplasm of unstimulated cells,

NF-κB is bound to a second protein, IκBα. Cell signalling results in phosphorylation of IκB and the release of NF-κB, which is then translocated to the nucleus where it activates the genes, producing a range of cytokines. Glucocorticoids may increase transcription of the gene controlling IκB, with the result that its cytoplasmic concentration increases, promoting the binding of NF-κB. Less NF-κB is then available to enter the nucleus and initiate cytokine gene transcription.

Corticosteroid use

Corticosteroids are mainly active in suppressing acute inflammatory reactions and inhibiting the short-term consequences of dysregulated immune responses. They are used in a very wide variety of conditions, but in most cases they do not alter the underlying course of the disease or reduce concentrations of potentially harmful autoantibodies. Their side effects are well known, such that there is increasing interest in the use of steroid-sparing cytotoxic agents and other immunotherapeutic modalities to reduce the necessity for chronic steroid administration whenever possible.

Cytotoxic drugs

> **Cytotoxic drugs can be:**
>
> - phase specific (toxic for cells entering a particular phase of the cell cycle);
> - cycle specific (toxic for cells at all stages of the cell cycle).

Cytotoxic drugs all kill cells that are capable of self-replication. Lymphocytes are very susceptible to them, and the most commonly used cytotoxic drugs (cyclophosphamide, azathioprine, methotrexate and chlorambucil) are toxic to these

cells. However, these agents are not selective for lymphoid-proliferating cells, and they are certainly not selective for the lymphocyte subsets that might be responsible for producing harmful autoantibodies or other effects.

Cytotoxic drugs can be classified as phase specific or cycle specific.

- Phase specific: toxic for cells entering a particular phase of the mitotic cycle, eg azathioprine and methotrexate are cytotoxic for cells specifically when they are in the S (DNA synthesis) phase.

- Cycle specific: toxic for cells at all stages of the mitotic cycle, including the intermitotic G_0 phase, eg cyclophosphamide and chlorambucil. These drugs are more toxic for cells that are actively cycling than they are for resting cells.

A newer cytotoxic immunosuppressant that is more specific for lymphocytes is mycophenolate mofetil, whose active metabolite is mycophenolic acid, which inhibits the enzyme inosine monophosphate (IMP) dehydrogenase. By blocking *de novo* synthesis of guanosine and adenosine mycophenolate mofetil impairs DNA synthesis in lymphocytes, these lymphocytes (unlike other cells) being unable to use an alternative (salvage) pathway to generate the nucleotides.

Cytotoxic drug use

Detailed discussion of the use of particular cytotoxic drugs in different conditions is beyond the scope of this section, but there are a number of important underlying principles.

Inhibition of primary response

Primary immune responses are generally inhibited more easily than secondary ones, eg the primary immune response elicited by renal transplantation may be readily impaired by the use of azathioprine and corticosteroids. If a recipient has been presensitised, however, this type of immunosuppressive regimen is relatively ineffective.

Differential effect on lymphocytes

Immunosuppressive drugs can exert differential effects on T and B lymphocytes, as in the following examples.

- Cyclophosphamide particularly affects B cells rather than T cells and is most effective in diseases where antibody responses are thought to be critical. The drug is commonly used in conditions such as acute nephritis in patients with systemic lupus erythematosus.

- Azathioprine is regarded primarily as an inhibitor of T-cell responses.

Non-specificity

The non-specificity of all cytotoxic drugs results in their being potentially myelotoxic, so that close monitoring of peripheral blood leucocyte and platelet counts is imperative.

Ciclosporin and related compounds (Fig. 13)

In the normal state, activation of a T-cell receptor usually initiates an increase in intracellular calcium within the T cell. This activates calcineurin, which in turn dephosphorylates the cytoplasmic component of the nuclear factor of activated T cells (NF-ATc). NF-ATc is then translocated to the nucleus, where it combines with NF-ATn to form a complex that is able to initiate transcription of the IL-2 gene, which promotes the immune response.

Ciclosporin works by selectively inhibiting activation and proliferation of T cells as follows.

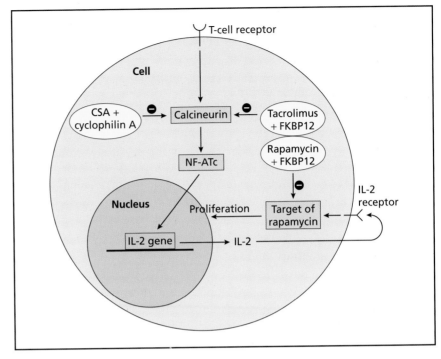

▲ **Fig. 13** Mechanism of action of ciclosporin and related agents. Tacrolimus and rapamycin both bind to the same immunophilin (FKBP12) but the resultant complexes act at different points to block cell proliferation. CSA, ciclosporin A; FKBP12, FK-binding protein 12 ('FK' refers to the original name of tacrolimus, FK506); NF-ATc, nuclear factor of activated T cells.

- It enters the cell cytoplasm and becomes activated after binding to cyclophilin, a member of a family of intracellular receptors called immunophilins.

- The drug–immunophilin complex binds to calcineurin, preventing it from dephosphorylating NF-ATc and interrupting the process of the immune response.

Related drugs such as tacrolimus (FK506) and sirolimus (rapamycin) have similar (but not identical) action (Fig. 13). Ciclosporin and such agents are commonly used as inhibitors of organ transplant rejection and are increasingly used in the treatment of autoimmune or vasculitic conditions.

Therapeutic antibodies or soluble ligands/receptors

Agents acting on lymphocytes

Antithymocyte serum (also called antithymocyte globulin, ATG) is a preparation of polyclonal antibodies made by immunising animals with human lymphocytes. It is not selective for T cells and can cause damage to other cells, including platelets. Its most common use is in the treatment of transplant organ rejection. Administration may cause serum sickness. The preparations currently available are poorly standardised and expensive; it is likely that their use will be supplanted in the future by monoclonal antilymphocyte antibodies (Table 12).

There has also been much interest in mimicking co-stimulatory CTLA4–B7 interactions with CTLA4-Ig, which is a CTLA4–immunoglobulin fusion molecule that activates B7 molecules. Although initial studies of CTLA4-Ig (abatacept) in primate models of transplantation were disappointing, a high-affinity form of the molecule (belatacept) has been shown to be similar in efficacy to ciclosporin in

TABLE 12 THERAPEUTIC MONOCLONAL ANTIBODIES THAT ACT ON LYMPHOCYTES

Target	Expression	Therapeutic antibody	Clinical application
CD25	Activated T cells Regulatory T cells (some)	Basiliximab (Simulect) Daclizumab (Zenapax)	Transplantation: induction of immunosuppression
CD52	T cells B cells	Alemtuzumab	Autoimmune disease: rheumatoid arthritis, multiple sclerosis Haematological malignancy: B-cell chronic lymphoid leukaemia Transplantation: induction of immunosuppression
CD20	B cells	Rituximab	Autoimmune disease: lupus, vasculitis and rheumatoid arthritis Haematological malignancy: non-Hodgkin's lymphoma Transplantation: role to be determined
CD3	T cells	OKT3	Transplantation: treatment of rejection; induction of immunosuppression

renal transplantation. More importantly, abatacept has been approved for the treatment of rheumatoid arthritis, with effects similar to those seen with tumour necrosis factor (TNF) blockade.

Anticytokine agents

The key pro-inflammatory cytokine is TNF. Antibodies to this factor have been shown to be effective in patients with rheumatoid arthritis; they are also effective in Crohn's disease complicated by the formation of fistulae. Agents approved for use include the monoclonal antibodies infliximab and adalimumab, also the soluble receptor etanercept.

Therapeutic antibodies in oncology

Clearly the use of antibodies as therapeutic agents goes beyond immunomodulation, and the largest field for their use is oncology. Several tumours have been targeted with antibodies against cell-surface markers specific for a given cancer.

One example is trastuzumab (Herceptin) for breast cancers expressing HER2. Two antibodies approved for use in colon cancer are cetuximab (Erbitux), a monoclonal antibody to epidermal growth factor, and bevacizumab (Avastin), a monoclonal antibody to vascular endothelial growth factor.

Drug combinations

It is becoming increasingly recognised that combinations of immunosuppressive drugs are effective in some conditions, particularly chronic rheumatic disorders such as refractory rheumatoid arthritis, eg ciclosporin in combination with methotrexate. Other combinations tested in small series include azathioprine and methotrexate, cyclophosphamide and azathioprine, and ciclosporin with other disease-modifying antirheumatic agents such as sulfasalazine. It may be that the need for such combinations of immunosuppressive drugs will

be abrogated by the use of anticytokine therapy or other biological agents in the future.

The future

The hope for the future is that much more specific immunosuppressive and anti-inflammatory agents will become available. The possibilities include the following.

- Targeting of mediators known to be critical in causing tissue damage and systemic upset in autoimmune diseases, eg using anticytokine reagents such as anti-TNF.

- Inhibiting the production of specific autoantibodies or facilitating the removal of these antibodies (or the immune complexes that they form) from the circulation.

- Developing an understanding of the fundamental mechanisms by which tolerance is lost to self antigens in order to facilitate the development of immunisation strategies that might prevent the development of disease at a much earlier stage.

FURTHER READING

Akira S. Mammalian Toll-like receptors. *Curr Opin Immunol* 2003; 15: 5–11.

- - - - - - - - - - - - - - - - -

Albert LJ and Inman RD. Molecular mimicry and autoimmunity. *N Engl J Med* 1999; 341: 2068–74.

- - - - - - - - - - - - - - - - -

Benschop RJ and Cambier JC. B-cell development: signal transduction by antigen receptors and their surrogates. *Curr Opin Immunol* 1999; 11: 143–51.

- - - - - - - - - - - - - - - - -

Bluestone JA, St Clair EW and Turka LA. CTLA4Ig: bridging the basic immunology with clinical application. *Immunity* 2006; 24: 233–8.

- - - - - - - - - - - - - - - - -

Breedveld FC. Therapeutic monoclonal antibodies. *Lancet* 2000; 355: 735–40.

Brekke OH and Sandlie I. Therapeutic antibodies for human diseases at the dawn of the twenty-first century. *Nat Rev Drug Discov* 2003; 2: 52–62.

Carroll MC and Janeway CA Jr. Innate immunity. *Curr Opin Immunol* 1999; 11: 11–12.

Chapel H, Haeney M, Misbah S and Snowden N, eds. *Essentials of Clinical Immunology*, 5th edn. Oxford: Blackwell Publishing, 2006.

Denton MD, Magee CC and Sayegh MH. Immunosuppressive strategies in transplantation. *Lancet* 1999; 353: 1083–91.

Frenette PS and Wagner DD. Adhesion molecules: part 1. *N Engl J Med* 1996; 334: 1526–9.

Frenette PS and Wagner DD. Adhesion molecules: part 2. *N Engl J Med* 1996; 335: 43–5.

Gabay C and Kushner I. Acute-phase proteins and other systemic responses to inflammation. *N Engl J Med* 1998; 340: 448–54.

Janeway CA, Travers P, Walport MJ and Shlomchik M. *Immunobiology: the Immune System in Health and Disease*, 6th edn. London: Garland Science, 2005.

King C and Sarvetnick N. Organ-specific autoimmunity. *Curr Opin Immunol* 1997; 9: 863–71.

Luster AD. Chemokines: chemotactic cytokines that mediate inflammation. *N Engl J Med* 1998; 338: 436–45.

Rossi D and Zlotnik A. The biology of chemokines and their receptors. *Annu Rev Immunol* 2000; 18: 217–42.

Sallusto F and Mackay CR. Chemoattractants and their receptors in homeostasis and inflammation. *Curr Opin Immunol* 2004; 16: 724–31.

Sayegh MH and Turka LA. The role of T-cell costimulatory activation pathways in transplant rejection. *N Engl J Med* 1998; 338: 1813–21.

Wraith DC, Nicolson KS and Whitley NT. Regulatory CD4+ T cells and the control of autoimmune disease. *Curr Opin Immunol* 2004; 16: 695–701.

Yu Z and Lennon VA. Mechanism of intravenous immune globulin therapy in antibody-mediated autoimmune diseases. *N Engl J Med* 1999; 340: 227–8.

9.1 Self-assessment questions

Question 1

Which one of the following statements is true of the immune system?

Answers

A B cells and T cells are both activated in lymph node follicles

B The thymus atrophies and stops functioning in adult life

C The bone marrow is the source of stem cells for B cells but not T cells

D Mucosal-associated lymphoid tissue is found in the respiratory and gastrointestinal tracts, but not the urogenital tract

E B cells only express one immunoglobulin molecule and T cells express only one T-cell receptor

Question 2

Which one of the following statements about Toll-like receptors (TLRs) is true?

Answers

A TLRs and proteins structurally related to them are only present in mammals

B They are only expressed on leucocytes

C TLR3 recognises Gram-negative endotoxin

D TLR9 recognises bacterial DNA

E They affect the innate immune response but have little effect on the adaptive immune response

Question 3

Which one of the following is *not* expressed by T cells?

Answers

A MHC class I

B CD3

C CD20

D CD25

E CD45

Question 4

Which one of the following statements about T cells is *false*?

Answers

A Mature T cells that do not express CD4 or CD8 have not been described

B Natural killer T cells develop in the thymus

C CD28 is important in T-cell co-stimulation

D Th2 T cells produce high levels of interleukin-4

E Th1 T cells produce high levels of interferon-γ

Question 5

Which one of the following statements about antigen presentation is true?

Answers

A MHC class I loci include A, B and DR

B CD8-positive T cells recognise peptide bound to MHC class II

C Peptide that is bound to MHC class I is usually derived from exogenous antigen

D The invariant chain is involved in the presentation pathway for MHC class II

E DM is involved in the presentation pathway for MHC class I

Question 6

Which one of the following statements about B cells is *false*?

Answers

A Selective IgA deficiency is not an X-linked condition

B The antigen-binding region of an antibody is located in a domain on the heavy chain rather than the light chain

C CD22 is a negative regulator of B cells

D CD79 is important for B-cell antigen–receptor signalling

E CD40 plays a role in antibody class switching

Question 7

Which one of the following statements about complement is true?

Answers

A Decay accelerating factor is a soluble regulator of the complement system

B CD59 inhibits the early classical pathway

C C4 deficiency is associated with neisserial infections

D Factor I cleaves C3b but not C4b

E C3 nephritic factor is an autoantibody

Question 8

Which one of the following statements is true of inflammation?

Answers

A Myeloperoxidase is found in neutrophils and macrophages

B ICAM-1 is a member of the immunoglobulin superfamily

C RANTES is an example of a C-X-C chemokine

D Radiolabelled serum amyloid P component may be detected in AA amyloid but not AL amyloid

E LFA-1 is a $\beta 1$ integrin

Question 9

Which one of the following statements does *not* correctly link an immunosuppressive treatment with its mechanism of action?

Answers

A Mycophenolic acid and inosine monophosphate dehydrogenase

B Daclizumab and CD25

C Rapamycin and FK-binding protein 12

D Basiliximab and interleukin 2

E Abatacept and tumour necrosis factor

Question 10

Which one of the following statements about anti-inflammatory and immunosuppressant drugs is true?

Answers

A Ciclosporin binds directly to calcineurin

B Cyclophosphamide has a major effect on B cells

C Calcineurin inhibitors act to a similar degree on B cells and T cells

D Corticosteroids do not affect NF-κB activity

E Ciclosporin and tacrolimus have identical mechanisms of action

9.2 Self-assessment answers

Answer to Question 1

E

B cells are activated in lymphoid follicles, whilst the T-cell area is the deep cortex of lymph nodes. Although the thymus atrophies and becomes less active, it continues to produce T cells throughout adult life. All blood cells originate from stem cells in the bone marrow: B cells also mature in the bone marrow whereas T cells mature in the thymus. Mucosal-associated lymphoid tissue is found in all of the stated tracts. Allelic exclusion (one receptor to one cell) applies to B and T cells.

Answer to Question 2

D

Toll-like receptors have emerged as a crucial mechanism for sensing microbial products. They are named after a protein found to have a developmental role in *Drosophila* (the fruit fly). They are found on leucocytes and also stromal cells, with wide-ranging effects on both innate and adaptive immunity. TLR3 recognises double-stranded viral RNA.

Answer to Question 3

C

CD20 is B-cell marker. MHC class I is found on all nucleated cells. CD3 is expressed on most T cells. CD25 is expressed on activated T cells, and constitutively on a type of regulatory T cell. Different forms of CD45 are expressed on T cells depending on whether they are naive or have encountered antigen.

Answer to Question 4

A

Natural killer T cells may be negative for CD4 and CD8 or express intermediate levels of CD4. Like all T cells, natural killer T cells develop in the thymus. The interaction of T-cell CD28 with antigen-presenting cell B7.1 or B7.2 is one of the most important co-stimulatory interactions. Interleukin-4 and interferon-γ characterise Th2 and Th1 T cells respectively.

Answer to Question 5

D

DR is an MHC class II locus. CD8-positive T cells recognise antigen bound to MHC class I, and CD4-positive T cells recognise antigen bound to MHC class II. The class I antigen presentation pathway is primarily for presentation of newly synthesised endogenous protein, whereas the class II pathway is for presentation of exogenous protein. DM and the invariant chain are both involved in processing for the class II pathway.

Answer to Question 6

B

Selective IgA deficiency is one of the most common immunodeficiencies but is not X-linked, whereas agammaglobulinaemia is X-linked. The variable regions of heavy and light chains combine to form the antigen-binding region. The other statements about CD molecules are all true.

Answer to Question 7

E

Decay accelerating factor is a complement regulator but is membrane bound. CD59 inhibits

131

insertion of the membrane attack complex into the cell membrane. Neisserial infections occur in patients with deficiency of the terminal pathway components. Factor I cleaves both C3b and C4b. C3 nephritic factor is an autoantibody that stabilises the alternative pathway C3 convertase; it is found in mesangiocapillary glomerulonephritis type II.

Answer to Question 8

B

Myeloperoxidase is found in neutrophils but not macrophages.

RANTES is a C-C chemokine. Serum amyloid P is found in both forms of amyloid and so the scan is useful for either. LFA-1 is a β2 integrin.

Answer to Question 9

E

Daclizumab and basiliximab both bind to CD25, the interleukin-2 receptor on T cells. The statements regarding mycophenolic acid and rapamycin are correct. Abatacept is a form of CTLA4-Ig, a soluble blocker of T-cell co-stimulation, not to be confused with etanercept which blocks tumour necrosis factor.

Answer to Question 10

B

Ciclosporin and tacrolimus are both calcineurin inhibitors but have different mechanisms of action, with the former binding first to cyclophilin and the latter to FK-binding protein 12. They both act primarily on T cells. One of the major effects of corticosteroids is on the activity of the transcription factor NF-κB. Cyclophosphamide inhibits cell replication non-specifically, but has a more pronounced effect on B cells than on T cells.

ANATOMY

Author:

S Jacob

Editor:

JD Firth

Editor-in-Chief:

JD Firth

Surface anatomy of the heart

The anterior surface with right, inferior and left borders (Fig. 1) consists of:

- the right atrium;

- the right ventricle;

- a narrow strip of left ventricle on the left border;

- the left auricle in the upper part of the left border.

The surface marking of the three borders is as follows.

- The right border (made up entirely of the right atrium) extends from the third to the sixth right costal cartilage, approximately 3 cm to the right of the midline.

- The inferior border (right ventricle and apex of the left ventricle) extends from the lower end of the right border to the apex (inside the mid-clavicular line of the fourth to fifth left intercostal spaces).

- The left border (narrow strip of left ventricle and the left auricle) extends from the apex to the second left intercostal space, approximately 3 cm from the midline.

Apex beat

This is defined as the lowest and most lateral cardiac pulsation in the precordium. The normal site is inside the mid-clavicular line of the fourth to fifth left intercostal spaces, moving to the anterior axillary line when lying on the left side.

The following are the recognised abnormal forms of the apex beat.

- Heaving: forceful and sustained in hypertension and aortic stenosis (pressure overload).

- Thrusting – forceful but not sustained as in mitral or aortic regurgitation (volume overload).

- Tapping: sudden but brief pulsation as in mitral stenosis.

- Missing: obesity, pleural effusion, pericardial effusion, emphysema.

Coronary arteries

The coronary arteries are shown in Fig. 2.

Right coronary artery

The origin is in the right coronary sinus. It descends in the right atrioventricular groove, supplies the right atrium and right ventricle, and continues as the posterior descending artery, supplying the posterior aspect of the interventricular septum and left ventricle.

Left coronary artery

The origin is in the left coronary sinus. Its parts and branches include:

- left main coronary artery;

- left anterior descending (LAD) branch, which supplies the anterior wall of both ventricles and most of the interventricular septum;

- circumflex (Cx) branch, which lies in the left atrioventricular groove and supplies the left atrium and left ventricle; in 10% of individuals, the posterior descending artery may be a continuation of the circumflex.

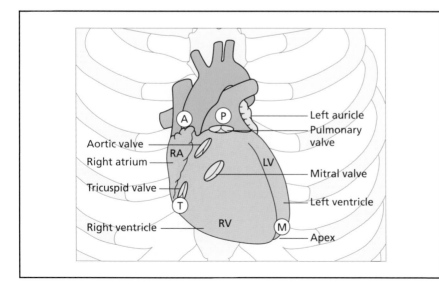

▲**Fig. 1** Surface projections of the heart. A, P, T and M indicate auscultation areas for the aortic, pulmonary, tricuspid and mitral valves, respectively.

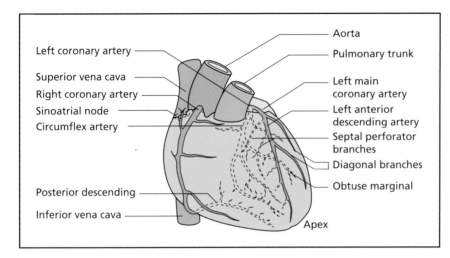

▲ **Fig. 2** The coronary arteries.

• Innervation: of fibrous pericardium and parietal layer of serous pericardium by phrenic nerves.

Pericardial pain originates in the parietal layer and is transmitted by the phrenic nerves.

The pericardium is closest to the surface at the level of the xiphoid process of the sternum and the sixth costal cartilages.

Blood supply of the conducting system

• Sinoatrial (SA) node: in 60% of individuals by the right coronary artery.

• Atrioventricular (AV) node: in 90% of individuals by the right coronary artery.

• Right coronary artery occlusion leads to inferior myocardial infarction, often associated with sinoatrial or atrioventricular dysrhythmia.
• Occlusion of the left coronary artery or its branches leads to anterior and/or lateral myocardial infarction, often with substantial ventricular damage and poor prognosis.

Pericardial cavity

The pericardial cavity is shown in Fig. 3. It consists of an outer fibrous pericardium and an inner serous pericardium; the latter has an outer parietal and an inner visceral layer, which enclose the pericardial cavity.

Relationships of the pericardial cavity

• Anterior: sternum, third to sixth costal cartilages, lungs and pleura.

• Posterior: oesophagus, descending aorta, vertebrae T5–T8.

• Lateral: root of the lung, mediastinal pleura, phrenic nerve.

Pericardiocentesis

A needle is inserted into the angle between the xiphoid process and the left seventh costal cartilage; it is then directed upwards at an angle of 45° towards the left shoulder. The needle passes through the central tendon of the diaphragm. Inadvertent puncture of the right ventricle is possible.

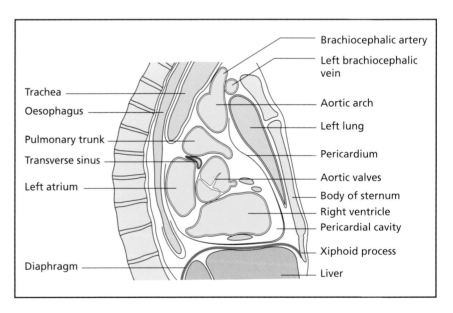

▲ **Fig. 3** Sagittal section through the thorax showing the relationship of the heart and pericardial cavity.

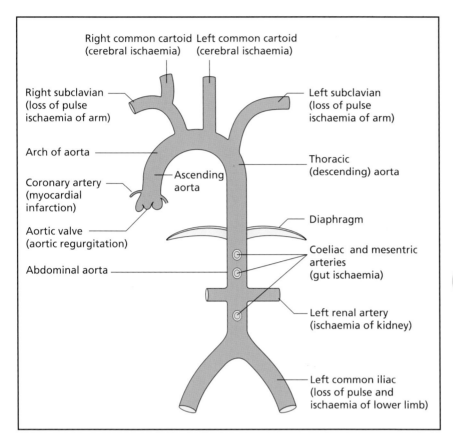

Right common cartoid
(cerebral ischaemia)

Left common cartoid
(cerebral ischaemia)

Right subclavian
(loss of pulse
ischaemia of arm)

Left subclavian
(loss of pulse
ischaemia of arm)

Arch of aorta

Ascending
aorta

Thoracic
(descending) aorta

Coronary artery
(myocardial
infarction)

Diaphragm

Aortic valve
(aortic regurgitation)

Coeliac and mesentric
arteries
(gut ischaemia)

Abdominal aorta

Left renal artery
(ischaemia of kidney)

Left common iliac
(loss of pulse and
ischaemia of lower limb)

▲ **Fig. 4** Parts and branches of the aorta. The effects of dissection and occlusion are given in parentheses.

Aorta

The anatomy of the aorta is shown in Fig. 4. In a dissecting aneurysm, which most commonly affects the thoracic aorta, the media (the middle layer of the arterial wall) splits into two layers creating a false lumen. Entry of blood into this cavity can occlude branches of the aorta, leading to ischaemia in the territory of any artery so affected. Figure 4 shows the branches of the aorta and the effects of occlusion.

⚠ The most common cause of severe central chest pain is myocardial ischaemia, but it is always important to consider aortic dissection. Did the pain come on suddenly? Was it tearing? Did it radiate to the back? Is the left radial pulse as strong as the right? Is the blood pressure in the left arm the same as in the right? Is the mediastinum widened on CXR? All these features suggest dissection.

Lungs and pleural cavities

The surface markings of the lungs and pleural cavities are shown in Fig. 5. The right lung has three lobes (upper, middle and lower) and the left lung usually has only two (upper and lower).

- The apex of the lung and the surrounding pleural cavity extend about 3 cm above the medial part of the clavicle.

- The oblique fissure lies along the sixth rib and separates the lower lobe from the upper lobe (and the middle lobe on the right).

- The horizontal fissure on the right side extends from the mid-axillary line along the fourth rib. It may be visible on a plain radiograph of the chest.

- The upper and middle lobes, which are in front of the lower lobe, are related to the anterior chest wall.

- The lower borders of the lungs cross the eighth ribs in the mid-axillary lines and the middle of the tenth ribs at the back.

- The lower margin of the pleura is about two ribs lower than the lower margin of the lung.

The lower parts of the lung and pleura overlap abdominal organs such as the liver, kidney and spleen. When the lung fields are markedly hyperinflated, the liver is pushed down by the diaphragm and may be palpable. The subclavian vessels and the brachial plexus lie on the apical pleura.

> ⚠ As the subclavian vein lies on the apical pleura, attempts to cannulate it may inadvertently produce a pneumothorax. A CXR is always required after this procedure to check for such a complication. Similar complications may also occur during a liver biopsy.

Trachea, bronchi and bronchioles

As the trachea descends into the chest, it moves slightly to the right of the midline, dividing at the carina into right and left main bronchi, the right main bronchus being more vertical than the left.

The right main bronchus divides into three lobar bronchi (upper, middle and lower), whereas the left divides into only two (upper and lower). Each lobar bronchus divides into segmental and subsegmental bronchi. There are about 25 generations of bronchi and bronchioles between the trachea and alveoli, the first 10 being bronchi and the rest bronchioles (Fig. 6).

The bronchi have:

- walls consisting of cartilage and smooth muscle;

- epithelial lining with cilia and goblet cells;

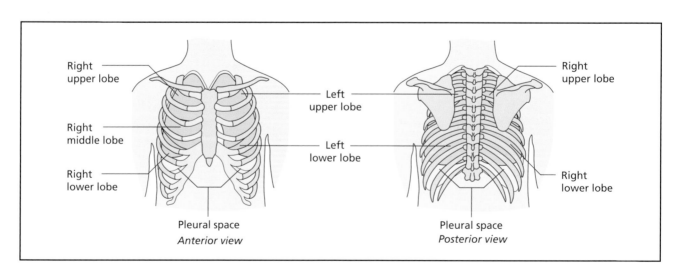

Right upper lobe — Left upper lobe — Right upper lobe

Right middle lobe

Right lower lobe — Left lower lobe — Right lower lobe

Pleural space
Anterior view

Pleural space
Posterior view

▲**Fig. 5** The surface markings of the lungs and pleura.

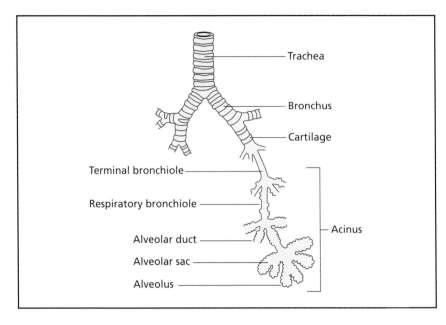

▲**Fig. 6** The segments of the airway from the trachea to the alveolus.

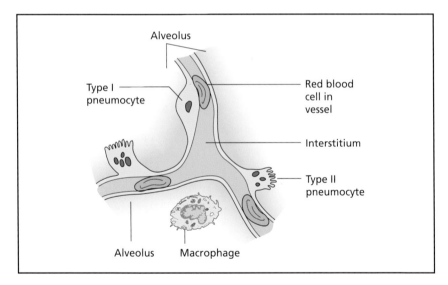

▲**Fig. 7** The anatomy of the alveolus.

- submucosal mucous glands;

- endocrine cells containing serotonin (5-hydroxytryptamine or 5HT).

The bronchioles are tubes that are less than 2 mm in diameter and are also known as small airways. They have:

- no cartilage or submucosal glands;

- Clara cells secreting a surfactant-like substance;

- a single layer of ciliated cells but only a few goblet cells.

As the right main bronchus is more vertical than the left, inhaled material is more likely to pass into it.

Alveolar ducts and alveoli

Each respiratory bronchiole supplies approximately 200 alveoli via alveolar ducts. There are about 300 million alveoli (Fig. 7) in each lung and their walls have type I and type II pneumocytes. Type II pneumocytes are the source of surfactant; type I pneumocytes and the endothelial cells of adjoining capillaries constitute the blood–air barrier, which has a thickness of about 0.2–2 µm.

Blood supply

About 25% of the total blood supply of the liver reaches it via the hepatic artery and the remaining 75% through the low-pressure portal vein (Fig. 8). Blood leaves the liver through the hepatic veins, which join the inferior vena cava. Besides the three major hepatic veins, there are a number of small veins draining the right lobe that enter the inferior vena cava directly. These may be the only veins draining the liver when the main veins are thrombosed, as in Budd–Chiari syndrome.

Bile duct

The right and left hepatic ducts collect the bile from the liver and join to form the common hepatic duct, which in turn is joined by the cystic duct from the gallbladder to form the common bile duct (Fig. 8). The common bile duct lies in the free border of the lesser omentum, along with the hepatic artery and the portal vein. Lower down, it passes behind the first part of the duodenum and the head of the pancreas. Tumours of the head of the pancreas can obstruct the common bile duct.

Pancreatic duct

The common bile duct is joined close to its end by the pancreatic duct to form the ampulla of Vater. The ampulla and the ends of the two ducts are surrounded by sphincteric muscles, the whole constituting the sphincter of Oddi. The hepatopancreatic ampulla terminates at the papilla of Vater on the posteromedial wall of the second part of the duodenum, about 10 cm distal to the pylorus.

Intrahepatic circulation

Blood from the branches of the hepatic artery and portal vein flows through the sinusoids towards the central terminal venules, which are tributaries of the hepatic veins. The sinusoids are bordered by plates of hepatocytes that are one cell thick.

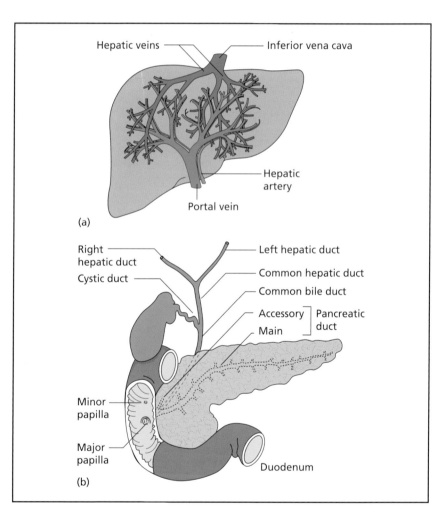

▲ **Fig. 8** Blood supply (**a**) and biliary drainage (**b**) of the liver.

Blood flowing through the sinusoids is separated from the hepatocytes by fenestrated endothelial cells, phagocytic Kupffer cells and the subendothelial space of Disse (Fig. 9).

The space of Disse contains the stellate cells of Ito, which are converted into myofibroblasts during liver injury. Proliferation of myofibroblasts leads to deposition of collagen, increasing the resistance to blood flow and resulting in portal hypertension.

Portosystemic anastomoses and portal hypertension

When portal venous pressure rises above 10–12 mmHg (normal 5–8 mmHg) the sites of portosystemic anastomoses (Fig. 10) dilate, most importantly causing oesophageal varices, which can haemorrhage dramatically. Splenomegaly is also a feature of portal hypertension.

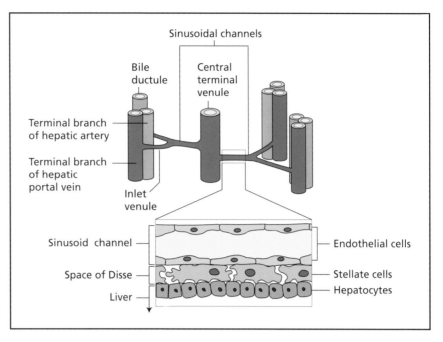

▲ **Fig. 9** The intrahepatic circulation.

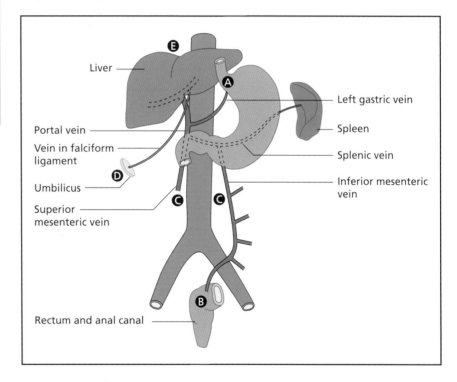

▲ **Fig. 10** The sites of portosystemic anastomoses. A, between the oesophageal branch of the left gastric vein and the oesophageal veins of the azygos system. B, between the superior haemorrhoidal branch of the inferior mesenteric vein and the inferior haemorrhoidal veins draining via the internal pudendal veins into the internal iliac vein. C, between portal tributaries in the mesentery and mesocolon and retroperitoneal veins communicating with renal, lumbar and phrenic veins. D, between portal branches in the liver and the veins of the abdominal wall via veins passing along the falciform ligament to the umbilicus. This may lead to a caput medusae. E, between the portal branches in the liver and the veins of the diaphragm across the bare area of the liver.

Posterior, superior and lateral to the spleen are the left diaphragm, pleura, lung and 9th, 10th and 11th ribs; anteriorly across the lesser sac is the stomach; medially is the left kidney; inferiorly is the splenic flexure of the colon. The splenic vessels and nerves enter or leave at the hilum, where the tail of the pancreas abuts the spleen. The splenic artery is one of the three main branches of the coeliac axis; the splenic vein is joined by the superior mesenteric vein to form the portal vein.

The normal spleen is not palpable. If the spleen enlarges, it does so posteriorly and superiorly before becoming palpable subcostally. It has to enlarge to two to three times its normal size before this happens (Fig. 11).

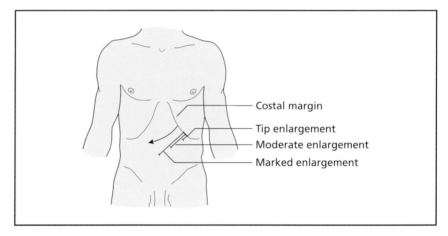

Costal margin
Tip enlargement
Moderate enlargement
Marked enlargement

▲ **Fig. 11** The direction of enlargement of the spleen. The spleen has a characteristic notched shape and moves downwards and to the right during full inspiration.

How can you tell whether a mass in the left upper quadrant is a spleen?

- The direction of splenic enlargement from the subcostal region is downwards and towards the right iliac fossa, and it moves in this direction on inspiration (a kidney moves up and down, not across).
- The upper border of the enlarged spleen cannot be felt (it is usually possible to reach above a kidney).
- The spleen is not bimanually palpable (ballotable) (an enlarged kidney is).

- The spleen is dull on percussion (a kidney is usually resonant).
- A notch may often (not always) be felt in the lower medial border of the spleen.

The spleen has a thin tense capsule and is the commonest intra-abdominal viscus to be ruptured by blunt trauma.

The kidneys are retroperitoneal on the posterior abdominal wall. Each is about 11 cm in length, with the right placed 1–2 cm inferior to the left. They lie within a fatty cushion of perinephric fat contained within the renal fascia. Posterior to the kidney from superior to inferior are the diaphragm, 12th rib and the muscles of the posterior abdominal wall (psoas, quadratus lumborum, transverses abdominis). Anterior to the right kidney is the liver, second part of the duodenum and the ascending colon; anterior to the left kidney is the stomach, pancreas, spleen and descending colon. An adrenal gland lies on the upper of each kidney.

Many chronic renal diseases cause the kidneys to shrink. A patient definitely has chronic renal disease if on ultrasound scanning their kidneys are less than 9 cm in length.

The renal hilum lies medially, where from anteriorly to posteriorly the renal vein, renal artery and pelvis of the ureter enter or leave the kidney. Renal lymphatics and nerves (sympathetic) also enter at the hilum. The renal artery arises directly from the aorta and the renal vein drains directly into the inferior vena cava. The left renal vein passes in front of the aorta and the right renal artery passes behind the inferior vena cava.

The anatomy of the pelvis of the ureter is very variable: it may be completely outside the substance of the kidney or be buried within the renal hilum. Within the kidney the pelvis of the ureter divides into two or three major calyces, each of which divides into a number of minor calyces, where collecting ducts discharge urine at the surface of the renal papilla.

The normal kidney is not usually palpable, except in thin patients.

How can you tell whether a mass in the left upper quadrant is a kidney?

- The kidney moves down with respiration (the spleen moves down and to the right).
- The upper border of the kidney can usually be felt (this is never possible with the spleen).
- The kidney is bimanually palpable (ballotable) (the spleen is not).
- The kidney is resonant on percussion (the spleen is dull).
- The kidney does not have a notch.

Thyroid gland

The thyroid is a bilobed structure in the lower part of the neck; the two lobes are joined by an isthmus that lies across the trachea below the cricoid cartilage. The gland weighs about 20–40 g and is wrapped around the front and sides of the larynx, to which it is bound by the cervical fascia (Fig. 12). During swallowing the larynx is elevated; hence, the thyroid gland also moves during swallowing. This is an important clinical sign in the diagnosis of a mass in the neck such as a thyroid swelling.

An enlarged thyroid gland can cause pressure effects by compressing the structures to which it is related, resulting in the following.

- Dysphagia: caused by compression of the oesophagus.

- Stridor: due to tracheal compression.

- Change in voice: caused by compression of the recurrent laryngeal nerves (which can also be damaged during thyroid surgery).

- Weakness of the carotid pulse: due to compression of the artery.

- Horner's syndrome: caused by compression of the sympathetic trunk which lies behind the carotid sheath.

The thyroid develops from the back of the tongue as the thyroglossal duct, which descends down to the neck. The descent may go further into the mediastinum, giving rise to a mediastinal thyroid and a mediastinal goitre.

Microanatomy

The thyroid gland is composed of thyroid follicles, which are spherical structures surrounded by cuboidal cells. The lumen of the follicles contains colloid. Parafollicular cells secrete calcitonin. The follicular cells, which become columnar when stimulated by thyroid-stimulating hormone, have the following functions:

- secrete thyroglobulin and iodine into the colloid;

- absorb thyroglobulin from the colloid;

- secrete thyroid hormones directly into the bloodstream.

Parathyroid glands

There are usually four parathyroid glands, lying deep in the posterior part of the thyroid gland; they develop from the third and fourth branchial pouches. Glands from the third pouch become the inferior glands and those from the fourth pouch become the superior glands. The blood supply to the glands is from the inferior thyroid artery. The epithelial cells of the gland are of two types: chief cells with clear cytoplasm; and oxyphilic cells with eosinophilic granular cytoplasm.

Blood supply of the parathyroid glands

Of patients undergoing thyroidectomy with preservation of the parathyroid glands, 30–40% develop hypocalcaemia. This is the result of spasm of the inferior thyroid artery, which supplies both the thyroid and the parathyroid glands. Most recover after a month or so.

Adrenal gland

Histologically, there is an outer cortex and an inner medulla; the cortex has three zones, glomerulosa, fasciculata and reticularis. Each

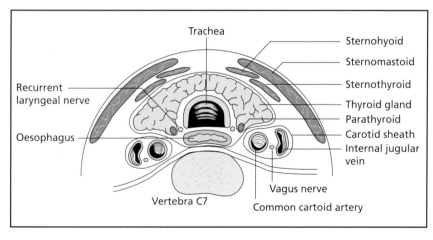

Trachea

Sternohyoid

Sternomastoid

Sternothyroid

Thyroid gland

Parathyroid

Carotid sheath

Internal jugular vein

Recurrent laryngeal nerve

Oesophagus

Vagus nerve

Vertebra C7

Common cartoid artery

▲ **Fig. 12** The thyroid gland and its relationships.

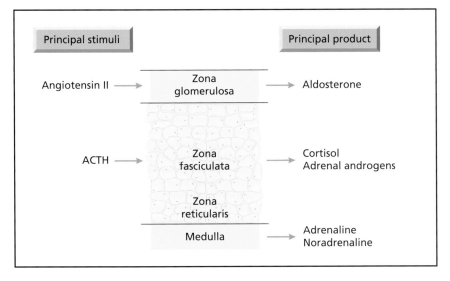

▲ **Fig. 13** Structure and function of the adrenal gland. ACTH, adrenocorticotrophic hormone.

zone has specific functions (Fig. 13).

Cortical steroids are delivered to the medulla through a unique arrangement of the blood supply (Fig. 14). The cortical arterioles form a subcapsular plexus, with some arterioles passing directly to the medulla, although capillaries supplying the cortex also join to form vessels that reach the medulla and then break up again into capillaries. Through this portal system, glucocorticoids are delivered to the medulla and induce the methyltransferase enzyme, leading to conversion of noradrenaline to adrenaline.

The medulla produces adrenaline and noradrenaline. In humans, only a small proportion of circulating noradrenaline is derived from the adrenal gland; most comes from the sympathetic nerve endings.

The breast

The breast or mammary gland consists of 15–20 lobes, with a lactiferous duct opening from each lobe at the apex of the nipple. It undergoes a variety of changes at various developmental stages.

- In childhood: the gland is inactive, with ducts being the principal glandular tissue.

- At puberty: oestrogens and progesterone secreted cyclically by the ovaries influence the growth of the duct system, fat and connective tissue.

- Pregnancy: in the early stages ducts proliferate further and form buds that expand to become the alveoli. In the second half of pregnancy, glandular proliferation slows, but alveoli enlarge and begin to form secretory material. Oestrogen and progesterone from the ovaries and placenta, as well as prolactin from the anterior pituitary, influence these changes.

- At parturition: oestrogen and progesterone levels fall, which increases prolactin secretion and induces lactation. Maintenance of lactation requires continued prolactin secretion, after cessation of which the gland undergoes regressive changes and returns to a resting state.

- After the menopause: the gland involutes, leaving only a few remnants of the ducts.

Ovary and uterus

Ovary

The ovary lies on the lateral wall of the pelvis and is attached to the broad ligament by the mesovarium. The normal ovary cannot be palpated, either through the anterior abdominal wall or by vaginal examination. Inflammation or enlargement causes pain that is poorly localised and may mimic appendicitis.

The ovary contains Graafian follicles at various stages of development, corpora lutea and corpora albicans (Fig. 15). Until puberty the ovary contains only primordial follicles. After the menopause, it becomes small and shrivelled, follicles disappearing completely in old age.

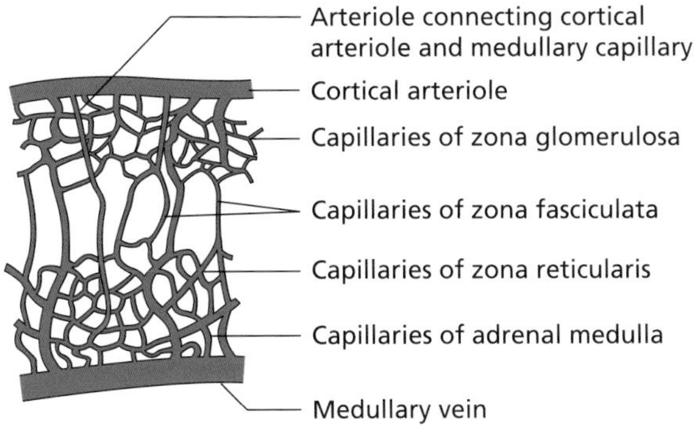

Arteriole connecting cortical arteriole and medullary capillary
Cortical arteriole
Capillaries of zona glomerulosa
Capillaries of zona fasciculata
Capillaries of zona reticularis
Capillaries of adrenal medulla
Medullary vein

▲ **Fig. 14** The blood supply of the adrenal gland.

145

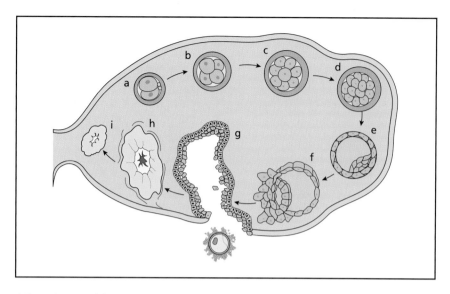

▲ **Fig. 15** Diagram of the ovary showing the development and fate of ovarian follicles: (**a**) oogonium, surrounded by follicular cells; (**b**) primordial follicle; (**c–e**) growing follicles; (**f**) Graafian follicle; (**g**) ruptured follicle; (**h**) corpus luteum; (**i**) corpus albicans.

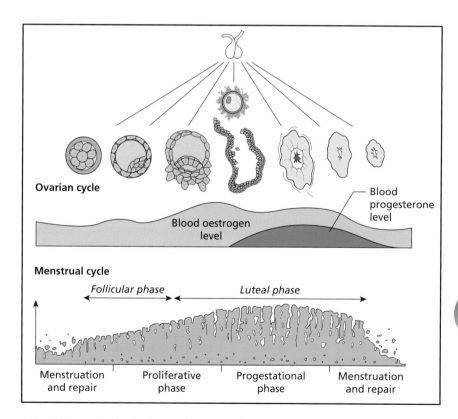

▲ **Fig. 16** Diagram showing the changes of the ovary and endometrium during a menstrual cycle.

Uterus

Four stages of cyclical change in the endometrium are recognised (Fig. 16).

1. Menstrual stage: during which there is external menstrual discharge.

2. Follicular (proliferative) stage: associated with maturation of the Graafian follicle and secretion of oestrogen.

3. Luteal (progestational) stage: concurrent with an active corpus luteum secreting progesterone.

4. Premenstrual stage: there is intermittent constriction of the arteries leading to ischaemia.

Testis

The normal testes are found in the scrotum at a temperature 2–3°C below body temperature. The left testis is usually at a lower level than the right.

The epididymis lies on the posterolateral aspect of the testis and is suspended by the spermatic cord which contains its arterial supply, venous and lymphatic drainage, and nerve supply. The vas deferens (ductus deferens) connects the epididymis to the prostatic urethra and transports spermatozoa. The epididymis and the vas deferens store spermatozoa.

The testis develops in the L2–L3 vertebral region and drags its vascular, lymphatic and nerve supply from this region to the scrotum. Testicular pain may therefore radiate to the loin, and renal pain is often referred to the scrotum.

Oesophageal sphincters and gastro-oesophageal reflux

There are two main anatomical sphincters, the mechanisms of which prevent gastro-oesophageal reflux.

- Lower oesophageal sphincter: the most important anatomical mechanism.

- External 'sphincter': formed by crural fibres of the diaphragm.

Lower oesophageal sphincter

The lower oesophageal sphincter is formed of specialised circular muscle fibres that pass through the diaphragm and the intra-abdominal oesophagus. It is kept closed by tonic muscle contractions and relaxes only during swallowing or vomiting. The tone of the sphincter is controlled via an intramural plexus of the enteric nervous system.

> ⚠ Neural release of nitric oxide may aid relaxation of the lower oesophageal sphincter, which explains why nitrates can sometimes relieve oesophageal symptoms and cannot be used as a 'diagnostic test' of coronary ischaemia.

External sphincter

This sphincter is less important, but also controversial. The phreno-oesophageal membrane connects the oesophagus to the surrounding right crus of the diaphragm. The tone of the diaphragm, which is increased with its contraction during inspiration and when intra-abdominal pressure is raised, exerts a sphincteric effect.

Gastro-oesophageal reflux

The factors associated with gastro-oesophageal reflux are shown in Fig. 17.

Peptic ulceration

Peptic ulcers may be found in the:

- oesophagus;

- stomach (areas most susceptible are shown in Fig. 18);

- duodenum;

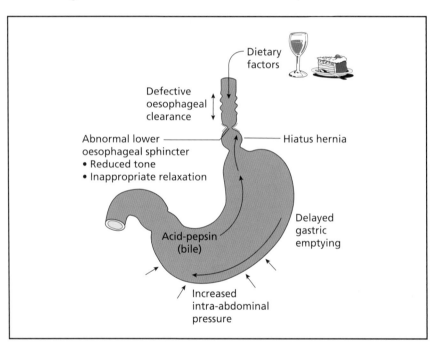

▲ **Fig. 17** Factors associated with the development of gastro-oesophageal reflux disease.

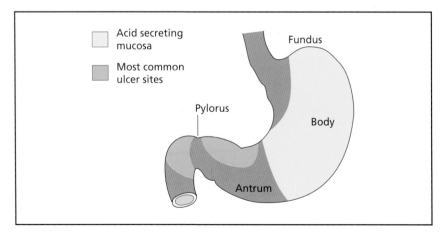

▲ **Fig. 18** Areas of the stomach most prone to ulcer formation.

- jejunum (after gastrojejunostomy);
- ileum (in Meckel's diverticulum).

Lesser sac of the peritoneum and pseudo-pancreatic cyst

The lesser sac lies behind the stomach and in front of the pancreas and extends upwards behind the liver and downwards into the layers of the greater omentum. Only a layer of parietal peritoneum intervenes between the lesser sac and the pancreas and other retroperitoneal structures (Fig. 19).

A collection of pancreatic juice and debris, which can develop in the lesser sac of the peritoneum after rupture of the pancreatic duct in acute pancreatitis, forms a pseudo-pancreatic cyst.

Structures felt on internal examination

Rectal examination

The structures felt on rectal examination are shown in Fig. 20 and include the following.

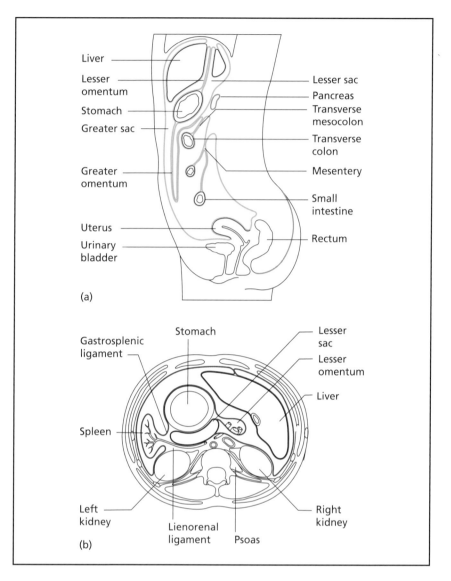

▲ Fig. 19 The peritoneum and peritoneal cavity: (**a**) midline sagittal section; (**b**) transverse section at the level of vertebrae T12.

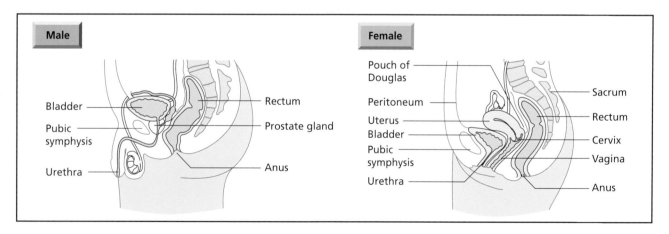

▲ Fig. 20 The structures felt on rectal examination.

- Male: the prostate and, rarely, the seminal vesicles.

- Female: the cervix, perineal body and, rarely, the ovaries.

- Both sexes: the anorectal ring, coccyx and sacrum, and ischial spines.

Vaginal examination

The structures felt on vaginal examination are shown in Fig. 21 and include the following.

- Cervix of the uterus and fornices of the vagina.

- Anteriorly: the urethra, bladder and symphysis pubis.

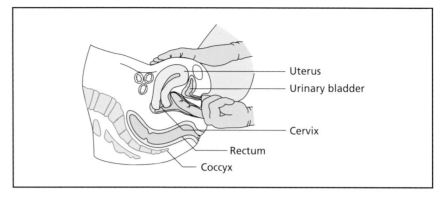

▲ **Fig. 21** The structures felt on vaginal examination.

- Posteriorly: the rectum; collection of fluid and malignant deposits in the pouch of Douglas.

- The body of the uterus, ovaries and the uterine tubes may also be felt with pressure applied to the lower abdominal wall.

Retina

When the retina is studied with an ophthalmoscope, the following should be examined (Fig. 22):

- the optic disc;
- the macula lutea;
- the retinal arteries and veins.

Optic disc

The optic disc lies medial (nasal) to the posterior pole of the eye and is circular or oval; it is more oval if astigmatism is present. It is paler than the rest of the retina, which is brick-red in colour but becomes pinker than normal when there is papilloedema. The physiological cup is a central depression, which is paler than the rest of the disc. This cup is deeper in glaucoma.

Macula lutea

The macula lutea lies lateral to the disc, almost at the posterior pole. It is the site of central vision. A depression in its centre is the fovea centralis, which has a glistening appearance and is devoid of blood vessels.

Retinal vessels

The central artery of the retina emerges from the disc and divides into upper and lower branches; each of these then divides into nasal and temporal branches. There are no anastomoses between the branches.

The retinal arteries are accompanied by the retinal veins. The arteries look brighter red than the veins, are narrower than them and have a brighter longitudinal streak caused by light reflection from the wall. The retinal veins normally pulsate, but arteries do not. This pulsation is absent in papilloedema. Spontaneous arterial pulsation is an abnormal finding, but may be seen in glaucoma and aortic regurgitation.

At the points where the arteries cross the veins, 'nicking' of the veins may be visible in hypertension. This is largely the result of an optical illusion caused by increased thickening of the arterial walls.

Lens

The lens is biconvex and placed in front of the vitreous humour (Figs 23 and 24). Its posterior surface is more convex than the anterior surface. It lies within a capsule. The refractive index of the lens is higher than that of the aqueous and vitreous humours, contributing 15 D (dioptres) out of a total refractive power of about 58 D.

The lens is suspended from the ciliary body by the suspensory ligament. Tension in this ligament flattens the lens. In accommodation, contraction of ciliary muscles reduces the circumference of the ciliary ring and slackens the suspensory ligament, so that the lens becomes more spherical, with an increased refractive index.

The chambers

The anterior and posterior ocular chambers, separated by the iris and pupil, contain aqueous humour (Figs 23 and 24). This is produced in the posterior chamber by filtration and secretion at the ciliary processes; it then passes through the pupil to enter the anterior chamber, situated between the cornea and the iris. At the iridocorneal angle, about 90% of the aqueous humour is absorbed into the canal of Schlemm,

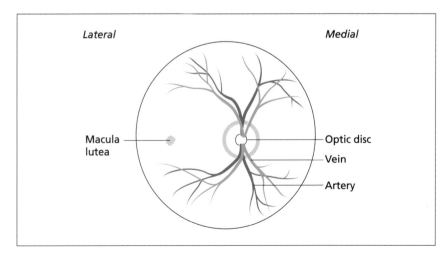

Lateral *Medial*

Macula lutea —

Optic disc
Vein
Artery

▲**Fig. 22** The fundus as seen by ophthalmoscopy.

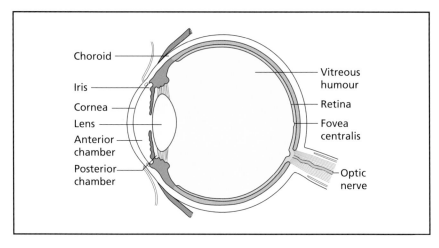

▲ **Fig. 23** Horizontal section through the eyeball.

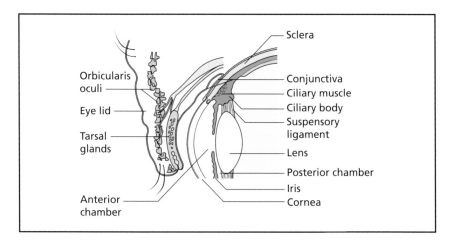

▲ **Fig. 24** The anterior and posterior chambers.

through which it passes into the scleral veins. It is not known how the remaining 10% is reabsorbed. The aqueous humour contributes to intraocular pressure, which maintains the geometry of the eyeball, and it also nourishes the lens and cornea.

Changes after cataract surgery

After cataract surgery, there is an inability on the part of the implanted lens to accommodate, but the convergence and pupillary constriction components of accommodation remain normal. There is also slight astigmatism caused by incision and suturing of the sclerocorneal junction.

Blood supply to the brain

Arterial supply

Circle of Willis The two internal carotids and the two vertebral arteries form an anastomosis on the inferior surface of the brain known as the circle of Willis (Fig. 25). Each half of the circle is formed by:

- an anterior communicating artery;
- an anterior cerebral artery;
- an internal carotid artery;
- a posterior communicating artery;
- a posterior cerebral artery.

Although most of the branches are therefore interconnected, there is normally only minimal mixing of the blood that passes through them, but when one artery is blocked the arterial circle may provide collateral circulation.

Posterior cerebral arteries The posterior cerebral arteries are the terminal branches of the basilar artery. They supply the occipital lobe, including the visual area, as well as the temporal lobe (Fig. 26). Occlusion of a posterior cerebral artery causes blindness in the contralateral visual field.

Anterior cerebral artery The anterior cerebral artery is the smaller of the two terminal branches of the internal carotid artery. It supplies the medial part of the inferior surface of the frontal lobe, the medial surface of the frontal and parietal lobes, the corpus callosum, and a narrow strip on the upper part of the lateral surface of the brain (see Fig. 26). The motor and sensory areas of the leg are supplied by this artery, resulting in characteristic paralysis when it is occluded.

Middle cerebral artery The middle cerebral artery is the larger of the terminal branches of the internal carotid artery. It lies in the lateral sulcus and its branches supply the lateral surface of the frontal, parietal and temporal lobes, except the narrow strip in the upper part supplied by the anterior cerebral artery (see Fig. 26). Occlusion of a middle cerebral artery results in contralateral motor and sensory paralysis of the face, arm and, usually to a lesser degree, leg.

Venous system

The cranial venous sinuses are situated within the dura mater. They are devoid of valves and drain eventually into the internal jugular vein. The following are the cranial venous sinuses (Fig. 27):

- superior sagittal sinus;
- inferior sagittal sinus;
- straight sinus;
- transverse sinus;
- sigmoid sinus;
- confluence of sinuses;
- occipital sinus;
- cavernous sinus.

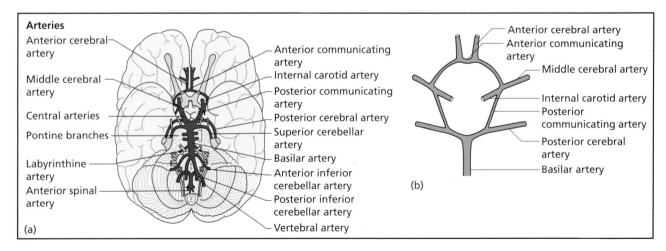

Arteries

Anterior cerebral artery
Middle cerebral artery
Central arteries
Pontine branches
Labyrinthine artery
Anterior spinal artery

Anterior communicating artery
Internal carotid artery
Posterior communicating artery
Posterior cerebral artery
Superior cerebellar artery
Basilar artery
Anterior inferior cerebellar artery
Posterior inferior cerebellar artery
Vertebral artery

(a)

Anterior cerebral artery
Anterior communicating artery
Middle cerebral artery
Internal carotid artery
Posterior communicating artery
Posterior cerebral artery
Basilar artery

(b)

▲**Fig. 25** The circle of Willis: the central arteries supply the corpus striatum, internal capsule, diencephalon and midbrain.

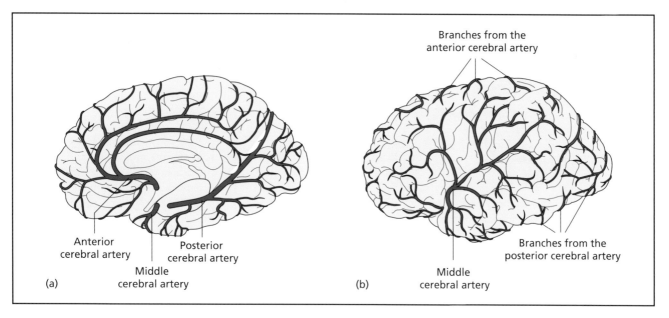

▲ **Fig. 26** Arterial supply of the cerebral hemisphere: (**a**) medial view; (**b**) lateral view.

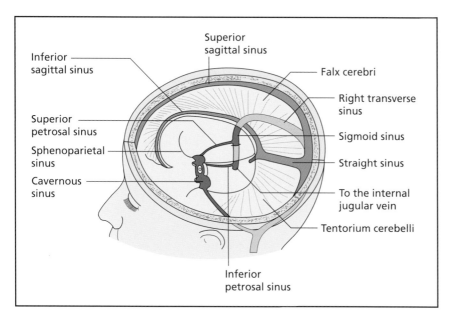

▲ **Fig. 27** The cranial venous sinuses.

Cavernous sinus The relationships of the cavernous sinus are shown in Fig. 28. It is related medially to the pituitary gland and the sphenoid sinus, and laterally to the temporal lobe of the brain. On its lateral wall, from above downwards, lie the oculomotor, trochlear and ophthalmic nerves. The internal carotid artery and the abducens nerve pass through the sinus.

Drainage of the cavernous sinus The connections of the cavernous sinus are shown in Fig. 29. Posteriorly it drains into the transverse/sigmoid sinus through the superior petrosal sinus and via the inferior petrosal sinus, passing through the jugular foramen into the internal jugular vein. The ophthalmic veins drain into the anterior part of the sinus.

Emissary veins passing through the foramina in the middle cranial fossa connect the cavernous sinus to the pterygoid plexus of veins and to the facial veins. Infection from the face can spread to the cavernous sinus via this route. The superficial middle cerebral vein drains into the cavernous sinus from above. The two cavernous sinuses are connected to each other by anterior and posterior cavernous sinuses, which lie in front of and behind the pituitary.

The meninges and haemorrhages

There are three layers of the meninges: dura mater, arachnoid mater and pia mater. There are three meningeal spaces, as follows.

- Extradural (epidural) space: between the cranial (spinal) bones and the endosteal layer of dura mater. This is a potential space, which becomes a real space when there is an extradural haemorrhage from a torn meningeal vessel.

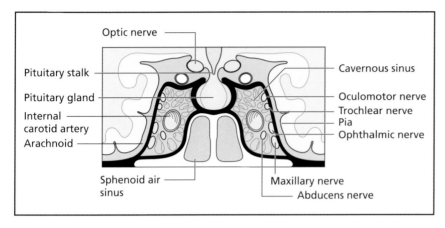

▲ **Fig. 28** The hypophysis and cavernous sinus.

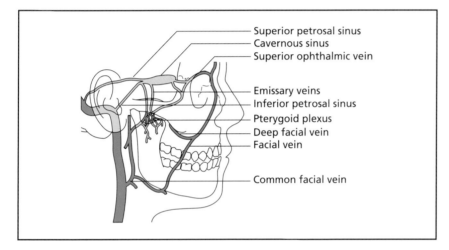

▲ **Fig. 29** The connections of the cavernous sinus.

• Subdural space: between the dura and the arachnoid mater. The cerebral veins traverse this space to reach the dural venous sinuses.

• Subarachnoid space: between the arachnoid and the pia mater. It contains cerebrospinal fluid (CSF) and the major vessels supplying the brain.

Extradural haemorrhage

Bleeding into the extradural space typically occurs after injury to the middle meningeal artery as a result of fracture of the temporal bone (Fig. 30a). The haematoma between the dura and the skull bone compresses the brain.

🔑 In extradural haemorrhage, there is typically a lucid interval, followed by deepening coma resulting from rapid increase in intracranial tension as the haematoma expands. Transtentorial herniation may occur, causing brainstem compression and (often) death.

Subdural haemorrhage

Subdural haemorrhage is usually caused by bleeding from small bridging veins crossing the subdural space (Fig. 30b). Acute haemorrhage is usually caused by trauma, but people with coagulation

disorders (including therapeutic anticoagulation) are particularly at risk.

🔑 Chronic subdural haemorrhage may happen in elderly people after trivial head injury; this is believed to be because the bridging veins are more vulnerable as a result of brain shrinkage.

Subarachnoid haemorrhage

The causes of bleeding into the subarachnoid space between the arachnoid and pia mater (Fig. 30c) include:

• rupture of a berry aneurysm;

• rupture of vascular malformation;

• hypertensive haemorrhage;

• coagulation disorders;

• head injury.

About 15% of subarachnoid haemorrhages are instantly fatal and a further 45% die because of rebleeding or vascular spasm. In survivors, organisation of blood clot can obliterate the subarachnoid space, causing hydrocephalus.

Cranial nerves

Olfactory nerve (cranial nerve I)

Axons from the olfactory mucosa in the nasal cavity pass through the cribriform plate of the ethmoid to end in the olfactory bulb. A cuff of dura, lined by arachnoid and pia mater, surrounds each bundle of nerves, establishing a potential communication and a route of infection between the subarachnoid space and the nasal cavity. The olfactory cortex consists of the uncus and the anterior perforated substance.

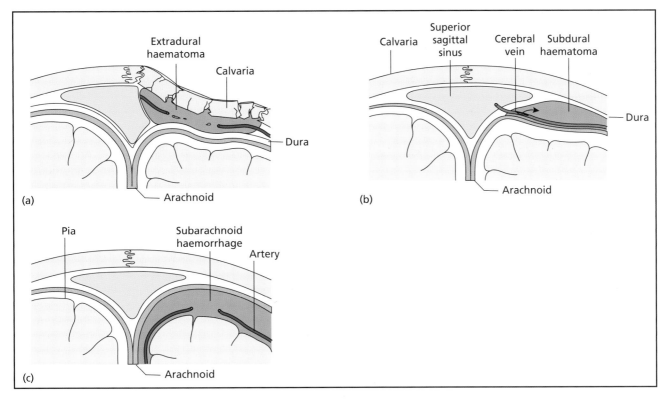

▲ **Fig. 30** Head injuries with various types of intracranial haemorrhage: (**a**) extradural haematoma; (**b**) subdural haematoma; (**c**) subarachnoid haemorrhage.

- Bilateral anosmia caused by transection of the olfactory nerves may be produced in head injuries with a fracture of the anterior cranial fossa.
- Unilateral anosmia may be a sign of a frontal lobe tumour.
- An uncinate type of fit is characterised by olfactory hallucinations.
- Involuntary chewing movements associated with unconsciousness may be a sign of a tumour in the olfactory cortex.

Optic nerve (cranial nerve II)

Impulses produced in the rods and cones of the retina by light reach the visual cortex through the visual pathway (Fig. 31), which consists of the following:

- optic nerve;
- optic chiasma;
- optic tract;
- lateral geniculate body;
- optic radiation;
- visual cortex.

Optic nerve The optic nerve starts at the lamina cribrosa, where the axons of the ganglion cells of the retina pierce the sclera. The nerve fibres, about 1–1.2 million of them, acquire a myelin sheath at this point. The optic nerve, covered by the dura, arachnoid and pia maters, runs in the orbit to enter the middle cranial fossa. The ophthalmic artery accompanies the nerve. In the middle cranial fossa, the two optic nerves unite to form the optic chiasma.

Optic chiasma In the optic nerve, nerve fibres from the temporal half of the retina lie laterally and those from the nasal half lie medially. These medial fibres cross over (decussate) in the chiasma. The left optic tract thus contains fibres from the temporal half of the left retina and the nasal half of the right retina, ie it transmits information from the right half of the visual field (and the right tract from the left half of the visual field).

- The sella turcica containing the pituitary gland lies inferior to the optic chiasma. A tumour of the pituitary may press on the optic chiasma, leading to bitemporal hemianopia.
- The internal carotid artery lies lateral to the optic chiasma. Aneurysm of the artery at this level can rarely compress the lateral fibres in the chiasma, leading to a nasal field defect in the eye on the affected side.

Optic tract The optic tract passes posterolaterally from the chiasma. It forms the anterolateral boundary of

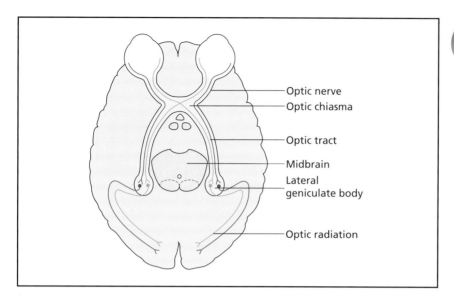

▲ **Fig. 31** The visual pathway.

the interpenduncular fossa, crossing the cerebral peduncle to terminate in the lateral geniculate body. Some fibres enter the midbrain, ending in the superior colliculus or the pretectal nucleus and forming the afferent limb of the light reflex (Fig. 32).

Lateral geniculate body and visual cortex Most fibres in the optic tract end in the lateral geniculate body, which has six layers and, along with the visual cortex, point-to-point representation of the retina. From the lateral geniculate body, fibres

of the optic radiation sweep laterally and backwards to the visual cortex in the occipital lobe (Fig. 31).

The visual cortex lies above and below the calcarine sulcus as well as on the walls of the sulcus. The upper half of the retina is represented on the upper lip of the calcarine fissure and the lower half on the lower lip. The macular region has a greater cortical representation than the peripheral retina, facilitating acuity of vision for the macular region.

Oculomotor nerve (cranial nerve III)

The oculomotor nerve contains two major components:

- somatic motor fibres, which supply the superior, inferior and medial recti, the inferior oblique and the levator palpebrae superioris muscles.

- parasympathetic fibres, which supply the ciliary muscles and the constrictor pupillae.

The path of the oculomotor nerve is shown in Fig. 33. The somatic efferent nucleus and the Edinger–Westphal nucleus (parasympathetic) lie in the midbrain at the level of the superior colliculus. The nerve emerges between two cerebral peduncles, passes between the posterior cerebral and superior cerebellar arteries and runs forwards in the interpeduncular cistern on the lateral side of the posterior communicating artery. It then pierces the dura mater lateral to the posterior clinoid process to lie on the lateral wall of the cavernous sinus (see Fig. 28), before dividing into small superior and large inferior divisions that enter the orbit through the superior orbital fissure.

The superior division of the oculomotor nerve supplies the superior rectus and the levator palpebrae superioris; the inferior division supplies the medial rectus,

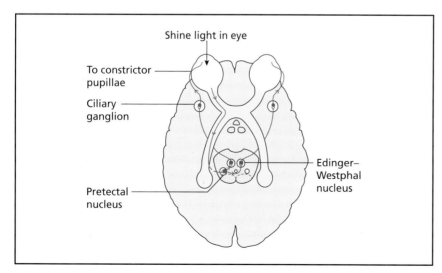

▲ **Fig. 32** The pathway of the light reflex.

inferior rectus and inferior oblique. The parasympathetic fibres from the Edinger–Westphal nucleus leave the branch to the inferior oblique to synapse in the ciliary ganglion. Postganglionic fibres supply the ciliary muscles and sphincter (constrictor) pupillae via the short ciliary nerves.

Complete division of cranial nerve III results in the following.

- Diplopia.
- Ptosis: due to paralysis of the levator palpebrae superioris.
- Divergent squint: caused by unopposed action of the lateral rectus and superior oblique.
- Dilatation of the pupil: results from the unopposed action of dilator pupillae supplied by the sympathetic fibres.
- Loss of accommodation and light reflexes: caused by paralysis of the ciliary muscles and constrictor pupillae (see Fig. 32).

The oculomotor nerve can be paralysed by:

- aneurysms of the posterior cerebral, superior cerebellar or posterior communicating arteries;
- raised intracranial pressure, especially associated with herniation of the uncus into the tentorial notch;
- tumours and inflammatory lesions in the region of the sella turcica.

Trochlear nerve (cranial nerve IV)

The trochlear nerve is the smallest of the cranial nerves. Its somatic motor fibres supply the superior oblique muscle.

The path of the trochlear nerve is shown in Fig. 34. Its nucleus lies in the midbrain at the level of the inferior colliculus; from here axons pass dorsally around the cerebral aqueduct to decussate at the posterior aspect of the brainstem. The nerve then passes anteriorly, lying in the lateral wall of the

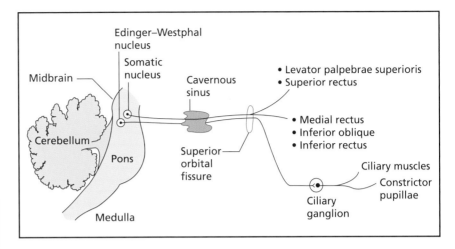

▲**Fig. 33** The path of the oculomotor nerve.

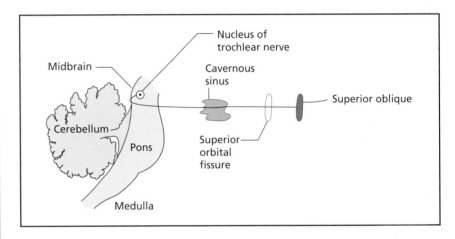

▲**Fig. 34** The pathway of the trochlear nerve.

cavernous sinus below the oculomotor nerve and above the ophthalmic division of the trigeminal nerve (see Fig. 28). It enters the orbit to reach the superior oblique muscle.

When the trochlear nerve is injured, diplopia occurs on looking down and the patient complains of difficulty walking down stairs.

Trigeminal nerve (cranial nerve V)

This is the principal sensory nerve of the head and also innervates the muscles of mastication. It is associated with four

parasympathetic ganglia. Its distribution is as follows:

- sensory to the face, scalp, teeth, mouth, nasal cavity, paranasal sinuses and most of the dura mater;
- motor to the muscles of mastication, mylohyoid, anterior belly of digastric, tensor tympani and tensor palati;
- ganglionic connections to the ciliary, sphenopalatine, otic and submandibular ganglia.

The trigeminal nerve nuclei, ganglion, branches and distribution are shown in Figs 35, 36 and 37.

Motor nucleus The motor nucleus of the trigeminal nerve, which gives

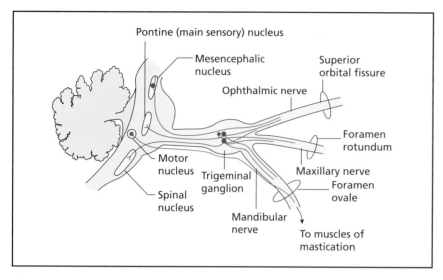

▲ **Fig. 35** The trigeminal nerve nuclei, ganglion and branches.

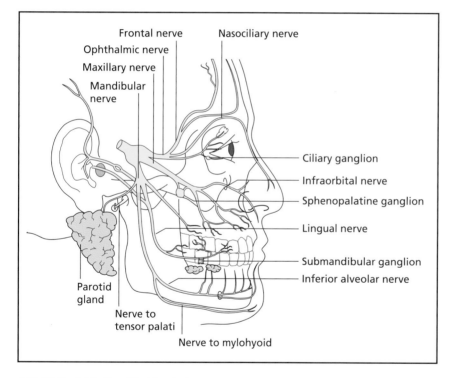

▲ **Fig. 36** The distribution of the trigeminal nerve.

rise to fibres supplying the muscles of mastication and the other muscles listed above, is situated in the upper part of the pons (Fig. 35).

Sensory nuclei There are three sensory nuclei in the brainstem that receive the general somatic afferent fibres of the trigeminal nerve (Fig. 35).

- Mesencephalic nucleus: concerned with proprioception; located in the midbrain.

- Pontine (main sensory) nucleus: concerned with touch, tactile discrimination and position sense.

- Nucleus of the spinal tract: concerned with pain and temperature sensation; located in

the medulla, extending caudally into the upper segments of the spinal cord.

Trigeminal ganglion Most of the cell bodies of the sensory root are located in the trigeminal ganglion, which is also called the semilunar ganglion or the Gasserian ganglion (see Fig. 35). From the convex surface of the ganglion, the ophthalmic, maxillary and mandibular nerves emerge. The motor root joins the mandibular branch.

Ophthalmic nerve This nerve enters the cavernous sinus, lying on its lateral wall (see Fig. 28), and passes to the orbit through the superior orbital fissure (see Fig. 36). Branches supply the conjunctiva, cornea, upper eyelid, forehead, nose and scalp (see Fig. 37). The ciliary ganglion in the orbit is connected to the ophthalmic nerve.

Maxillary nerve From the middle cranial fossa, the maxillary nerve enters the pterygopalatine fossa through the foramen rotundum. It then passes through the inferior orbital fissure, lies on the floor of the orbit as the infraorbital nerve, and passes through the maxillary sinus, emerging on the face through the infraorbital foramen (see Fig. 36). Its branches supply the cheek, lateral aspect of the nose, lower eyelid, upper lip, upper jaw and teeth (see Fig. 37). The sphenopalatine ganglion is connected to the maxillary nerve in the pterygopalatine fossa.

Mandibular nerve This nerve, having both motor and sensory fibres, leaves the skull through the foramen ovale.

- The sensory fibres innervate the auricle and external acoustic meatus, the skin over the mandible, the cheek, the lower lip, the tongue and the floor of the mouth, the lower teeth and the gums (see Fig. 37).

- The motor fibres supply the muscles of mastication, namely the temporalis, masseter, medial pterygoid and lateral pterygoid. Branches from the mandibular division also innervate the tensor tympani and tensor palati, as well as the anterior belly of the digastric and the mylohyoid muscles. Proprioceptive fibres are also contained in the branches innervating the muscles. The submandibular ganglion is connected to the lingual nerve, which is a branch of the mandibular nerve.

The angle of the jaw is supplied by nerve roots C2 and C3, not the trigeminal nerve. In patients with non-organic facial sensory loss, that loss usually extends to the edge of the jaw.

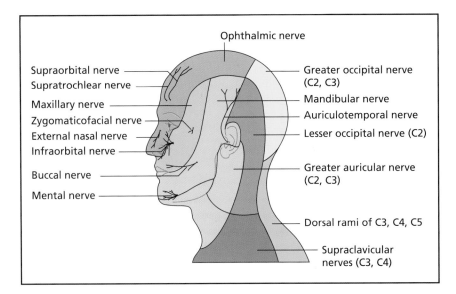

▲ **Fig. 37** The cutaneous supply of the head and neck.

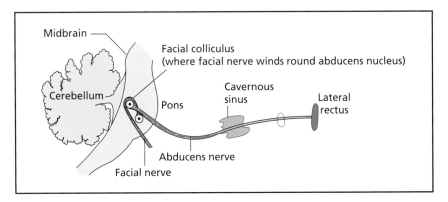

▲ **Fig. 38** The path of the abducens nerve.

Abducens nerve (cranial nerve VI)

The abducens nerve contains somatic motor fibres that supply the lateral rectus muscle. Its path is shown in Fig. 38. Its nucleus lies in the floor of the fourth ventricle in the upper part of the pons, with the fibres of the facial nerve winding around the nucleus to form the facial colliculus (Fig. 39). The abducens nerve emerges on the brainstem at the junction between the medulla and the pons. It then passes forward through the pontine cistern and pierces the dura mater to enter the cavernous sinus, where it lies on the inferolateral aspect of the internal carotid artery (see Fig. 28). The nerve enters the orbit through the tendinous ring at the superior orbital fissure and supplies the lateral rectus muscle.

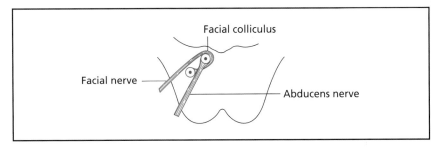

▲ **Fig. 39** Section of the lower part of the pons where the facial nerve winds around the nucleus of the abducens nerve to produce the facial colliculus.

Facial nerve (cranial nerve VII)

The facial nerve supplies the muscles of facial expression. It also conveys parasympathetic fibres to the lacrimal gland, glands in the nasal cavity, and submandibular and sublingual glands, and transmits taste fibres from the anterior two-thirds of the tongue.

The motor nucleus is situated in the lower part of the pons. From here, motor fibres loop around the nucleus of the abducens nerve to form the facial colliculus (Fig. 39) and emerge at the cerebellopontine angle, along with the nervus intermedius, which contains the sensory and parasympathetic fibres.

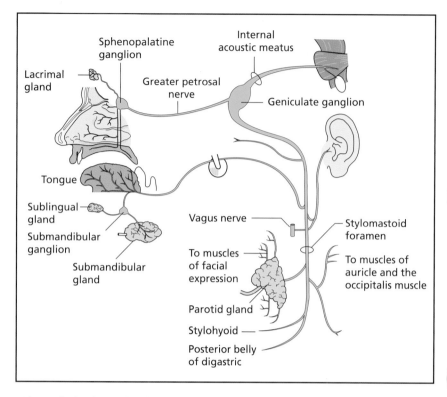

▲**Fig. 40** The distribution of the facial nerve.

The sensory fibres in the nervus intermedius are the central processes of the geniculate ganglion, which synapse in the nucleus of the tractus solitarius in the pons. The nervus intermedius lies lateral to the motor fibres of the facial nerve, in between the facial and the vestibulocochlear nerves. The autonomic fibres originate from the superior salivatory nucleus in the pons.

The distribution of the facial nerve is shown in Fig. 40. The motor fibres and the nervus intermedius pass through the pontine cistern and enter the internal acoustic meatus, where the two join to form the facial nerve. This nerve then passes through the facial canal in the petrous temporal bone, runs laterally over the vestibule to reach the medial wall of the middle ear, where it bends sharply backwards over the promontory. This bend, the genu, is the site of the geniculate ganglion.

From here the nerve passes downwards on the posterior wall of the middle ear, to emerge through the stylomastoid foramen at the base of the skull.

In the petrous temporal bone, the facial nerve produces three branches.

- The greater petrosal nerve transmits preganglionic parasympathetic fibres to the sphenopalatine ganglion. The postganglionic fibres supply the lacrimal gland and the glands in the nasal cavity.

- The nerve to stapedius.

- The chorda tympani nerve carries parasympathetic fibres to the submandibular and sublingual glands, as well as taste fibres from the anterior two-thirds of the tongue.

After emerging from the stylomastoid foramen, the nerve enters the parotid gland and divides

into temporal, zygomatic, buccal, marginal mandibular and cervical branches. These supply the muscles of facial expression. Before entering the parotid gland, the nerve supplies a branch to the posterior belly of the digastric, the stylohyoid and the muscles of the auricle.

- A pontine lesion at the level of the facial colliculus will cause facial nerve paralysis associated with that of the abducens nerve.
- Tinnitus and deafness, along with weakness of the facial muscles and loss of taste sensation, are signs of an acoustic neuroma.

Supranuclear innervation of the facial nerve nucleus

The part of the facial nerve nucleus that supplies the lower part of the face receives input from the opposite cerebral hemisphere; the part supplying the upper part of the face receives bilateral input. Hence:

- in a lower motor neuron facial lesion, the whole of the face is affected;
- in an upper motor neuron facial lesion, only the lower part of the face is affected.

Vestibulocochlear nerve (cranial nerve VIII)

The vestibulocochlear nerve, attached to the brainstem lateral to the facial nerve at the cerebellopontine angle, enters the internal acoustic meatus. At the base of the internal acoustic meatus it breaks up into many rootlets which then pierce the thin medial wall of the vestibule. The vestibular fibres enter the vestibular ganglion, from which fibres pass to innervate the maculae of the utricle and saccule and the cristae of the semicircular ducts.

The cochlear fibres pass into the core of the modiolus and enter the osseous spiral lamina, where the nerve has its spiral ganglion. From this ganglion, fibres pass through the osseous spiral lamina to innervate the hair cells of the organ of Corti (Fig. 41).

Impulses from the auditory nerve reach the auditory nuclei in the brainstem and are transmitted to the inferior colliculus and medial geniculate body of both sides through the trapezoid body and the lateral lemnisci. From here they reach the auditory cortex via auditory radiations (Fig. 42).

Glossopharyngeal nerve (cranial nerve IX)

The glossopharyngeal nerve contains sensory fibres (including taste) from the posterior third of the tongue and the oropharynx (tonsillar fossa). The nerve also supplies the stylopharyngeus muscle, contains parasympathetic fibres innervating the parotid gland, and innervates the carotid sinus and carotid body (Fig. 43).

In the medulla, the glossopharyngeal nerve has the following nuclei.

- Nucleus ambiguus: supplies nerve fibres to the stylopharyngeus muscle. This nucleus, via branches of the vagus nerve, also innervates the muscles of the soft palate, pharynx and larynx.

- Inferior salivatory nucleus: innervates the parotid gland.

- Nucleus of the tractus solitarius: receives taste fibres via the glossopharyngeal nerve (also via the facial nerve).

- Dorsal nucleus of the vagus: the ninth nerve shares, with the vagus, general sensation from the posterior third of the tongue and the oropharynx.

Cranial nerve IX leaves the skull though the jugular foramen and enters the pharynx in the upper part of the neck. Its terminal branches supply the posterior third of the tongue and the tonsillar fossa (Fig. 43).

Vagus nerve (cranial nerve X)

The vagus nerve contains the following sensory fibres:

- fibres from the mucosa of the pharynx and larynx, and those transmitting visceral sensation of the organs in the thorax and abdomen;

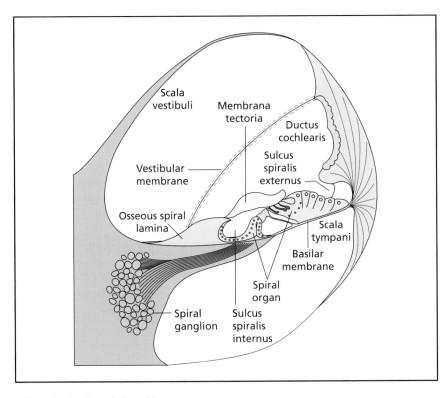

▲ **Fig. 41** Section through the cochlea.

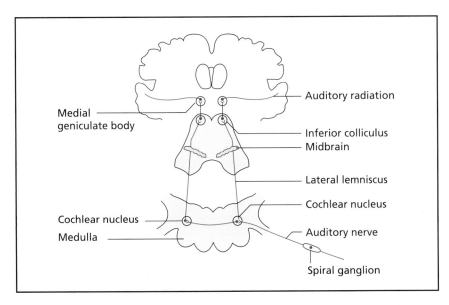

▲ **Fig. 42** The auditory pathway.

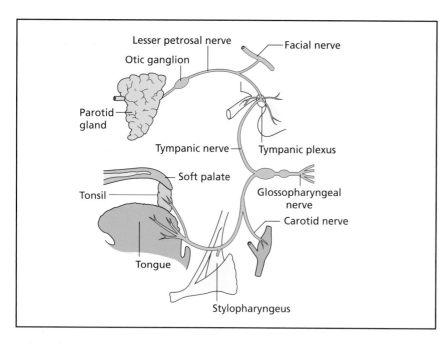

▲ **Fig. 43** The distribution of the glossopharyngeal nerve.

- fibres carrying general sensation from the dura, parts of the external auditory meatus and the external surface of the tympanic membrane;

- fibres carrying taste sensation from the epiglottis.

The vagus nerve also contains preganglionic parasympathetic fibres that go to all the thoracic and abdominal viscera up to the splenic flexure. The cranial part of the accessory nerve, which innervates the muscles of the soft palate,

pharynx and larynx, is also distributed via the vagus.

The following nuclei are associated with the vagus nerve in the brainstem (Fig. 44).

- Dorsal nucleus: situated in the floor of the fourth ventricle in the medulla; it receives general visceral sensation from the various organs supplied by the vagus. Its motor component gives rise to the preganglionic parasympathetic fibres in the vagus.

- Nucleus of the tractus solitarius: shared with the facial nerve and the glossopharyngeal nerve for taste fibres.

- Nucleus ambiguus: from this the fibres of the cranial part of the accessory nerve originate; these are then distributed along with the vagus nerve.

Bulbar and pseudobulbar palsies cause paralysis of these nuclei and hence vagal paralysis.

The vagus emerges from the brainstem in the groove between the olive and the inferior cerebellar peduncle, below the rootlets of the glossopharyngeal nerve; it then passes through the jugular foramen. It bears two ganglia: the superior in the foramen and the inferior after emerging from the foramen. Beyond the inferior ganglion, the cranial part of the accessory nerve joins the vagus.

Branches and distribution The following are the branches of the vagus nerve (Fig. 45).

- Meningeal branch: arises from the superior ganglion and supplies the dura of the posterior cranial fossa.

- Auricular branch: also originates from the superior ganglion and supplies small areas on the medial aspect of the auricle, external auditory meatus and the outer surface of the tympanic membrane.

- Pharyngeal branch: arises from the inferior ganglion and supplies muscles of the soft palate and pharynx.

- Superior laryngeal nerve: divides into the external laryngeal nerve (supplying the cricothyroid muscles) and the internal laryngeal nerve (the sensory nerve of the laryngeal part of the

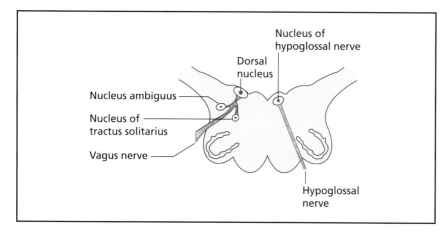

▲ **Fig. 44** Section through the upper part of the medulla showing the nuclei of the vagus and hypoglossal nerves.

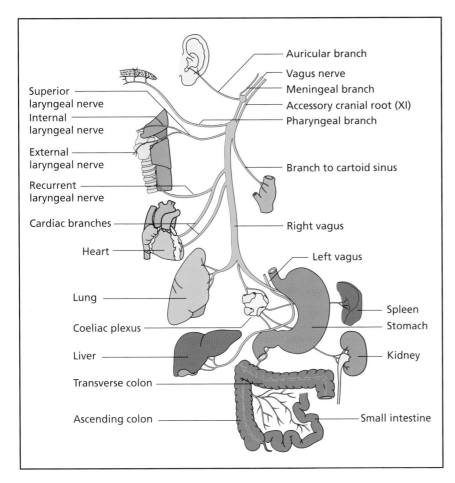

Superior laryngeal nerve
Internal laryngeal nerve
External laryngeal nerve
Recurrent laryngeal nerve
Cardiac branches
Heart
Lung
Coeliac plexus
Liver
Transverse colon
Ascending colon

Auricular branch
Vagus nerve
Meningeal branch
Accessory cranial root (XI)
Pharyngeal branch
Branch to cartoid sinus
Right vagus
Left vagus
Spleen
Stomach
Kidney
Small intestine

▲ **Fig. 45** The distribution of the vagus nerve.

pharynx and the laryngeal mucosa above the level of the vocal cords).

- Recurrent laryngeal nerve: the left nerve winds around the ligamentum arteriosum and the right around the subclavian artery. On both sides, the nerve lies in the groove between the trachea and the oesophagus. The nerves supply all the intrinsic muscles of the larynx, except the cricothyroid, and provide sensory innervation to the mucosa of the larynx below the vocal cords and to the mucosa of the trachea and oesophagus.

- Cardiac branches.

- Pulmonary branches.

- Branches to the abdominal viscera.

Accessory nerve (cranial nerve XI)

The accessory nerve has a small cranial and a larger spinal root.

Cranial root The cranial root arises from the nucleus ambiguus. It joins the spinal root for a short distance and then branches off to rejoin the

vagus and be distributed to the muscles of the soft palate, pharynx and larynx.

Spinal root The spinal root arises from the upper five segments of the cervical part of the spinal cord and enters the skull; here it joins the cranial root and leaves the skull through the jugular foramen. Immediately below the jugular foramen, the spinal root passes backwards to supply the sternocleidomastoid and trapezius muscles.

Hypoglossal nerve (cranial nerve XII)

The hypoglossal nerve supplies all the extrinsic and intrinsic muscles of the tongue. Its nucleus, which gives rise to the somatic motor fibres, lies in the medulla in the floor of the fourth ventricle (Fig. 44). The nerve leaves the skull through the hypoglossal canal.

Pituitary gland

The pituitary gland lies within a bony fossa known as the sella turcica (Fig. 46). The diaphragma sellae, a fold of dura mater, is the roof of the sella turcica and separates the pituitary gland from the optic chiasma.

The pituitary has two main parts: anterior (adenohypophysis) and

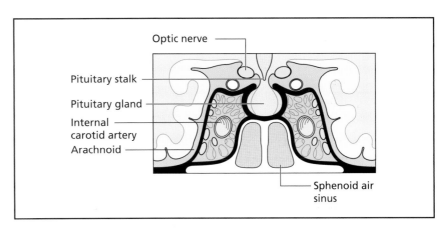

Optic nerve
Pituitary stalk
Pituitary gland
Internal carotid artery
Arachnoid
Sphenoid air sinus

▲ **Fig. 46** Coronal section through the cavernous sinus showing the structures related to the pituitary gland.

posterior (neurohypophysis). There is also a small intermediate lobe.

The relationship of the pituitary to the hypothalamus is shown in Fig. 47. An extensive vascular communication between the two, the hypothalamo-hypophyseal portal system, brings the anterior pituitary under the influence of the hypothalamic hormones. Posterior pituitary hormones are synthesised in the hypothalamic nuclei and reach the posterior pituitary, where they are stored.

A tumour of the pituitary may make the diaphragma sellae bulge or the tumour may break through it, pressing on the optic chiasma and causing characteristic visual field defects.

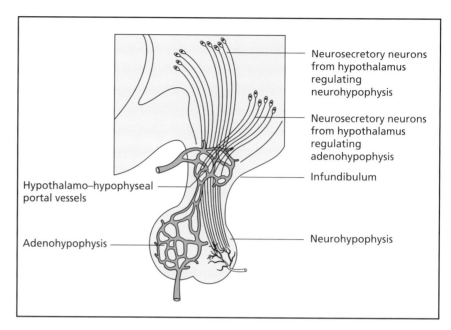

▲ **Fig. 47** The relationship of the pituitary gland to the hypothalamus.

The spinal cord

The spinal cord extends from the lower end of the medulla oblongata, at the level of the foramen magnum, to the lower border of L1 or the upper border of L2 (Fig. 48). The lower part of the cord is tapered to form the conus medullaris, from which a prolongation of pia mater, the filum terminale, passes downwards to attach to the coccyx. The subarachnoid space, which contains CSF, extends to the level of S2. The epidural space outside the dura contains fat and the components of the vertebral venous plexus.

The area of the spinal cord from which a pair of spinal nerves arises is defined as a spinal cord segment. The cord has 31 pairs of spinal nerves and hence 31 segments: 8 cervical, 12 thoracic, 5 lumbar, 5 sacral and 1 coccygeal. The lumbar and sacral nerve roots below the termination of the cord form the cauda equina. A cross-section of the

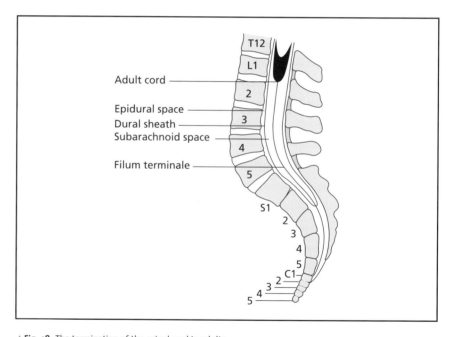

▲ **Fig. 48** The termination of the spinal cord in adults.

spinal cord, showing the meninges, is shown in Fig. 49.

Internal structure of the spinal cord

The grey matter, which contains the sensory and motor nerve cells, is surrounded by the white matter containing the ascending and descending tracts (Fig. 50). The central canal is continuous above with the fourth ventricle. The posterior (dorsal) horn of the grey matter contains the termination of the sensory fibres of the posterior (dorsal) root. The larger anterior (ventral) horn contains motor cells, which give rise to fibres of the anterior (ventral) roots. In the thoracic and upper lumbar regions, there are lateral horns containing the cells of origin of the preganglionic sympathetic fibres.

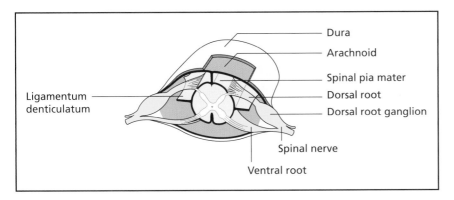

▲ **Fig. 49** The spinal meninges.

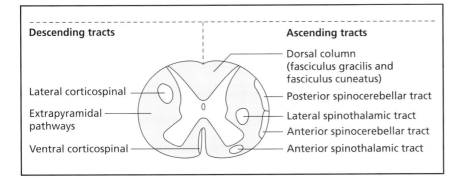

▲ **Fig. 50** Location of the spinal tracts. The descending tracts are shown on the left, the ascending tracts on the right.

The white matter is divided into the dorsal, lateral and ventral funiculi, each containing a number of ascending and descending fibre tracts. Some of the main tracts are briefly described below.

Fasciculus gracilis and fasciculus cuneatus These two tracts form the major components of the dorsal funiculus or dorsal column. They contain fibres that provide fine and discriminative tactile sensation as well as proprioception. The fasciculus gracilis deals mainly with sensations from the lower limb and the cuneate fasciculus with those from the upper limb. Fibres in the dorsal column are uncrossed, carrying sensation from the same side of the body.

Lateral corticospinal tract The corticospinal tracts control skilled voluntary movements and consist of the axons of neurons in the frontal and parietal lobes. These tracts descend through the internal capsule, the basis pedunculi of the midbrain, the pons and pyramid of the medulla, and then cross in the motor decussation in the lower part of the medulla oblongata. Most fibres cross to the opposite side and terminate in laminae IV–VII and IX, forming synaptic connections with motor neurons. The lateral corticospinal tract thus contains axons of the neurons in the contralateral cerebral hemisphere. The fibres in the tract are somatotopically arranged, those for the lower part of the cord being lateral and those for the upper levels medial.

Spinothalamic tract The spinothalamic tract conducts pain and temperature sensation as well as some tactile sensations. It contains crossed ascending axons of the neurons lying in the grey matter of the opposite half of the spinal cord. These axons cross in the midline, close to the central canal in the ventral grey commissure. Many of the fibres give collaterals to the reticular nuclei in the brainstem as they ascend, and they finally terminate in the thalamic nuclei. The fibres are somatotopically arranged; those for the lower limb are superficial and those for the upper limb deepest.

Fibres carrying pain and other sensations from the internal organs are carried in the spinoreticular tract, which terminates in the reticular formation in the medulla and pons.

Ventral corticospinal tract The ventral corticospinal tract, which lies in the ventral funiculus, contains corticospinal fibres that remain uncrossed in the motor decussation in the medulla. These fibres eventually cross the midline at segmental levels and terminate close to those in the lateral corticospinal tract.

Blood supply of the spinal cord

The blood supply of the spinal cord is derived from the anterior and posterior spinal arteries. The anterior spinal artery supplies the whole of the cord in front of the posterior grey column. The posterior spinal arteries, usually one on either side posteriorly, supply the posterior grey columns and the dorsal columns on either side.

The spinal arteries are reinforced at segmental levels by radicular arteries from the vertebral, ascending cervical, posterior intercostal, lumbar and sacral arteries. The radicular arteries enter the vertebral canal through the intervertebral foramina, accompanying the spinal nerves and their ventral and dorsal roots. These arteries may be compromised in resection of segments of the aorta in aneurysmal surgery.

> Occlusion of the anterior spinal artery, caused by infarcts or fracture of the vertebral body, can result in an anterior cord syndrome with paralysis and loss of pain and temperature sensation below the level of the lesion. However, there is preservation of light touch and proprioception, because these are carried in the dorsal columns that are supplied by the posterior spinal artery.

Segmental innervation

Knowledge of the dermatomes (segmental innervation of the skin) and myotomes (segmental innervation of muscles) is important when testing for nerve root compression and assessing the level of spinal cord injuries (Fig. 51).

Upper limb The dermatomes of the brachial plexus are as follows:

- upper segments (C5, C6) are on the lateral aspect;

- lower segments (C8, T1) are on the medial aspect;

- C7 is in the middle.

There is considerable overlap across adjoining dermatomes, but there is no overlap across the axial line.

The pattern of the myotomes is more complex, but there is a proximal to distal gradient.

- Shoulder: C5.

- Elbow flexors (biceps): C5 and C6.

- Elbow extensors (triceps): C7 and C8.

- Intrinsic muscles of the hand: T1.

Lower limb The dermatomes of the lower limb lie in a numerical

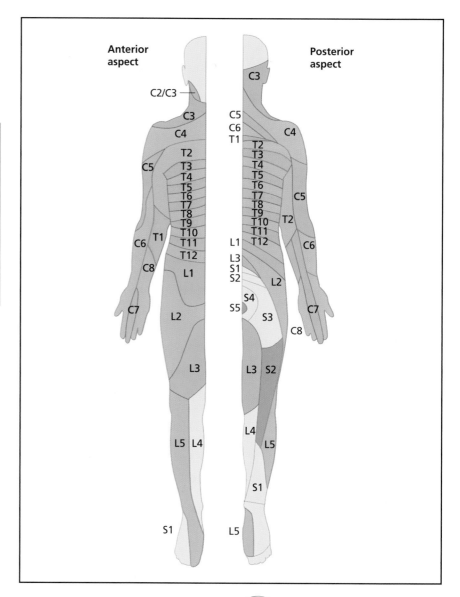

▲ **Fig 51** The dermatomes of the body.

sequence downwards at the front of the limb and upwards on its posterior aspect. The myotomes are as follows.

- Hip: L2 and L3 are flexors; L4 and L5 are extensors.

- Knee: L3 and L4 are extensors; L5 and S1 are flexors.

- Ankle: L4 and L5 are dorsiflexors; S1 and S2 are plantar flexors.

Hence the segments tested by the knee jerk are L3 and L4 and by the ankle jerk S1 and S2.

> **Distribution of dermatomes**
> - C7: middle finger.
> - T4: nipple.
> - T10: umbilicus.
> - L1: inguinal region.
> - S1: sole of the foot.

FURTHER READING

General anatomy
Ellis H. *Clinical Anatomy: a Revision and Applied Anatomy for Clinical Students*, 11th edn. Oxford: Blackwell Science, 2006.

- - - - - - - - - - - - - -

Neuroanatomy
Patten J. *Neurological Differential Diagnosis*, 2nd edn. London: Springer-Verlag, 1996.

10.1 Self-assessment questions

Question 1
The left anterior descending artery:

Answers
A Is a branch of the right coronary artery
B Supplies all of the interventricular septum
C Gives off the acute marginal artery
D Gives off the diagonal artery
E Supplies the sinoatrial node in 90% of individuals

Question 2
With regard to the intrahepatic circulation:

Answers
A Of the total blood supply of the liver, 25% is carried by the portal vein and the remaining 75% by the hepatic artery
B The central terminal veins are tributaries of the portal vein
C The sinusoids drain into the portal vein
D The sinusoids are also called spaces of Disse
E The space of Disse is bordered by hepatocytes and endothelial cells

Question 3
Regarding the parathyroid glands:

Answers
A There are usually two glands
B They develop from the third and fourth branchial pouches
C They are supplied by the superior thyroid artery
D They lie in the anterior part of the thyroid gland
E The oxyphil cells of the gland produce thyrocalcitonin

Question 4
The posterior cerebral artery:

Answers
A Is a branch of the internal carotid artery
B Is connected to the internal carotid artery by the anterior communicating artery
C Supplies the visual cortex
D If occluded unilaterally, causes bitemporal hemianopia
E Is closely related to the trochlear nerve

Question 5
Complete transection of the oculomotor nerve results in:

Answers
A Inability to shut the eye
B Convergent squint
C Constriction of pupil
D Loss of accommodation but not light reflex
E Diplopia

Question 6
The facial nerve:

Answers
A Emerges through the jugular foramen
B Lies deep to the parotid gland
C Parasympathetic fibres synapse in the geniculate ganglion
D The chorda tympani nerve is one of its branches
E If the upper part of the face is spared, the lesion is at the facial colliculus

Question 7
With regard to the retina:

Answers
A The optic disc lies medial to the macula lutea
B The optic disc is paler in colour than normal when there is papilloedema
C Its blood supply comes from the branches of the choroidal arteries and the central artery of the retina
D Branches of the arteries anastomose
E Arteries normally pulsate but veins do not

Question 8
The subarachnoid space:

Answers
A Lies between the dura and the arachnoid mater
B Extends along the whole length of the optic nerve
C Contains the cerebral arteries but not the veins
D Contains the choroid plexus producing the cerebrospinal fluid
E Does not extend beyond the lower end of the spinal cord

Question 9
With regard to the anatomy of the bronchial tree:

Answers

A The left main bronchus is more vertical than the right one

B The left main bronchus divides into three lobar bronchi, whereas the right only into two

C The bronchi and bronchioles have walls consisting of cartilage and smooth muscle

D The bronchi have submucous glands but not the bronchioles

E The arterial supply is derived from the pulmonary arteries

Question 10

On palpation there is a mass in the left flank. Which one of the following statements is *not* correct?

Answers

A The spleen moves on respiration, but the kidney does not

B The spleen can have a notch, but the kidney does not

C The spleen cannot be balloted, but the kidney can

D The spleen is dull to percussion, but the kidney is resonant

E It is impossible to palpate above the spleen

10.2 Self-assessment answers

Answer to Question 1

D

The left anterior descending artery is a branch of the left coronary. It gives off the obtuse marginal artery and the diagonal arteries. The interventricular septum is supplied both by anterior and posterior (often from the right coronary) descending branches. The sinoatrial node is supplied by the right coronary or the circumflex branch of the left.

Answer to Question 2

E

The portal vein transports about 75% of blood to the liver and about 25% is supplied via the hepatic artery. The terminal veins into which the sinusoids drain are tributaries of the hepatic veins.

Answer to Question 3

B

There are usually four parathyroid glands. They are located towards the posterior aspect of the thyroid gland and are supplied by branches from the inferior thyroid artery.

Answer to Question 4

C

The posterior cerebral artery is the terminal branch of the basilar artery, which in turn is formed by the union of the two vertebral arteries. The posterior communicating artery connects the internal carotid artery and the posterior cerebral. It is closely related to the oculomotor nerve. If occluded it causes contralateral homonymous hemianopia.

Answer to Question 5

E

Oculomotor nerve paralysis causes ptosis, divergent squint due to unopposed action of lateral rectus and superior oblique, and dilatation of pupil. Both accommodation and light reflexes are lost. Shutting the eye is a function of the facial (VII) nerve.

Answer to Question 6

D

Sparing the upper part of the face is a sign of an upper motor neuron facial lesion. A lesion at the facial colliculus will cause a lower motor neuron paralysis of the facial and abducens nerves. After emerging from the stylomastoid foramen the nerve runs within the parotid gland.

Answer to Question 7

A

The optic disc lies medial to the macula. It is normally paler in colour compared with the rest of the retina but becomes pinker when there is papilloedema. The arterial supply of the retina is solely from the central artery, with no anastomosis between its branches. The retinal arteries do not normally pulsate but the veins do.

Answer to Question 8

B

The subarachnoid space between the arachnoid and the pia extends along the whole length of the optic nerve. It contains the cerebral arteries and veins and the cerebrospinal fluid. The choroid plexuses are in the ventricles.

Answer to Question 9

D

The right bronchus is more vertical and divides into three lobar bronchi. Bronchioles do not have cartilage on their walls but do have smooth muscle. The bronchi have submucous glands but not the bronchioles.

Answer to Question 10

A

The spleen moves towards the right iliac fossa on inspiration, whereas the kidney moves straight up and down.

PHYSIOLOGY

Authors:

JD Firth, SJ Fowler, M Gurnell, GM Hirschfield, PR Roberts and NS Ward

Editor:

JD Firth

Editor-in-Chief:

JD Firth

1.1 The heart as a pump

For over 70 years, in many cases, the human heart beats at an average of 70 bpm and pumps about 5–6 L of blood around the body each minute. This requires the following:

- a robust electrical means of generating the heartbeat;

- a mechanism for transmitting this information to the muscle pump in a coordinated way;

- a muscle that does not get tired.

Generation of the heartbeat

Pacemaker tissue

Specialised cells in the heart have an inherent ability to discharge rhythmically. After each impulse their membrane potential declines spontaneously to reach the threshold for the action potential, and another impulse is generated. This is shown in Fig. 1.

The mechanism of this behaviour is as follows.

1. At the peak of each impulse an outward potassium current (I_K) begins and causes repolarisation, whereupon it declines.

2. Transient (T) calcium channels then open and an inward calcium current leads to gradual depolarisation of the membrane, the 'prepotential'.

3. When the membrane has depolarised to a critical degree, long-lasting (L) calcium channels open and an increased inward calcium current generates the action potential. The inward sodium current plays little part in this tissue.

Pacemaker cells are found in the following.

- Sinoatrial node: these pacemaker cells have the fastest rate of spontaneous depolarisation and normally set the pace of the heart.

- Atrioventricular node and Purkinje tissue: these cells depolarise spontaneously at a slower rate than those in the sinoatrial node. They take over if the sinoatrial node ceases to function, or control the ventricular rate if the atrioventricular node fails to conduct atrial impulses into the ventricle (complete heart block).

Cardiac action potential

The mechanism of the nerve action potential is discussed in detail in Section 4.1. The action potential in the His–Purkinje system and atrial and ventricular myocardium is similar to this, ie rapid depolarisation is caused by a fast inward sodium current, but an important difference is that the cardiac action potential lasts much longer: 200–300 ms compared with a few milliseconds. The form of the action potential in the cardiac myocyte is shown in Fig. 2.

Electrical conducting system of the heart

The impulse-generating and -conducting system of the heart is shown in Fig. 3. The sequence of events is as follows.

1. The sinoatrial node in the upper right atrium depolarises.

2. The action potential spreads across the atrial syncytium, causing atrial systole.

3. Conduction to the ventricles occurs only through the atrioventricular node.

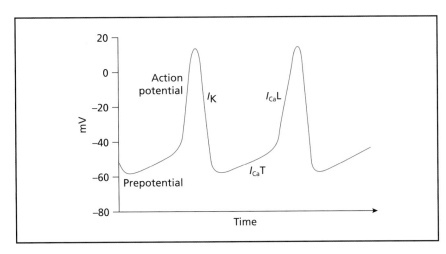

▲ **Fig. 1** The membrane potential of pacemaker tissue. I_{Ca}L, inward calcium current through long-lasting channels; I_{Ca}T, inward calcium current through transient channels; I_K, outward potassium current.

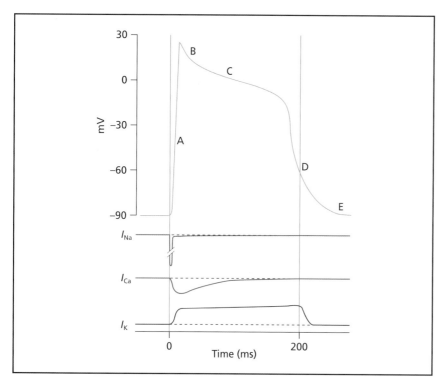

▲ **Fig. 2** Phases of the action potential of a cardiac muscle fibre. (A) Depolarisation results from Na⁺ influx through rapidly opening Na⁺ channels. (C) Ca²⁺ influx through more slowly opening calcium channels produces the plateau. (B, D, E) Polarisation is caused by K⁺ efflux through several different types of K⁺ channel.

4. The impulse passes down the bundle of His, into the right bundle branch and the two branches of the left bundle, to the Purkinje fibres and then to the cardiac myocytes.

Cardiac muscle

The pumping of blood by the heart is driven by contraction of cardiac myocytes, which are arranged in bundles called myofibres. Each cardiac myocyte contains many contractile elements called myofibrils. Sarcomeres are the functional subunits of the myofibrils and are made up of thick and thin filaments (Fig. 4).

Every thick filament is composed of about 300 myosin molecules, each of which ends in a bilobed myosin head. Each thin filament has a tropomyosin backbone around which are wound two helical chains of actin. Troponin complexes (T, C and I) are positioned every 38 nm:

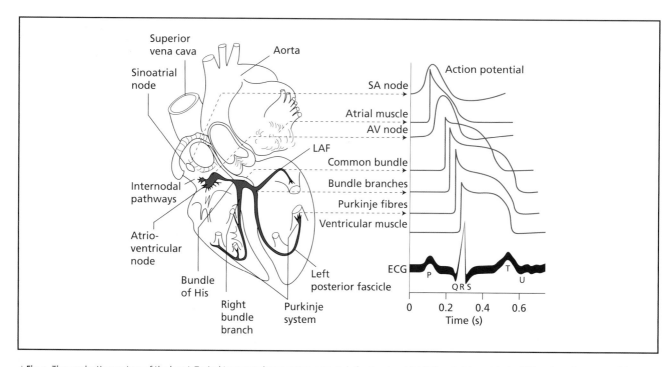

▲ **Fig. 3** The conducting system of the heart. Typical transmembrane action potentials for the sinoatrial (SA) and atrioventricular (AV) nodes, other parts of the conduction system, and the atrial and ventricular muscles are shown, along with the correlation to the ECG. LAF, left anterior fascicle.

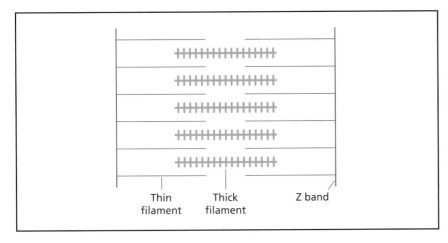

Calcium promotes the binding of myosin heads (thick filaments) to actin (thin filaments). A calcium-sensitive ATPase in the myosin heads generates the energy required for relative motion of thick and thin filaments, leading to contraction of the muscle.

The cardiac cycle

The events of the cardiac cycle are shown in Fig. 5.

▲ **Fig. 4** Schematic diagram of sarcomere structure. Movement of thick and thin filaments relative to one another leads to muscle contraction.

- troponin T binds the whole troponin complex to tropomyosin;

- troponin I inhibits contraction;

- troponin C binding counteracts (and therefore regulates) troponin I.

The thin filaments are anchored to the Z line at one end and interdigitate with thick filaments at the other.

> Bedside tests for the measurement of serum troponin levels can be used to diagnose myocardial infarction; negative testing in appropriate clinical circumstances indicates patients at very low risk of coronary events (see *Cardiology*, Sections 1.4.3, 2.1.2 and 2.1.3).

Mechanism of contraction

As indicated in Fig. 2, depolarisation opens calcium channels in the myocyte cell membrane to admit a small amount of extracellular calcium. This triggers sudden release of much more calcium from intracellular stores in the sarcoplasmic reticulum.

▶ **Fig. 5** Events of the cardiac cycle at a heart rate of 75 bpm. The phases of the cardiac cycle are (A) atrial systole (AS), (B) isovolumic ventricular contraction, (C) ventricular ejection, (D) isovolumic ventricular relaxation and (E) ventricular filling. See text for further details.

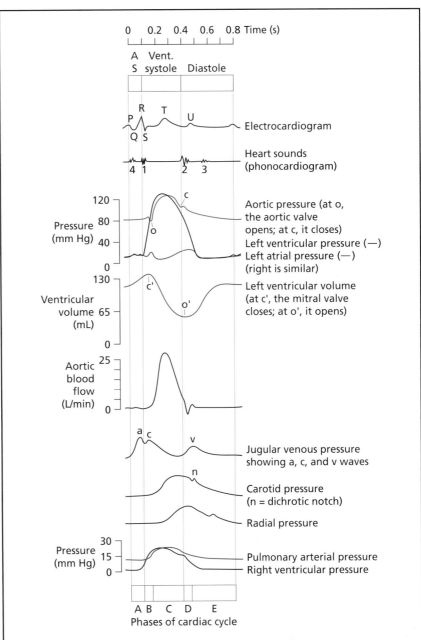

A Atrial contraction provides a final boost to left ventricular (LV) filling just before the onset of LV contraction.

B The left ventricle begins to contract and rising LV pressure closes the mitral valve (MV). This produces the first heart sound and marks the onset of cardiac systole. Isovolumic contraction refers to the build-up of LV pressure after MV closure, but before aortic valve opening.

C Aortic valve opening is followed by rapid ejection, during which LV pressure reaches a peak and then begins to fall. When pressure in the aorta exceeds that in the left ventricle, the aortic valve closes. This produces the aortic component of the second heart sound and marks the end of systole.

D Isovolumic relaxation refers to the continued relaxation of the ventricle after aortic valve closure, but before MV opening.

E When LV pressure falls below left atrial (LA) pressure, the mitral valve opens and early filling occurs. As LA and LV pressures equalise, filling stops (diastasis).

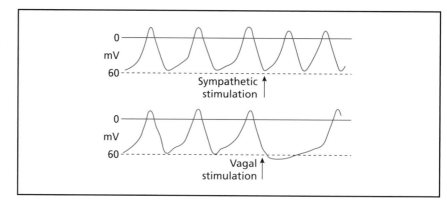

▲ **Fig. 6** Effect of sympathetic (noradrenergic) and vagal (cholinergic) stimulation on the membrane potential of the sinoatrial node.

- Most LV filling occurs during the rapid or early phase of diastole and it is this that produces a physiological third heart sound.
- Atrial systole becomes important when a high cardiac output is required or when there is impaired LV relaxation, eg hypertrophy.
- The ECG R wave occurs just before mitral valve closure and therefore marks the end of cardiac diastole.

Physiological factors governing cardiac output

Variation in cardiac output can be produced by changes in:

- heart rate;
- Stroke volume.

Control of cardiac rate

The heart rate under physiological circumstances varies between about 45 and 200 bpm, although fit athletes may have a resting pulse rate slower than this. An increase in heart rate is the usual and most effective way of increasing cardiac output and is determined primarily by cardiac innervation.

- Parasympathetic nerves: under normal conditions, the vagus actively slows the heart rate (Fig. 6). Atropine, which blocks the action of acetylcholine (the chemical released by vagal nerve endings in the heart), causes an increase in heart rate.

- Sympathetic nerves: activation leads to an increase in heart rate (Fig. 6).

Control of stroke volume

Starling's law

Within wide limits, the output of the heart is independent of arterial resistance and temperature; up to a certain point, the output of the heart is proportional to the venous inflow.

The stroke volume of the heart is governed by the following.

- Preload: the pressure that fills the ventricles. Stretch induces fibre lengthening and enhances contractility, as stated by Starling. It probably does this by increasing the sensitivity of the myofilaments to calcium.

- Afterload: the resistance against which the ventricles pump.

- Inotropic state: a positive inotrope is something that makes the ventricle work harder with a given filling pressure; a negative inotrope has the opposite effect. Sympathetic nerve stimuli have a positive inotropic action, while parasympathetic nerve stimuli are negatively inotropic.

The effects of varying preload and of inotropes on cardiac work are shown in Fig. 7.

Catecholamines

Catecholamines, such as adrenaline (epinephrine) and noradrenaline, act on the heart through β-adrenergic receptors (predominantly β_1). They increase contractility (inotropic) and heart rate (chronotropic). Second messengers (intracellular signal transduction) include G proteins, adenylyl cyclase, cyclic AMP and protein kinase A, which act in concert to increase intracellular calcium. They can, within limits, improve the performance of a failing heart (see Fig. 7) up to a point.

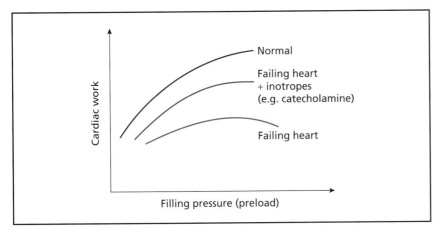

▲ **Fig. 7** Relationship between preload and cardiac work.

Response of the heart to stress

Cardiac myocytes are incapable of dividing (except in the fetal heart) and so any increase in heart muscle mass is accomplished by an increase in cardiac myocyte size, ie hypertrophy rather than hyperplasia (Table 1). The heart responds to any kind of long-term stress (physiological or pathological) by undergoing hypertrophy (Table 2 and Fig. 8).

- Hypertrophy occurs as a response to virtually any heart muscle disorder: initially compensatory, but then detrimental with diastolic dysfunction and increased risk of dysrhythmia.
- Concentric and eccentric hypertrophy are named after the effect that they have on the position of the apex beat. Concentric hypertrophy occurs in a pressure-overloaded ventricle, eg hypertension, aortic stenosis. The apical impulse is prominent but not displaced. Eccentric hypertrophy occurs in a volume-overloaded ventricle, eg mitral or aortic regurgitation. The apical impulse is prominent but is also displaced laterally.

TABLE 1 **FEATURES OF HYPERTROPHY AT VARIOUS ANATOMICAL LEVELS IN THE HEART**

Anatomical level	Manifestation of hypertrophy
Cellular (cardiac myocyte)	Induction of early response genes encoding transcription factors Induction of genes normally only expressed in fetal life, eg atrial natriuretic factor in the ventricle Up-regulation of contractile protein genes General increase in cell protein/RNA
Tissue	Increase in size but not number of cardiac myocytes Increased number of non-myocytes, eg fibroblasts Increased production of extracellular matrix
Organ	Increased muscle mass Initial compensation for stress/heart muscle injury Diastolic dysfunction[1] Arrhythmic tendency[1]

1 In pathological hypertrophy only.

TABLE 2 **TYPES OF CARDIAC MYOCYTE GROWTH RESPONSE**

Type of growth response	Manifestation of growth response
Hyperplasia	Increased cardiac myocyte number during growth *in utero*
Maturational growth	Increased cardiac myocyte size during cardiac growth in childhood
Physiological hypertrophy	Increased cardiac myocyte size during adaptation to physical training
Pathological hypertrophy	Increased cardiac myocyte size to compensate for heart muscle damage (eg myocardial infarction) or excessive cardiac workload (eg hypertension, valve dysfunction)

FURTHER READING

Ganong WF. *Review of Medical Physiology*, 22nd edn. London: Lange Medical Books, 2005.

Hunter JJ and Chien KR. Signalling pathways for cardiac hypertrophy and failure. *N Engl J Med* 2000; 341: 1276–83.

Opie LH. Mechanisms of cardiac contraction and relaxation. In: Zipes DP, Libby P, Bonow RO and Braunwald E, eds. *Braunwald's Heart Disease: a Textbook of Cardiovascular Medicine*. Philadelphia: Elsevier Saunders, 2005: 457–89.

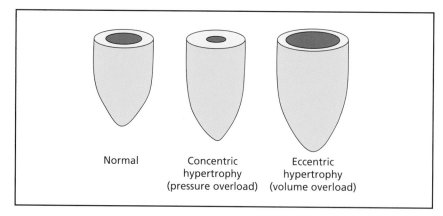

▲ **Fig. 8** Patterns of left ventricular hypertrophy. In concentric hypertrophy, the ventricular wall thickens with a relative diminution of the lumen. Eccentric hypertrophy is characterised by a thickened ventricular wall accompanied by dilatation of the lumen.

1.2 The systemic and pulmonary circulations

The cardiovascular system exists to satisfy the metabolic requirements of the tissues via the maintenance of adequate cardiac output and therefore of blood pressure.

Blood pressure (BP) and cardiac output (CO) are related by the following formula:

$$BP = CO \times TPR$$

where TPR is the total peripheral resistance of the circulation.

The circulation is made up of several different types of blood vessel, each with its own function. Normal pressures at different sites in the circulation are shown in Table 3.

Systemic circulation

Large conduit arteries
These arteries are elastic in order to absorb the pressure peaks associated with intermittent cardiac ejection and thus convert pulsatile flow to continuous distal flow.

Resistance vessels
These smaller arteries and arterioles are the major contributors to peripheral resistance because resistance and vessel radius are related as follows:

$$\text{Resistance} \propto 1/\text{radius}^4 \text{ (Laplace's law)}$$

Thus, a small decrease in radius causes a very large increase in resistance.

Differential resistance throughout the arterial tree allows differential distribution of the circulation in response to local metabolic requirements. Systemic vasomotor activity is controlled by:

- the autonomic nervous system;

- local endothelial and vascular smooth muscle factors (see Section 1.3).

Capillaries
These form a large total surface area for blood/tissue exchange. Fluid transfer across the vascular endothelium depends on the balance between outward haemodynamic pressure and inward oncotic pressure (Starling's law).

Veins
These are thin-walled capacitance vessels holding two-thirds of the blood volume at any time. They return blood to the heart by the external pump of skeletal muscle contraction, aided by one-way valves.

Pulmonary circulation
The lungs receive venous blood for gas exchange from the pulmonary arteries and their own small arterial supply through the bronchial circulation.

The normal pulmonary circulation:

- is high flow;

- is low resistance;

- accommodates increases in cardiac output, with minimal change in pressure.

As in the systemic circulation, the major contributors to vascular resistance are the small arteries and arterioles. Pulmonary vascular resistance is normally only about 10% of systemic vascular resistance.

The most potent stimuli of pulmonary vasoconstriction are hypoxia and acidosis. In contrast

TABLE 3 NORMAL PRESSURES IN THE CIRCULATION			
Site in circulation	Systolic (mmHg)	Diastolic (mmHg)	Mean (mmHg)
Right atrium			0–8
Right ventricle	15–30	2–10	
Pulmonary artery	15–30	8	
Left atrium			1–10
Left ventricle	100–140	3–12	
Aorta	100–140	60–90	70–105

to the systemic circulation, the autonomic nervous system has no significant role in controlling pulmonary vascular resistance.

1.3 Blood vessels

The blood vessels comprising the circulation are not just conduits conveying blood to and from tissues; they possess complex and finely balanced systems for controlling blood flow and preventing thrombosis and haemostasis. They participate in several metabolic pathways and can respond to injury by releasing pro-inflammatory mediators and directing inflammatory cells to where they are needed. Most of these functions are orchestrated by the endothelium.

Anatomy

Arteries are composed of three main histological layers.

1. Intima: a layer of tightly bound endothelial cells separates the lumen from the basal elastic lamina. This lamina, made up of areolar and elastic tissue, is more prominent in medium and large arteries, reflecting their role as conduits.

2. Media: layers of vascular smooth muscle cells secrete, and are embedded within, a dense matrix of collagen, elastin and glycosaminoglycans. The thickness of this layer varies with the size of the artery. An external elastic lamina separates the adventitia from the media.

3. Adventitia: this outermost layer contains fibroblasts within a meshwork of elastin, collagen and smooth muscle fibres.

Blood supply

The adventitia and outer layers of the media receive their blood from the vasa vasorum, small arteries that enter from outside the vessel. The inner layers of the media and the intima are supplied by intimal blood.

Endothelium

The endothelium comprises one of the largest organs in the body, with a total luminal surface area greater than 500 m². Its major function is to mediate communication between the blood and vessel walls. Endothelial cells detect physical and chemical signals in the lumen, translating them into chemical messages that are understood by the underlying smooth muscle or passing blood cells. Large numbers of receptors for circulating hormones, local mediators and vasoactive factors are expressed on the endothelial cell membrane. Physical stimuli,

such as membrane stretch or shear stress, lead to the opening of specific cation channels which hyperpolarise the cell.

Smooth muscle cell layer

The vascular smooth muscle provides the tone of the vessel and secretes a complex matrix that gives the vessel its tensile strength and elasticity. The walls of large conduit arteries, eg the aorta, contain more elastic tissue, whereas resistance vessels are more muscular.

Regulation of vascular tone is immensely complex and the end-result of the integration of a large number of competing vasoconstrictor and vasodilator forces (Table 4).

The endothelium

The key to the function of blood vessels is the endothelium. Changes in vascular tone, controlled by

TABLE 4 REGULATION OF VASCULAR TONE. THE REGULATION OF VASCULAR TONE IS IMMENSELY COMPLEX. VESSELS ARE RICHLY INNERVATED AND A WIDE VARIETY OF NON-ADRENERGIC NON-CHOLINERGIC (NANC) NERVES HAVE CENTRAL AND/OR PERIPHERAL ACTION, MOST OF WHICH ARE POORLY UNDERSTOOD

Response	Type	Example
Vasoconstriction	Mechanical	Intrinsic mycocyte response to stretch
	Endothelial	Endothelin Angiotensin-converting enzyme Some prostanoids, eg thromboxane
	α-Adrenoceptor activation	Sympathetic nervous system
	Hormonal	Angiotensin II Vasopressin (ADH)
Vasodilatation	Endothelial	Nitric oxide Some prostanoids, eg prostacyclin, PGE_2 Other substances
	β-Adrenoceptor activation	Occurs in muscles in exercise
	Hormonal	Atrial natriuretic peptide
	Metabolic	Adenosine

ADH, antidiuretic hormone; PGE_2, prostaglandin E_2.

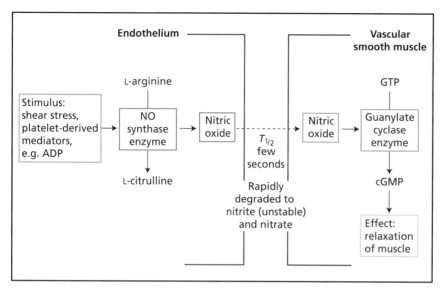

▲**Fig. 9** Production and action of nitric oxide (NO) as a vasodilator. ADP, adenosine diphosphate; cGMP, cyclic guanosine monophosphate; GTP, guanosine triphosphate.

release of vasoconstrictor and vasodilator mediators, allows the vessel to respond to changes in the local environment.

Vasodilator function

The main vasomotor influence of the endothelium is as a dilator. If the layer of endothelial cells is removed, the vessel constricts. The continuous basal release of vasodilator agents from the endothelium counteracts the tonic constriction produced by the sympathetic nervous system.

The major vasodilator is nitric oxide, synthesised from L-arginine by the action of nitric oxide synthase (Fig. 9). Nitric oxide has a half-life of only a few seconds and is produced continuously by the endothelium. The physiological stimuli underlying this process are largely unknown, although shear stress and platelet-derived mediators are thought to have a role. Several pharmacological agents also stimulate nitric oxide release, namely acetylcholine, bradykinin and substance P; these are used in the experimental assessment of endothelial function.

Vasoconstrictor function

The main vasoconstrictor released by the endothelium is endothelin-1 (Fig. 10), which is the most potent vasoconstrictor known. In healthy vessels, its concentration is too low to promote constriction.

Hypoxia, thrombus and transforming growth factor (TGF)-β are physiological stimuli for the release of endothelin-1. It may have a role in some diseases, in particular myocardial infarction, hypertension, diabetes, renal failure and Raynaud's disease.

Regulation of platelet function and haemostasis

The healthy endothelium releases a variety of mediators that are antithrombotic and prevent the formation of thrombus on healthy vessel walls, whereas damaged endothelium produces prothrombotic factors to effect haemostasis (Fig. 11). Platelets are particularly important in this process. They respond to damaged endothelium by changing their shape, transforming from a discoid shape to a sphere with dendritic extensions that facilitate adhesion to the damaged endothelium. Platelets have a major role in

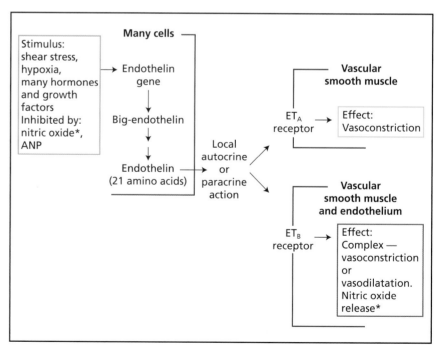

▲**Fig. 10** Production and action of endothelin as a vasoconstrictor. There are three separate endothelin genes encoding three separate endothelins. Differences (if any) between the actions of these isoforms are not well understood. Asterisks indicate negative feedback system. ANP, atrial natriuretic peptide.

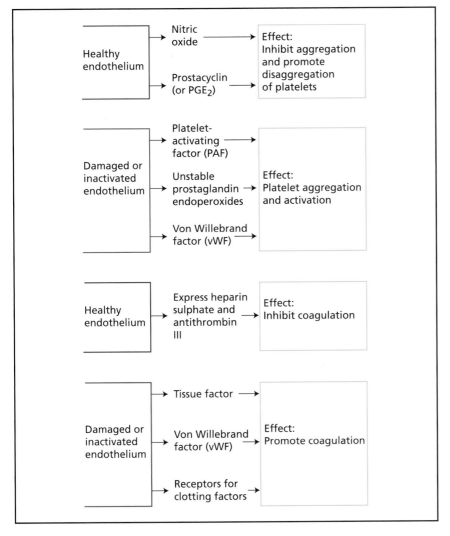

Fig. 11 Effect of endothelium on platelets and coagulation. The endothelium also releases thrombolytic (eg urokinase, tissue plasminogen activator) and antithrombolytic (eg plasminogen activator inhibitor) factors. In health, thrombolytic factors are dominant.

thrombus formation associated with acute coronary syndromes. This has led to the widespread use of antiplatelet agents in these clinical circumstances, including aspirin, clopidogrel and glycoprotein IIb/IIIa inhibitors, eg abciximab and tirofiban.

Cellular adhesion
The resting endothelium prevents cells from adhering fully to, or migrating into, the vessel wall, although leucocytes are allowed to roll along its surface. In response to damage or inflammation, the endothelium attracts and encourages the passage of appropriate cell types into the vessel wall (Fig. 12).

Cell growth
In the healthy artery, proliferation of vascular smooth muscle is actively inhibited.

- Vasodilators released by the endothelium and antiplatelet and antithrombotic mediators, particularly heparan sulphate and

TGF-β, inhibit proliferation of underlying smooth muscle.

- Damaged and activated endothelial cells may produce vasoconstricting prothrombotic mediators, which will promote smooth muscle proliferation.

Cytokines
The endothelium participates in the inflammatory response, producing several cytokines and other pro-inflammatory molecules. Receptors for a broad range of cytokines are present, allowing modulation of endothelial activity.

- In response to endotoxin, endothelial cells release interleukin (IL)-1, IL-6 and IL-8. In a similar fashion, tumour necrosis factor (TNF) is released by vascular smooth muscle cells.

- Circulating and locally produced cytokines alter the balance of vasoactive mediators, thrombotic activity and the expression of adhesion molecules, eg IL-1 and TNF both increase nitric oxide synthesis.

Transport and metabolism
The endothelium closely controls the passage of molecules into the vessel wall and participates in lipid metabolism. Small molecules can enter the vessel wall in the gaps between the tight junctions of the endothelial cells, but larger molecules such as insulin have to be transported actively across the endothelial cell by transcytosis. Lipoprotein lipase is expressed on the luminal endothelial cell surface and receptors for low-density lipoproteins are present in varying amounts. In the healthy endothelium these receptors are present at low levels, inhibiting the entry of low-density lipoprotein into the vessel wall.

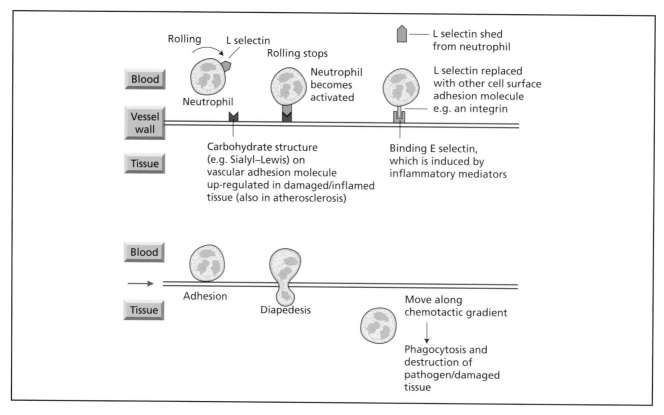

▲ **Fig. 12** How a neutrophil enters the tissue in the acute inflammatory response.

1.4 Endocrine function of the heart

The physiological function of the heart is influenced by a large number of hormonal substances, including catecholamines. The pathophysiology of the cardiovascular system is significantly affected by a number of natriuretic peptides: atrial natriuretic peptide (ANP), brain-type natriuretic peptide (BNP), C-type natriuretic peptide (CNP) and urodilatin.

BNP was first described in 1988 and has subsequently been proven to originate from the heart and is a cardiac hormone. The interaction of these cardiac hormones is illustrated in Fig. 13.

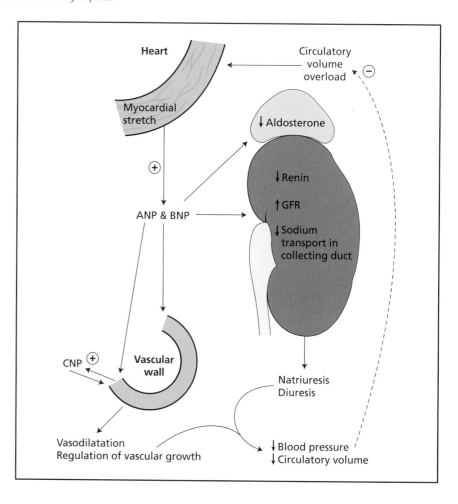

▶ **Fig. 13** Interactions of atrial natriuretic peptide (ANP), brain natriuretic peptide (BNP) and C-type natriuretic peptide (CNP). GFR, glomerular filtration rate.

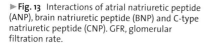

Pathophysiology

BNP is synthesised and secreted from the ventricular myocardium whereas ANP is produced primarily in the atria and released when atrial wall tension is increased. The main stimulus for BNP release is ventricular wall stress. Its release into the blood provides a major marker for heart failure.

Therapeutic use of BNP

BNP can now be measured by fully automated and commercially available assays. It can be used to confirm a diagnosis of heart failure and assess treatment as the level correlates with the degree of heart failure, ie New York Heart Association (NYHA) class and ejection fraction. The level of BNP has also been shown to correlate strongly with prognosis.

FURTHER READING

Knight CJ. Antiplatelet treatment in stable coronary artery disease. *Heart* 2003; 89: 1273–8.

Weber M and Hamm C. Role of B-type natriuretic peptide (BNP) and NT-ProBNP in clinical routine. *Heart* 2006; 92: 843–9.

2.1 The lungs

Main functions of the lungs

- Transport of oxygen from the environment to the pulmonary circulation.
- Excretion of carbon dioxide from the pulmonary circulation.
- Contribution to acid–base balance.

Resting minute ventilation in a healthy adult is approximately 5 L/min, but this may rise to as much as 150 L/min during heavy exercise. Peak exercise performance is probably less important nowadays than it may have been earlier in evolutionary history, but many lung diseases cause dyspnoea, most commonly by causing disruption to the process of pulmonary ventilation.

Successful gas exchange relies on:

- pulmonary ventilation, ie air has to pass from the mouth to the alveolus;
- diffusion of gases across the alveolar–capillary junction;
- an intact pulmonary circulation;
- intact control mechanisms.

Pulmonary ventilation

Structure of the lung and thorax

Thorax The lungs are enclosed in a bony structure (the vertebrae and the 12 ribs), which serves to protect the heart and lungs against injury. Inferiorly, the thoracic cavity is separated from the abdominal compartment by the diaphragm. The respiratory muscles move the thoracic cage outwards and thus create subatmospheric pressure within, producing inspiratory airflow.

The most important respiratory muscle in humans is the diaphragm, which accounts for about 70% of minute ventilation. Diaphragmatic contraction results in downward movement of the central tendon. This creates negative pressure within the thorax and positive pressure in the abdomen. This pressure is transmitted across the diaphragm muscle via the 'zone of apposition' to the lower ribs, causing outward movement (Fig. 14). Co-contraction of the upper thoracic muscles (eg the scalenes) results in movement outward and upward of the upper thorax.

Diaphragmatic paralysis

- Difficulty in breathing when lying down: pulmonary oedema is not the only cause of orthopnoea.
- Paradoxical abdominal movement on inspiration: the abdomen goes in instead of out.

Spinal injury sparing the diaphragm may cause paradoxical inward movement of the upper thorax during inspiration.

Lung The trachea divides into two main bronchi. The right main

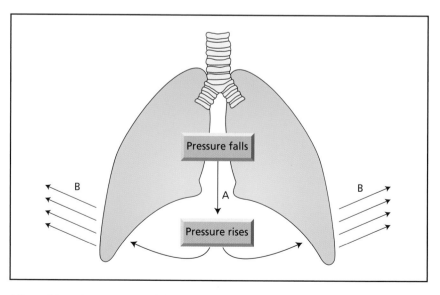

▲ **Fig. 14** Schematic representation of the action of the diaphragm. Diaphragm contraction (A) results in caudal movement of the central tendon. This causes a rise in intra-abdominal pressure and a fall in intrathoracic pressure. Over the zone of apposition (arrows), the ribcage directly overlays the abdominal compartment with the diaphragm interposed. (B) Therefore the consequence of the rise in intra-abdominal pressure is outward movement of the ribcage which further lowers pressure in the thorax.

bronchus then divides to enter three separate lobes (upper, middle and lower), whereas the left divides into two, the upper and lower. Successive dichotomous (ie into two) branching leads to approximately 20,000–30,000 terminal bronchioles.

The terminal bronchiole is the segment proximal to the respiratory bronchiole, which is defined as a bronchiole to which alveoli are directly connected; each terminal bronchiole has a diameter of 0.5 mm and supplies a fundamental unit, the acinus.

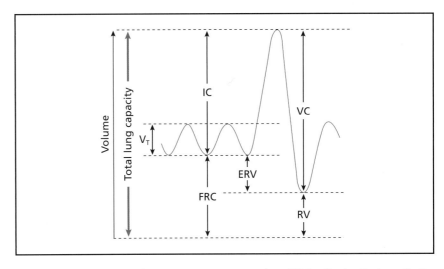

▲ **Fig. 15** Subdivisions of lung volume. ERV, expiratory reserve volume; FRC, functional residual capacity; IC, inspiratory capacity; RV residual volume; VC, vital capacity; V_T, tidal volume.

Normal physiology

Two different forces act on the lungs.

1. The lungs themselves exert a positive (ie inward) recoil pressure at all lung volumes, a fact proven by every pneumothorax.

2. The chest wall exerts a negative recoil pressure at low lung volumes and a positive recoil pressure at high lung volumes.

These relationships are known as the pressure–volume curves. The neutral point of the respiratory system is the functional residual capacity (FRC). At this point, the positive lung recoil pressure is exactly equal to the negative chest wall pressure. This is the point reached by taking a small breath in and then exhaling without any active effort.

Various lung volumes can be measured. The simplest measurement of pulmonary physiology is to measure the volume of air during inspiration (or expiration), which can be done as follows.

*   Tidal volume (V_T): the volume of air inspired during a quiet breath.

*   Inspiratory capacity: volume change going from FRC to a maximal inspiration.

*   Vital capacity (VC): the volume exhaled during a forceful expiration from a full inspiration (ie total lung capacity, TLC) to full expiration.

Even at full expiration, gas remains within the thoracic cavity and this is termed the residual volume (RV) (Fig. 15).

Physiological limits to ventilation

Sometimes ventilation is limited by the drive to breathe, which may be altered by neurological disease or much more often by drugs, eg opiates.

More commonly, lung disease itself imposes a limit to respiration. Broadly speaking, disease may affect pulmonary physiology by:

*   imposing a restricting effect on ventilation;

*   presenting an obstruction to expiratory airflow.

Both restrictive and obstructive defects may give a small VC and, although restrictive and obstructive defects may coexist, it is customary

to separate them on the basis of TLC (Fig. 16), although this measurement is not universally available:

*   diseases that are restrictive give a low TLC;

*   diseases that are obstructive give an increased TLC.

Pathophysiology

Chronic obstructive pulmonary disease (COPD) is especially important because it is very common.

To understand dyspnoea in COPD, it is necessary to consider the flow–volume (FV) loop. Representative examples are shown in Fig. 17. In both Fig. 17a and Fig. 17b the FV loop during a maximal effort is shown as the blue line at the periphery. The smallest red loop in the centre of each diagram represents quiet breathing, and the loops of increasing size around these correspond to increased ventilation at increased exercise loads.

*   Figure 17a is from a healthy young adult: with increasing exercise, end-expiratory lung volume (EELV) moves closer to

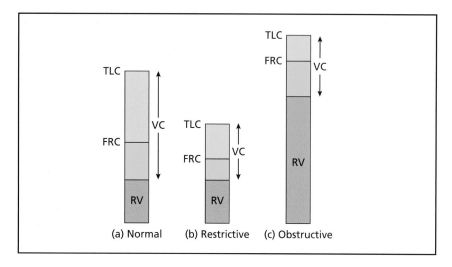

▲ Fig. 16 Schematic representation of the difference between (**b**) restrictive and (**c**) obstructive lung disease. In both obstructive and restrictive conditions, VC is reduced, although in obstructive conditions this is because of difficulty in breathing out (which forces the patient to a higher lung volume) whereas in restrictive disease the patient is unable to inspire to a normal TLC. Note that obstructive and restrictive conditions may coexist. FRC, functional residual capacity; RV, residual volume; TLC, total lung capacity; VC, vital capacity.

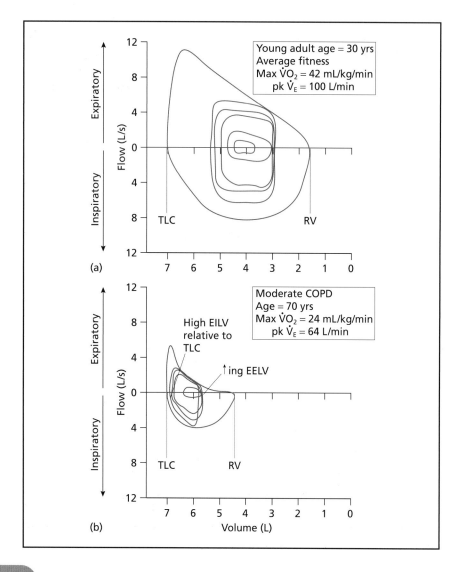

RV and the loop expands, only touching the maximal envelope at peak exercise.

- Figure 17b is from a patient with COPD: this touches the maximal envelope at the lowest level of exercise. As minute ventilation rises with increasing exercise, the patient is obliged to increase end-inspiratory lung volume (EILV), thereby shifting the loop to the left and allowing greater expiratory flow. At these increased lung volumes, the mechanics of the lung are such that increased muscular effort is required to generate the same minute ventilation, and the patient is closer to the actual ceiling of TLC.

Diffusion of gases

Once oxygen enters the terminal acinus, the predominant mode of transport is diffusion. Three factors influence the efficiency of this process:

- ventilation–perfusion matching;

- diffusion of gas from the alveolus to the red blood cell;

- uptake of oxygen by the red blood cell.

The actual diffusive process is not a limiting factor for gas exchange in normal lungs, but becomes so in diseases that impair this process, eg pulmonary fibrosis. Mismatching of ventilation with perfusion on a regional basis is a frequent problem in pulmonary disease, for example:

- in COPD, regions of the lung may be underventilated;

◄ Fig. 17 Flow–volume loops from (**a**) a healthy young adult and (**b**) a patient with chronic obstructive pulmonary disease (COPD). See text for explanation. EELV, end-expiratory lung volume; EILV, end-inspiratory lung volume; RV, residual volume; TLC, total lung capacity.

- in pulmonary embolic disease, areas of lung may be adequately ventilated but not perfused.

Uptake of oxygen by the red cell depends on its ambient partial pressure. It can also be modified by the presence of fetal haemoglobin, as with thalassaemia major, or a lack of 2,3-diphosphoglycerate, as in transfused blood.

Measurement of diffusing capacity

In clinical practice, diffusion capacity is, of necessity, measured for the whole lung. The gas used for measurement is carbon monoxide (CO) because of its very high affinity for haemoglobin, meaning that uptake is therefore limited only by diffusion capacity.

The essence of the single-breath T_{LCO} (diffusing capacity for CO) test is as follows.

- The patient inhales rapidly from RV to TLC from a reservoir containing a known composition of CO and helium. The purpose of including helium is that this gas, being insoluble, does not cross from the alveolus to the capillary. Calculation of the change in helium concentration therefore allows, with knowledge of the inspired volume, calculation of the functional volume of gas in the lung, ie alveolar volume (V_A), which should be similar to TLC in normal subjects.

- The rate constant for alveolar capillary CO transfer (K_{CO}) is obtained by measuring the change in CO concentration between the inspired and expired gas.

- To obtain T_{LCO}, K_{CO} is multiplied by V_A and divided by barometric pressure. It is often not appreciated that the primary measurements are of K_{CO} and V_A.

Control mechanisms

The primary function of the respiratory system is blood gas homeostasis. An adequate control mechanism is required, in addition to an intact gas exchange mechanism and respiratory muscle pump. The basic circuitry surrounding the control of breathing is shown in Fig. 18.

It is hard to measure the mechanisms of automatic ventilatory control because of the difficulty in eliminating overriding cortical effects. In research studies, it is possible to measure electrical activity of the respiratory muscles (at one extreme) or minute ventilation (at the other). In clinical practice, none of these factors are usually measured and control problems are inferred from measurement of the arterial partial pressure of carbon dioxide (Pa_{CO_2}); if this rises without other explanation, then the rise is attributed to a problem with the mechanisms controlling ventilation.

Two stimuli of respiratory drive are of particular importance: the hypoxic drive and the CO_2 drive. Ventilation increases during exercise but the stimulus for this, at least initially, is thought to be neural. The stimulus presented by a rise in H^+ (caused by acidosis from CO_2 or another acid) is a potent drive to hyperventilation, mediated via areas located on the ventrolateral surface of the medulla.

Patients who have continuous exposure to high levels of CO_2, such as those with chronic respiratory failure, become relatively insensitive to CO_2 and rely on their hypoxic drive. Hypoxic drive is mediated via the carotid body, the

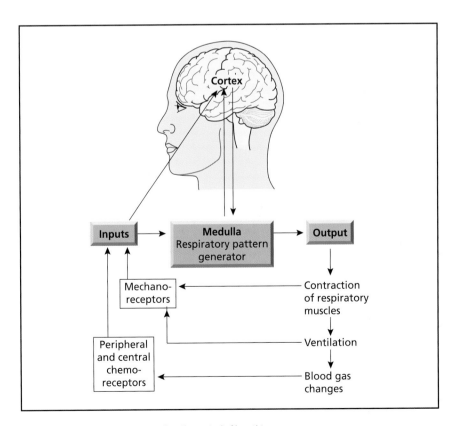

▲ **Fig. 18** The basic circuitry surrounding the control of breathing.

discharge of which is increased linearly in response to falling arterial oxygen saturation (Sao_2) (and hyperbolically to Pao_2); this response is magnified by concomitant hypercapnia. In practice, ventilation does not increase until Pao_2 is less than 8 kPa (or Sao_2 <92%).

⚠ Administration of high-flow oxygen to a patient with significant prior hypercapnia may result in significant type II respiratory failure. This was considered to be a result of depression of respiratory drive, but an alternative explanation is that oxygen results in reversal of regional hypoxic vasoconstriction and therefore causes poor ventilation–perfusion (V/Q) matching.

Many drugs depress respiratory drive, common examples being sedatives, opiates (prescription and 'street' drugs) and alcohol.

FURTHER READING

Hughes JMB and Pride NB, eds. *Lung Function Tests: Physiological Principles and Clinical Applications*. Edinburgh: WB Saunders, 1999.

3.1 The gut

> 🔑 **Main functions of the gut**
>
> - Absorption of water, nutrients, minerals and vitamins.
> - Barrier function.
> - The gastrointestinal tract (as well as the liver) also plays an important role in the immune system, with numerous lymphocytes and antigen-presenting cells.
>
> Because the gut has both absorptive and barrier functions, different tasks are performed at specialized sites along its length.
>
> - Stomach: this acts as a reservoir for ingested food, mechanically grinding it to an appropriate size before delivering it in a controlled manner to the small intestine.
> - Small bowel: contains long finger-like villi and crypts to create an extraordinarily large surface area which, in conjunction with surface digestive enzymes, bile and pancreatic juices, allows the effective absorption of protein, fat and carbohydrate.
> - Large bowel: the colon is chiefly concerned with the absorption of salt and water from the ileal effluent. It also plays a small role in energy intake via the active absorption of short-chain fatty acids following bacterial fermentation of non-absorbable dietary fibre.

Innervation of the gut
The gut has a large degree of autonomy, mostly as a result of the possession of its own nervous system, the enteric nervous system. This comprises a complex of nerve and nerve-associated cells situated in two planes in the gut wall:

- the submucosa (submucous plexus);

- between the inner circular muscle and outer longitudinal muscle layers (myenteric plexus), from where both sensory and motor nerves spread out to reach the muscles and mucosa.

The ability of the enteric nervous system to operate independently depends to a large extent on the self-generation of periodic depolarisation and repolarisation ('slow waves'), which trigger smooth muscle contraction and hence peristalsis. A specialised group of cells, the interstitial cells of Cajal, are thought to be responsible for this inherent rhythmicity and are intimately associated with the enteric nervous complex. Thus, when the small intestine is divided, isolated segments are able to cycle independently. However, the enteric nervous system does not work in isolation and receives modulatory input from the central nervous system (CNS), as shown in Fig. 19. The 'brain–gut axis' is a very important component of functional bowel disorders, which are the commonest gastrointestinal complaints in clinical practice.

Small bowel
The best-defined pattern of electrical activity in the gut is the migrating myoelectrical (motor) complex. This occurs in the fasted gut and is characterised by a cyclical migrating burst of intense electrical and contractile activity. The cycle is divided into four parts (Fig. 20).

1. Quiescence, lasting 30–50 minutes.

2. Irregular sporadic spiking activity, lasting 20–40 minutes.

3. Intense maximal spiking activity, lasting 5–6 minutes (often referred to as the 'migrating motor complex' or MMC).

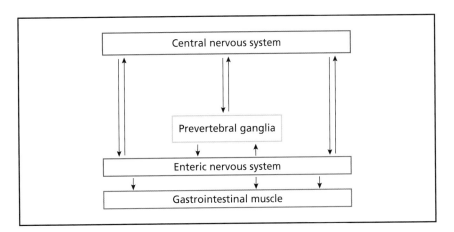

▲ **Fig. 19** Innervation of the gut.

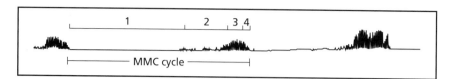

▲ **Fig. 20** Migrating motor complex (MMC) recorded in the small intestine of a dog. See text for further explanation.

4. Transition back to quiescence, lasting about 5 minutes.

In humans, the periodicity is 90–100 minutes and the velocity 1–5 cm/min. Most MMCs start from either the oesophagus or the duodenum, and migrate through the small bowel; most fail to reach the terminal ileum. They are thought to act as 'housekeepers', clearing the intestine of any residue, and are quickly abolished by ingestion of a meal.

Large bowel

High-amplitude propagated contractions (HAPCs) occur at a frequency of 2–10 per 24 hours: these travel distally at a rate of 1 cm/s and are readily invoked by purgatives. They probably cause mass movement of colonic contents, propelling large amounts of stool ready for evacuation.

Transit through the gut

Stomach

Transit through the stomach depends on the consistency, size and type of food ingested. Liquid meals pass through the stomach rapidly, being half emptied in 30–60 minutes, whereas solid meals take approximately twice as long to pass through. Fat markedly delays gastric emptying by stimulating duodenal receptors.

Small bowel

Transit through the small intestine takes around 2–4 hours.

Large bowel

Transit through the colon is very variable both between and within individuals, with a range of 5–70 hours.

Regulation of transit and food processing

Swallowing (deglutition)

After mastication of food, swallowing is initiated by a voluntary phase, followed by an involuntary pharyngeal phase, which transmits the food through the pharynx into the oesophagus, and an involuntary oesophageal phase, which propels food into the stomach.

Primary peristalsis carries food along the oesophagus to the stomach in around 10 seconds, with secondary peristalsis, stimulated by distension from any remaining food debris, quickly clearing the remainder. The lower oesophageal sphincter, which is normally hypertonic, relaxes upon initiation of swallowing to allow easy passage of food into the stomach.

> • An incompetent or lax lower oesophageal sphincter may contribute towards gastro-oesophageal reflux disease.
> • Failure of the lower oesophageal sphincter to relax on swallowing, together with heightened sphincteric pressure, is characteristic of achalasia.

Stomach

- Acts as a storage vessel, permitting controlled release of contents into the small intestine for digestion and absorption.

- Mechanically breaks food into small particles.

- Secretes acid, pepsinogen and intrinsic factor.

Gastric motility (emptying) and secretion are controlled by the following neural and hormonal mechanisms (Fig. 21):

- cephalic mechanisms;

- gastric mechanisms;

- intestinal mechanisms.

Cephalic phase The cephalic response, ie increased secretion in anticipation of food, is vagally mediated. Vagal fibres:

- directly stimulate parietal cells to secrete acid and pepsinogen;

- stimulate gastrin release (via gastrin-releasing peptide, GRP), which in turn stimulates secretion of acid from parietal cells via gastrin receptors.

The low pH changes pepsinogen to the active pepsin moiety.

Gastric phase The gastric phase is the most important mechanism, accounting for around 70% of the total meal-associated gastric secretion. As food enters the stomach, it initiates long vagovagal reflexes and local enteric reflexes that stimulate gastric secretion. Amino acids also directly stimulate gastrin production.

Intestinal phase The intestinal phase is largely inhibitory and mediated by nerves and hormones.

- Acidity, protein breakdown products and fat all initiate local enterogastric neural reflexes,

Although fats are almost all completely degraded to free fatty acids and monoglycerides by the pancreatic lipases, proteins and carbohydrates require further degradation by enzymes within the brush borders of the enterocytes. Lactase, sucrase, maltase and peptidases break down disaccharides, peptides and polypeptides into their base units for absorption.

The terminal ileum also has two specialised absorptive functions:

- active uptake of the vitamin B_{12}–intrinsic factor complex;
- active reabsorption of bile salts.

This enterohepatic circulation results in about 94% of bile salts being conserved.

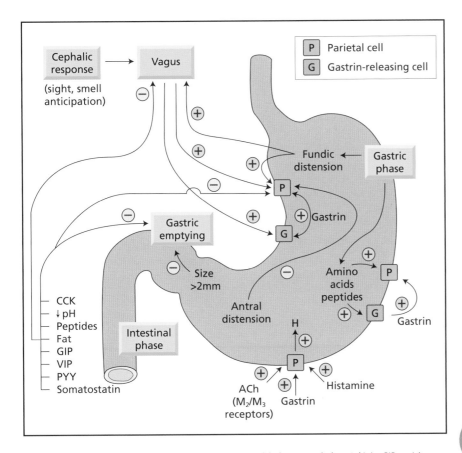

▲ **Fig. 21** Control of gastric motility and secretion. ACh, acetylcholine; CCK, cholecystokinin; GIP, gastric inhibitory polypeptide; M_2/M_3, muscarinic receptors; PYY, peptide YY; VIP, vasoactive intestinal polypeptide.

reducing acid secretion and delaying gastric emptying. Longer extrinsic neural reflexes to the prevertebral sympathetic ganglia are also involved.

- Cholecystokinin (CCK), released from the jejunal mucosa in response to fat, is a potent inhibitor of gastric motility and secretion.

- Secretin, gastric inhibitory polypeptide and peptide YY may also have inhibitory roles.

Intrinsic factor is produced by the parietal cells and binds to ingested vitamin B_{12}. The complex is then taken up via receptors in the terminal ileum.

Small bowel
The small intestine is primarily involved in the digestion and

absorption of food and water. Contact of food with the duodenal mucosa results in the release of CCK and secretin from the duodenum and jejunum.

Cholecystokinin

- Inhibits gastric emptying.
- Causes contraction of the gallbladder, emptying bile into the duodenal lumen, where it acts as a detergent, breaking the fat into micelles.
- Stimulates the exocrine pancreas to produce proteases (trypsin, chymotrypsin), lipases and amylases.

Secretin

- Stimulates bicarbonate secretion by the pancreas, which neutralises the acidic gastric effluent and provides an optimum pH for pancreatic digestive enzyme function.

- Always be alert to the possibility of subsequent vitamin B_{12} deficiency after extended right hemicolectomies: it may take up to 5 years to become apparent, but its effects can be devastating.
- Bile salts in the colon act as cathartics; Crohn's disease of the terminal ileum, ileal resection and right hemicolectomies may all cause diarrhoea as a result of bile salt malabsorption. Investigation is with a bile malabsorption study (SeHCAT scan), although empirical treatment with a bile salt-binding resin such as cholestyramine is often trialled.

Large bowel

The colon is primarily concerned with the absorption of salt and water from the 1.5 L of chyme that enter it daily. This process is very efficient, resulting in only 100 mL of water loss per day, on average, via the faeces; the colon is capable of absorbing up to 6 L/day.

Colonic bacteria ferment non-absorbable dietary fibre into the short-chain fatty acids (SCFAs) butyrate, propionate and acetate. Butyrate appears to be important for the well-being of colonocytes, and SCFA absorption may contribute up to 10% of the energy supplies to the body. This energy supply may be particularly important when the absorptive function of the small bowel is compromised (eg short bowel syndrome).

FURTHER READING

Degen LP and Phillips SF. Variability of gastrointestinal transit in healthy women and men. *Gut* 1996; 39: 299–305.

Kellow JE, Borody TJ, Phillips SF, Tucker RL and Haddad AC. Human interdigestive motility: variations in patterns from esophagus to colon. *Gastroenterology* 1986; 91: 386–95.

Nightingale JM, Lennard-Jones JE, Gertner DJ, Wood SR and Bartram CI. Colonic preservation reduces the need for parenteral therapy, increases incidence of renal stones, but does not change high prevalence of gallstones in patients with a short bowel. *Gut* 1992; 33: 1493–7.

Sanders KM. A case for interstitial cells of Cajal as pacemakers and mediators of neurotransmission in the gastrointestinal tract. *Gastroenterology* 1996; 111: 492–515.

3.2 The liver

The liver has complex functions including metabolism of carbohydrates (see *Biochemistry and Metabolism*, Crbohydrates). It is also involved in the metabolism and excretion of drugs (see *Clinical Pharmacology*, Sections 2.4 and 2.5).

> **Main functions of the liver**
>
> - Production of bile, which contains bilirubin and bile acids.
> - Synthesis of plasma proteins and lipids.
> - Metabolism of drugs, carbohydrates and amino acids.
> - Clearance of waste products and drugs: metabolic products excreted via the urine or into the bile.

Clearance function

Clearance is achieved by:

- metabolism of substances to enhance their elimination into the urine or bile;

- direct excretion of substances into the bile.

Bile

Normal bile contains water, bicarbonate, bile acids and bile salts, cholesterol and bilirubin. Some drugs also undergo biliary excretion.

Some 600 mL of bile is produced daily, 150 mL of which comes from bile ductules; these modify the bile as it passes from the biliary canaliculi into the common bile duct.

> **Cholestasis**
>
> Failure of normal amounts of bile to reach the duodenum, as a result of pathology anywhere between the hepatocyte (ie sepsis) and the ampulla of Vater, is known as cholestasis. This causes:
>
> - jaundice (rise in serum bilirubin);
> - elevated alkaline phosphatase and γ-glutamyltransferase (GGT);
> - elevated cholesterol level.

Bile acids/salts and the enterohepatic circulation The main function of bile salts is to form micelles with cholesterol and phospholipid. This leads to the emulsification of fats, assisting their absorption in the small bowel.

The primary bile acids, synthesised from cholesterol in the liver, are cholic acid and chenodeoxycholic acid. Cholic acid predominates in human bile. In the liver, bile acids are conjugated with glycine and taurine to form bile salts, after which they cannot be absorbed by the bile ducts or jejunum. However, they are absorbed further down the gut, mainly by the terminal ileum. This is the basis of the enterohepatic circulation, which transports bile salts back to the liver and thereby recycles the entire bile salt pool 2–15 times every day.

Note the following.

- The rate of bile acid secretion is dependent on the rate of reabsorption of bile salts and their transport back to the liver.

- Bile salts not absorbed in the ileum undergo 7α-dehydroxylation by colonic bacteria, producing secondary bile acids (deoxycholic acid).

- Bacteria in the small bowel can deconjugate bile acids, resulting in malabsorption of fats.

- If there is a block to the excretion of bile acid into the bile (cholestasis), bile acids are excreted in the urine.

Figure 22 shows some of the transporters involved in the excretion of bile acids and other endogenous/exogenous compounds.

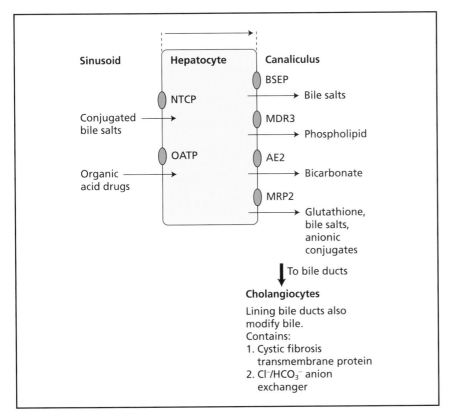

▲ **Fig. 22** Some of the transporters involved in hepatobiliary transport of substances from the sinusoids into bile. Variable degrees of cholestasis (jaundice, itching, increased alkaline phosphatase) occur with disruption to one or more of these transporters. AE2, anion exporter; BSEP, bile salt exporter pump; MRP2, MDR3, multidrug-resistant peptides; NTCP, Na$^+$ taurocholate cotransporter polypeptide; OATP, organic ion transporter proteins.

Mechanism of intrahepatic cholestasis and jaundice

- Reduced Na$^+$ taurocholate cotransporter polypeptide (NTCP): sepsis (endotoxin, oestrogens).
- Reduced bile salt exporter pump (BSEP): progressive familial intrahepatic cholestasis (Byler's syndrome).
- Reduced multidrug resistant peptide (MRP2): Dubin–Johnson syndrome.

The tertiary bile acid ursodeoxycholic acid is more hydrophilic and less toxic to cells than other bile salts. This is the rationale for its use in chronic cholestatic conditions such as primary biliary cirrhosis. It also interferes with the terminal ileal absorption of cholic acid and chenodeoxycholic acid.

Bile salts increase the biliary excretion of water, conjugated bilirubin and cholesterol (mainly derived from high-density lipoprotein). Hydrophobic bile acids, such as taurodeoxycholic acid and taurochenodeoxycholic acid, cause cell toxicity, which partially explains the bile duct and hepatocyte damage seen in cholestasis.

Bilirubin Bilirubin is formed when the ring structure of haem is broken open by microsomal haem oxygenase. It is then transferred to the liver bound to albumin, where it is conjugated, allowing secretion into the bile (Fig. 23).

There can be no urobilinogen in the urine if jaundice is caused by biliary obstruction.

Several inherited conditions can cause impaired conjugation of bilirubin and failed excretion of conjugated bilirubin resulting in jaundice (Table 5). In Gilbert's syndrome, unconjugated hyperbilirubinaemia is the result of impaired function of the bilirubin enzyme uridine diphosphate (UDP) glucuronosyltransferase 1 (UGT1). The gene for this is on chromosome 2 and the genetic defect is the insertion of a pair of nucleotides (thymidine and adenosine) in the gene promoter, which affects binding of transcription factors and reduces UGT1 production.

Synthetic function

Plasma proteins

Important substances produced by the liver include:

- albumin, which functions as a transport protein;
- coagulation factors;
- other acute-phase reactants such as C-reactive protein (CRP).

During the acute-phase response, interleukin (IL)-1, IL-6 and tumour necrosis factor (TNF)-α cause a fall in hepatic albumin synthesis and a rise in acute-phase proteins, including CRP, fibrinogen and serum amyloid A protein.

Albumin The liver produces 10 g of albumin every day. Its plasma half-life is 22 days.

The serum albumin is usually normal in acute liver failure, and it is one of the few clinical conditions where CRP production does not occur to any great extent.

Coagulation factors All clotting factors, with the exception of von Willebrand's factor, are synthesised in the liver. The liver also produces

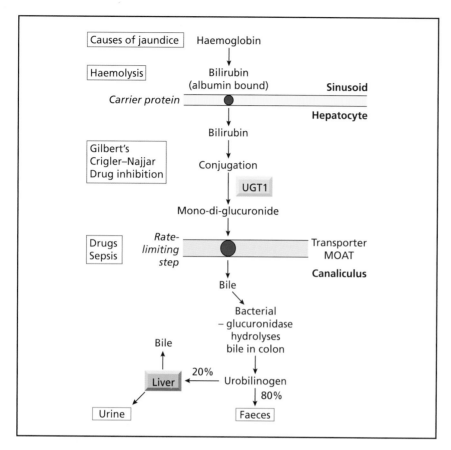

▲ **Fig. 23** Bilirubin metabolism. UGT1, uridine diphosphate glucuronosyltransferase 1; MOAT, multispecific organic anion transporter.

the inhibitors of coagulation, including antithrombin III, proteins C and S, as well as factors involved in fibrinolysis.

α₁-Antitrypsin This is produced by the liver and makes up 80–90% of serum α₁-globulin. It is an inhibitor of trypsin. The normal phenotype is MM. The abnormal protein, ZZ, cannot be excreted by the endoplasmic reticulum and accumulates in the liver, resulting in a hepatitic illness in children with subsequent hepatic fibrosis. Cirrhosis in adults can occur as well.

Metabolism

Carbohydates

The liver is the principal source of blood sugar, with glucose-6-phosphatase producing glucose for peripheral use.

- After an overnight fast, 75% of blood glucose comes from glycogenolysis and 25% from gluconeogenesis, using substrates including lactate.

- Of body lactate, 60–70% is removed by the liver.

- Hypoglycaemia and lactic acidosis occur when only 20% of liver function remains, ie acute liver failure.

- In contrast, cirrhosis is complicated by peripheral insulin resistance and hyperglycaemia. Hyperglycaemia also occurs because of hyperinsulinaemia resulting from a failure of clearance and degradation of insulin.

Amino acids

The liver receives amino acids from the diet and from tissue breakdown. Some amino acids are metabolised to urea and creatinine.

TABLE 5 FAMILIAL HYPERBILIRUBINAEMIAS. ALL ARE AUTOSOMAL RECESSIVE

Clinical condition	Defect	Mechanism	Presentation
Gilbert's syndrome	Unconjugated hyperbilirubinaemia	Low UGT1 Promotor gene defect	Intermittent jaundice No liver disease
Crigler–Najjar type 1	Unconjugated hyperbilirubinaemia	No UGT1 Gene mutation	Kernicterus in infancy
Crigler–Najjar type 2	Unconjugated hyperbilirubinaemia	10% of UGT1	Survive into adult life
Dubin–Johnson	Conjugated hyperbilirubinaemia	Impaired transport protein MRP2 deficient	Intermittent jaundice Black pigmented liver
Rotor	Conjugated hyperbilirubinaemia	Unknown Normal liver	Intermittent jaundice

MRP2, multidrug resistance protein 2; UGT1, UDP glucuronosyltransferase 1.

> 🔑 The rate of urea synthesis is reduced in cirrhosis and serum urea levels may be less than 1 mmol/L. Serum ammonia levels rise, particularly if there is severe portal hypertension.

FURTHER READING

Bosma PJ, Chowdhury JR, Bakker C, *et al*. The genetic basis of the reduced expression of bilirubin UDP-glucuronosyltransferase 1 in Gilbert's syndrome. *N Engl J Med* 1995; 333: 1171–5.

– – – – – – – – – – – – – – – –

Kullak-Ublick GA, Beuers U and Paumgartner G. Hepatobiliary transport. *J Hepatol* 2000; 32 (Suppl. 1): 3–18.

– – – – – – – – – – – – – – – –

Sherlock S and Dooley J. *Diseases of the Liver and Biliary System*, 11th edn. Oxford: Blackwell Science, 2002.

3.3 The exocrine pancreas

The pancreas has both endocrine and exocrine functions. These two roles are not entirely discrete because some of the hormones secreted by the islets of Langerhans may have paracrine effects on acinar secretion (eg somatostatin, pancreatic polypeptide).

The exocrine function of the pancreas involves the production and secretion of proteases, amylase and lipase, which play a central role in digestion.

Anatomy

The functional unit of the exocrine pancreas is the acinus and the accompanying ductule. Pancreatic acinar cells synthesise and secrete digestive enzymes, which drain via the ductule and interlobular ducts into the main pancreatic duct. The main pancreatic duct empties into the duodenum via the ampulla of Vater.

Constituents of pancreatic juice

- Bicarbonate.

- Chloride.

- Amylase: digests starch and glycogen.

- Lipases: lipase, phospholipase A, carboxylesterase.

- Proteases: trypsinogen, chymotrypsinogen, proelastase, procarboxypeptidase (A and B).

- Trypsin inhibitor.

Control of exocrine function

Various hormones and neurotransmitters act on the acinar cell:

- vasoactive intestinal polypeptide;

- secretin;

- cholecystokinin;

- acetylcholine.

- gastrin-releasing peptide;

- substance P.

> 🔑 The clinical hallmark of disordered pancreatic exocrine function is steatorrhoea with associated malabsorption (see *Gastroenterology and Hepatology*, Sections 2.4.2 and 3.2). This was classically detected by faecal fat estimation but this has been superseded by faecal elastase measurement in the first instance.

Exocrine pancreatic function may be impaired in chronic pancreatitis (common) and cystic fibrosis (uncommon). For a description of endocrine pancreatic function, see *Physiology*, Section 5.4.

4.1 The action potential

The neuron is the fundamental unit of the nervous system; it transfers information by using an electrical signal, the action potential. Action potentials are derived from changes in the resting membrane potential (RMP) of the neuron, which is about –90 mV (negative on the inside of the cell).

Establishing the resting membrane potential

• A Na⁺/K⁺-ATPase pump transports three sodium ions out of the cell for every two potassium ions transported in. Thus, at rest, potassium ions are predominantly intracellular and sodium ions extracellular, creating a concentration gradient; in addition, an electrochemical gradient across the cell membrane is created with a relative negative charge inside the cell.

• Each ion tends to diffuse down its own concentration gradient, but only to a point where the electrochemical gradient is balanced. If the cell membrane were permeable only to sodium, then this equilibrium RMP (E-Na) would be about +60 mV (positive on the inside of the cell); if permeable only to potassium ions, the RMP (E-K) would be about –95 mV (Fig. 24).

• At its resting state the cell membrane is very permeable to potassium but not to sodium ions, so the RMP is closer to the equilibrium potential of potassium.

• When a nerve impulse is transmitted, the situation is reversed and for about 0.5 ms the cell membrane is much more permeable to sodium than to potassium. Thus, the membrane potential at the peak of an action potential, the reversal potential, becomes closer to the equilibrium potential of sodium.

• The RMP is set up by the Na⁺/K⁺-ATPase pump as an electrogenic phenomenon, but the instantaneous changes that occur during the action potential are related to changes in diffusion across voltage-gated channels.

For further discussion of these issues, see *Cell Biology*, Ion Transport.

> • A voltage-dependent pump transports three sodium ions out of the cell for every two potassium ions transported in.
> • The cell membrane is far more permeable to potassium than to sodium at rest.
> • This pattern reverses during depolarisation.

Initiating the action potential

Any factor such as electrical stimulation or mechanical compression may cause increased permeability to sodium ions by opening sodium channels. The following processes then occur.

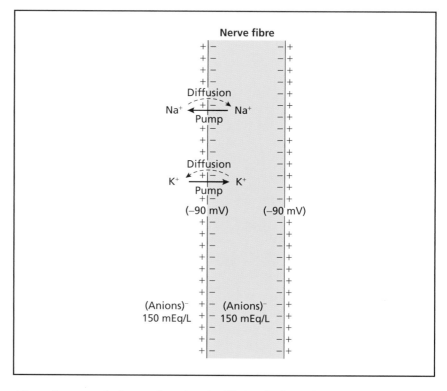

▲ **Fig. 24** The process of active pumping and passive diffusion of sodium and potassium ions in establishing the resting membrane potential of a normal nerve fibre.

- The membrane potential becomes less negative as a result of some sodium influx; at a threshold of about –60 mV, the increased permeability to sodium ions becomes subject to positive feedback processes, accelerating the influx of sodium ions and resulting in depolarisation (Fig. 25).

- The reversal potential is about +45 mV, the amplitude and duration of the action potential being fixed ('all or nothing').

- Almost immediately, the sodium channels close and the membrane becomes more permeable to potassium than normal. The positive charge inside the cell results in potassium moving out, leading to repolarisation. The potassium channels remain open for longer, explaining the 'positive' (as measured from outside the cell) after-potential.

Refractory period

The absolute refractory period follows each action potential, and is a period during which a second action potential cannot be initiated. There then follows a relative refractory period during which a larger than normal stimulus is required to initiate an action potential. These refractory periods are a result of two processes.

- The overshoot of potassium influx that results in repolarisation causes the membrane potential temporarily to move further away from the threshold potential.

- The sodium channels close and cannot be opened again to initiate an action potential until the membrane potential has returned to the RMP.

Propagating the action potential

The depolarisation spreads laterally to neighbouring areas of the neuron,

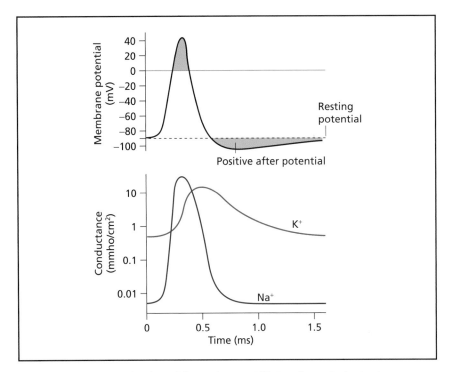

▲ **Fig. 25** The action potential and causal changes in permeability to sodium and potassium ions.

resulting in the opening of sodium channels and the initiation of depolarisation (Fig. 26). This process can be speeded up by the following.

- Increasing the diameter of the axon, although this would create problems of size.

- Myelination: many mammalian axons are myelinated, which increases membrane resistance and decreases capacitance, thereby enhancing conduction velocity without increasing size.

The nodes of Ranvier are excitable areas of membrane between myelin cells. Depolarisation spreads from one node to another, and at any one time up to 40 nodes may be involved in an action potential (Fig. 26). This spreading from node to node is known as the saltatory conduction of the action potential.

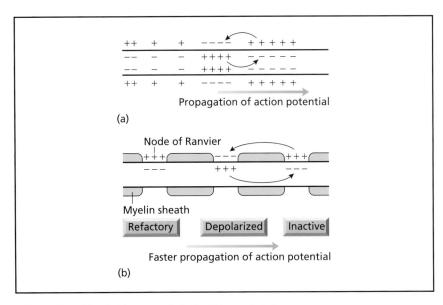

▲ **Fig. 26** Current flow in (**a**) an unmyelinated and (**b**) a myelinated axon.

TABLE 6 CLASSIFICATION OF NERVE FIBRES*			
Fibre type	Conduction velocity (m/s)	Diameter (μm)	Function
Aα	70–120	12–20	Proprioception, somatic motor
Aβ	30–70	5–12	Touch, pressure
Aγ	15–30	3–6	Motor to muscle spindles
Aδ	12–30	2–5	Pain, temperature
B	3–15	1–3	Preganglionic autonomic
C	0.5–2	0.2–2	Postganglionic autonomic, pain, temperature, pressure

* Adapted from Lamb JF, Ingram CG, Johnston IA and Pitman RM. *Essentials of Physiology*. Oxford: Blackwell Scientific Publications, 1980.

Some peripheral neuropathies affect predominantly large or small fibres. From Table 6, it is possible to see why each type of neuropathy has the characteristics that are clinically observed (see *Neurology*, Sections 2.1.1 and 2.1.2).

- Large-fibre neuropathy: reduced proprioception and power, areflexia, minimal loss of pinprick (pain) sensation.
- Small-fibre neuropathy: selective loss of pain and temperature sensation, normal strength, normal power, preserved reflexes.

Calcium is important in maintaining the membrane's impermeability to sodium ions. In hypocalcaemic states, the probability of depolarisation being initiated in response to any stimulus is higher, which can result in frequent spontaneous action potentials and muscle contraction, ie tetany.

Local anaesthetics such as lidocaine (lignocaine) also reduce membrane permeability to sodium ions, reducing the chances of action potentials propagating through the anaesthetised area.

FURTHER READING

Hodgkin AL and Huxley AF. A Quantitative description of membrane current and its application to conduction and excitation in nerve. *J Physiol* 1952; 117: 500–44.

4.2 Synaptic transmission

Neurons transmit information by means of the action potential and communicate with each other via connections called synapses. A typical neuron in the central nervous system (CNS) will have inputs from many sources and have many synaptic outputs, eg an anterior horn cell in the spinal cord may have up to 50,000 synaptic connections. These are located mainly on the cell body or dendrites. There are two types of synapse.

- Electrical synapses: these are rare, but allow the direct transmission of current from presynaptic to postsynaptic neurons.
- Chemical synapses: the usual form of communication between neurons.

Chemical synaptic transmission

Neurotransmitter release

- An action potential arrives in a nerve terminal, resulting in an influx of calcium ions.
- Within the nerve terminals, chemicals termed 'neurotransmitters' are found in

vesicles. These can be situated in the 'active zone' or bound to actin filaments in a reserve pool (Fig. 27). The calcium influx initiates fusion of the vesicles to the presynaptic plasma membrane, releasing the neurotransmitter contents by exocytosis. Calcium influx also dissociates the vesicles from actin filaments, allowing more neurotransmitter to be available for exocytosis.

- The vesicles then form clathrin-coated pits, which are recycled to form new vesicles.

Receptor sites

Neurotransmitters diffuse rapidly across the synaptic cleft and act on receptors that may be directly or indirectly linked to membrane channels.

- Direct: the receptor may be part of the channel complex (ionotropic), when the time from nerve terminal excitation to permeability change in the postsynaptic membrane (synaptic delay) is short (about 0.5 ms).
- Indirect: the receptor may act indirectly with ion channel(s) via G proteins (metabotropic). This leads to longer synaptic delay (>1 ms). For further discussion, see *Cell Biology*, Ion Transport

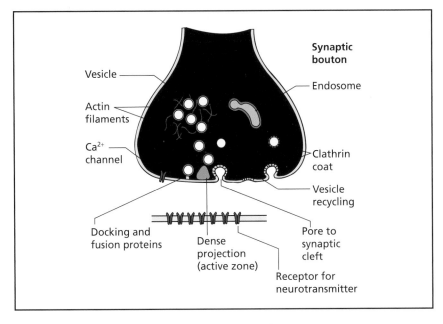

▲ **Fig. 27** Release of neurotransmitter from a presynaptic terminal.

Postsynaptic potentials

Interaction of a neurotransmitter with its appropriate receptor causes a local synaptic potential. These local potentials last longer than an action potential and can summate with one another (Fig. 28).

and Receptors and intracellular signalling.

Synaptic potentials may cause depolarisation or hyperpolarisation, depending on whether the postsynaptic membrane potential becomes more or less negative.

- An excitatory postsynaptic potential (EPSP) results from increased permeability to all ions (in contrast to an action potential).

This causes a small depolarisation as a result of the net influx of sodium ions; the potassium ions do not move greatly because the resting membrane is already relatively permeable to them.

- An inhibitory postsynaptic potential (IPSP) results from increased permeability to only potassium and chloride ions. As the equilibrium potential of both these ions is negative, hyperpolarisation results.

A combination of EPSPs and IPSPs on the same cell will summate to move the membrane potential closer or further away from the threshold potential for initiation of an action potential (Fig. 29).

Excitatory postsynaptic potentials

- Summate in order to evoke an action potential.
- Have no refractory period.
- Are not propagated along the axon.
- Increase membrane permeability to potassium and sodium simultaneously (not sequentially as in an action potential).

Function of synapses

Synapses may facilitate both excitation and inhibition, acting on axonal cell bodies to initiate or prevent the formation of an action potential. In addition, a synapse may be formed between an inhibitory presynaptic terminal and the presynaptic terminal of another neuron (Fig. 30), resulting in a reduction in the number of vesicles released by each impulse. This system allows more selective, controlled inhibition.

The various possible patterns of neuronal circuits allow the complexity and subtlety of organisation of neurons in the CNS to become immense (Fig. 31).

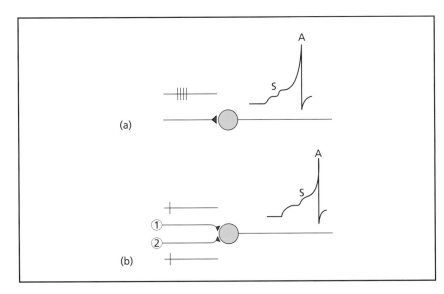

▲ **Fig. 28** Postsynaptic potential summation via single or multiple inputs: (**a**) temporal summation; (**b**) spatial summation. S, local synaptic potentials; A, action potential.

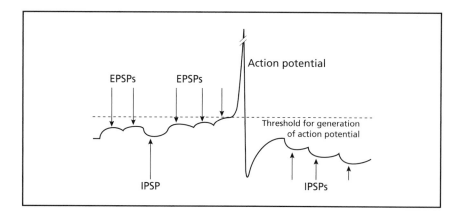

Fig. 29 Postsynaptic potentials generating an action potential. EPSPs, excitatory postsynaptic potentials; IPSPs, inhibitory postsynaptic potentials.

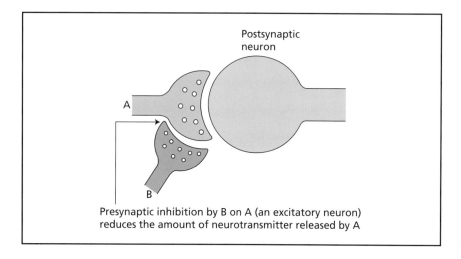

Fig. 30 Presynaptic inhibition.

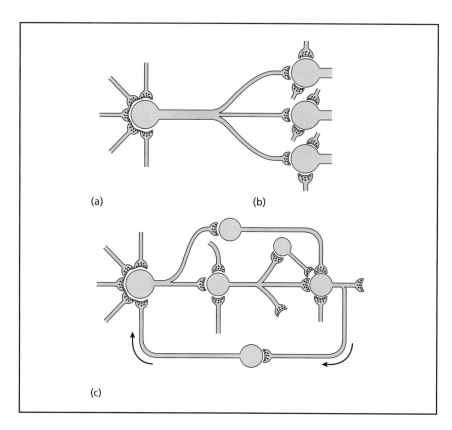

Fig. 31 Neuronal circuits: (a) convergence; (b) divergence; (c) feedback loop.

4.3 Neuromuscular transmission

Anatomy

Skeletal muscle is innervated by large-diameter myelinated nerve fibres that originate in the anterior horn cells of the spinal cord. Each fibre branches to innervate from three (eye muscles) to several hundred (gastrocnemius) muscle fibres, called the motor unit.

The motor neuron forms terminal branches of small-diameter unmyelinated fibres, each of which innervates only one muscle fibre; the junction is situated in its centre. Numerous folds in the surface of the muscle fibre increase the surface area of contact greatly.

Each axon terminal contains about 300,000 vesicles, which in turn contain the neurotransmitter acetylcholine (ACh) (Fig. 32).

Release of acetylcholine

Every action potential that arrives at the neuromuscular junction is followed by a muscle action potential; this is a system that has a high safety factor and is unlikely to fail under normal circumstances. The mechanism is as follows.

- About 300 vesicles containing ACh are released into the synaptic cleft in response to increased amounts of intracellular calcium, which is far greater than the number of vesicles released during transmission of impulses between neurons.

- ACh diffuses across the synaptic cleft and binds to the postsynaptic nicotinic ACh receptor.

- Within 1 ms, most ACh is destroyed by acetylcholinesterase, which is found in high concentrations at the motor end-plates.

End-plate potential

- Stimulation of the nicotinic postsynaptic receptor results in increased permeability to sodium, potassium and calcium ions.

- The influx of cations moves the end-plate potential (EPP) closer to the threshold of spontaneous depolarisation (about –50 mV), at which point an action potential sweeps across the muscle membrane.

- Single vesicles of ACh are released spontaneously and randomly every second or so.

- These 'quanta' of ACh cause miniature end-plate potentials (MEPPs) of about 1 mV. This results in about 1,000 channels opening for 1 ms each, allowing 40,000 ions through each channel, in order to produce a depolarisation of 1 mV.

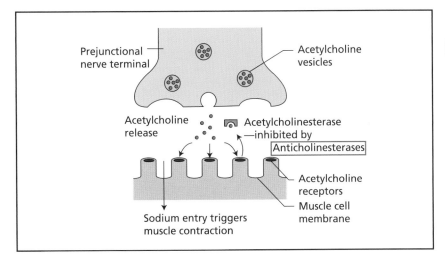

In addition to the presence of antibodies directed against ACh receptors in myasthenia gravis, the morphology of the neuromuscular junction is abnormal. The synaptic cleft is widened and there are far fewer folds in the surface of the muscle fibre, reducing the surface area of contact between nerve and muscle. It is therefore much harder to raise the EPP to the threshold of stimulating the muscle fibre, resulting in clinical weakness. See *Neurology*, Section 2.2.5.

▲ **Fig. 32** The neuromuscular junction.

PHYSIOLOGY: **SECTION 5**
ENDOCRINE PHYSIOLOGY

5.1 The growth hormone–insulin-like growth factor 1 axis

The growth hormone (GH)–insulin-like growth factor (IGF)-1 axis is illustrated in Fig. 33. Hypothalamic growth hormone-releasing hormone (GHRH) and somatostatin are key regulators of pituitary GH secretion. A potent endogenous growth hormone secretagogue (GHS), ghrelin, has recently been identified from the stomach and is probably a new member of the brain–gut peptide family. GHSs appear to act to promote GH release through coordinated effects at both hypothalamic and pituitary levels.

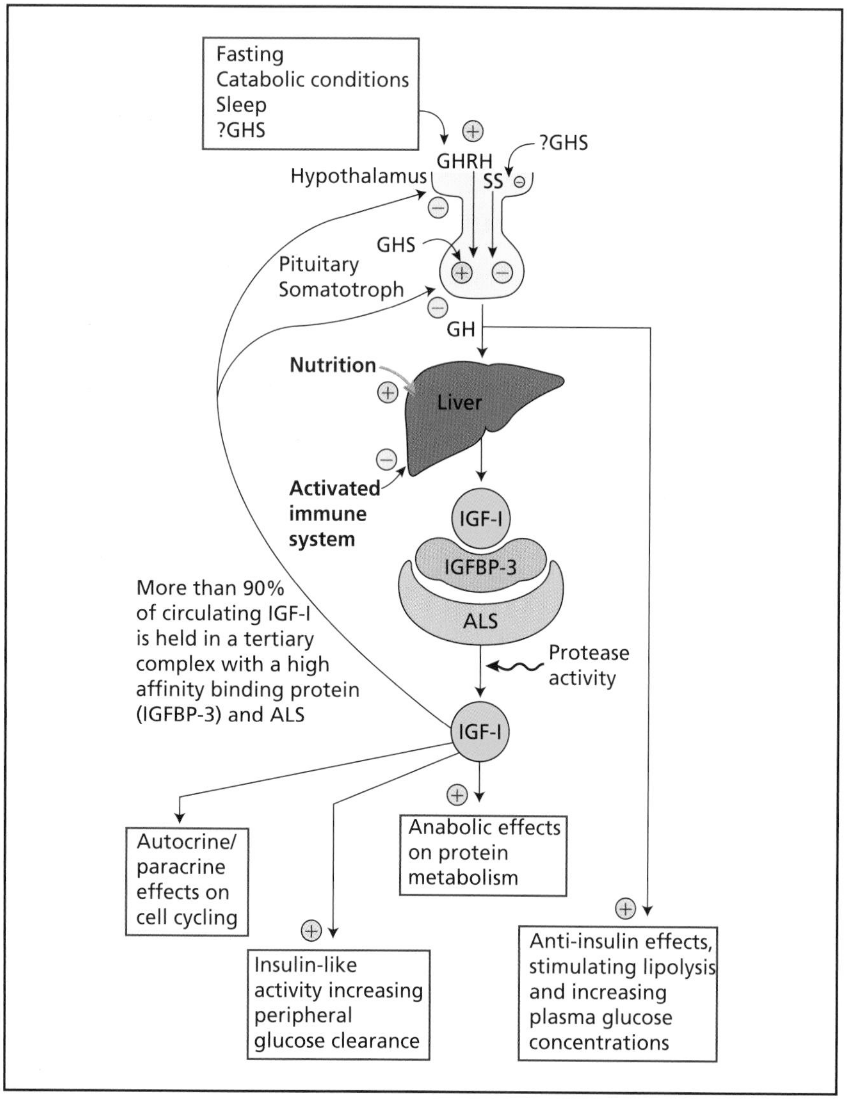

▲**Fig. 33** The growth hormone (GH)–insulin-like growth factor (IGF)-I axis. ALS, acid-labile subunit; GHRH, growth hormone-releasing hormone; GHS, growth hormone secretagogue; IGFBP-3, IGF-binding protein-3; SS, somatostatin.

Growth hormone itself has direct 'anti-insulin' effects, whilst its anabolic actions are mediated principally through IGF-1 which is produced by the liver.

The large circulating pool of IGF-1 is bound to high-affinity binding proteins, predominantly IGF-binding protein (IGFBP)-3. When IGFBP-3 is proteolytically cleaved, its affinity for IGF-1 is reduced, releasing the IGF-1 to bind to its cell-surface receptors. The IGFs have endocrine, paracrine and autocrine effects, regulating metabolism, cell survival, differentiation and cell death.

5.2 The hypothalamic–pituitary–adrenal axis

The hypothalamic–pituitary–adrenal axis is illustrated in Fig. 34. About 80% of the total circulating cortisol is bound to cortisol-binding globulin, 10% is bound to albumin and 10% is free (metabolically active).

Normal cortisol secretion follows a circadian rhythm, with a peak shortly before waking followed by a decline as the day progresses to reach a trough at night; this should be borne in mind when prescribing cortisol replacement therapy.

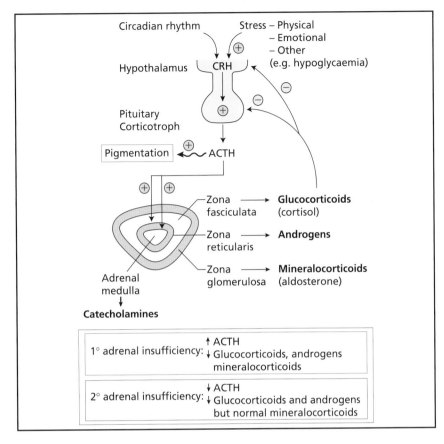

▲**Fig. 34** The hypothalamic–pituitary–adrenal axis. CRH, corticotrophin-releasing hormone; ACTH, adrenocorticotrophic hormone.

Cortisol has many vital metabolic and immunomodulatory effects, and is important in the maintenance of normal circulatory function. Sustained high levels of glucocorticoids (eg long courses of high-dose prednisolone, chronic severe illness, or Cushing's syndrome) have catabolic effects and are immunosuppressive.

Aldosterone production by the zona glomerulosa of the adrenal cortex is regulated by the renin–angiotensin system and not by adrenocorticotrophic hormone (ACTH). Secretion of catecholamines by the adrenal medulla is stimulated via the splanchnic nerves.

regulate a diverse array of physiological processes ranging from normal growth and development, through aspects of homeostasis

(eg energy and heat production), to cardiac contractility.

Thyroid hormone structure, synthesis and secretion

T_4 and T_3 are both derived via iodination of the phenolic rings of tyrosine residues in thyroglobulin to form monoiodotyrosine or diiodotyrosine, which are coupled to form T_3 or T_4 (Fig. 35). A number of the steps of this process are under direct regulation by thyroid-stimulating hormone (TSH) from the anterior pituitary (Fig. 36).

- Autoantibodies targeted against thyroid peroxidase (anti-TPO/antimicrosomal antibodies) are found in the serum of many patients with autoimmune thyroid disease (especially hypothyroidism).
- A small amount of unhydrolysed thyroglobulin is released from the thyroid follicular cell and can be detected in serum. This may be increased in some situations, eg differentiated thyroid malignancy, where it can serve as a useful tumour marker.

5.3 Thyroid hormones

Thyroid hormones, namely thyroxine (T_4) and 3,5,3′-triiodothyronine (T_3),

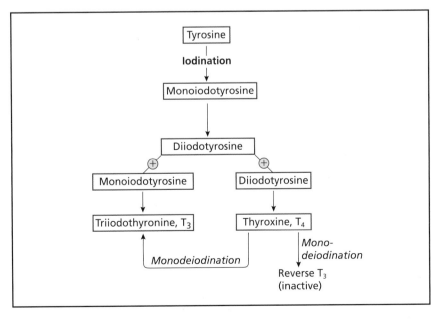

▲**Fig. 35** Synthesis of thyroid hormones.

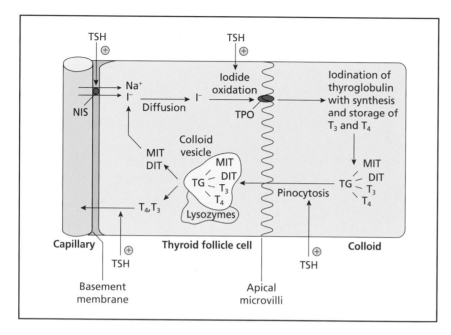

▲ **Fig. 36** Thyroid hormone synthesis in a thyroid follicle cell. I⁻, iodide ion; NIS, sodium (Na⁺) iodide (I⁻) symporter; TPO, thyroid peroxidase; TG, thyroglobulin; MIT, monoiodotyrosine; DIT, diiodotyrosine; T₄, thyroxine; T₃, triiodothyronine; TSH, thyroid-stimulating hormone; ⊕, direct stimulation by TSH.

Wolf–Chaikoff effect

Small increases in available iodide permit increased organification and thyroid hormone formation, but beyond a critical level the high intrathyroidal I⁻ content appears to block organification with a subsequent fall in hormonogenesis (Wolff–Chaikoff effect). This phenomenon appears to be transient, with the normal thyroid gland able to 'escape' from the I⁻ effect through inhibition of the iodide trap and consequent reduction in intrathyroidal iodide levels. Failure of the gland to undergo this adaptation, as may occur in some patients with autoimmune thyroid disease, can lead to iodide-induced hypothyroidism.

Jod–Basedow effect

Excessive thyroid hormone synthesis can occur in response to an iodide load in some people. This is more common in iodine-deficient regions and may be due to unmasking of latent thyroid disease (Jod–Basedow effect).

Thyroid hormone action

Most of the circulating T_3 and T_4 (>99%) are bound to plasma proteins [thyroxine-binding globulin (TBG), prealbumin and albumin] and are physiologically inactive.

Changes in the concentrations of these binding proteins affect measurements of total thyroid hormone concentrations, and hence most laboratories now routinely measure free thyroid hormone levels (FT_4 and FT_3), which are a more reliable indicator of thyroid status.

Although the concentration of T_4 in blood is greater than that of T_3, it is the latter which acts as the biological effector hormone. Most T_3 is derived by peripheral deiodination of T_4 in target tissues. Once inside the cell, T_3 binds to specific nuclear receptors that regulate the rate of transcription of a wide variety of target genes. The resultant effects include:

- regulation of energy expenditure;
- catabolic effects on carbohydrate and fat metabolism;
- reduction in serum cholesterol;
- normal fetal brain and skeletal development.

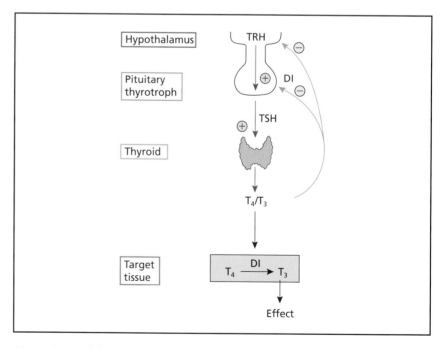

▲ **Fig. 37** The hypothalamic–pituitary–thyroid axis. TRH, thyrotrophin-releasing hormone; TSH, thyroid-stimulating hormone; T₃, triiodothyronine; T₄, thyroxine; DI, deiodinase. Note that the pituitary expresses a distinct (type 2) deiodinase enzyme that allows conversion of T₄ to T₃ in order to facilitate negative feedback.

The hypothalamic–pituitary–thyroid axis

The hypothalamic–pituitary–thyroid axis is shown in Fig. 37.

> ⚠ TSH levels are an unreliable indicator of the state of the hypothalamic–pituitary–thyroid axis in central hypothyroidism. If this is a possibility, request measurement of free thyroid hormone levels (FT_4 and FT_3).

5.4 The endocrine pancreas

The pancreas comprises two distinct functional organs:

- the exocrine pancreas, a major source of digestive enzymes;

- the endocrine pancreas.

Four major cell types have been identified within the islets of Langerhans that make up the endocrine pancreas:

- A (α) cells that secrete glucagon;

- B (β) cells that secrete insulin;

- D (δ) cells that secrete somatostatin;

- F (PP) cells that secrete pancreatic polypeptide.

Together these hormones regulate not only the rate of absorption of various dietary constituents but also their cellular storage and metabolism.

Insulin

Insulin synthesis and secretion

The human insulin gene is located on chromosome 11. The initial gene product, a precursor molecule preproinsulin, is cleaved almost immediately after synthesis to proinsulin, which is stored in secretory granules. Subsequent processing of proinsulin releases insulin and a smaller connecting peptide (C-peptide) through cleavage at two sites within proinsulin (Fig. 38). The insulin molecule comprises two peptide chains (A and B) that are connected by two disulphide bridges (Fig. 38).

Glucose is the most potent stimulus of insulin release, entering the pancreatic β cell both by diffusion and via a glucose transporter (GLUT-2). Insulin secretion in response to glucose occurs in a biphasic manner: the early (first) phase response, which is relatively short-lived, occurs almost immediately with rising glucose levels, but if glucose levels are maintained then a late-phase response is seen that is more gradual in onset but sustained.

A number of other factors have been shown to regulate insulin release in humans including:

- dietary components, eg amino acids;

- hormones, such as incretins (eg glucagon-like peptide-1), secretin, gastrin, cholecystokinin;

- drugs, eg diazoxide, somatostatin analogues.

> 🔑 Both diazoxide and somatostatin analogues inhibit insulin release and are therefore potentially useful in ameliorating the symptoms associated with insulinoma prior to surgical removal.

Insulin action

Insulin exerts its effects through binding to specific receptors on the surface membrane of the target cell. These receptors are membrane glycoproteins composed of α (extracellular) and β (predominantly cytoplasmic) subunits. Binding of insulin triggers a cascade of intracellular signalling pathways that ultimately facilitate transport of nutrients into insulin target tissues, an important mechanism being the migration of the GLUT-4 glucose transporter to the cell surface that promotes glucose uptake.

Insulin is an anabolic hormone with the following actions:

- promotion of the uptake of glucose into cells and its conversion into glycogen and lipids;

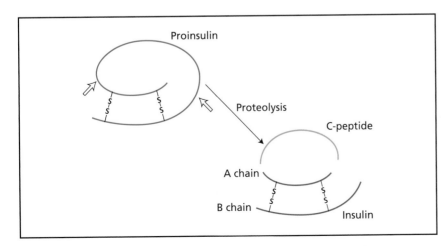

▲ **Fig. 38** Proteolytic cleavage of proinsulin to insulin and C-peptide. Open arrows indicate sites of proteolysis.

- increase in amino acid uptake by the liver and muscle;

- inhibition of catabolic processes, including hepatic glycogenolysis, lipolysis and gluconeogenesis.

In contrast, lack of insulin leads to increased glycogenolysis, lipolysis and gluconeogenesis, leading to hyperglycaemia (resulting in polyuria due to osmotic diuresis) and hyperketonaemia (resulting in potentially fatal ketoacidosis).

Insulin metabolism

First-pass metabolism in the liver removes half of the insulin in the hepatic portal vein. Within the plasma it circulates in unbound form, is freely filtered by the glomeruli and then rapidly reabsorbed and metabolised by the renal tubules. The plasma half-life of insulin is approximately 5 minutes.

> ⚠ Metabolism of insulin by the kidneys is impaired in renal failure, so diabetics may be at risk of hypoglycaemia if they remain on their 'normal treatment' regimen in the face of deteriorating renal function. Close monitoring and often a reduction in the dosage of oral hypoglycaemic agents or insulin is required.

Glucagon

Glucagon release from the pancreatic α cells occurs in response to falling blood glucose levels (<5 mmol/L). Its primary site of action is within the liver, where it promotes mobilisation of glycogen and gluconeogenesis.

Glucose homeostasis

Figures 39 and 40 outline the important steps involved in the maintenance of normal blood glucose levels during the fed and fasting states respectively.

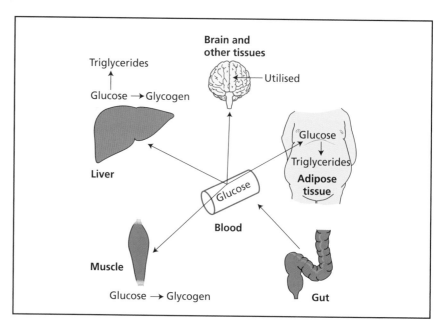

▲ **Fig. 39** Glucose homeostasis during the fed state.

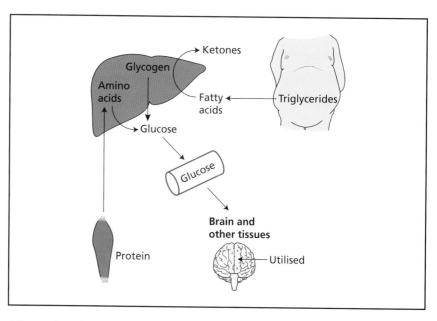

▲ **Fig. 40** Glucose homeostasis during the fasting state.

5.5 The ovary and testis

The key steps in the sex steroid biosynthetic pathways are shown in Fig. 41, together with an outline of the steroid ring structure. In general, the major pathways are similar in the adrenal, ovary and testis.

Ovary

Figures 42 and 43 illustrate the hypothalamic–pituitary–ovarian axis and plasma hormone levels during a menstrual cycle respectively. In the ovary, luteinising hormone (LH) induces ovulation of the mature follicle and stimulates oestrogen production by promoting the synthesis of androgen precursors

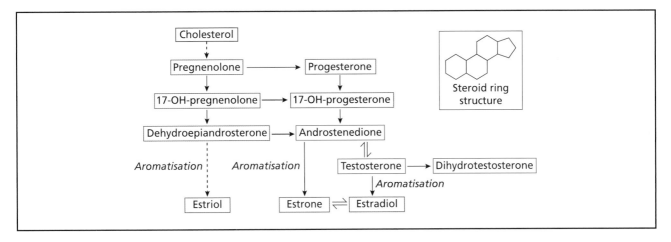

▲ **Fig. 41** Sex steroid biosynthesis.

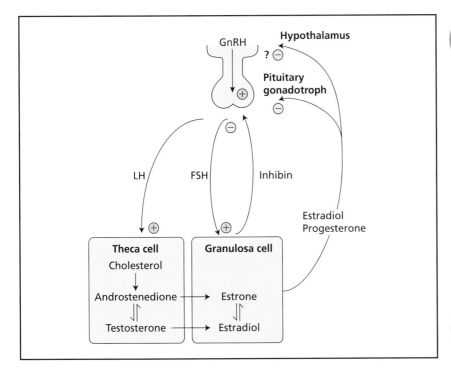

▲ **Fig. 42** The hypothalamic–pituitary–ovarian axis. FSH, follicle-stimulating hormone; GnRH, gonadotrophin-releasing hormone; LH, luteinising hormone.

> ⚠ Concentrations of LH and FSH may reach 'postmenopausal' levels during the ovulatory surge, so repeat measurements together with a paired oestradiol sample should be checked before making a diagnosis of premature ovarian failure.

Progesterone is produced by the corpus luteum and has 'progestational' effects inducing secretory activity in the endometrium.

> 🔑 A high mid-luteal phase progesterone concentration indicates that the cycle was ovulatory.

in theca cells. Diffusion of these androgens into adjacent granulosa cells is followed by aromatisation into oestrogens under the influence of follicle-stimulating hormone (FSH). LH also helps to sustain the corpus luteum during the second half of the cycle by stimulating progesterone synthesis. In addition to the role outlined above, FSH is responsible for the development of the mature follicle which ovulates in response to the LH surge in mid-cycle.

About 2% of total circulating oestradiol is unbound, with the remainder bound to albumin (~60%) and sex hormone-binding globulin (SHBG) (~38%).

In addition to the hormones shown in Fig. 43, non-steroidal hormones and growth factors (including insulin and the IGFs) have autocrine and paracrine effects in the regulation of ovarian function, follicular maturation and steroidogenesis.

Figure 44 outlines the ovarian and adrenal sources of circulating androgens in women.

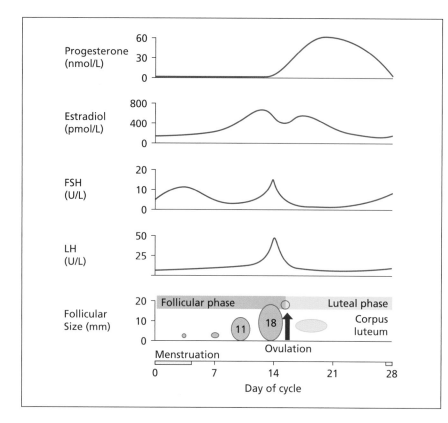

▲ **Fig. 43** Plasma hormone concentrations during a menstrual cycle.

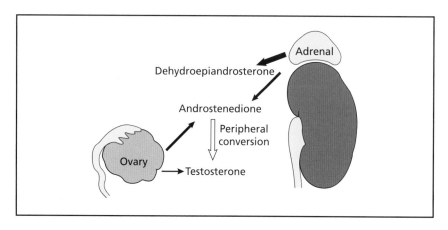

▲ **Fig. 44** Normal sources of circulating androgens in women. Note that there is no negative feedback loop directly regulating androgen production in women.

Testis

Figure 45 illustrates the hypothalamic–pituitary–testicular axis. LH predominantly acts to promote testosterone production by the Leydig cells. FSH appears to be important in the initiation of spermatogenesis, possibly through increasing intratubular concentrations of dihydro-testosterone (the active form)

via an effect on Sertoli cells, with subsequent stimulation of spermatozoa production from spermatogonia that lie between the Sertoli cells in the seminiferous tubules.

About 2% of total circulating testosterone is unbound, with the remainder bound to albumin (~55%) and SHBG (~43%).

5.6 The breast

Hormonal regulation of breast development

Several hormones and growth factors act synergistically to promote ductal and alveolar development of the mammary gland. These include prolactin, estradiol, progesterone, GH, IGF-1 and other growth factors. Physiological involution of the mammary gland occurs after lactation and after the menopause. In men, gynaecomastia may result from an increase in the net effective oestrogen/androgen ratio acting on the breast.

> High levels of placental estradiol and progesterone during pregnancy prime the breast for milk formation but inhibit lactation, so the combined oral contraceptive pill should not be used in lactating women.

Lactation

After parturition the sudden withdrawal of estradiol and progesterone releases the inhibition of lactation that has occurred during pregnancy. Both the anticipation of nursing (including the sight and sound of the baby) and nipple stimulation promote oxytocin release from the posterior pituitary, resulting in myoepithelial contraction and milk expulsion. The 'milk ejection reflex' can be inhibited by stress.

Prolactin is released from the anterior pituitary in response to nipple stimulation and maintains lactogenesis. It also inhibits hypothalamic secretion of gonadotrophin-releasing hormone (GnRH) and gonadal steroid production, thus inhibiting ovulation, although women should

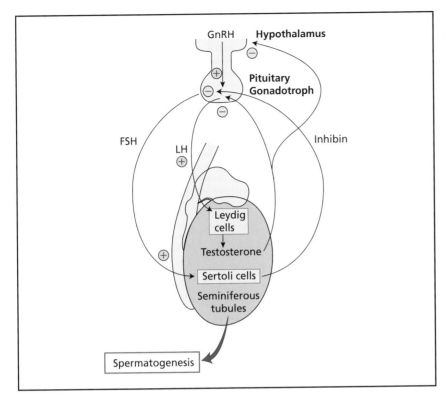

▲**Fig. 45** The hypothalamic–pituitary–testicular axis. FSH, follicle-stimulating hormone; GnRH, gonadotrophin-releasing hormone; LH, luteinising hormone.

🔑 Dopaminergic agonists such as bromocriptine inhibit prolactin production and may be used in the treatment of pathological hyperprolactinaemia and after a stillbirth.

⚠ Drugs that enter breast milk in significant quantities may be toxic to the infant. Some examples are listed in the *British National Formulary*, but the general advice should be that only essential drugs are given to lactating women.

still be advised to use appropriate contraceptive precautions while breast-feeding. The regulation of prolactin secretion is illustrated in Fig. 46.

The removal of milk (by the infant suckling) is essential to the maintenance of milk secretion, so early support to establish successful breast-feeding is critical to avoid failure of lactation. Continued nipple stimulation after weaning may result in unwanted postpartum galactorrhoea.

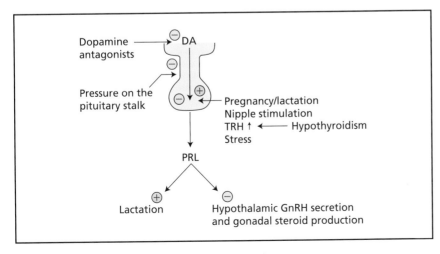

▲**Fig. 46** Regulation of prolactin secretion. DA, dopamine; GnRH, gonadotrophin-releasing hormone; PRL, prolactin; TRH, thyrotrophin-releasing hormone.

5.7 The posterior pituitary

The posterior pituitary secretes two nine-amino-acid peptides, arginine vasopressin (also known as antidiuretic hormone, ADH) and oxytocin. Both are synthesised in nerve cell bodies in the supraoptic and paraventricular nuclei of the hypothalamus as large precursor molecules comprising a signal peptide, the active nonapeptide, and a specific neurophysin (carrier protein). They are processed as they pass along the nerve axons and are secreted, separate from their neurophysins, from the posterior pituitary into the systemic circulation or from the median eminence into the portal blood to influence anterior pituitary function.

Antidiuretic hormone
ADH has a half-life in the circulation of 5–15 minutes and is metabolised in the liver and kidneys. Its main function under physiological

conditions is the control of blood osmolality.

Control of ADH secretion

ADH release is stimulated by:

- increase in blood osmolality;

- hypotension/intravascular volume depletion;

- nausea/vomiting;

- pain.

Actions of ADH

The principal action of ADH is to reduce the renal excretion of water. It has pressor actions at very high serum concentrations, eg when stimulated by hypotension /intravascular volume depletion.

- Deficiency of ADH leads to the syndrome of cranial diabetes insipidus, which is one of the causes of polyuria.
- The commonest cause of normovolaemic hyponatraemia is the syndrome of inappropriate antidiuresis (SIAD) due to posterior pituitary or ectopic secretion of ADH.

Oxytocin

The effects of oxytocin are mainly confined to pregnancy and the postpartum period.

- Stimulation of the nipple leads to oxytocin secretion and milk ejection from the lactating breast (the suckling reflex).

- Release of oxytocin following distension of the cervix of the pregnant uterus is involved in the initiation of parturition.

There are no known physiological actions of oxytocin in men or non-pregnant, non-lactating women.

Infusion of oxytocin is used routinely to initiate and maintain labour.

By modifying the volume and content of the urine, the kidneys play a dominant role in determining the fluid and electrolyte constitution of the body. This function is vital. Many different sensors monitor the volume and composition of the various body fluid compartments and feed this information to the kidneys, via the renal nerves or by the mediation of hormones. An integrated response modulates the excretion of fluid and electrolytes with astonishing precision. If the sensors transmit erroneous information, the renal response may seem inappropriate, eg in cardiac failure there is retention of sodium and water. If kidney function is impaired, homeostasis fails, eg in chronic renal failure there can be retention of sodium, potassium and water.

6.1 Blood flow and glomerular filtration

The nephron and its blood supply
The nephron and its blood supply are shown in Fig. 47.

The anatomical arrangements are highly specialised. Countercurrent flow of tubular fluid in the loops of Henle, which allows the development of a standing gradient of osmolality, is essential for the mechanism of urinary concentration and dilution. This can be maintained only if the blood supply follows a similar path, and there is countercurrent flow in the vasa rectae. An inevitable consequence of this is the formation of a standing gradient of oxygen tension in the kidney, such that in the normal renal medulla the partial pressure of oxygen is as low as 1–2 kPa.

The kidneys have the highest blood flow, weight for weight, of any large organ. Of the normal total cardiac output of about 5 L/min, about 25% (1.25 L/min) goes to the kidneys. All this blood passes through the glomeruli, where capillary pressure is high (45–60 mmHg), driving the formation of glomerular filtrate at the rate of about 100 mL/min in a young adult. Water, electrolytes and small molecules pass through freely; larger molecules are retarded in proportion to their size and negative charge (the more negative are retarded the most).

Glomerular filtration rate
The glomerular filtration rate (GFR) is the rate at which an ultrafiltrate of plasma passes through the glomerular capillaries into the renal tubule. It is most commonly determined clinically by the measurement of creatinine clearance.

Principle of clearance measurement
If a compound is freely filtered at the glomerulus (not secreted, reabsorbed or metabolised by the kidney), is physiologically inert, and can be measured in plasma and urine, the GFR can be calculated from the rate at which the compound is excreted in the urine:

Plasma concentration (P) × GFR = Urine concentration (U) × Urine volume (V)

GFR = (Urine concentration × Urine volume)/Plasma concentration

$$\mathrm{GFR} = UV/P$$

Creatinine clearance
Creatinine (molecular weight 113) satisfies most of the criteria listed above as necessary for clearance of a compound to be used as a measure of GFR. It is a product of the metabolism of creatine in muscle, this being synthesised from amino acids (L-arginine, glycine and L-methionine) in kidney, liver and pancreas and transported to skeletal muscle and other tissues where it is metabolised to phosphocreatine, a major energy storage form in the body.

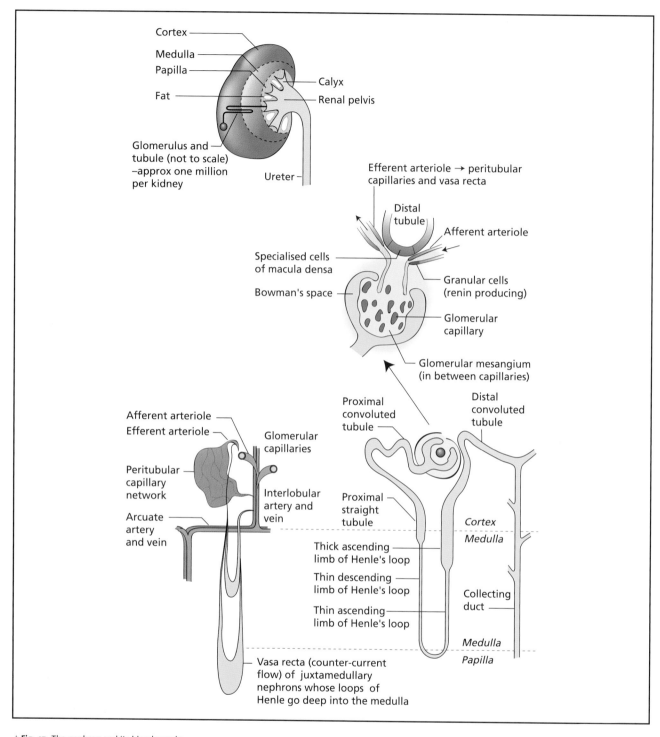

▲ **Fig. 47** The nephron and its blood supply.

Creatinine clearance declines with age (Table 7). As most creatinine is the product of metabolism in muscle, the rate of its production varies considerably between individuals. A large muscular man has much more muscle than a frail old woman, so that

the same serum creatinine value indicates a very different level of renal function. This is now recognised by the increasingly routine reporting of estimated GFR (eGFR) and chronic kidney disease (CKD) stage whenever a blood sample is sent for measurement of serum creatinine.

A serum creatinine measurement within the normal range does not necessarily mean normal renal function.

TABLE 7 AVERAGE VALUES OF SERUM CREATININE AND CREATININE CLEARANCE IN MEN AND WOMEN OF DIFFERENT AGES

Sex	Age (years)	Creatinine (μmol/L)	Creatinine clearance (mL/min)
Male	25	100	110
	45	110	90
	65	115	70
	85	105	50
Female	25	90	95
	45	100	80
	65	100	65
	85	105	45

6.2 Function of the renal tubules

As the glomerular filtrate passes down the renal tubules, its volume and content are modified substantially. Transfer of large quantities of water, electrolytes and other solutes occurs in the proximal tubule. Fine tuning of excretion occurs in the distal tubule.

In addition to being filtered at the glomerulus, some substances are secreted directly into the tubules, eg potassium, cations and organic anions such as bile salts.

The tubule handles different substances differently, but all are subject to rigorous control.

- Glucose: 100% normally reabsorbed.

- Water and sodium: 90–99.9% normally reabsorbed.

- Potassium: 80–90% reabsorbed on a normal diet, but can reabsorb 99% in potassium deficiency, and excrete more than 100% in potassium excess (implying net tubular secretion).

Control of glomerular and tubular function

> Glomerular and tubular function are tightly controlled.
>
> - 'Autoregulation' keeps the GFR constant.
> - 'Tubuloglomerular balance' enables the function of a tubule to compensate automatically for the fluctuation in filtration rate of the glomerulus to which it is attached.

It is absolutely critical that tubular and glomerular functions are matched. If the tubules were to fail and if glomerular filtration persisted at its normal rate, urine would be produced at a rate of 100 mL/min. This could not be sustained for long!

As might be expected for the crucial task of controlling glomerular and tubular function, control is not left in the hands of a single mechanism. Several mechanisms operate in parallel, acting to stabilise the rate of glomerular filtration and to match tubular function to it, while allowing adjustment of rates of urinary excretion of water and electrolytes to fulfil the homeostatic requirements of the body as a whole.

Autoregulation

Glomerular blood flow and filtration rate vary little when arterial pressure alters. How does this happen?

Myogenic response An increase in pressure leads to stretching of the smooth muscle cells in arterial/arteriolar walls. These constrict, reducing lumen size and preventing increased flow.

Tubuloglomerular feedback Increased delivery of filtrate (particularly chloride) to the macula densa (specialised cells in the distal tubule where it abuts the glomerulus) leads to contraction of mesangial cells in the glomerulus. This increases renal arteriolar resistances and reduces the area of the glomerulus available for ultrafiltration, thereby reducing glomerular plasma flow and GFR.

Glomerulotubular balance

If the filtration rate increases in a glomerulus, the rate of reabsorption increases in the proximal tubule connected to that glomerulus. How does this happen?

1. Blood flow around a proximal tubule is derived from the efferent arteriole of the glomerulus attached to that tubule.

2. If glomerular blood flow is held steady (see above), an increase in the amount of glomerular filtrate formed can occur only because of an increase in filtration fraction (the fraction of blood filtered in its passage through the glomerulus).

3. If filtration fraction increases, then because proteins are excluded from the glomerular filtrate, the oncotic pressure of the plasma in the efferent arteriole must increase.

4. When this plasma with increased oncotic pressure passes on into the peritubular capillary network, it encourages (via Starling's forces) reabsorption of fluid from the tubule, balancing the effect of the initial increase in glomerular filtration.

Influences from outside the kidney

A wide variety of neurohumoral mechanisms modulates glomerular and tubular function, enabling them to satisfy the homeostatic demands of the whole body. This is discussed in more detail below.

Sodium transport along the nephron

Of filtered sodium, 90–99.9% is reabsorbed by the renal tubule. In balance, sodium excretion equals sodium intake, with urinary sodium excretion varying from 50 to 250 mmol/day depending on the diet. Different mechanisms are responsible for sodium reabsorption in different segments of the nephron, and these are shown in Fig. 48.

Proximal tubule

Of the sodium filtered at the glomerulus, 75% is reabsorbed in the proximal tubule. Water is reabsorbed in proportion to sodium by transcellular and paracellular routes so that the fluid in the proximal tubule remains isotonic.

Thick ascending limb of the loop of Henle

Loop diuretics (furosemide, bumetanide) act on the $Na^+/K^+/2Cl^-$ cotransporter in this segment of the nephron. Mutations in the gene for this protein (and also those of some other ion channels in the thick ascending limb) cause Bartter's syndrome, which presents with profound hypokalaemia in infancy.

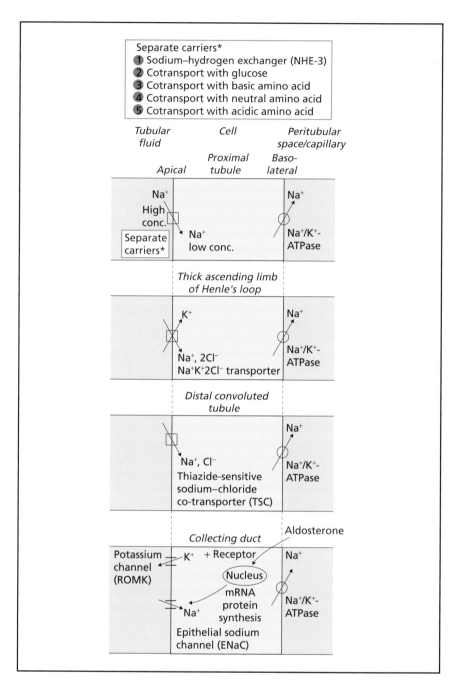

▲ **Fig. 48** Main mechanisms of sodium reabsorption in different segments of the nephron.

Distal convoluted tubule

Thiazide diuretics act on the Na^+/Cl^- cotransporter in this segment of the nephron. Metolazone is chemically a thiazide but also acts at other sites along the tubule, making it an extremely powerful diuretic. Mutations in the gene encoding the Na^+/Cl^- cotransporter cause Gitelman's syndrome, the most

common of the genetic causes of hypokalaemia in adults.

Collecting ducts

The collecting ducts are where 'fine tuning' of sodium excretion occurs. The sodium channel is under the influence of aldosterone (see below). Spironolactone binds to the cytoplasmic mineralocorticoid

TABLE 8 FACTORS MODULATING THE RENAL CIRCULATION AND SODIUM EXCRETION BY THE KIDNEY

Monitors of blood volume	Intermediary	Effect on kidney
Receptors (poorly characterised) in arterial and venous systems detect 'filling' of the vascular tree (systemic and pulmonary)	Sympathetic nervous system activated by perception of underfilling (also other systems, eg brain natriuretic peptides)	Activation of sympathetic nervous system leads to sodium retention
Cardiac atria monitor filling of venous system	Atrial stretch leads to secretion of atrial natriuretic peptide (also other systems, eg sympathetic nervous system)	Atrial natriuretic peptide acts on distal nephron segments to increase sodium excretion
Sensors of adequacy of renal perfusion	Renin–angiotensin–aldosterone system	If perfusion is inadequate, sodium is retained

receptor, preventing the action of aldosterone. The sodium channel itself is blocked by amiloride. As sodium reabsorption in the collecting duct is associated with potassium excretion, both spironolactone and amiloride are 'potassium-sparing' diuretics.

For many years, the existence of specific sodium channels in different nephron segments was surmised from physiological and pharmacological experiments. Molecular biological techniques (see *Genetics and Molecular Medicine*, Techniques in Molecular Biology) applied to families with rare mutations have allowed many of these sodium channels to be cloned; this has enormously advanced our understanding of the physiology of the kidney. Studies of rare genetic conditions can lead to discoveries of wide significance.

Factors modulating the renal circulation and sodium excretion

A wide variety of factors affect sodium excretion by the kidney. The main monitors of circulating volume, intermediaries and the renal effects of those intermediaries are shown in Table 8. Figure 49 shows how the renin–angiotensin–aldosterone system operates in response to a decrease or increase in renal perfusion.

Circulatory compromise

When the circulation is under stress (eg hypotension, dehydration), renal perfusion and glomerular filtration are maintained by homeostatic mechanisms (Table 8 and Fig. 49). Some pharmacological agents can prevent these from working, particularly the following.

- Converting enzyme inhibitors block the conversion of angiotensin I to angiotensin II.

- Angiotensin II receptor antagonists block the effect of angiotensin II.

- NSAIDs block the production of vasodilator prostaglandins.

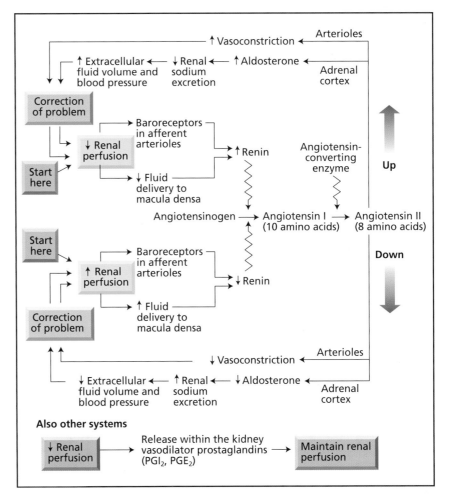

▲ **Fig. 49** The renin–angiotensin–aldosterone system. PGE$_2$, prostaglandin E$_2$; PGI$_2$, prostacyclin.

These agents can therefore contribute to the development of haemodynamically mediated acute renal failure ('acute tubular necrosis') and should be stopped when this is likely, unless there are pressing reasons for not doing so.

> Angiotensin-converting enzyme inhibitors, angiotensin II receptor antagonists and NSAIDs should generally be stopped in patients with circulatory compromise that is affecting renal function.

Sodium-retaining states

The body retains sodium, manifest as oedema, in a wide range of clinical conditions. The complexity of the arrangements for control of sodium excretion makes it very difficult indeed to work out why this happens. The following are the currently favoured hypotheses.

- Cardiac failure: impaired pump function leads to a perception that the circulation is 'underfilled' and activates homeostatic mechanisms, leading to sodium retention.

- Hepatic failure: abnormal vascular tone leads to perception of 'underfilling' and activation of sodium-retaining mechanisms.

- Nephrotic syndrome: in children hypoalbuminaemia leads to intravascular volume depletion via alteration of Starling's forces; this activates the renin–angiotensin–aldosterone system and hence sodium retention. The situation in adults is more complex and this simple analysis rarely applies.

Potassium transport along the nephron

Almost all filtered potassium is reabsorbed before the collecting tubules. Potassium excretion is then governed by the rate of its secretion into the distal nephron. Figure 50 shows the mechanisms involved.

Modulation of renal potassium excretion

Aldosterone is the main regulator of potassium homeostasis and hypokalaemia directly stimulates aldosterone production by the adrenal gland. The action of aldosterone on the collecting duct is shown in Fig. 51.

The following are other factors that influence potassium excretion.

- Alkalosis: this increases apical potassium channel and basolateral Na^{+2}/K^{+2}-ATPase activity and promotes potassium excretion.

- High urinary flow rate: this decreases the concentration of potassium in the tubular fluid, thus increasing the concentration gradient for, and stimulating, potassium excretion.

- Chronic changes in potassium intake: these can profoundly modify renal capacity to conserve or excrete potassium. The mechanism involves aldosterone but is not fully understood.

Hyperkalaemia

Rarely a clinical problem except in patients with renal failure, when it can kill suddenly and without warning.

> All physicians need to know how to recognise the ECG manifestations and treatment of hyperkalaemia. See *Acute Medicine*, Section 1.2.19 and *Nephrology*, Section 1.4.1.

Hypokalaemia

The most common causes of hypokalaemia are diuretics and gastrointestinal fluid loss, in particular vomiting. The concentration of potassium in vomitus is relatively low, and patients with vomiting become hypokalaemic because of increased renal losses of potassium. Why does this happen? The answer is because considerations of acid–base homeostasis dominate those of potassium homeostasis.

- Loss of gastric acid leads directly to alkalosis.

- Volume depletion leads to activation of the renin–angiotensin–aldosterone system.

- To correct alkalosis, the kidney excretes bicarbonate.

- This excretion has to be in combination with sodium or potassium.

- High aldosterone levels encourage potassium excretion.

Urinary concentration and dilution

In humans, serum osmolality (concentration of solutes) is maintained between 285 and 295 mosmol/L. To achieve this, urinary osmolality can vary between 50 mosmol/L (very dilute) and 1,200 mosmol/L (very concentrated) in the absence (dilute urine) or presence (concentrated urine) of antidiuretic hormone (ADH).

A rise in serum osmolality stimulates the release of ADH, which regulates excretion of water by the kidney (Fig. 52). A rise in serum osmolality also stimulates thirst and fluid intake, but note that drinking in humans is normally driven by social rather than osmotic stimuli, eg the cup of coffee after the ward round.

Urinary concentrating and diluting mechanism

The means by which the kidney can generate concentrated or dilute

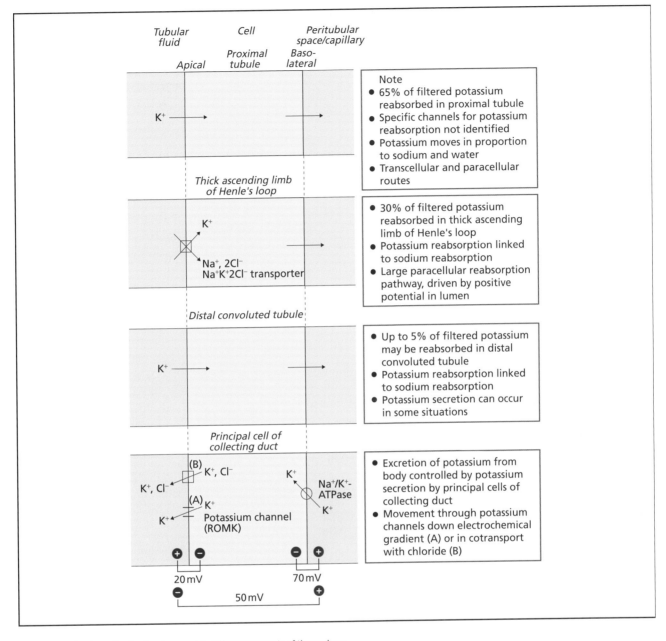

▲ **Fig. 50** Mechanisms of potassium transport in different segments of the nephron.

urine are complex and difficult to understand, but depend on the following.

- Fluid within the nephron is always hypotonic by the time it reaches the distal convoluted tubule.

- Osmolality in the interstitium of the renal medulla is permanently high.

- Permeability of the collecting ducts to water is variable.

- Without ADH: the collecting ducts are not permeable to water and hypotonic fluid passes from the distal convoluted tubule and out of the nephron without water being removed so that dilute urine is excreted.

- With ADH: the collecting ducts are permeable to water, which is removed as fluid passes through them, and concentrated urine is excreted.

More details of the renal mechanism are shown in Fig. 53.

In those diseases that affect mainly the renal medulla, eg chronic interstitial nephritis, the osmolality gradient in the medulla is impaired and patients cannot concentrate and dilute their urine normally ('salt-wasting nephropathy'), putting them at risk of dehydration and volume depletion.

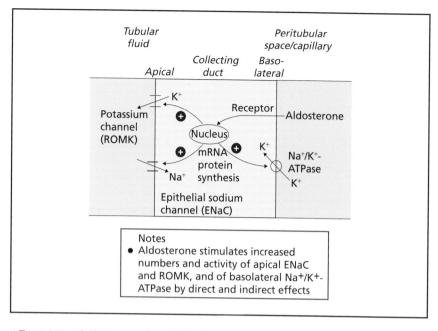

▲ **Fig. 51** Action of aldosterone on the collecting duct. ENaC, epithelial sodium channel; ROMK, potassium channel.

Non-osmotic stimuli for ADH release

Non-osmotic stimuli for ADH release are much more potent than osmotic stimuli, and the highest levels are seen with volume depletion, pain, nausea and anaesthesia. This has very important clinical implications.

After anaesthesia and surgical operations, the levels of ADH are extremely high and patients (particularly women) are unable to excrete a water load for 24–48 hours. Severe hyponatraemia and death can follow the inappropriate administration of hypotonic fluids, the usual culprit being 5% dextrose.

Intravascular volume depletion must be excluded (jugular venous pulse not low, no postural hypotension, urinary sodium concentration not very low, ie not less than 20 mmol/L) before a diagnosis of 'syndrome of inappropriate antidiuresis' (SIAD) is made. Concentrated urine is appropriate to intravascular volume status, if not to serum osmolality, if the patient is hypovolaemic.

Renal contribution to acid–base balance

On a normal Western diet, the body produces 50–100 mmol of acid per day. This is excreted by the kidneys, which also reabsorb all the bicarbonate filtered at the glomerulus, because loss of this would induce acidosis. The following are the three main renal processes involved in acid–base homeostasis:

- reabsorption of filtered bicarbonate;
- excretion of titratable acid;
- excretion of ammonia.

Reabsorption of filtered bicarbonate

Most bicarbonate is reabsorbed in the proximal tubule. The mechanism is shown in Fig. 54. Inhibition of carbonic anhydrase explains (in part) the diuretic properties of acetazolamide. This process of bicarbonate reabsorption is deficient in 'bicarbonate-wasting' renal tubular acidosis (proximal, type 2).

Excretion of titratable acid

Urinary pH is almost always less than that of plasma, with a normal

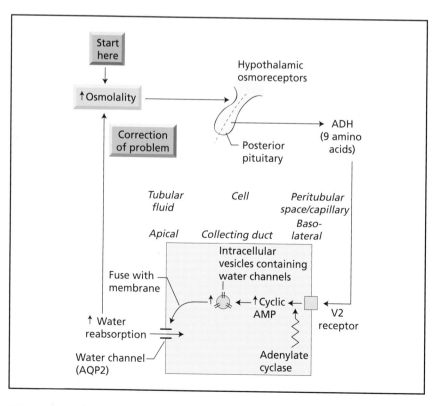

▲ **Fig. 52** Control of serum osmolality by antidiuretic hormone (ADH). AMP, adenosine monophosphate; AQP2, aquaporin 2.

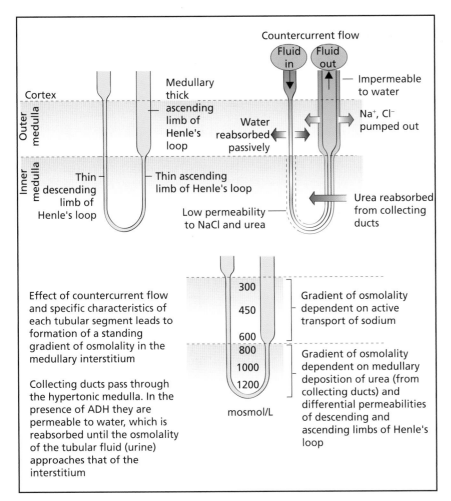

▲ **Fig. 53** Tubular mechanism of urinary concentration and dilution. ADH, antidiuretic hormone.

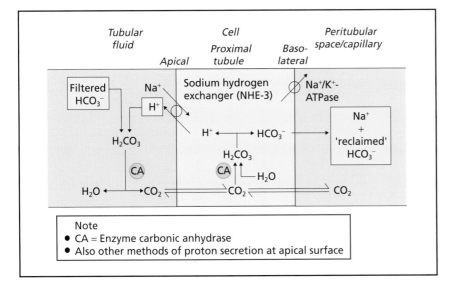

▲ **Fig. 54** Tubular reabsorption of filtered bicarbonate.

minimum value of about 4.5 (compared with plasma pH of 7.35–7.45). The amount of alkali required to titrate the urine back to pH 7.40 is the amount of 'titratable acid' (mostly HPO_4^{2-} and SO_4^{2-}) that it contains. This accounts for 25% of acid load excretion. The mechanism is shown in Fig. 55.

Excretion of ammonia

The mechanism is shown in Fig. 56 and accounts for 75% of acid load excretion. In both Figs 55 and 56, it can be seen that proton secretion at the apical membrane is required. In the proximal and early distal tubule, this is accomplished by the Na^+/H^+ exchanger; in the late distal tubule and type A intercalated cells of the collecting duct, H^+-ATPase is responsible.

Inability to excrete protons or maintain the proton concentration gradient in the distal tubule leads to distal renal tubular acidosis (type 1).

6.3 Endocrine function of the kidney

The kidney is the source or target of action of many hormones (Table 9).

Vitamin D metabolism and parathyroid hormone

Vitamin D metabolism

The metabolism of vitamin D is shown in Fig. 57. The main active metabolite is 1,25-dihydroxycholecalciferol, which acts on several tissues, always with the effect of increasing serum calcium and phosphate.

• Gut: increases calcium and phosphate absorption.

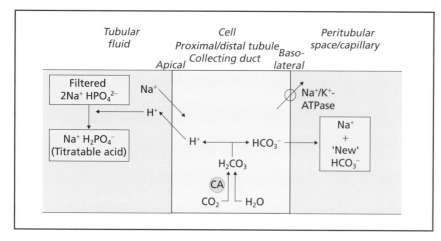

▲ **Fig. 55** Tubular excretion of titratable acid. CA, carbonic anhydrase.

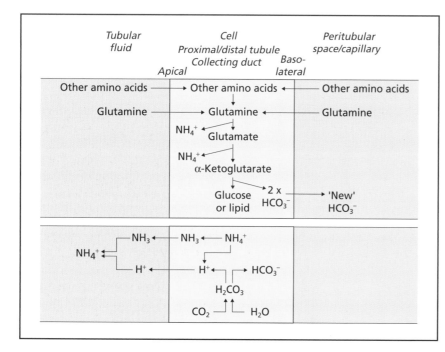

▲ **Fig. 56** Tubular excretion of ammonia.

TABLE 9 ENDOCRINE FUNCTIONS OF THE KIDNEY

Endocrine function	Hormone/mediator	Action
Kidney produces	Renin	Affects sodium excretion
	1,25-dihydroxycholecalciferol	Affects calcium/phosphate homeostasis
	Erythropoietin	Regulation of red blood cell count
Kidney target	Antidiuretic hormone	Controls water excretion
	Aldosterone	Alters sodium handling
	Atrial natriuretic peptide	Alters sodium handling
	Parathyroid hormone	Affects calcium and phosphate handling
Local autocrine and paracrine systems	Prostaglandins	Vascular and tubular function
	Endothelins	Vascular and tubular function
	(Many others)	

- Bone: enhances the action of parathyroid hormone (PTH), resulting in net bone resorption.

- Kidney: stimulates reabsorption of calcium and phosphate.

Parathyroid hormone

This is a protein of 84 amino acids and is secreted by the chief cells of the parathyroid gland in response to a fall in serum ionised calcium. The actions of PTH include the following.

- Stimulation of osteoblasts and thereby osteoclasts, resulting in net bone resorption with release of calcium and phosphate.

- Increased 1α-hydroxylase activity in cells in the proximal renal tubule, which enhances production of 1,25-dihydroxycholecalciferol.

- Reduced phosphate reabsorption by the renal tubule.

- Increased calcium reabsorption by the renal tubule.

Abnormalities of vitamin D metabolism and PTH secretion occur in renal failure, appearing when GFR falls below about 40 mL/min. If untreated, these abnormalities can lead to severe bone disease ('renal osteodystrophy'). Treatment with active metabolites of vitamin D (most commonly 1α-hydroxycholecalciferol) is used to prevent this, but sometimes parathyroidectomy is necessary.

Erythropoietin

The kidney is the main source of erythropoietin, a heavily glycosylated hormone consisting of 165 amino acids which controls production of red blood cells (Fig. 58).

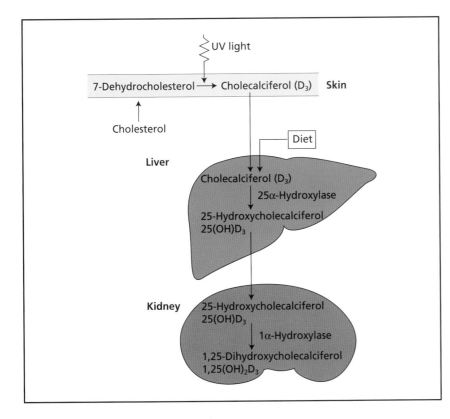

▲**Fig. 57** Formation of the active metabolites of vitamin D.

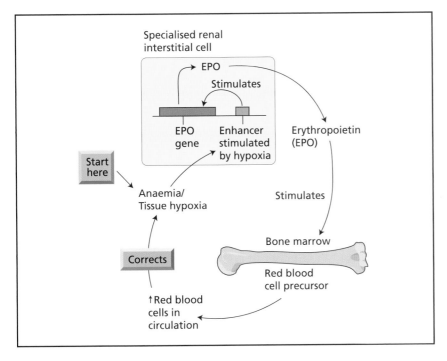

▲**Fig. 58** Production and control of erythropoietin.

Erythropoietin production is deficient in advanced renal failure and leads to anaemia. This can be treated effectively with erythropoietin injections, which are one of the main advances in renal medicine in the last 15 years.

FURTHER READING

Arieff AI. Hyponatremia, convulsions, respiratory arrest, and permanent brain damage after elective surgery in healthy women. *N Engl J Med* 1986; 314: 1529–35.

Arieff AI and Ayus JC. Hyponatremia. *N Engl J Med* 2000; 343: 886.

Brater DC. Diuretic therapy. *N Engl J Med* 1998; 339: 387–95.

Davison AM, Cameron JS, Grünfeld J-P, et al., eds. *Oxford Textbook of Clinical Nephrology*, 3rd edn. Oxford: Oxford University Press, 2005.

Scheinman SJ, Guay-Woodford LM, Thakker RV and Warnock DG. Genetic disorders of renal electrolyte transport. *N Engl J Med* 1999; 340: 1177–87.

Schrier RW. Pathogenesis of sodium and water retention in high-output and low-output cardiac failure, nephritic syndrome, cirrhosis, and pregnancy (1). *N Engl J Med* 1988; 319: 1065–72.

Schrier RW. Pathogenesis of sodium and water retention in high-output and low-output cardiac failure, nephritic syndrome, cirrhosis, and pregnancy (2). *N Engl J Med* 1988; 319: 1127–34.

Valtin H. *Renal Function: Mechanisms Preserving Fluid and Solute Balance in Health*, 3rd edn. Boston: Little, Brown, 1995.

7.1 Self-assessment questions

Question 1

The average cardiac output of a man at rest is:

Answers

A 1–2 L/min
B 3–4 L/min
C 5–6 L/min
D 7–8 L/min
E 9–10 L/min

Question 2

In the pacemaker tissue of the heart the action potential is generated by:

Answers

A Outward movement of potassium
B Outward movement of chloride through B channels
C Inward movement of sodium through A channels
D Inward movement of calcium through T channels
E Inward movement of calcium through L channels

Question 3

Which of the following best describes the constituents of the thin filament of a cardiac myofibril?

Answers

A Myosin
B Myosin and actin
C Actin
D Actin and tropomyosin
E Actin, tropomyosin and troponin

Question 4

Starling's law (of the heart) states that cardiac output is:

Answers

A Proportional to heart rate
B Proportional to venous inflow
C Proportional to inotropic state
D Inversely proportional to arterial pressure
E Inversely proportional to cardiac work

Question 5

The vasodilator nitric oxide is normally synthesised from which of the following:

Answers

A L-Alanine
B L-Arginine
C Threonine
D Tryptophan
E Tyrosine

Question 6

Resting minute ventilation in a healthy adult is:

Answers

A 2 L/min
B 5 L/min
C 8 L/min
D 12 L/min
E 20 L/min

Question 7

The functional residual capacity of the lung is reached by the patient:

Answers

A Taking the biggest possible breath in
B Taking the biggest possible breath out

C Taking a small breath in and then exhaling without any active effort
D Taking a small breath in without any active effort
E At the mid-point of a respiratory cycle without any active effort

Question 8

In obstructive lung disease, which one of the following statements is true?

Answers

A Total lung capacity is reduced, functional residual capacity is increased, and residual volume is reduced
B Total lung capacity is reduced, functional residual capacity is reduced, and residual volume is increased
C Total lung capacity is reduced, functional residual capacity is increased, and residual volume is reduced
D Total lung capacity is increased, functional residual capacity is reduced, and residual volume is increased
E Total lung capacity is increased, functional residual capacity is increased, and residual volume is increased

Question 9

The hypoxic drive to breathe is mediated by:

Answers

A Carotid body
B Aortic arch baroreceptors
C Areas on ventrolateral surface of the medulla

D Hypothalamus

E Pulmonary nerves

Question 10

In restrictive lung disease, which one of the following statements is true?

Answers

A Total lung capacity is reduced, functional residual capacity is reduced, and residual volume is normal

B Total lung capacity is reduced, functional residual capacity is increased, and residual volume is increased

C Total lung capacity is reduced, functional residual capacity is reduced, and residual volume is reduced

D Total lung capacity is increased, functional residual capacity is reduced, and residual volume is reduced

E Total lung capacity is reduced, functional residual capacity is increased, and residual volume is normal

Question 11

Which cells are responsible for the inherent rhythmicity of the contraction that causes peristalsis of the small intestine?

Answers

A Purkinje cells

B Langerhan cells

C Paget cells

D Ito cells

E Interstitial cells of Cajal

Question 12

Transit through the small intestine takes how long?

Answers

A 1–2 hours

B 2–4 hours

C 4–6 hours

D 6–8 hours

E 10–14 hours

Question 13

Cholecystokinin is released from the:

Answers

A Liver

B Gallbladder

C Stomach

D Jejunum

E Ileum

Question 14

In man, bile salts are mainly synthesised by:

Answers

A Conjugation of chenodeoxycholic acid with glycine and taurine

B Conjugation of cholic acid with glycine and taurine

C Conjugation of bilirubin with glycine and taurine

D Conjugation of bilirubin by glucuronyltransferase

E Conjugation of chenodeoxycholic acid by glucuronyltransferase

Question 15

Gilbert's disease is caused by a defect in:

Answers

A Uridine diphosphate glucuronosyltransferase 1

B Organic anion transporter protein

C Multispecific organic anion transporter

D Multidrug resistant peptide

E Bile salt exporter pump

Question 16

The resting membrane potential of a neuron is:

Answers

A Inside –90 mV

B Inside –60 mV

C Inside –30 mV

D Zero

E Inside +30 mV

Question 17

The sodium-potassium (Na^+/K^+)-ATPase transports:

Answers

A Two sodium ions out of the cell for every three potassium ions transported in

B Three sodium ions out of the cell for every three potassium ions transported in

C One sodium ion out of the cell for every two potassium ions transported in

D Two sodium ions out of the cell for every two potassium ions transported in

E Three sodium ions out of the cell for every two potassium ions transported in

Question 18

Conduction of a nerve impulse by a myelinated axon is described as saltatory. The term 'saltatory' is used because the action potential in a myelinated axon:

Answers

A Requires greater sodium influx than in an unmyelinated axon

B Requires lesser sodium influx than in an unmyelinated axon

C Employs faster sodium influx than in an unmyelinated axon

D Employs slower sodium influx than in an unmyelinated axon

E Spreads from one node of Ranvier to the next

Question 19

An inhibitory postsynaptic action potential results from increased permeability to:

Answers

A Sodium and potassium

B Potassium

C Potassium and chloride

D Sodium

E Sodium and chloride

Question 20

Stimulation of the nicotinic postsynaptic receptor results in increased permeability of the muscle cell membrane to:

Answers

A Sodium, potassium and calcium

B Sodium and calcium

C Sodium and potassium

D Sodium

E Calcium

Question 21

If the concentration of a compound in the plasma is P and in the urine is U, and the urinary volume is V, then which formula correctly gives the clearance rate of the compound from plasma?

Answers

A $U \times V \times P$

B $(U \times V)/P$

C $U/(P \times V)$

D $P/(U \times V)$

E $(P \times V)/U$

Question 22

Which of the following mechanisms for reabsorbing sodium from the nephron is the main target for loop diuretics?

Answers

A Na^+/H^+ exchanger

B $Na^+/K^+/2Cl^-$ cotransporter

C Na^+/Cl^- cotransporter

D Epithelial sodium channel

E Na^+/K^+-ATPase

Question 23

Which of the following statements best describes the circumstances that lead vomiting to cause hypokalaemia?

Answers

A High concentration of potassium in vomitus; low concentration of potassium in urine; low concentration of chloride in the urine

B High concentration of potassium in vomitus; high concentration of potassium in urine; high concentration of chloride in the urine

C High concentration of potassium in vomitus; low concentration of potassium in urine; high concentration of chloride in the urine

D Low concentration of potassium in vomitus; high concentration of potassium in urine; low concentration of chloride in the urine

E Low concentration of potassium in vomitus; high concentration of potassium in urine; high concentration of chloride in the urine

Question 24

Which one of the following is *not* a stimulus for release of antidiuretic hormone?

Answers

A Pain

B Nausea

C Intravascular volume depletion

D Fever

E High serum osmolality

Question 25

The main site of action of aldosterone is on which part of the nephron?

Answers

A Proximal convoluted tubule

B Descending limb of loop of Henle

C Thick ascending limb of loop of Henle

D Distal convoluted tubule

E Collecting duct

Question 26

The amino acid that acts as the immediate source of ammonium (NH_4^+) ions for excretion by the renal tubule is:

Answers

A Glutamine

B Arginine

C Ornithine

D Cystine

E Tryptophan

Question 27

The main biologically active form of vitamin D is:

Answers

A Cholecalciferol

B 1-Hydroxycholecalciferol

C 25-Hydroxycholecalciferol

D 24,25-Dihydroxycholecalciferol

E 1,25-Dihydroxycholecalciferol

Question 28

Erythropoietin is normally produced by which cell type within the kidney?

Answers

A Interstitial cell

B Glomerular mesangial cell

C Proximal tubular cell

D Distal convoluted tubular cell

E Collecting duct tubular cell

Question 29

The anabolic effects of growth hormone are mediated by:

Answers

A Growth hormone binding directly to growth hormone receptors

B Insulin

C Glucagon

D Dihydrotestosterone

E Insulin-like growth factor 1

Question 30

Which part of the adrenal gland is mainly responsible for the production of glucocorticoids?

Answers

A Medulla

B Zona reticularis

C Zona fasciculata

D Zona glomerulosa

E Zona cushingosa

Question 31

Thyroxine (T_4) is synthesised from:

Answers

A Two molecules of monoiodotyrosine
B One molecule of monoiodotyrosine and one molecule of diiodotyrosine
C Two molecules of diiodotyrosine
D One molecule of triiodothyronine and one molecule of monoiodotyrosine
E One molecule of triiodothyronine and one molecule of diiodotyrosine

7.2 Self-assessment answers

Answer to Question 1

C

Cardiac output at rest is 5–6 L/min.

Answer to Question 2

E

After the pacemaker tissue has repolarised following an action potential, transient (T) calcium channels open and an inward calcium current leads to gradual depolarisation of the membrane (the 'prepotential'). When the membrane has depolarised to a critical degree, long-lasting (L) calcium channels open and an increased inward calcium current generates the action potential. The inward sodium current plays little part in the action potential of this tissue.

Answer to Question 3

E

The thick filaments of cardiac myofibrils are made of myosin. Each thin filament has a tropomyosin backbone, around which are wound two helical chains of actin, with troponin complexes (T, C and I) positioned every 38 nm. The thin filaments are anchored to the Z line at one end and interdigitate with thick filaments at the other.

Answer to Question 4

B

Starling's law states that 'within wide limits, the output of the heart is independent of arterial resistance and temperature; up to a certain point, the output of the heart is proportional to the venous inflow'.

Answer to Question 5

B

Nitric oxide is the main endogenous vasodilator, which is synthesised from L-arginine by the action of nitric oxide synthase, generating L-citrulline in the process. Nitric oxide has a half-life of only a few seconds and is produced continuously by the vascular endothelium.

Answer to Question 6

B

Resting minute ventilation in a healthy adult is approximately 5 L/min, but this may rise to as much as 150 L/min during heavy exercise.

Answer to Question 7

C

A defines total lung capacity, B defines residual volume. The neutral point of the respiratory system is the functional residual capacity (FRC), when the positive lung recoil pressure is exactly equal to the negative chest wall recoil pressure. It is reached by taking a small breath in and then exhaling without any active effort.

Answer to Question 8

E

In obstructive lung disease the patient has difficulty breathing out. This forces the patient to a higher lung volume, an increased functional residual capacity (the point reached by taking a small breath in and then exhaling without any active effort) and an increased residual volume (the point reached after maximal expiration). Vital capacity, the difference between total lung capacity and residual volume, is decreased.

Answer to Question 9

A

Acidosis from CO_2 or another acid is a potent drive to hyperventilation, mediated via areas located on the ventrolateral surface of the medulla. Hypoxic drive is mediated via the carotid body, the discharge of which is increased linearly in response to falling arterial oxygen saturation (Sao_2) (and hyperbolically to Pao_2); this response is magnified by concomitant hypercapnia. In practice ventilation does not increase until Pao_2 is less than 8 kPa (or $Sao_2 < 92\%$).

Answer to Question 10

A

In restrictive lung disease the patient is unable to inspire to a normal total lung capacity. Thus the patient has a reduced functional residual capacity (the point reached by taking a small breath in and then exhaling without any active effort) but a normal residual volume (the point reached after maximal expiration). Vital capacity, the difference between total lung capacity and residual volume, is decreased.

Answer to Question 11

E

The ability of the enteric nervous system to operate independently depends to a large extent on the self-generation of periodic depolarisation and repolarisation ('slow waves'), which trigger smooth muscle contraction and hence peristalsis. A specialised group of cells, the interstitial cells of Cajal, are thought to be responsible for this inherent rhythmicity and are intimately associated with the enteric nervous complex.

Answer to Question 12

B

Transit through the stomach depends on the consistency, size and type of food ingested. Liquid meals pass through rapidly, being half emptied in 30–60 minutes, whereas solid meals take about twice as long to pass through. Fat markedly delays gastric emptying by stimulating duodenal receptors. Transit through the small intestine takes around 2–4 hours. Transit through the colon is very variable both between and within individuals, with a range of 5–70 hours.

Answer to Question 13

D

Cholecystokinin, released from the jejunal mucosa in response to fat, is a potent inhibitor of gastric emptying, causes contraction of the gallbladder, and stimulates the exocrine pancreas to produce proteases, lipases and amylases.

Answer to Question 14

B

The primary bile acids, synthesised from cholesterol in the liver, are cholic acid and chenodeoxycholic acid. Cholic acid predominates in human bile. In the liver, bile acids are conjugated with glycine and taurine to form bile salts, after which they cannot be absorbed by the bile ducts or jejunum. However,

they are absorbed further down the gut, mainly by the terminal ileum. This is the basis of the enterohepatic circulation, which transports bile salts back to the liver and thereby recycles the entire bile salt pool 2–15 times every day.

Answer to Question 15

A

In Gilbert's syndrome, unconjugated hyperbilirubinaemia is the result of impaired function of the bilirubin enzyme uridine diphosphate (UDP) glucuronosyltransferase 1 (UGT1). The gene for this is on chromosome 2 and the genetic defect is the insertion of a pair of nucleotides (thymidine and adenosine) in the gene promoter, which affects binding of transcription factors and reduces UGT1 production.

Answer to Question 16

A

In its resting state the cell membrane is very permeable to potassium ions but not to sodium ions, so the resting membrane potential is close to the equilibrium potential of potassium, which is about –95 mV.

Answer to Question 17

E

By transporting three sodium ions out of the cell for every two potassium ions transported in, the Na$^+$/K$^+$-ATPase establishes the concentration gradients of sodium (high extracellular/low intracellular) and potassium (low extracellular/high intracellular) that, along with the differential permeability of the resting cell membrane to sodium (relatively impermeable) and potassium (relatively permeable), form the basis of the resting membrane potential.

Answer to Question 18

E

Myelination increases membrane resistance and decreases capacitance, enhancing conduction velocity without increasing an axon's size. The nodes of Ranvier are excitable areas of membrane between myelin cells. Depolarisation spreads from one node to another, a process known as saltatory conduction.

Answer to Question 19

C

An excitatory postsynaptic action potential is the result of increased permeability to sodium and potassium. The equilibrium potentials of both potassium and chloride are more negative than the resting membrane potential (–90 mV), so increase in permeability to these ions leads to hyperpolarisation of the membrane (inside becomes more negative) and a reduced likelihood of an action potential being initiated (hence inhibitory postsynaptic action potential).

Answer to Question 20

A

Stimulation of the nicotinic postsynaptic receptor results in increased permeability of the muscle cell membrane to sodium, potassium and calcium. The net effect of this is to cause influx of cations, moving the end-plate potential towards the threshold for spontaneous depolarisation (about –50 mV), at which point an action potential is generated and sweeps across the muscle membrane.

Answer to Question 21

B

(U × V)/P defines the clearance of a substance from plasma. If the substance is freely filtered at the glomerulus and not secreted, reabsorbed or metabolised as it passes down the nephron, then its clearance can be used to estimate glomerular filtration rate. In routine clinical practice creatinine clearance is often used for this purpose.

Answer to Question 22

B

The Na^+/H^+ exchanger is the main mechanism for sodium reabsorption in the proximal tubule, the $Na^+/K^+/2Cl^-$ cotransporter (target for loop diuretics) in the loop of Henle, the Na^+/Cl^- cotransporter (thiazide diuretics) in the distal convoluted tubule, and the epithelial sodium channel (spironolactone and amiloride) in the collecting duct. The Na^+/K^+-ATPase is found predominantly on the basolateral surface of all tubular cells and pumps sodium from within the cells into the peritubular space/capillaries.

Answer to Question 23

D

The concentration of potassium in vomitus is relatively low and patients with vomiting become hypokalaemic because of increased renal losses of potassium. Loss of gastric acid and chloride in vomitus leads directly to alkalosis and volume depletion, which stimulates the renin–angiotensin–aldosterone system. To correct alkalosis the kidney excretes bicarbonate, which must be accompanied by a cation, either sodium or potassium. High aldosterone levels favour potassium loss. Chloride is conserved, with urinary concentration falling to very low levels.

Answer to Question 24

D

Pain, nausea and intravascular volume depletion are much more

potent stimuli for antidiuretic hormone (ADH) release than is the osmotic stimulus of a high serum osmolality. This explains why ADH levels are very high after surgery and why severe hyponatraemia can result from inappropriate administration of 5% dextrose intravenously in the postoperative period. Fever is not a direct stimulus for ADH release.

Answer to Question 25

E

Aldosterone acts on the collecting duct where it binds to an intracellular mineralocorticoid receptor, the effect (via direct and indirect mechanisms) being to stimulate increased numbers and activity of apical epithelial sodium channels and potassium channels, and of basolateral Na^+/K^+-ATPase.

Answer to Question 26

A

The conversion of glutamine to glutamate and the conversion of glutamate to α-ketoglutarate each liberates one ammonium ion within tubular cells. Excretion of these ions is accompanied by the generation of one 'new' bicarbonate ion (HCO_3^-) that is reabsorbed. Failure of this mechanism leads to one of the types of renal tubular acidosis.

Answer to Question 27

E

Cholecalciferol (Vitamin D_3) is consumed in the diet and produced in the skin by the action of light on 7-dehydrocholesterol. It undergoes 25α-hydroxylation in the liver and then 1α-hydroxylation in the kidney to form the main active metabolite. Patients with renal failure who are deficient in vitamin D are given either 1α-hydroxycholecalciferol or

1,25-dihydroxycholecalciferol to circumvent their deficiency of 1α-hydroxylase.

Answer to Question 28

A

Erythropoietin is produced by a specialised cell within the renal interstitium, where its production is stimulated by hypoxia. It acts directly on the bone marrow to stimulate the production of red blood cells.

Answer to Question 29

E

Growth hormone has direct 'anti-insulin' effects, but its anabolic actions are mediated through insulin-like growth factor 1, which is produced in the liver and binds directly to cell-surface receptors to exert its actions.

Answer to Question 30

C

The adrenal medulla is responsible for catecholamine production, the zona reticularis for androgen production, the zona fasciculata for glucocorticoid production and the zona glomerulosa for mineralocorticoid production.

Answer to Question 31

C

Thyroxine (T_4) is synthesised from two molecules of diiodotyrosine. Most triiodothyronine is derived by peripheral deiodination of T_4 in target tissues, but some is synthesised directly from one molecule of monoiodotyrosine and one molecule of diiodotyrosine.

THE MEDICAL MASTERCLASS SERIES

Haematology and Oncology

HAEMATOLOGY

PACES Stations and Acute Scenarios 1

ONCOLOGY

Cardiology and Respiratory Medicine

CARDIOLOGY

Gastroenterology and Hepatology

GASTROENTEROLOGY AND HEPATOLOGY

PACES Stations and Acute Scenarios 3

Diseases and Treatments 60

Neurology, Ophthalmology and Psychiatry

NEUROLOGY

Endocrinology

ENDOCRINOLOGY

PACES Stations and Acute Scenarios 3

Nephrology

NEPHROLOGY

Rheumatology and Clinical Immunology

RHEUMATOLOGY AND CLINICAL IMMUNOLOGY

PACES Stations and Acute Scenarios 3

INDEX

Note: page numbers in *italics* refer to figures, those in **bold** refer to tables.